MEDIEVAL
MILITARY
TECHNOLOGY

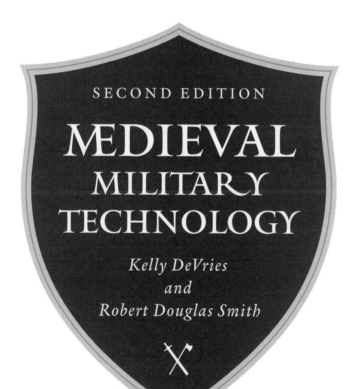

SECOND EDITION

MEDIEVAL
MILITARY
TECHNOLOGY

Kelly DeVries
and
Robert Douglas Smith

UNIVERSITY OF TORONTO PRESS

Library and Archives Canada Cataloguing in Publication

DeVries, Kelly Robert, 1956–
          Medieval military technology / Kelly DeVries and Robert Douglas Smith.—2nd ed.

Includes bibliographical references and index.
Issued also in electronic formats.
ISBN 978-1-4426-0497-1

1. Armor, Medieval. 2. Artillery—History. 3. Fortification—History. 4. Warships—History.
5. Military history, Medieval. I. Smith, Robert Douglas II. Title.

U810.D48 2012   355.009'02   C2012-902147-4

We welcome comments and suggestions regarding any aspect of our publications—please feel free to contact us at news@utphighereducation.com or visit our Internet site at www.utppublishing.com.

NORTH AMERICA
5201 Dufferin Street
North York, Ontario, Canada,
M3H 5T8

2250 Military Road
Tonawanda, New York, USA, 14150

Orders
PHONE: 1–800–565–9523
FAX: 1–800–221–9985
E-MAIL: utpbooks@utpress.utoronto.ca

UK, IRELAND, AND CONTINENTAL EUROPE
NBN International
Estover Road, Plymouth, PL6 7PY, UK

Orders
PHONE: 44 (0) 1752 202301
FAX: 44 (0) 1752 202333
E-MAIL: enquiries@nbninternational.com

Every effort has been made to contact copyright holders; in the event of an error or omission, please notify the publisher.

The University of Toronto Press acknowledges the financial support for its publishing activities of the Government of Canada through the Canada Book Fund.

Printed in Canada

CONTENTS

ILLUSTRATIONS

ACKNOWLEDGMENTS

IT MAY BE MORE DIFFICULT TO WRITE THE ACKNOWLEDGEMENTS OF THE second edition of a book than it is the first edition. Having to combine the reasons why a book was initially written, and thanking those who helped in that initial writing, with what prompted a second edition to be written, with those who helped there, is not easy. Often, lots of time has passed between the two editions, twenty years in the case of this book, and many things change during that time. (For one thing, the authorship of this book has gone from one to two.) Perhaps that is why so many authors simply attach their new acknowledgements to the bottom of their original ones. To keep from repeating things, as well as try to express thanks to people who have helped me both before the appearance of the first book, and since, I will try to combine the two sets of acknowledgements. As the first acknowledgements were written alone by me, Kelly DeVries, I am writing these, with some comments by Robert Douglas Smith added at the end.

This book was first suggested to me in 1988, when I was teaching as a sessional lecturer in the Department of History at the University of British Columbia, by my department chairman, Professor Richard W. Unger, whose own works on the history of medieval technology have established (and continue to establish) him as one of the "giants" in the field. As he pointed out to me, the history of medieval military technology has been largely left up to amateur historians and antiquarians whose interests in the field were derived largely from their desires to replicate, in re-enactments and wargames, the arms, armor, and castles of the medieval warrior. Numerous books and articles from professional medieval and arms and armor historians have appeared, it is true, but no one book had been devoted to an overview of all medieval military technology. This was further emphasized in studying the then-profusion of recent general works on technology and war, all of which give but little space to the discussion of the Middle Ages, especially in comparison to ancient and modern military technology. To Professor Unger for suggesting this to me, I give special thanks.

In the original acknowledgements, I also thanked my mentor in the history of technology, Professor Bert S. Hall, then Professor at the Institute of History and Philosophy of Science and Technology at the University of Toronto. In carrying on the tradition of his own mentor, Lynn White, Jr., his discussions with me, both in graduate school and since my graduation, and with Bob, since meeting him more than a decade ago, have been of untold assistance as we puzzled through the intricacies of studying a historical genre in which one frequently must look beyond the written text. His encouragement of us in this and many other endeavors, as well as his diligence in scrutinizing whatever we send him, has been invaluable. Bert has, since the original edition of this book, retired from full-time teaching at the University of Toronto, but he continues to be the fount of technological knowledge we turn to often.

In the first edition, I also praised the Centre for Medieval Studies at the University of Toronto, my graduate school, for preparing me with the linguistic and historical necessities medieval historians need to research in medieval history. Now, as it nears 25 years since that graduation date, I look back with an extremely fond remembrance of what may have been the best years of my life, living in one of the great cities in the world, Toronto, which provided then, and continues to provide now, such a great base for engulfing oneself completely in the Middle Ages, and working with some of the best professors and fellow students in the field. One of the greatest thrills in my professional life was returning to campus after about fifteen years and meeting with some of these professors, and to be told by two of them how proud they were of what I had accomplished with what they had taught me. I know I can speak for all of the University of Toronto alumni in thanking you, kind and diligent men and women, for being such influences and examples.

While visiting one of the earliest International Medieval Congresses, sponsored each summer by the University of Leeds, I had the great fortune to meet Bob Smith and his wife, Ruth Brown. The Royal Armouries, at which Bob was the Head of Conservation, had just moved to Leeds, and he came to the Congress to speak on early gunpowder weapons, something I had considered up to then that I had a pretty good knowledge of. Within only a few minutes of his presentation, and in several discussions since, I realized that I was but an amateur in the field. This meeting almost immediately bore fruit, as a couple of school years later, 1998–99, was my first sabbatical at Loyola College (now University) where I became employed the year that this book was published. That sabbatical year soon turned into eighteen months when, added to the honor of holding a Senior Fellowship at the Dibner Institute for the History of Science and Technology, Massachusetts Institute of Technology, I received a Professional Development Fellowship by the National Science Foundation, Science and Technology Studies to study the history of gunpowder weapons with Bob at the Royal Armouries, the idea being to marry my expertise as a historian with his as an artefactual scholar. We have never looked back. The work done that year eventually resulted in our first book together, *The Artillery of the Dukes of Burgundy, 1363–1477*, published by Boydell Press in 2005. Three more have followed: *Medieval Weapons, An Illustrated History of their Impact* (ABC-CLIO, 2007); *The Sieges of Rhodes in 1480 and 1522: A New History* (History Press, 2011); and now this volume. I wish to thank him and Ruth for everything: housing, hospitality, fun, visits to foreign and English sites, good movies, good food and drink, insightful discussion, and friendship.

In the past twenty years I have also amassed enormous debts. First, thanks to Loyola University: to my colleagues in the History Department (for their intelligence, friendship, respect and indulgence in sometimes picking up the pieces of my teaching when I have been delayed on flights, etc.); to our Administrative Assistant, Joanne Dabney (for her cheerfulness, advice and insight, not just in dealing with the University, but also with the more important things in life—she is, in her own just words, my guruess); and to the four Deans and three Presidents that I have had at Loyola over the past two decades (whose support, especially financial, has assisted my career immensely).

Second, thanks must also go to the Midgley Family of Menston, Yorkshire, for their love, support, and attic. There were only four children when I first met them, but now there are five, plus one more marrying into the family this year. They never judge me, but no doubt question how it is possible for someone to do what I do and still get paid. I will admit that it beats working. I can never repay their love.

Thanks to the Royal Armouries. I have benefitted from my association with the many valued friends I have among the staff; especially valuable is the library, where I have spent many, many productive hours. Thanks to Bob, Karen, Thom, Philip, Graeme, John, Guy, Andy, Stuart, Chris, and Stuart—I am sure I've missed more than one on this list, and for that I apologize.

The Royal Armories and the Center for Humanities of Loyola University Maryland supplemented the cost of reproducing illustrations for this book, which is greatly appreciated.

To the editors of Broadview Press, and now the University of Toronto Press, thanks for your patience. I hope this is worth it.

Finally, in the original edition of this book, I thanked my wife, Barbara Middleton, for her patience and hard work in getting the book to a publishable state. Circumstances have led to our no longer being together, but for 28 years she stood by me, allowing me to make the frequent trips from home which have been so important to my career. I owe her much thanks and love. She is also the mother of my three children, Beth, Michael, and Catie. All three were quite young at the time this book originally appeared, and all now have grown and are fine adults. Beth has brought Jonathan Peart into our family as her husband, and now also Ian, my beautiful, intelligent grandson. By the time this appears, she has told me I will be a grandfather yet again. I dedicated the first edition of this book "Aan mijn gezin" (to my family), and I do so with this edition as well.

Robert Douglas Smith would like to acknowledge and thank Ruth Brown for her continued help and assistance in every aspect of this work—without her support it would be significantly the poorer. He would also like to express his thanks and admiration to his fellow writer, Kelly, who always manages to keep his cool and remain an oasis of calm.

INTRODUCTION

THE IMAGE OF THE MEDIEVAL KNIGHT IN SHINING ARMOR, THE CASTLE, THE catapult, and the long- or crossbowman has become the portrait of medieval society most indelibly imprinted on our mind by popular cinema and literature. Even the United States Marines have seen fit to advertise their corps by using the depiction of a medieval knight wielding his sword, hoping by this, no doubt, to connect some sort of historical precedent to their recruitment drive. And, if this were not enough, on almost any given Saturday across North America, England, and Continental Europe, groups of mock medieval warriors spar and tourney in an effort to recreate what they imagine to have been an age of chivalry, where strict laws of war prohibited unequal military conflict. There is even a professional jousting circuit, with tournaments held primarily in Europe, but also in the United States and Australia. They are matched endlessly by wargamers, who started with *Dungeons and Dragons*, played on 25-cent pads of paper with their friends around tables in dorms and basements, and have graduated to *World of Warcraft*, *Final Fantasy* (now up to installment XIV) and, still, *Dungeons and Dragons*, played on $1,000 computers on the internet with people over the entire globe. For them, too, the Middle Ages was a time of intricate (and exciting) military technology.

But they are not alone in their search for the coupling of war and technology. Professional historians are also studying what they view as an unalterable historical dependency. Perhaps responding to Lewis Mumford's question, "how far shall one go back in demonstrating the fact that war has been the chief propagator of the machine,"[1] a number of books have been published concerning the relationship between technology and warfare. However, most of these have taken a wide chronological and geographical sweep at the subject, choosing to analyze military technology over the ages and around the world rather than focusing on a narrower time and place. This is certainly the case in a number of prominent works of this genre, for example, Bernard and Fawn M. Brodie's *From Crossbow to H-Bomb*, William McNeill's *The Pursuit of Power: Technology, Armed Force, and Society since A.D. 1000*, Martin van Creveld's *Technology and War from 2000 B.C. to the Present*, and Robert L. O'Connell's *Of Arms and Men: A History of War, Weapons and Aggression*.[2] Consequently, the Middle Ages, as every other period, is dealt with in only a few pages, a short survey insufficient to meet the demands of a reader interested in studying military technology in the years between the Fall of Rome and the sixteenth century.

This book presents a short, but comprehensive, look at military technology during the Middle Ages. It concentrates on the invention, manufacture, and use of the technologies that made medieval warfare the material for legends and movies. It discusses the arms and armor that once determined the death or life of soldiers and now fill our museums, artillery that once shook the walls of towns and fortresses and now are reconstructed for television documentaries, the castles and fortifications that once protected the population and now serve as tourist havens, and ships that served as vehicles for trade as well as war and now serve as sites for the dives of underwater archaeologists. While technical when required, this book is directed mainly at the general reader with the intention of serving as a textbook and as a reference guide for medieval scholars.

The book is divided into four parts, each of which is further divided into chapters. Part One examines the technology of arms and armor during the Middle Ages. Chapter One discusses the offensive weapons of the medieval soldier: the spear, lance, axe, sword, dagger, staff-weapon, mace, hammer, sling, bow (both short and long), and crossbow. Chapter Two deals with armor, including shields, helmets, and body armor. And Chapter Three discusses the debate that arose with Lynn White's article on the stirrup's role in the origin of feudalism: "Stirrup, Mounted Shock Combat, Feudalism, and Chivalry."

Part Two examines the technology of artillery. Chapter Four discusses the history and use in battle and at sieges of non-gunpowder artillery: *ballistae*, *onagers*, and traction and counterweight trebuchets, as well as that very curious incendiary (or probably incendiaries) known as Greek Fire. Chapter Five deals with gunpowder artillery, its invention, proliferation, and use before 1500. And Chapter Six discusses other medieval siege machines.

Part Three examines the technology of fortifications. It is divided into four chapters. Chapter Seven discusses the continued use of Roman fortifications as well as the construction of new fortifications in the Early Middle Ages. Chapter Eight deals with the motte-and-bailey castle, a fortification built from earth and wood. Chapter Nine, the longest in this section, discusses stone castles. And, finally, Chapter Ten discusses urban fortifications and fortified residences.

The final section of this book, Part Four, is concerned with the construction of warships during the Middle Ages. It is divided into two chapters, Chapter Eleven dealing with early medieval warships from the late Roman period to the eleventh century and Chapter Twelve discussing later medieval warships beginning with Crusader technology. The two chapters detail the inventions and innovations in shipbuilding that affected naval warfare throughout these periods and discuss the weaponry that was invented or adapted for use in fighting at sea.

What this book does not want to be is overly deterministic. It is said that only non-historians of technology believe in technological determinism. Whether this is the case is perhaps more easily discussed on conference panels and at professional historical roundtables; this book aims only to present the current historical thought or, in many instances, debate on medieval military technology.[3] I hope I have done this without showing any prejudices, although that may be virtually impossible.

The above introduction is a minor reworking of that of the first edition of this book, published in 1992, then by just one of the present authors, Kelly DeVries, a historian. In this, the second edition, almost all of the original text has been substantially rewritten with the collaboration of a second author, Robert Douglas Smith, an artefactual scholar, whose expertise has come from more than a quarter of a century of studying, curating, and conserving the very arms, armor, and artillery presented in the book. Of course, the medieval military technology described is still the same, and this has allowed the organization of the book to remain unaltered. However, the interpretation of this technology has changed and developed. Since the first edition many historians and artefactual experts have made medieval military history and technology one of the liveliest and most interesting fields in all of historical research and scholarship, let alone in the fields of medieval and military history. Many of these scholars have retrodden old ground, although more often than not presenting new ideas and interpretations of it, but many others have opened new roads of research. Their activity alone warrants a frequent updating of this synthesis, and while a period of 20 years between editions might not be considered by anyone as "frequent," this edition will, we hope, keep the editors of the University of Toronto Press and military historians and teachers happy for at least another decade.

Notes

1. Mumford (1934): 86.

2. Brodie and Brodie (1973); McNeill (1982); van Creveld (1989); O'Connell (1989). Boot (2006) does the same, but only for the period from 1500 to the present.

3. Two relatively recent articles that discuss medieval military technological determinism are Bartlett (1986) and Stone (2004).

PART I

Arms
and
Armor

IT MIGHT WELL BE AN EXAGGERATION TO CLAIM THAT THE MIDDLE AGES would mean little to the modern world without its characteristic offensive and defensive armaments. Yet, certainly for the purposes of modern culture as conveyed by fantasy novels, comics, and Hollywood films, is there anything more evocative of medieval society than the knight in shining armor, lance couched under his arm, bearing down on his tournament opponent, or the Viking warrior with his battle axe slicing through defenseless peasants and monks? Could King Arthur be the greatest king of England without his trusty sword, Excalibur, pulled from the rock as a symbol of his right to rule? Or Robin Hood without his longbow, sending its arrow to split an opponent's in the Sheriff of Nottingham's archery competition? Or Roland without his longsword, cutting a Muslim foe (and his horse) clean in half? Or Macbeth without his dagger, murdering Duncan, the king of Scotland? Truly, the Middle Ages without their distinctive arms and armor would lose some of their defining images and unique character.

Anthropologists have difficulty determining when the first armaments were invented. Some steadfastly adhere to the theory that warfare is a manmade activity, learned but not inherent, and that early weapons were initially invented as agricultural implements and not as tools of war. Others take the opposite side of the debate, arguing for an original invention of weapons.[1]

Whatever might be the answer, and it will probably never be known for sure, by the beginning of the Stone Age (c.70,000 BCE), early man had begun to use spears, fire, and stone clubs as protection against animals and other men. By the end of the Paleolithic Age (35,000–12,000 BCE), cave paintings show that Neanderthal and Cro-Magnon man had also begun to use strategy and tactics to integrate their weaponry with their combat, thus creating the first organized warfare. Their weaponry fitted into three categories: clubs, stone axes, and thrusting spears used for short-range warfare; throwing spears (javelins) for medium-range warfare; and throwing stones for longer-range warfare.[2]

The Mesolithic Age (12,000–7000 BCE) saw the first real development in arms: the invention of the sling and the bow and arrow. These increased the range, generally extending to around 100–200 meters, and the damage caused by their impact. They also allowed the user to remain concealed and, when used in a group, to unleash a barrage of missile fire. Only the biblical story of David and Goliath need be recalled to exemplify the fatal result of such a missile fired accurately from the smallest warrior against the largest foe. Seemingly of less importance was the invention of the mace and the rudimentary dagger, which also appeared at this time and quickly took the place of the club next to the traditional short-range thrusting spear and stone axe. Cave paintings also depict the introduction of protective clothing (proto-armor) worn by some of these late–Stone Age soldiers.[3]

Neolithic man began experimenting with the use of copper as early as 6000 BCE in Anatolia, but it took 2,000 years before the extraction and smelting of metals produced bronze strong enough (and cheap enough) to replace traditional stone tools and armaments. Spears, javelins, arrows, maces, and axes were now crowned by a hard bronze head, which could be easily sharpened. Indeed, archaeological remains from Ancient Mesopotamia and Egypt show that the metallic axe was the most preferred weapon of these civilizations. Daggers were a more viable short-range weapon, especially when lengthened, as bronze now made possible, to produce a sword that could be used both to pierce and to slash an enemy. With bronze weaponry came the invention of stronger, more protective armor: helmets, shields, breastplates, and greaves. Chariots also appeared during the Bronze Age, used primarily as a mode of transportation to and around the battlefield or as mobile missile-launching platforms.[4]

Around 1200 BCE, iron began to replace bronze, and armies began to adopt more systematized armaments policies. Frequently, soldiers became known by the name of their armament—e.g., the Greek *hoplite* named after his distinctive shield, the *hoplon*; and the *cataphract*, the cavalryman called by the name of his heavy armor—while certain lands were known to produce mercenaries especially skilled in the use of a single weapon—e.g., Dahae Horse Archers, Numidian Light Cavalrymen, Rhodian or Balearic Slingers, Aetolian Javelinmen, and Cretan or Syrian Archers. The types of weapons, however, remained the same: the spear, sword, and axe were the primary short-range weapons; the javelin for medium range; and the sling and bow the primary long-range weapons. The only major changes came with the introduction of the staff-sling (the *fundibalus*), which was capable of throwing a 400-gram stone or a dart over 200 meters, and in the length of the spear, which expanded during the Macedonian period to a length of more than seven meters. This latter weapon (known as a *sarissa*) became the principal offensive armament of the armies of Philip of Macedon and Alexander the Great, who used it in their victories against Greece, Persia, the Middle East, Egypt, and the western portion of India.[5]

From the beginning of their history, Roman armies too were characterized largely by the use of a single weapon, the *pilum*, a heavy javelin, used either as a thrusting or a thrown weapon. The early Roman soldier also carried a dagger, a helmet, and a large, oblong shield called a *scutum*. This remained the standard equipment for the Roman soldier for more than a thousand years. Styles changed, armor for the torso was added, and a short sword (the *gladius*) replaced the dagger, but otherwise the standard equipment was little modified until the fourth or fifth centuries CE. And why should it have been? The Roman armies dominated the Mediterranean world from the time of their defeat of the Greeks and Carthaginians in the second century BCE until the invasions of barbarian tribes from across the Danube and Rhine rivers brought its fall in the late fourth and early fifth centuries.[6]

Trying to link the armaments of the ancient world with those of the medieval world is an impossible task. While the types of armament varied little between the two periods, and in fact varied little between the Stone Age and the twentieth century, their construction, conception, and tactical use varied considerably. The following three chapters will endeavor to explain these differences, following the development of offensive armaments thematically and the development of defensive armaments chronologically. A chapter will also attempt to summarize the theory, put forth by Lynn White, Jr., that the diffusion of the stirrup to Western Europe led to what has been called feudalism; both White's thesis and criticisms of it will be discussed.

Notes

1. Ferrill (1985): 15–16.
2. Ferrill (1985): 16–17.
3. Ferrill (1985): 18–26.
4. Ferrill (1985): 38–44.
5. On the weaponry of the Greek armies see Hanson (1989): 55–88 and Ferrill (1985): 99–102. On the weaponry of the Macedonian army see Ferrill (1985): 175–80. For both see A. Hall (1957): II: 695–700.
6. See Bishop and Coulston (1989): 17–62; Webster (1985): 127–29; and A. Hall (1957): II: 703–7.

CHAPTER I

ARMS

THE ROMAN SOLDIERS WHO FACED THE BARBARIAN INVASIONS OF THE
fourth and fifth centuries carried weapons that varied little from those carried
by the first-century legionnaires. The spear was still the major Roman infantry
weapon, although three different sizes of spear had replaced the earlier *pilum*:
the short *verutum*, having a head with an average measurement of 12.5 centimeters and a shaft measuring 60.5 centimeters; the long *spiculum*, with a head
23 centimeters long and a shaft 167.5 centimeters in length; and the *plumbata*, a
short javelin with a barbed and lead-weighted head. Swords were also carried
by infantry soldiers, although the *spathae*, as they were now called, were much
longer (72 centimeters) than the original *gladii*. Support troops continued to
use bows, slings, and staff slings.[1] Late Roman cavalry, which remained few
in number compared with the large number of infantry and were generally
manned by non-Italian soldiers, were equipped with a long spear (later called
a lance) and a long sword. Because the cavalry had no stirrups, both the spear
and sword were used primarily in close-combat situations.[2]

The barbarian soldiers whom they faced in the fourth and fifth centuries
had different weapons, and different attitudes toward these weapons, than did
the Romans. For one thing, there was little standardization among, or even
within, the various tribal armies that invaded the empire. The Visigoths and
Ostrogoths, who were successful in their initial conquests largely because of

Fig. 1.1: Barbarian horseman. Sandstone relief.

bpk, Berlin / Art Resource, NY.

their overwhelming numbers, probably had very few arms, acquiring most of their offensive weapons from trading with the Romans or from having taken them as booty. The Huns, on the other hand, were mostly horse archers, using the lance only as a secondary weapon. The Franks preferred the axe as their main offensive armament, both as a close-combat, handheld weapon and as a missile.[3]

Second, while first-century Roman writers such as Tacitus had been quite disparaging in their assessment of early barbarian armaments, by the time of the invasions, barbarian weaponry had improved in both quality and variety. The infantry still used spears as their chief weapon, but these had been improved with better and stronger iron heads. They also carried axes, bows with iron-tipped arrows, and swords. The chief weapon of the cavalry was a long, two-edged sword.[4] At least initially, although the weapons of the barbarians were not as strong or well-made as those of the Romans, the invaders seemed to recognize these limitations and were able to modify their tactics until they could more effectively use their "inferior" weapons. The Romans were unable to do the same, and this tactical failure may have added to their ultimate inability to defeat the invaders of the empire.[5]

Finally, barbarian soldiers generally carried a greater quantity of arms, often at the expense of armor. This characteristic especially astounded the late Roman chroniclers, as it was quite different from the tradition of their own soldiers. These authors describe at great length the large number of weapons carried by the barbarians. For example, Sidonius Apollinaris relates his first encounter with Frankish soldiers in 470:

> Their swords hung from their shoulders on baldricks, and
> round their waists they wore a belt of fur adorned with
> bosses. . . . In their right hands they held barbed lances and
> throwing-axes, and in their left shields, on which the light
> shone, white on the circuit and red on the boss, displaying
> both opulence and craftsmanship.

And Procopius, writing a century later, records a similar impression of the Franks:

> The military equipment of this people is very simple. . . .
> They do not know the use of the coat of mail or greaves and
> the head the majority leave uncovered, only a few wear the
> helmet. They have their chests bare and backs naked to the
> loins, they cover their thighs with either leather or linen. . . .
> Fighting on foot is both habitual and a national custom and
> they are proficient in this. At the hip they wear a sword and
> on the left side their shield is attached. They have neither
> bows nor slings, no missile weapons except the double
> edged axe and the *angon* which they use most often. The
> *angons* are spears which are neither very short nor very long;

they can be used, if necessary for throwing like a javelin, and also, in hand to hand combat.[6]

In the long term the barbarian tribes overran Europe, defeating the Romans, and their weaponry and warring traditions became the model for the Middle Ages. Almost all medieval weapons were known at the time of the barbarian invasions—spears, lances, axes, daggers, swords, clubs, slings and bows—and those which developed later—particularly staff-weapons and crossbows—generally evolved from these.

THE SPEAR/LANCE

Since the earliest times the spear, together with the sword, was the most important and widely used offensive weapon for both the infantry and cavalry. In the earlier medieval period it was used both as a handheld thrusting weapon and as a missile. Though the spear was used throughout the medieval period, the lance, used particularly by cavalry in the couched position, under the right arm, developed from the spear, and could deliver a more effective and harder strike.

The spear was the primary arm of the Roman legionnaire; it was also the principal weapon of their fourth- and fifth-century barbarian enemies. While these barbarian spears were technologically simpler than the *pila* used by the Romans, they were nevertheless effective on the battlefield. This was noted as early as the first century, when Tacitus wrote:

> Only a few of them use swords or large lances: they carry spears—called *frameae* in their language—with short and narrow blades, but so sharp and easy to handle that they can be used, as required, either at close quarters or in long-range fighting. Their horsemen are content with a shield and spear; but the foot-soldiers also rain javelins on their foes: each of them carries several, and they hurl them to immense distances . . . .[7]

Barbarian spears were not, however, uniform in size or shape. M. J. Swanton's impressive study, *The Spearheads of the Anglo-Saxon Settlements*, reveals that 12 different types of spearheads have been found in Anglo-Saxon archaeological excavations. These he further grouped into four main categories: derivative forms of Germanic spear-types prior to the Anglo-Saxon settlement in England; leaf-shaped blades; angular blades; and corrugated blades. While chronological and regional differences can account for some of the variations in spearhead styles, on the whole the conclusion must be that the Anglo-Saxons saw no need for consistency. Each smith probably created his own style of spearhead.[8] The same must also be true for early medieval spears across continental Europe. Although a study similar to the depth and mastery of Swanton's does not exist for continental or Scandinavian Europe, the archaeological remains of spearheads from these regions show a similar lack of uniformity.[9]

Sidonius Apollinaris, Procopius, and Gregory of Tours all note the spear as an important, if not *the* most important, weapon of the Frankish soldiers, but none of their descriptions suggests that it was a particularly special weapon. Agathias, writing at almost the same time as Procopius and Gregory of Tours, describes a weapon, which he calls an *angon*:

> The *angons* are spears which are neither short nor long; they can be used, if necessary for throwing like a javelin, and also, in hand to hand combat. The greater part of the *angon* is covered with iron and very little wood is exposed. Above, at the top of the spear, on each side from the socket itself where the staff is fixed, some points are turned back, bent like hooks, and turned toward the handle. In battle, the Frank throws the *angon*, and if it hits an enemy the spear is caught in the man and neither the wounded man nor anyone else can draw it out. The barbs hold inside the flesh causing great pain and in this way a man whose wound may not be in a vital spot still dies. If the *angon* strikes a shield, it is fixed there, hanging down with the butt on the ground. The *angon* cannot be pulled out because the barbs have penetrated the shield, nor can it be cut off with a sword because the wood of the shaft is covered with iron. When the Frank sees the situation, he quickly puts his foot on the butt of the spear, pulling down and the man holding it falls, the head and chest are left unprotected. The unprotected warrior is then killed either by a stroke of the axe or a thrust with another spear.[10]

It is unclear whether this is an accurate description of Frankish spears in general, but most modern historians accept it as such.[11] A similar spear is described

Fig. 1.2: Carolingian horse, from the *Golden Psalter* (*Psalterium aureum*).

Sankt-Gallen Stiftsbibliothek, Cod. Sang. 22, page 140 (digital version).

in the tenth-century poem *Waltheri*; it had three cords attached to its end so that, when it was stuck into an enemy's shield, these cords could be used to pull him over and kill him.[12]

Charlemagne (r.768–814), carried out a major restructuring of his army, not only reforming the command structure, organization, and tactics, but also attempting to establish a standardized weapons policy. As early as 792–93, the

Carolingian law known as *Capitulare missorum* stated that all horsemen must carry a spear, and this was repeated in capitularies of 804 and 811. The infantry was also required to carry spears, as directed in the *Aachen Capitulary*, decreed in 802–803.[13] Further evidence can be found in artistic sources, all of which show the spear as the predominant weapon carried by both the Carolingian cavalry and infantry.[14] The Carolingian spear appears not to have been a missile weapon; artistic and literary sources indicate that both the cavalry and the infantry used it primarily as a thrusting weapon. Indeed, after the middle of the eighth century, the Frankish javelin or *angon* is no longer found in archaeological excavations.[15]

The spear continued to be a simple thrusting weapon. It used just the weight and power of the individual infantry soldier, either thrusting downwards in a stabbing motion, or upwards in an attempt to strike an opponent under his armor or to lift him from his horse. However, for the cavalry, using the spear on horseback and holding it under his arm, in what came to be called the couched position, meant that a horseman could utilize the power and speed of his mount to produce a far greater impact at the point of attack than a manual thrust could.

This type of warfare has been called "mounted shock combat" by modern historians, a phrase that correctly recreates what must have been an extremely forceful and "shocking" attack. It clearly impressed medieval writers, many of whom recount this form of combat in graphic detail. Take, for example, the results of such an attack as described in *The Song of Roland*:

> He breaks his shield and bursts open his hauberk, cuts
> through his bones, and tears away the whole spine from his
> back; with his lance he casts out his soul; he thrusts it well
> home and causes his body to swing back and hurls him dead
> from his horse a full lance-length away.[16]

Although certainly exaggerating the effects of such an attack, the anonymous writer quite clearly shows the impression that contemporaries had of mounted shock combat, an impression that led the Byzantine princess Anna Comnena to believe that a Crusade horseman could "bore his way through the walls of Babylon."[17] As R.H.C. Davis has written, "The purpose of a charge was not just to hit one's opponent but to gallop through the enemy ranks so as to make them panic and flee."[18] It is likely that the spear underwent some development to enable it to be used in this new way. It was made stronger to withstand the additional impact; the head was usually leaf shaped with a sharp point,

Fig. 1.3: Infantry army from the eleventh century.

sometimes with "wings" at its base to prevent too deep a penetration; and a hand grip was made at the rear end.[19]

There is considerable uncertainty about when mounted shock combat was first practiced. Historians for many centuries assumed that the tactic was developed early in the Middle Ages, perhaps even as early as the battle of Adrianople (378). This was countered effectively in 1951, when D.J.A. Ross, in an article entitled *"Plein sa hanste"* ("The Couched Lance"), contended that the first descriptions of couched lances could not be found before the composition of the early *chansons de geste*, which he dated to 1050–1100.[20] This thesis in turn was rebutted in 1962 when Lynn White, Jr., published his *Medieval Technology and Social Change*. In a chapter entitled "Stirrup, Mounted Shock Combat, Feudalism, and Chivalry" (which will be discussed more thoroughly in Chapter Three below), White claimed that mounted shock combat was known much earlier than the date that Ross had established, possibly as early as the eighth century, the century that White believed saw the development of stirrups and the origin of the heavy cavalry-based army.[21]

But White's date for the origin of mounted shock combat did not stand long without criticism. Within a year, Ross had defended his 1951 thesis, using not only the *chansons de geste* but also the Bayeux Tapestry as evidence,[22] and this was echoed over the next two decades by a number of articles supporting him, all of which established the date of the introduction of mounted shock combat to sometime between c.1050 and c.1150: in 1965, François Buttin used a copious number of original narrative sources to claim a mid-twelfth-century date;[23] in 1980, David C. Nicolle affirmed an early-twelfth-century date based on the influence of Crusader couched-lance warfare against the Muslims;[24] in 1985, Bernard S. Bachrach established a twelfth-century date based upon the development of the high cantel and high pommel saddle;[25] the same year, Victoria Cirlot, using Catalan artistic, diplomatic, and literary sources, set the date at c.1140;[26] and in 1988, Jean Flori affirmed a date of c.1100 based on Christian and Muslim narratives, epics, and illustrated documents.[27]

Whatever the original date may have been, it seems certain that by the middle of the twelfth century the use of the couched lance had begun to dominate the battlefield, and that from then until the end of the Middle Ages, mounted shock combat was the only use of the lance from horseback. It was also a tactic universally employed throughout Western Europe. This is clearly seen in the large number of artistic sources from all western kingdoms depicting the cavalry lance held in a couched position.[28] Contemporary chronicles report that the lance was the principal offensive weapon of the Crusaders in the Holy Land, where the first attack in a battle was always a mounted shock combat charge.[29] In England, the 1181 Assize of Arms decreed by Henry II specifies only the lance as a required weapon for horsemen in battle.[30] A similar requirement was ordered of all cavalry soldiers in Florence in 1260.[31]

Despite its obvious simplicity, however, mounted shock combat was not an easy form of warfare to learn, and cavalry soldiers had to train extensively before they could wield the lance with dexterity and skill. R.H.C. Davis described how the lance was used:

If one was to hold a lance horizontal and steady while gal-
loping a horse, it was essential to secure the lance at more
than a single point. If it was well balanced, one could hold
it in one hand and tuck the rear end under one's armpit, but
even this position was hard on the wrist, and could not be
maintained for long. It was therefore normal for knights to
hold their lance upright, not only when on the march, but
also at the start of a charge, resting it (from the middle of
the twelfth to the fourteenth century) on a "fewter" or felt
butt on the saddle bow. As the charge developed, and at the
last moment, the lances were lifted off the fewters and their
points lowered or "couched." So as to ensure that the weight
of the lance and the force of its blow did not unbalance the
rider by being on his right side only, the point of the lance
was held to the left of the horse's head with the base secured
tightly under the rider's right armpit. Aim was taken by
steering the horse and, if necessary, by twisting one's whole
body in the saddle.[32]

Training for warfare was always a part of the education of the nobility, and
mock battles, or *melées*, developed very early as a means to hone the skills and
techniques needed in battle, particularly on horseback. To develop the skills
of using the couched lance, the tournament emerged in the very last decades
of the eleventh or first decades of the twelfth century.[33] In the twelfth and thirteenth centuries, jousters at these tournaments generally used the same lances
as they would on the battlefield, with the sharp lance head removed and a blunt
coronal replacing it if fighting in a tournament *à plaisance*; in a tournament *à out-
rance*, which more explicitly imitated warfare, the sharp warhead remained. The
coronal prevented the lancehead from piercing an opponent's armor, although
the impact was still usually forceful enough to knock him from his horse. The
lance was usually fitted with a small flared plate, the vamplate, just in front of
the hand grip to protect the hand. In the late medieval period breastplates were
fitted with a projection on the right side, which was used to enable the rider to
steady and aim the lance more accurately.[34]

While the cavalry lance went through several modifications as mounted
shock combat developed, the infantry spear remained relatively unchanged
between the time of Charlemagne and the fourteenth century. It continued to
be short, measuring usually no more than two meters in length, and was made

of light wood with an iron spearhead. Still, it remained the primary weapon of the infantry soldier on the battlefield.[35] In the fifteenth century the infantry spear lengthened to become a pike. In this form it continued to dominate infantry warfare until well into the eighteenth century.[36]

THE AXE

As a weapon of war the axe was used extensively throughout the medieval period. In the early Middle Ages it was both a smashing and missile weapon, although the two functions were fulfilled by axes of different sizes: the smaller, lighter axe was thrown and the larger, heavier axe was used in hand-to-hand combat. The axe also became associated especially with Viking and Anglo-Saxon elite warriors. In the high and later Middle Ages, although still used, it was not often the primary weapon of a soldier. It was also used almost exclusively as a close-quarter infantry weapon, with a few notable exceptions.

Technically quite sophisticated and able to smash and pierce armor, the barbarian axe (known as a *francisca*), had application both as a weapon and as a tool. Late Roman chroniclers were especially impressed with these axes, reporting that barbarian soldiers used axes both in close infantry combat and as missile weapons. As close-combat weapons, they were wielded by barbarian invaders in order to withstand and defeat imperial infantry while, when thrown in unison, they were capable of shattering Roman shields and sometimes killing the soldiers behind them.[37] Based on the large number of *franciscae* excavated from barbarian graves, the average throwing axe weighed 1.2 kilograms, the head accounting for between 300 and 900 grams. The handle measured 40 centimeters in length and the head 18 centimeters. Modern experiments have indicated how they were thrown: they could strike an opponent with significant force at four meters with a single rotation, at eight meters with a double rotation, and at 12 meters with a triple rotation.[38] The throwing axe remained important to barbarian soldiers until the beginning of the seventh century, when for some as yet undetermined reason it began to decline in use and eventually disappeared altogether.

The handheld battle axe, however, continued to be used as an infantry weapon throughout the rest of the Middle Ages. Perhaps nowhere and at no other time was it more popular than when used by Vikings.[39] It was certainly their chief weapon when they are recorded as attacking Lindisfarne Abbey in 793, and it continued until at least the end of the eleventh century. To the

Vikings, the long-handled, broad-edged battle axe was a symbol of warrior status and was often buried with its owner so that he might take it on his journey to Valhalla. To their victims, the Viking axe, typically called a "Danish axe" no matter who was wielding it, was a symbol of the bloodthirsty violence of marauding warriors.

There were two types of Viking battle axe. The first was known as the *skeggøx* or bearded axe, because its blade was drawn down like a beard. Archaeological specimens of this type have been dated as early as the eighth century, when they may have been primarily tools adapted for warfare, and they continued to be used well beyond the end of the Viking raids. The second type of battle axe used by the Vikings was the *breidøx* or broad axe. These had a more triangular-shaped head and were used almost exclusively as weapons. They do not appear until 1000, but after this time they seem to have been the axe of choice among Viking warriors. The cutting edge of the broad axe was often made of steel, low-carbon iron, which could be hardened and welded onto the head, and the blade and neck were sometimes decorated with silver or gold inlay.[40]

Once the Vikings conquered England, the battle axe also became popular among Anglo-Saxon warriors. The Anglo-Saxon battle axe was much the same as the Viking broad axe, although its effectiveness was increased by the organization and training of the Anglo-Saxon army. It was also the chief weapon carried by the Anglo-Saxon army at Hastings, as depicted in the Bayeux Tapestry; both professional Anglo-Saxon soldiers (the *huscarls*) and conscripts (the *fyrd*) are shown using it, and indeed William the Conqueror himself is shown wielding one in the Bayeux Tapestry.[41] The axe was also known across Western Europe and used extensively throughout the continent.

Following the conquest of England by William, the use of the battle axe among English soldiers diminished, but it did not die out completely. Norman Englishmen continued to use the weapon, and legend has it that Richard the Lionheart took one to the Holy Land on his Crusade, as his main weapon against the Saracens.[42]

Throughout the rest of the Middle Ages, literary, artistic, and archaeological evidence shows that the axe was still popular as a military weapon, especially for the infantry. It is mentioned often in medieval literature: for example, in the chivalric tale *Sir Gawain and the Green Knight*, the axe plays a principal role as the weapon of challenge from the Green Knight to Sir Gawain. (Gawain is challenged to behead the Green Knight with a battle axe and agrees to allow the Green Knight, should he survive this wound, to do the same a year later to Gawain.[43])

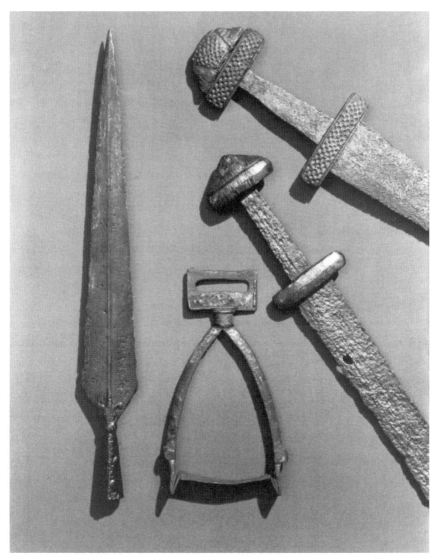

Fig. 1.4: Viking arms.

The Bridgeman Art Library International / Nationalmuseet, Copenhagen, Denmark.

In artistic sources the battle axe also appears frequently, in a variety of styles and lengths. Most are shaped like the bearded or broad axes of the Vikings and Anglo-Saxons, while others are shown with spikes, hammers or points at the opposite end to the axe head. Finally, a few are depicted with long axe heads, the tips of which are curved back and either resting on or attached to the haft in what may be a precursor to the staff-weapons that became common later.

Short-handled axes are also frequently depicted, although they were apparently not thrown.[44]

There are a large number of extant examples of medieval battle-axe heads. These date from the tenth to the fourteenth centuries and are found across Europe, although it is apparent from the large number of finds in Northern and Eastern Europe that the axe continued to be favored there more than in other European lands. Most of them reveal little more than what can be learned from artistic sources; they are all similar in size and shape to the axes of the Vikings and Anglo-Saxons, with only slight and limited changes. These included a sharply upward sweep in some axe blades of the twelfth and thirteenth centuries; the addition of a hammer on the back of some axe blades; and an increase in the thickness of some blades as plate armor began to develop and become more plentiful in the fifteenth century. However, axe heads found in Poland and Hungary remain comparatively thin.[45]

By the fourteenth century, the battle axe began to diminish greatly in popularity as pole-axes, halberds, and other staff-weapons, all of which had evolved from the battle axe, were used more frequently by infantry soldiers. However, at the same time as the infantry began to reject the axe, the cavalry developed a smaller, lightweight form as a close-combat weapon. The "horseman's axe," as it became known, had a small head with a curved blade and a hammer at the back. Its haft was the same length as the mace and war hammer, and it was probably wielded in a similar fashion to those other close-combat weapons.[46] This may be the type of axe reputedly used by Robert Bruce to kill Sir Henry de Bohun, earl of Lancaster, at the battle of Bannockburn in 1314.[47]

———

THE SWORD

Of all medieval weapons the sword was perhaps the most common, along with the spear in the earlier period, and certainly the most celebrated. At all times they ranged from the most utilitarian and cheap to the most intricately made and expensive—weapons to be passed down through the generations. They were also frequently named, with King Arthur's "Excalibur" and Roland's "Durendal" perhaps the most famous. A sword consisted of a single piece of iron forming the blade and tang fitted with a cross-guard, the form of which changed over the years, and a grip for the hand secured in place with a pommel at the end, the form of which changed largely with changes in fashion. Simple, cheap swords were made from iron, while better blades were edged with steel or made from intricately formed rods of iron forged together, the so-called pattern-welded blades. The form of the blade and its length varied over time to reflect both fashion and the enemy to be faced. All swords would have been kept in a scabbard, usually made from wood covered in leather, and hung at the side of the warrior.

The Romans of late antiquity had both long and short swords, which they used as secondary weapons to their *pila*. The existence of barbarian swords was reported by Tacitus, who in his derisive tone claimed that they had not many of them, as their iron "is not plentiful."[48] But if they were not numerous in the first century, they seem to have improved both in abundance and quality by the fourth and fifth centuries, for almost all barbarian soldiers were reported, by contemporary chroniclers, to have carried one.[49] This can also be seen in the numerous archaeological excavations of barbarian gravesites, almost all of which contain a sword. These barbarian swords were of varying length and type. A few, probably those owned by tribal military leaders, were long (75–100 centimeters), narrow (around 6 centimeters wide), heavy, and double-edged, and most were decorated. Others were shorter, measuring 40 centimeters in length. A third group was up to 85 centimeters in length with a width of between 4 and 6.5 centimeters, but, unlike the long swords, these were lighter and probably were meant to be wielded only with one hand. (These swords may correspond to the weapon known to contemporary chroniclers as the *seax*, *sax* or *scramasax*.) Small versions of the same sword, measuring around 20 centimeters in length, have also been found. Their pommels were of various sizes and shapes, and all had a hilt of wood covered with leather. They were made of finely forged iron of a quality equal or superior to contemporary Roman swords.[50]

Swords continued to be valued across Europe throughout the early Middle Ages. The Code of Ervig (680–687) even made the ownership of a sword mandatory for all men, Goth or Roman, joining the Visigothic army.[51] In Anglo-Saxon England the sword was held in a similarly high regard. As H.R. Ellis Davidson has shown in her study, *The Sword in Anglo-Saxon England*, it was an integral part of Anglo-Saxon military society. Relying on both literary and archaeological sources, she has determined that while the axe, spear, and bow were important weapons to the pre-Conquest English, "they had none of the richness of association possessed by the sword."[52]

The sword was often a potent symbol, especially of leadership in the ruling classes. One would be given to a boy as a gift at birth, at his naming or when he reached manhood. The child would grow up playing with it and with other, lighter swords, so that it became a weapon he could wield with strength and agility. In some cases the sword would not be new but would be a family treasure that had been passed down from one warrior to the next, a token of past wars fought, maybe for many generations. The sword could also be won by prowess in war or battle: Beowulf, for example, received a magnificent sword from the Danish leader, Hrothgar, to reward his defeat of Grendel and Grendel's mother. A sword could also be given as a mark of fealty or to reward service to a lord. The sword was the warrior's constant companion, carried at all times and, at his death, either buried with him or passed on to his son or close relative.[53]

High-quality swords were made in an intricate and complex way so that, on completion, they appeared to have what is often called a "watered" surface. Rods of iron were joined, forge-welded, edge-to-edge, and the subsequent billet twisted and folded and hammered out to the desired overall shape. Following grinding and polishing, the surface was then treated to reveal a fine pattern that has been compared to watered silk, today also called pattern-welding. A blade made in this way would have been extremely expensive and much prized. It would have been finished by adding a simple cross-guard to prevent an opponent's sword sliding up the blade, a wooden grip covered in leather, and a pommel, at this time generally of "brazil-nut" form. Often the blade was further decorated with an inlaid inscription, usually in silver, of the maker's name or a talismanic formula.[54] While Ellis Davidson's work is concerned solely with Anglo-Saxon swords, the social atmosphere which she found surrounding the possession of a sword existed everywhere throughout the early Middle Ages.

In Charlemagne's many capitularies referring to weaponry, the sword is always prominent. When a warhorse is owned, so too should a sword; in fact, in many sources the sword is reported to be the cavalry soldier's primary weapon. But while a new emphasis on ownership of the sword was present in Carolingian Europe, and the numbers of these weapons increased dramatically, the sword itself had not changed much from earlier Frankish examples. It was still usually a simple broad shape, either single- or double-edged, with a

Fig. 1.5: Seax.

ARMS AND ARMOR

rounded point made for slashing and cutting rather than thrusting. The hilt was usually fitted with a simple straight cross-guard, grip, and pommel. Both the long sword and the *seax* continued to be carried, as attested to in both literary and archaeological sources. However, the one-handed *seax* began to disappear at the end of the eighth century.

The only change that seems to have been made to Carolingian swords is in the shape of the blade. Earlier swords had edges that ran parallel for most of the length of the blade, converging only at the end to form a point. In the beginning of the ninth century, this construction was changed so that the blade tapered gradually from the hilt to the tip. This shifted the center of gravity closer to the sword grip and made the weapon more maneuverable and easier to handle in combat, while at the same time not losing any strength in the blade itself.

Carolingian swords were almost always inscribed with the name of the maker—Ulfberht and Ingelrii being the most famous—and sometimes, for the wealthiest owners, the hilt was decorated with gold, silver, gems or jewels. The scabbards, made of wood covered with leather, were also decorated, and these were hung on a sword-belt around the waist; earlier swords were hung either on a belt or from a baldrick across the shoulder.[55]

Carolingian swords were well known throughout Europe; examples from the ninth and tenth centuries have been found everywhere from Iceland to the Holy Land and from Spain to Russia. They were particularly favored among the Vikings who, despite using the axe and spear more frequently as infantry weapons, prized the sword above all other arms.[56] Carolingian swords also set the technological standard for sword making for several centuries, although this was mostly because of the large numbers being made rather than their comparative quality over earlier swords.[57] The swords on both sides of the Norman Conquest of England were Carolingian-influenced, either by direct diffusion or through their connection to the Vikings.[58] They were also the swords of the Spanish *Reconquista* and the First Crusade.[59] In all cases the sword was primarily a cavalry weapon, to be used in close combat, although infantry soldiers also could carry one if they could afford it.[60] The sword was the most expensive weapon.

From 800 to the eleventh century, swords did not differ in construction from the Carolingian archetype. This was probably because the mail armor that sword-bearers faced had not changed; it was difficult to penetrate at the best of times, but slashing at least gave the user a broader surface of attack. Sword blades remained flat and light, with sharper edges emphasized rather than a point. Only the size of the blade, the size of the hilt, and the style of pommel, cross-guard, grip, and scabbard changed, although generally for no other reason than personal preference.[61]

By the later eleventh century the sword usually consisted of a wide, double-edged blade with a somewhat rounded end, and a simple cross-guard and pommel. The sword was kept in a scabbard secured to a simple waist belt. This type of sword was used throughout the next two centuries, although not all swords in this period were identical. For example, there was considerable variation in length, from as short as 66 centimeters to as long as 96 centimeters. The cross-guard, although often just a plain straight crossbar of iron, could also be more elaborate: the ends might curve either away from or toward the hand, and it might be more ornately shaped and perhaps decorated. The pommel, too, tended to be relatively simple, with many swords having just a plain disc pommel, although some retained the so-called "brazil-nut" form common in the earlier medieval period.

The grip was usually short to fit the hand, although some swords had longer grips, which allowed them to be wielded with both hands to increase the power of attack. The grip was made from wood bound with leather and ranged from the simple to the very elaborately decorated high-status examples made for kings and nobles.

In the later thirteenth century the sword started to change, in response to changes in armor, it seems, from a slashing weapon with a relatively wide blade to a thrusting weapon where the point was used more than the edges. In the first half of the fourteenth century, sword blades were made narrower, tapered to the point, and of diamond or hexagonal cross section. The grip was also often lengthened and extended so that the sword could be used either in one or two hands. By the middle of the fifteenth century, the cross-guard was often curved toward the blade, and the disc and "brazil-nut" pommels were replaced by pommels of triangular, conical, or oval shape. National characteristics also emerged during this period, with swords of different designs developing in various areas of Europe.[62]

Over time more elaborate cross-guards developed. At first, an extra ring at the base of the blade was sometimes added through which the forefinger was inserted, and from the early fifteenth century an iron ring was also added to one side of the cross-guard as extra protection. From about 1450, a second ring was added to the other side. And by the end of the century pieces of iron, known as guards, were added from the cross-guard to the pommel to provide added protection for the hand. The hilt became increasingly more elaborate and additional guards were added, which in some cases almost enclosed the hand in a

ARMS AND ARMOR

Fig. 1.6: Sword with "brazil-nut" pommel—European, c. 1100.

Fig. 1.7: Sword with disc pommel—possibly English, c. 1325.

cage of iron bars. However, this development was neither straightforward nor regular, and many early features, such as a straight cross-guard, continued to be used on some types of sword.[63]

The falchion, a variation of the traditional longsword, was also introduced during the late Middle Ages. This was a short, single-edged weapon with a very broad, curved blade, shaped similarly to a modern machete. It also was primarily an infantry weapon and was not anywhere near as popular a sword as the more traditional style. However, in illustrations of the period, the falchion was often depicted as the sword of Muslim and Mongol warriors, or the sword used for executions.[64]

During the fifteenth century, there was also a tendency for swords to be made lighter, and, by the end of the century, they had become an essential part of everyday dress. As a result, these swords became more highly decorated and ornate, leading eventually to the development of the rapier in the sixteenth century, the civilian sword *par excellence*.[65] The thick, heavy, awkward, but finely crafted medieval sword passed into memory.

Training in the use of swords was of course very important, and swordsmanship was taught in a master/pupil relationship. From the early fourteenth century, the techniques of fighting with the sword started to be written down and illustrated, and there are manuscripts showing the various starting positions, called wards, and sequences of movements that were to be learned. Although only a few examples from the later Middle Ages survive, fencing books proliferated after the 1530s, when fencing became part of every gentleman's education.

During the early sixteenth century, a number of schools also began to be established throughout the capitals of Europe, and a number of different techniques developed.[66]

THE DAGGER

The dagger, essentially a very short sword, was a central element of a soldier's weapons, probably since antiquity, although evidence for it at that time is not always easy to find, a problem that exists throughout the Middle Ages as well. Moreover, it is often difficult to interpret what sources—written, archaeological, and artistic—there are: when, for instance, does a domestic knife, used for eating and in the kitchen, become a dagger for military use? This is almost impossible to tell, unless the dagger can be found used in military activity, and even then, who is to say that the two uses for this soldier were mutually exclusive? However, by the later medieval period the evidence becomes clearer, as daggers had assumed a much greater military importance, and many different types can be identified.

With respect to the early Middle Ages, the Visigoths, once they settled in Spain during the sixth century, began using daggers of a Hispano-Roman type.[67] The Franks also favored the weapon, with two of Charlemagne's capitularies, decreed in 804 and 811, requiring all cavalry soldiers to carry one.[68] In the north, both the Anglo-Saxons and the Vikings also commonly used the dagger. However, grave sites of both peoples show that short-bladed weapons were buried not only with male adults, but also with women and children. Indeed, according to a study by Heinrich Härke on knives in Anglo-Saxon burials, the size of the blade was related to the sex and age of the corpse: the male adult was buried with the largest, measuring an average of 170 millimeters; the female adult was buried with the second largest, an average of 130 millimeters; and children of both sexes were buried with the smallest, an average of 100–110 millimeters, although it is unlikely that the daggers buried with women and children were for military use.[69] In Byzantium, Emperor Justinian's sixth-century legal code, known as the *Institutes*, established that at least in that early medieval empire, the dagger was the preferred weapon of assassins.[70] Continental and Mediterranean archaeological remains from this period also show that the early medieval dagger was between 45 and 175 millimeters long, made of iron with a single sharp edge and a hilt of wood or bone.[71] Although the dagger does not appear on the Bayeux Tapestry, it was no doubt common by the eleventh century and, together with the sword, had become the primary weapon worn by those professional military men who would later become known as men-at-arms. With the sword portrayed in contemporary artworks almost always on the left hip, to be gripped in the right hand, the dagger could be worn vertically on the right hip or in front—to be gripped with the right hand—or almost horizontally behind the back—to be gripped with either hand. The latter meant that the dagger could be used either together with the sword or, when required, alone. Daggers are also depicted both with the blade pointed downwards, in a stabbing grip, and with the blade pointed upwards, in a thrusting grip. One or both edges could be sharpened.[72] Daggers were also frequently carried by civilians, with five of the characters in Geoffrey Chaucer's *Canterbury Tales* carrying one: the Yeoman, the shipman, the murderers of "The Pardoner's Tale," Simkin, and the Monk.[73]

After around 1250 a number of different types of dagger appeared across Europe. The first distinct type to appear was the cross-hilt or quillon dagger. It was so named by modern historians because of the characteristic cross-guard (quillons) that resembled the cross-guard of swords; in fact, artistic depictions and extant examples most often look like smaller versions of contemporary swords. The pommel could be of almost any shape: a disc, wheel, octagon or sphere. Early examples had pommels that curved away from the grip, the so-called antennae-pommel type, and quillons that swept down toward the blade, or pommels of crescent or ring form with straight quillons. The grip could be made in either one or two pieces and was usually wrapped in leather and wire. The blade was usually short and either double-edged, of flattened diamond section, or single-edged and triangular in shape, with a strong taper from the hilt to the point. Surviving scabbards are rare, especially early ones, but were probably made of leather with a metal throat and chape. Contemporary art has cross-hilt daggers used most often by knights and men-at-arms, and thus worn on the right side hanging from the sword belt on a cord or thong.[74]

A second type of dagger was the baselard, a contemporary name, from which it is thought to have originated in Basel, Switzerland, during the late thirteenth or early fourteenth century, and from where it quickly spread all over Europe. Very popular, these daggers had become so common by the early fifteenth century that an anonymous English poet wrote:

> There is no man worth a leke,
> Be he sturdy, be he meke,
> But he bear a basilard.

While in the fourteenth century the baselard was particularly an elite weapon, especially in southern Germany and Italy, by the fifteenth century, as suggested in the poem, it had become more of a commoner's weapon, to be used even by civilians. The hilt had a very characteristic form, with both the cross-guard and pommel ends giving it the shape of an 'H' on its side or a capital 'I'. The cross-guard pieces could be of equal length and quite small, but the typical baselard had a cross-guard that was slightly longer than the pommel. The grip was usually made of two pieces riveted through the tang, often with many rivets, and was made of wood, ivory, horn or bone. Although early examples have single-edged blades, most baselards were double-edged of flattened diamond form. Extant scabbards, again rare, were made from leather, with metal mounts at the throat, middle, and chape. Luxury versions of the baselard were also made, and a few have survived in which the scabbard is made of carved ivory or bone, or whose hilts are elaborately carved boxwood, bone, or ivory. Some have curved cross-pieces shod with metal.[75]

The rondel dagger, introduced probably around 1300, was in widespread use all over Western Europe by the middle of the century. The characteristic grip was usually placed between an equal-sized disk-shape pommel and cross-guard, or rondels, from which it derives its name. These rondels were generally made of wood faced with metal or solely in metal (steel, iron, or bronze), although horn, wood, and bone rondels have also been found. Usually slender and elegant in form, like the cross-hilt dagger, the rondel dagger was also a weapon for the elite soldiers. On early examples of this dagger, the blade was relatively short, double-edged, of flattened diamond section, and tapering from the hilt to the point. Later, the blades became longer, up to about 38–40 centimeters in length, and single-edged. Scabbards were usually just simple leather sheaths often with decorative tooling.[76]

Another common dagger, first appearing in about 1300, was the ballock dagger, a contemporary name derived from the shape of the hilt: two spherical cross-guard pieces placed alongside a long and fairly wide grip that tapers to a bulbous, although sometimes flat, knob at the top, thus resembling an erect penis and testicles. (More prudish historians in the nineteenth century called them kidney daggers.) The grip was usually made in one piece from plain wood, ivory, or horn, without metal, although later metal grips are known. Early examples have a single-edged blade of triangular section tapering evenly from the hilt to the point; however, from about 1400, double-edged versions appear. Scabbards were usually just leather with no metal mounts. The ballock dagger was worn on the left hip, hanging vertically at the front or sometimes horizontally at the back.[77]

Fig. 1.8: Ballock dagger—English, c. 1500.

The ear (or eared) dagger was developed in Spain at the end of the four-teenth century and then spread across Europe. Its name derives from the distinctive pommel, the two edges of which rise from the end of the grip in a "V"-shape, rather like two ears. In general, ear daggers were elegant and usually highly decorated, often containing a grip of bone or ivory with enamel, incised and colored decoration that was etched, damascened in gold or silver, with niello work and, in the sixteenth century, cast medallions. The cross-guard was usually of disc form, larger early on but reducing in size until it had almost completely disappeared. The blade was broad and double-edged. Sometimes the hilt was decorated with damascened gold.[78]

The final distinctive type of dagger, the so-called *cinquedea* (meaning five fingers), was almost solely a specialty of Italy. The very broad, flat blade tapered evenly from the hilt to the point, with a strong medial ridge and fluting. The flutes were almost always arranged in three layers running with the axis of the blade: two at the tip, three immediately behind them, and four near the hilt. The hilt was of two forms, either with a wheel pommel, a grip like a sword, and cross-guards curved toward the blade or, more commonly, it had an arched pommel with strongly down-curving cross-guards of rectangular cross sec-tion. *Cinquedeas* could be very long, but they were often short and always wide. Scabbards were usually made from *cuir boulli*, shaped to fit the blade, and often covered in tooled decoration.[79]

One other name is frequently associated with medieval daggers, the *miseri-cordia* (or *miséricorde*). Associated with mid-thirteenth-century cavalry, the name is said to have come from the "mercy" killing of a wounded man after a battle, but it is more likely to have come from being the weapon that was used to compel an opponent to surrender, to request "mercy." Hence, it may not have been a type of dagger at all, but merely a term used to describe the use of a dag-ger.[80] Of course, being merciful was not the dagger's function in battle; instead, most often, after an opponent had been debilitated with another weapon, it delivered the *coup de grâce* by being thrust under the armor into the neck, armpit or groin.

THE STAFF-WEAPON

The name staff-weapon, sometimes also called a polearm, is a generic term describing an entire category of offensive weapons that, in their simplest form, were a combination of the spear or lance and an axe, blade, and/or hammer. From relatively simple forms, a wide range of staff-weapons developed from about 1300, for example, the halberd, glaive, and partisan. The staff-weapon was the infantry weapon of choice and was used extensively on the battlefield across Europe from 1300 to the mid-sixteenth century. Although there were many variants and types, they were used, almost exclusively, by soldiers to thrust and slash at their opponents. Staff-weapons encouraged the development of large formations of soldiers working together as a coordinated group. Furthermore, developments in armor, leading to full-plate armor, meant that there was a need for an infantry weapon that was capable of both thrusting and cutting actions, since the ability of plate armor to resist penetration—together with its smooth, rounded surfaces, which tended to deflect attack—meant that the thrusting spear was less effective.[81]

Although most of these weapons date from the late Middle Ages, there are some earlier examples. The earliest is to be found in a Catalan document of 977 that refers to a *guisarme*, described as a long-hafted weapon with an extremely long, axe-shaped head.[82] A capital in the Church of St. Nectaire in France, carved in the late eleventh or early twelfth century, depicts two soldiers carrying long-hafted weapons, one of which has an axe head and the other what David C. Nicolle describes as "a mysterious glaive-like weapon."[83] Five other portrayals of staff-weapons can be dated to the twelfth and thirteenth centuries: a wall painting from the Ermita de San Badilio in Aragon from the early twelfth century depicts a long-hafted trident or military pick carried by a horsed hunter; an illumination from *Queen Melisende's Psalter* made in the Kingdom of Jerusalem between 1131 and 1143 shows a long-hafted war flail; a carved doorway from San Miguel de Uncastillo in Aragon displays a ball-and-chain on a medium-sized haft; a mosaic from the Cathedral of Monreale in Sicily dating from c.1180–90 depicts three long-hafted staff-weapons, one with a head similar to the glaive mentioned above and two others with long, hooked blade heads; and, finally, an illumination from the *Roman de Tristan*, made in France c.1260, portrays a long-hafted, elongated axe.[84]

In the early years of the fourteenth century, infantry armies armed predominantly with staff-weapons began to achieve their first substantial victories over

Fig. 1.9: Halberd—Swiss or German, c. 1480.

cavalry-based armies. The Flemings defeated the French at Courtrai in 1302 and at Arques in 1303; the Scots defeated the English at Loudon Hill in 1307 and at Bannockburn in 1314; and the Swiss defeated the Austrians at Mortgarten in 1315 and at Laupen in 1339. These victories were not, however, determined by weapons alone; considerable valor and bravery in the face of a cavalry charge by heavily armed knights atop well-trained warhorses, as well as battlefield tactics such as the construction of natural impediments to the charge, were just as important. However, the fact that infantry armies armed with this new hafted weapon could defeat cavalry was recognized and led to significant changes to battlefield tactics.[85]

From the very end of the thirteenth century a new type of staff-weapon started to appear: the halberd, combining the spear with the axe. At first it consisted of a fairly broad blade with a spike projecting from the top secured to the end of a long pole, around two meters in length. It could be used, like the spear, as a thrusting weapon, but it could also be swung over the head and brought down with considerable force. In addition to the socket into which the shaft fitted, the head was also secured in place with long langets, iron straps running down from the head, nailed to the haft. During the fifteenth century an extra spike was added to the rear of the axe portion of the head, making it an even more formidable weapon.[86]

A considerable number of other staff-weapons appeared in the late thirteenth and fourteenth centuries, some very characteristic of particular areas and some more widely distributed around Europe. The *goedendag* ("good day" or "hello"), used by the Flemings in their battles of the fourteenth century, far from being sophisticated or innovative, was basically a heavy headed club to which long iron spikes were attached. The glaive, a staff-weapon with a large cutting and thrusting blade and a convex front edge and a straight back, probably first appeared in Europe in the thirteenth century, although it was never very common. Later, in the sixteenth century, it came to be very much a ceremonial weapon carried by official guards and in procession. The bill, which consisted of a forward facing hook with one or more spikes projecting from the rear and/or front, was common throughout Europe.

Simple forms of the bill were very similar to halberds and were probably used in much the same way, but other, more complex types were developed in many areas. For example, the Welsh bill, which had a long slender curved blade with a right-angled spike, and the *roncone*, an Italian form of staff-weapon, had a long straight blade, a smaller curved hook, and backward facing spikes. The partizan was a later development, from about 1500, and was basically a long, flat blade tapering to a point, rather like an elongated spear. Its use was widespread throughout Europe.[87]

Another type of staff-weapon, which might have developed from the Flemish *goedendag*, was the *morgenstern*, of which there are several variants, but all had a head from which a number of spikes protruded. Although the term *morgenstern* is used for the whole group, it had a variety of local names such as morning star, holy water sprinkler, and *goupillon*. A further variant of the *morgenstern* was the *kettenmorgenstern*, which had a short length of chain at the end of the haft to which a spiked ball was attached. This ball-and-chain weapon has attracted a great deal of comment from modern historians, some claiming that it existed, with others dismissing it as a fantasy. It was likely that a weapon like this was used but was not common.[88] The military flail is another staff-weapon that has been much commented on, but it is uncertain exactly what it was or how it was used: either it was the same as the flail used by peasants to winnow grain or it was a shorter version adapted specifically for military service.

By 1400 the axe had developed into what was called the pollaxe, a weapon about 150 centimeters long with a head consisting of a small convex axe blade, a spike at the rear and a short top spike. The rear spike was often flat and hammer-like, and the head was usually attached to the haft with two or four long langets. It is generally believed that the pollaxe was used more for foot combats between two opponents or in tournaments than in general combat, but illustrations show them being used in battle as very effective close-combat weapons. Surviving pollaxes are usually of high quality and often decorated.[89]

THE MACE

The club, a heavy wooden stick often with a bulbous head, goes back into antiquity and has always been used on the battlefield by low status soldiers. A second weapon, the mace, also developed at some time in the distant past and consisted of a wooden handle with a separate head secured to it. Both weapons are difficult to trace in early sources.

Germanic and Celtic barbarian tribes used just the fire-hardened club, a weapon with which they had fought at least since the first century CE, if not earlier.[90] However, the earliest indication of maces and clubs used in warfare is found in the Bayeux Tapestry, where they are shown being carried by the Normans and Anglo-Saxons at Hastings. While some of the weapons shown are simple clubs that thicken toward the end, some have very definite mace-like heads.[91] Thus the mace was certainly being used by the eleventh century and thereafter developed into a subsidiary weapon, after the lance and sword, which could be used in close-quarter fighting. These later maces were often heavy and had pronounced edges and flanges that would have been effective against plate armor.

By the twelfth century, the club disappears from the sources, although it probably lingered on as a weapon for lower-status soldiers and militia. The mace became heavier and was then often made entirely of iron, as opposed to earlier versions that consisted of a copper alloy or iron head mounted on a wooden shaft. It was now more capable of inflicting greater damage, especially against more heavily armored foes. Two styles predominated. The first, and probably the earlier of the two, consisted of a knobbed head, while the second had a head formed into a number of flanges or wings equally set around a tubular core and sharp enough to inflict considerable damage on plate armor.[92]

Artistic and literary sources also establish the popularity of the mace as a weapon, and it is frequently depicted in medieval art of all kinds.[93] Literary sources are much more descriptive. As it became the secondary weapon of the tournament *melée*, behind the lance, there are many good descriptions of the sounds and destructive capabilities of the mace in action. The purpose of this weapon was well known to these authors, and they often emphasize its destructive capabilities. As Geoffrey Chaucer writes: "With mighty maces the bones they to-brest." He also records that a mace in combat "todashed" Troilus' shield.[94] But death and broken bones were the infrequent results of a mace attack. More often these resulted simply in a damaged or misshapen piece of armor. Even the great jouster William Marshal had to be extricated from his helm, crushed by his opponent's mace, on more than one occasion.[95]

One further note should be made concerning the medieval mace. It has always been suggested that the mace was used, if not entirely created for use, by ecclesiastics in military affairs. Scholars supporting this idea have frequently

Fig. 1.10: Mace head—European, twelfth–thirteenth century.

pointed to the Bayeux Tapestry for support, where Odo, the bishop of Bayeux and half-brother of William the Conqueror, is depicted with a club in his hand.[96] In reality, however, this seems to be more folklore than historical truth. It is more likely that Odo of Bayeux carried a club or mace not as a weapon, but as a symbol of office. The club, and later the mace, symbolized more than military prowess to the medieval warrior; it was, in fact, a symbol of his ruler-ship or nobility. The mace, then, was the precursor to the scepter. In the Bayeux Tapestry everyone who carries a club or mace, including Odo, does so to signify his leadership.[97]

THE WAR HAMMER

The medieval war hammer was not a widely used weapon, and there are no writ-ten accounts, few artistic sources, and even fewer extant exemplars to give us an indication that it was used at all, at least before the very end of the Middle Ages.

ARMS AND ARMOR

Fig. 1.11: War Hammer—German, 1500–50.

The earliest artistic rendering of the war hammer dates from c.1250, when it is found in the hand of an anonymous English knight's effigy in the Malvern Priory Church. This is a short-hafted weapon with a square hammer head on one side and a short, slightly curved pick on the other. This single example is the only one for the thirteenth century, and the next depiction does not appear for more than 100 years, when four can be seen in Spanish paintings dating c.1350–1500. The heads of these weapons are all similar to the English knight's hammer, but two of them have long hafts, both carried by standing figures. This may indicate that the hammer, while not used often in battle, could be carried by both infantry (long-hafted hammers) and cavalry (short-hafted hammers).[98]

An extant medieval war hammer, dating from around 1450 in the holdings of the Wallace Collection in London, differs little from these artistic renderings. The hammer head is still square in shape, although turned at a 45-degree angle to present a diamond-shaped front; the pick is short, slightly curved, and equal in length to the head. The head is also separate from the haft, which is of modern construction, and is attached to it by a cubical box of steel that is placed over the intersection of the haft and head. The haft may have been metal, but was probably wood, and its length cannot be determined. A second hammer in the Wallace Collection, dated to c.1490, is the same shape and size, indicating perhaps that there was less variation in these weapons than in others from the same period.[99]

While apparently not a popular medieval weapon, the war hammer became much more common in the sixteenth and seventeenth centuries.[100]

THE SLING

Often disregarded in studies of warfare, the sling was used all the way to the end of the medieval period to throw projectiles of stone or lead, although, especially in the later medieval period, it was never a common weapon. Of extremely simple construction, they were made from knotted string and leather, and used exclusively by the common soldier. Unfortunately, the nature of these materials means that no examples have survived, although there are illustrations of their use.

Both the handheld and staff slings were very popular missile weapons in the ancient world; however, they seem to have been unknown to the barbarians, but this may be a consequence of a lack of surviving evidence. Muslim armies used the weapon, although also apparently as infrequently as the Christians.[101]

There are very few literary or artistic references to the medieval sling, but, again, this is probably because they have not been looked for. The sling is listed as a weapon in the laws of Justinian, written in sixth-century Byzantium, but only in a reference that specifies weapons mentioned by Xenophon, who lived in the fourth century BCE.[102] It is also the answer to one of *Aldhelm's Riddles*, composed in Anglo-Saxon England sometime in the seventh or early eighth century, but it almost certainly refers only to the weapon used by David to slay Goliath, with perhaps no contemporary equivalent.[103] Finally, Chaucer mentions a staff sling held by a giant facing Sir Topas, as well as a number of simple slings in his story of Troilus and Criseyde, but they are never used by the heroes of these stories.[104] Slings also can be seen in a number of illustrations showing the confrontation between David and Goliath.[105] And a manuscript illumination of the *Historia Anglorum* of Matthew Paris, made in England c.1255, shows two staff slings in the hands of naval soldiers who are operating them in an attack of a coastal fortification.[106]

In the later medieval period, slings were still being used on the battlefield, although they remained uncommon and their use infrequent. Stones were the main ammunition, although, later on, they were also used to throw incendiary weapons: for example, the early-sixteenth-century military engineer Biringuccio has them being used to throw firepots. These were fitted with a fuse that was lit before throwing, and, upon shattering, the contents were ignited, spreading fire and confusion.[107]

THE BOW

Although the bow was used from ancient times to the end of the medieval period, it acquired almost mythical status in the twentieth century as the weapon of Robin Hood, whose deadly accuracy could put one arrow into another, and in the hail of arrows unleashed at the Battle of Agincourt in the films of *Henry V* made by Laurence Olivier in 1945 and by Kenneth Branagh in

one absq; tumultu ꝛuiolenta ꝺepdatione. ut soli
filio ꝺei uictoria ascribatur. Et cum caperetur aui
taus maculis noꝙs babilonis. ñ fuit aususf more solito xpi
amor aggreди. s; confusus anfugienf jꝺa castra combur
sit. Eo itaꝙ due milites xpi ꝺamuerani ingressi. pla

Turris damiate

Fig. 1.12: Staff sling shown in Matthew Paris's *Historia Major*, c. 1219.

The Bridgeman Art Library International / Corpus Christi College, Cambridge, UK. Ms. 16, Roll 178.

1989. It was also the weapon of the Huns, the Seljuk and Ottoman Turks, and the Mongols, who used it to terrifying effect from horseback, and it was the weapon that dominated the battlefields of France in the fifteenth century.

The use and form of the medieval bow, especially that used by the English from the late thirteenth century, have attracted a great deal of comment from, and debate among, historians, especially since the discovery and excavation of a large number of longbows from the wreck of the *Mary Rose*, which sank in 1545. Since the 1980s this debate has concentrated primarily on the draw weight of the bow, that is, the force needed to draw the string back to the firing position, but even the firing position has been the topic of much debate: whether the string was pulled back to the chest, the chin or the ear.[108] Most recently, although certainly not finally, a very detailed and lengthy study has also called into question the long-held belief that most earlier bows were short and that the longbow was a later development, arguing instead that the bow was always long.[109]

There is also some question about the extent and importance of the bow among the barbarian tribes at the time of their invasions of the Roman Empire. Ancient authors claimed that the Visigoths were proficient archers, the first to use the bow, and the best at it, a claim that the large number of arrowheads found in Visigothic grave sites seems to confirm. They carried the recurved, composite bow and shot iron-tipped arrows from horseback, although it is apparent that the weapon was secondary to the spear in battle.[110] The Huns, too, were proficient horse archers, avoiding open battle but using the bow for raids and skirmishes against light cavalry.[111]

On the other hand, the Ostrogoths, Franks, Angles, and Saxons, although employing the weapon, did not use it as much as the other barbarian tribes. The Franks preferred the throwing axe as a missile weapon, although a large number of arrowheads have been found in Frankish grave sites, while the Ostrogoths held the bow in such low esteem that Totila, the king of the Ostrogoths during the sixth-century Byzantine invasion of Italy, refused to allow his army to use bows against the invaders.[112] As for the Angles and Saxons, grave sites in England show that they did indeed use the bow, although the small number of arrowheads found in these graves—only 1.1 per cent of Anglo-Saxon warriors' graves contain arrowheads—suggests that the weapon was not valued as much as their other offensive armaments.[113] Perhaps this is the reason why an Anglo-Saxon riddle was written, the author calculating that most would not know the weapon. He even had to give an internal clue to help one discover the answer to the riddle: the first word is the Old English word for bow, *boga*, although it has been reversed:

> *Agob*'s my name, if you work it out;
> I'm a fair creature fashioned for battle.
> When I bend, and shoot a deadly shaft
> from my stomach, I desire only to send
> that poison as far away as possible.
> When my lord, who devised this torment for me,
> releases my limbs, I become longer
> and, bent upon slaughter, spit out
> that deadly poison I swallowed before.
> No man's parted easily from the object
> I describe; if he's struck by what flies
> from my stomach, he pays for its poison
> with his strength—speedy atonement for his life.
> I'll serve no master when unstrung, only when
> I'm cunningly notched. Now guess my name.[114]

The Vikings also used the bow on the battlefield, although they undoubtedly preferred to use the axe and the spear. The bow appears to have been used primarily for hunting, as established by literary and archaeological sources, but it always played a minor role in Viking military tactics.[115] The bow excavated at Hedeby also shows that Viking bows must be characterized as longbows, as it measures 192 centimeters in length and was made of yew, although there is likely no connection to the later English longbows.[116]

By the time of Charlemagne and the establishment of the Carolingian Empire with its professional army, the bow returned to favor with an importance not previously seen among the Franks. This might have been, as François Ganshof and Simon Coupland insist, the result of Charlemagne's wars against the Avars and Slavs, tribes that had used the bow since ancient times. Their proficiency with the weapon, although certainly not decisive, may have inspired the Carolingians to adopt it. In a decree known as the *Aachen Capitulary*, of 802–803, Charlemagne ordered that the bow should become the army's chief infantry weapon, with infantry soldiers ordered to carry it, a spare string, and 12 arrows (the contents of one quiver). He followed this, in 806, with a decree demanding that each horseman should also be equipped with a bow as well as several quivers of arrows. Both decrees were further confirmed in an 811 capitulary.

The earlier Franks had used longbows, D-shaped, perhaps as long as two meters. In Charlemagne's time the composite, recurved bow adopted from the Avars and Slavs was added, with the result that both bows were probably common in the Carolingian army. Also, both barbed and non-barbed Carolingian arrowheads have been found, indicating their simultaneous use. Although none have been discovered dating before the Tudor period in England, from medieval illustrations it can be seen that the quiver was probably made of wood and leather, covered with a domed lid to protect the arrows, with a long strap so that it could be slung across the archer's back.[117]

The bow had a resurgence in popularity during the eleventh and twelfth centuries. In Spain units of mounted archers formed part of the Christian *reconquistador* armies. These mounted archers shot their light, composite bows backward over the rear of the horse, a tactic that they had probably adopted from their Muslim enemies. They also deployed infantry archery units, their weapons being similar, although heavier and probably longer, to those used by mounted archers.[118]

In France at this time, the bow also played a major military role. The army of William, Duke of Normandy, later called the Conqueror, included archers who accompanied him on his invasion of England in 1066. Evidence, although not undisputed, suggests that Harold, the Anglo-Saxon king opposing William, died when struck in the eye by a Norman arrow at the battle of Hastings. The Bayeux Tapestry depicts these Norman infantry archers, not wearing armor, with quivers at their right hips.[119] The Normans also used archers in their attacks and conquests of Sicily in the eleventh century, including "Saracen" archers.[120]

By the twelfth century, continental European armies were discarding their regular bows and adopting crossbows instead. Only in Spain and England did the bow continue to be used for warfare. Spanish soldiers, both infantry and cavalry, used the recurved bow until the end of the Middle Ages. The English also continued to use the bow and with it achieved several successes in twelfth- and thirteenth-century warfare, most notably at the battle of the Standard, fought in 1138, when English archers decimated the charging Scottish line. By the middle of the thirteenth century, the bow had become so important in England that the Assize of Arms of 1242 named archers as the second most important class of soldiers after the mounted knight.[121]

From the beginning of the fourteenth century it is clear that archery was making a significant difference in medieval battles and sieges, enabling the English to dominate in their wars with France. How and why this occurred is still highly controversial. The traditional view is that the English had been using a shorter type of bow and that it was their encounters with the Welsh that introduced them to the so-called longbow. Although made in a similar way to the English bow, the Welsh bow was thought to be longer, and the arrow was pulled back farther—to the ear instead of to the chest—making it more powerful. This improved the range of the bow, and the English army quickly adopted the longbow and recruited large numbers of Welsh and Cheshire archers proficient in the weapon.[122] However, this has recently been challenged. Matthew Strickland and Robert Hardy make the case that the short bow never existed, that bows were always relatively long, and that they were always pulled back to the ear; they contend that the pictorial evidence has been misinterpreted.[123] But, if this were the case, what could have led to the relatively sudden phase of successes by the English, with victories over the Scots at Dupplin Moor in 1332, Halidon Hill in 1333, and Neville's Cross in 1346, and the French at Sluys in 1340, Morlaix in 1342, Crécy in 1346, Poitiers in 1356, and Agincourt in 1415? In the past, many have concluded that it was the English longbow that made the difference—the longbow that was, supposedly, developed from the Welsh bow and that was more powerful and longer ranged.[124] But if the bow had not really changed at all, what *did* lead to these victories?

Fig. 1.13: Battle of Agincourt, *Chroniques de Froissart*, fifteenth century, from H.W. Kock, *Medieval Warfare*.

Among the first to challenge the accepted theory of the "invincibility" of the English longbow were two military historians, John Keegan and Claude Gaier. Keegan, in particular, in a study of the battle of Agincourt, has shown that the tactical use of the English archers at this battle, and, for that matter, in all of the battles since the beginning of the fourteenth century, with the longbowmen either skirmishing in a "shoot-out" with their opponents' archers or flanking their infantry troops, could not have caused the losses of life attributed to them by historians. In fact, there is little evidence that the longbowmen, needing to fire with an extremely steep arc to cover the distance between themselves and the enemy and thus unable to penetrate their opponents' armor, did any more damage than the killing of a few horses and the wounding of even fewer men. While the archers did not kill many men, however, they did harass their enemy to such an extent that they broke into a disordered charge, a charge narrowed by continual flanking fire until it reached and stopped at the solid infantry line. This, then, caused the victory—not the archery fire itself, but the archery-induced disordered charge into a solid infantry line, which was neither penetrated nor defeated.[125]

This thesis, that the successes of the English army were due to a change in tactics and not in weapons, has been accepted by other recent historians—although not by all.[126] Those who support the argument suggest that no longer was the first phase of a battle marked by a charge of the English cavalry, the mounted men-at-arms. Instead, the army formed a defensive position of dismounted men-at-arms, armed with pikes and spears, with archers on their flanks. The attack of the enemy was met by the lines of men-at-arms and held at a relative stand-still while the archers maintained a constant barrage of arrows to their flanks. When more charges were made, mayhem ensued, as the previous attackers could not now retreat and subsequent ones were forced to a halt by the mass of men and horses in front of them. The archers were able to pick off attackers at will.[127]

Contemporary illustrations from the fourteenth century give us some idea of what the bow looked like, but we can also get some information from contemporary documents.[128] An important source for the medieval bow comes from a court case in 1315 following the murder of Robert of Essington. The weapons used by his assailants are described, the first being "a bow of Spanish yew, two ells in length, and of the thickness of four men's thumbs," which shot an arrow called a "clotharewe." This bow was some 2.3 meters in length and some 10 centimeters thick. Two other assailants had bows of Irish yew while another had one of elm. Finally, Roger of Byshebury used "a bow called Turkeys," made of Spanish yew, one and a half ells long (1.7 meters), and shooting a barbed arrow called a "wolfarewe," which was made of ash and was three quarters of an ell (74 centimeters) in length. Although this bow was called "Turkeys," the fact that it was made of yew probably means that it was not the recurved, composite bow.[129] Clearly, therefore, there was more than one type of bow in use, the choice in all probability being related to fashion, personal taste, and cost.

Like many aspects of the medieval bow, its range and effectiveness have been much discussed and debated over the years, and there are still no clear conclusions. What is clear, however, is that the longbow was an effective weapon against both mail and plate armor. It is unlikely that arrows were able to penetrate armor, except at relatively short range, i.e., less than 50 yards (45 meters), but it must always be remembered that injuring a soldier was often the same as killing him; debilitating a man took him out of the conflict.

By the end of the fifteenth century, the use of the longbow in battles had declined significantly. Why this happened is unclear, but it is certain that by this time there was a serious shortage of archers in England. The kingdom had, in the two centuries before, weathered shortages of bows and arrows: on one occasion, in 1356, the Black Prince was compelled to order the arrest and forced labor of all fletchers in Cheshire until his store of arrows was recouped.

The supply of bows and arrows had declined from a total of 11,000 bows and 23,600 sheaves of arrows (each sheaf with 24 arrows) in 1360 to a total of only 1,000 sheaves of arrows and no bows in 1381. However, in neither of these cases was the problem a shortage of materials; rather, it was a lack of trained manpower. That changed in the fifteenth century, however. When Edward IV demanded that 20,000 archers be recruited in 1453, he was forced to drop his request to 13,000 archers, and even this number proved too high.[130] Despite even proscribing the playing of football and golf in 1456 until archers once again became skilled with the longbow, neither Edward IV nor any other king would ever again be able to use either the quantity or quality of longbow archers that had once proved to be so effective in previous battles.[131]

One possible reason, although probably not the only one, for the decline in the longbow was that by the beginning of the fifteenth century another military technology had developed to challenge its superiority: the handgun. By 1400, handheld gunpowder weapons were being used on the battlefield and, although not common until later in the century, handgunners began to take their place in the ranks of almost all continental European armies. As their numbers rose, the number of archers declined until, by the beginning of the sixteenth century, archers had essentially disappeared from the battlefields of Europe. Still, the mystique of the longbow persisted: some English commanders in the sixteenth century were even reluctant to accept the handgun in the English army, believing that it could never duplicate the successes of the longbow.[132]

THE CROSSBOW

The crossbow was, for much of the High and Late Middle Ages, widely used by all armies across Western Europe. It consisted of a short, heavy bow to the center of which was attached a stock. A release mechanism was fitted to the stock to which the string of the bow was pulled, or spanned, by either manual or mechanical means. The top of the stock was usually grooved to take the short arrow, quarrel, or bolt, the end of which rested on the drawn-back string. Operating the trigger, often a lever on the underside of the stock, released the string and fired the bolt. The release mechanism usually consisted of a rotating disc of hard material, often horn or ivory, called the nut, set so that it protruded above the top of the stock and was held in place by a rod attached to the trigger. A groove in the nut was positioned so that when it was "cocked," the string of the bow was held fast. The string was pulled back to the firing position either by hand, with the aid of a stirrup at the end of the bow and a simple claw secured to the user's belt or, later on, by mechanical means using a cranequin or windlass mechanism.[133]

The advantages and disadvantages of the crossbow and longbow have never been fully resolved by modern historians. It is often said that the crossbow was more powerful than the longbow and that it could be prepared, in the shooting position, ahead of time and held there until ready to shoot (the longbow archer had to release his arrow at the moment of reaching full draw). The crossbow also demanded little if any training, while it took the archer many years to be fully proficient in the longbow. However, the major advantage of the longbow was the rate of fire. A crossbowman could shoot, at best, probably one shot per minute, while the longbowman could fire as many as 10 arrows in the same time, although in a battle he would likely not do so, his supply of arrows so small that he would not have wanted to shoot them all too rapidly. It is also likely that the longbow was cheaper to produce than the crossbow, although good comparative figures are not easy to find.[134]

The crossbow probably descended from the ancient Greek *gastaphretes* (or "belly bow") and was also used in both ancient Rome and China. However, it does not seem to have become popular in Western Europe until the eleventh century, perhaps because the barbarian invaders never learned the technology nor perceived it to be an effective weapon within their cultural traditions. Some historians have argued that the crossbow was used, albeit sparingly, by the Franks throughout the Early Middle Ages. If this thesis is not accepted, however, it is difficult to understand how the crossbow spread to Western Europe in the eleventh century.[135] It seems almost certain that it was used frequently by either the Muslims or the Byzantines. At least, Anna Comnena, the daughter of one Byzantine emperor and sister to another, seemed completely overwhelmed by the weapon, which was carried by the First Crusaders. This is her intricate description of the crossbow:

> The crossbow is a weapon of the barbarians, absolutely
> unknown to the Greeks. In order to stretch it one does
> not pull the string with the right hand while pushing the
> bow with the left away from the body; this instrument of
> war, which shoots missiles to an enormous distance, has
> to be stretched by lying almost on one's back; each foot
> is pressed forcibly against the half-circles of the bow and
> the two hands tug at the bow, pulling it with all one's

ARMS AND ARMOR

Fig. 1.14: Crossbow—German, 1500.

strength towards the body. At the mid-point of the string is a groove, shaped like a cylinder cut in half and fitted to the string itself; it is about the length of a fair-sized arrow, extending from the string to the centre of the bow. Along this groove, arrows of all kinds are shot. They are very short, but extremely thick with a heavy iron tip. In the shooting the string exerts tremendous violence and force, so that the missiles wherever they strike do not rebound; in fact they transfix a shield, cut through a heavy iron breastplate and resume their flight on the far side, so irresistible and violent is the discharge. An arrow of this type has been known to make its way right through a bronze statue, and when shot at the wall of a very great town its point either protruded from the inner side or buried itself in the wall and disappeared altogether. Such is the crossbow, a truly diabolical machine. The unfortunate man who is struck by it dies without feeling the blow; however strong the impact he knows nothing of it.[136]

The Church, however, did not have the same regard for the weapon as did soldiers. Because of its brutality in war, both Pope Urban II (1096–97) and the Second Lateran Council (1139) condemned its use among Christians. However, this condemnation was rarely heeded, and by the end of the century the crossbow had become popular in Europe. King Richard I of England, for one, used it widely; tradition holds that it was he who introduced it to the French, who quickly adopted it. Ironically, Richard himself was killed by a crossbow bolt. In 1200, the Church relaxed its denunciation of the weapon, allowing its use against infidels, pagans, and Cathars, and in the case of a "just war."[137]

After the twelfth century, the use of the crossbow increased markedly, especially in continental Europe, where most kings and nobles used crossbowmen in their armies, frequently employing mercenaries (principally Gascons and Genoese) when they failed to recruit sufficient numbers of these troops from among their own subjects. These crossbowmen were used tactically at the beginning of a battle and on the flanks to harass opposing forces.[138]

Over the course of the later medieval period, the crossbow developed considerably from its relatively simple beginnings. The first bows were made from wood, but later ones were made either of a composite of sinew, horn, and wood, or of steel, both latter types being more powerful and effective weapons.[139]

David Bachrach has identified three different types of English crossbow in the thirteenth century and three different materials. The first, the "one-foot" crossbow, is thought to have had a stirrup at the front of the stock for one foot of the crossbowman while he was drawing back the string. "Two-foot" crossbows are more difficult to identify, but they may refer to a larger stirrup into which two feet could be inserted. However, there is no evidence of crossbows with a stirrup for two feet, from either pictorial or surviving crossbows, and the exact meaning is still in some doubt.[140] The third type, the crossbow *ad turnum*, is also somewhat problematic. Bachrach identifies it as a large crossbow, mounted on a stand, which needed a mechanical device to span it; he suggests a windlass. However, there is also little evidence to substantiate this interpretation. He goes on to say that each type could have either a wooden or a composite bow.[141]

Just when the change from wooden to composite bows took place is uncertain, but even at the beginning of the fourteenth century both were still being used, and there is evidence that the English Crown was ordering them in roughly equal quantities, due probably in part to the higher cost of the composite bow. This is borne out by data for the costs of the different types of crossbow during the reign of Edward I (1270–1307): "one-foot" crossbows cost around 18 pence, "two-foot" crossbows about four shillings (48 pence), and the cross-bow *ad turnum* as much as 10 shillings (120 pence) each.[142]

Over the course of the fourteenth century the composite crossbow completely replaced the wooden crossbow, and in the fifteenth century the steel crossbow was introduced, probably from Germany initially. This increased the bow's power markedly, giving it a greater range and ballistic impact than any other bow known in the Middle Ages. Estimates as to the range vary from 370 to 500 meters, with sufficient force to pierce even the best plate armor.[143]

As the power of the crossbow increased, the method of drawing the string back to the shooting position had to change. At first the string could be drawn back by hand, with a stirrup added at the end of the twelfth century to the front of the stock so that the crossbow could be held down with the foot while pulling the string back. A simple hook attached to a belt around the waist of the crossbowman was used to increase his pulling power: holding the crossbow with his foot, the crossbowman bent over, slipped the string over the hook on his belt and, by standing upright, his powerful leg muscles pulled the string back to the firing position.[144]

However, as the bow was made more powerful, it became insufficient to load by this method, and a simple lever mechanism was introduced: the goat's-foot lever. This was a simple folding device that, when placed over the stock and the string fitted to it, could be unfolded to pull the string back to the shooting position. For the very powerful bows of the fifteenth century, this too was found to be inadequate, so two mechanical devices were developed: the crane-quin, a device working on the rack-and-pinion principle, used gears to increase the force available to draw back the string; and the windlass, which used a series of pulleys to much the same effect. As the power of the crossbow increased, and it became necessary to use a cranequin or windlass, the speed of spanning the crossbow decreased, although well-trained crossbowmen could probably still maintain a reasonable rate of fire.[145]

The quarrel, or bolt, was about 40 centimeters in length and was made of ash or yew with a flattened or tapered rear and some form of fletching; feathers, thin wood, and leather were all used. A number of differently shaped heads were also used, depending on the target, but in warfare the usual form was diamond shaped in cross section.[146] When needed, crossbow bolts were made both quickly and well, as evidenced in the order of 100,000 crossbow bolts by the king of Aragon, James the Conqueror, in the mid-thirteenth century.[147]

Most crossbows had no form of sighting, and it was probable that accuracy depended on the skill of the crossbowman. On some a backsight was fitted, often just a strip of wood with notches in it fixed to the rear of the stock.[148]

Crossbows were used both on the battlefield and in sieges. However, the larger crossbow, the crossbow *ad turnum*, could be shot only from castle and town walls, and there is evidence that, by the early thirteenth century, the openings for crossbows were designed to allow for a more systematic flanking fire against besiegers.[149] Crossbows were also used on ships to improve their offensive capability.[150]

It should also be noted that although the crossbow was normally an infantry weapon, it could also be shot from horseback, and there are a number of instances where this was specifically noted: Philip Augustus of France used them in his early-thirteenth-century wars against King John of England; Frederick II of Germany employed a corps of mercenary Hungarian mounted crossbowmen in 1238; and Pope Gregory IX (despite the Church's prohibition) used Provençal mounted crossbowmen against the Lombard League in 1239.[151]

From the late fourteenth century, gunpowder weapons began to replace crossbows, particularly for the defense of castles but also, occasionally, on the battlefield. But this was a slow transition, taking many decades. This change may have been responsible for a decline in the skill of shooting a crossbow, and, as with the longbow, steps were taken to halt such decline. For example, in 1384 Charles V of France prohibited the playing of any game, except for shooting with a bow or crossbow, and in the 1440s Charles VII set up companies of crossbowmen, called *franc-archers*. However, the crossbow did not survive the influx of handguns and, although still used for hunting and sport, by 1550 it—like so many other medieval weapons—had all but disappeared from the battlefield.[152]

Notes

1. Bishop and Coulston (1989): 63–65. On the *plumbata* see also P. Barker (1979) and Sherlock (1979).

2. Ferrill (1986): 48–49.

3. E. Thompson (1958): 6–7; Ferrill (1986): 143–44; and B. Bachrach (1970b): 436–37.

4. E. Thompson (1958): 3–6.

5. Contamine (1984): 12.

6. Apollinaris is translated in Davis (1970): 108–9, Procopius in B. Bachrach (1970b): 436–37. See also Agathias in B. Bachrach (1970b): 436. On the *angon*, see the Agathias quotation on p. 9.

7. Tacitus (1970): 105–6.

8. Swanton (1973).

9. J. Cirlot (1967): 8–14; Bruhn de Hoffmeyer (1972): 86–88; and Brønsted (1960): 122–23.

10. B. Bachrach (1970b): 436–37.

11. See Contamine (1984): 176–77.

12. Contamine (1984): 177.

13. Coupland (1990): 30; Ganshof (1968): 65; and Beeler (1971): 14.

14. Coupland (1990): 47.

15. Coupland (1990): 47.

16. Ross (1951): 10.

17. Comnena (1969): 316–17.

18. Davis (1989): 19.

19. Ascherl (1989): 271.

20. Ross (1951).

21. L. White (1962): 1–38.

22. Ross (1963).

23. Buttin (1965).

24. Nicolle (1980).

25. B. Bachrach (1985b): 744–48.

26. V. Cirlot (1985).

27. Flori (1988).

28. See the numerous examples in Nicolle (1988).

29. Smail (1956): 112–13 and Contamine (1984): 67.

30. Contamine (1984): 67 and Beeler (1971): 186.

31. Contamine (1984): 67.

32. See Davis (1989): 19–22.

33. Crouch (2005): 2–9.

34. Crouch (2005) and Barber and Barker (1989).

35. See Mann (1957): 66–67 and Bruhn de Hoffmeyer (1972): 126–31.

36. Oakeshott (1980): 44–47 and Contamine (1984): 135–36.

37. E. Thompson (1958): 5; B. Bachrach (1970b): 436–37; Contamine (1984): 12, 176; Ferrill (1986): 145.

38. Contamine (1984): 176. See also Härke (1990): 34.

39. Contamine (1984): 20.

40. Pedersen (2002): 29–31; Brønsted (1960): 122; Poertner (1975): 150; and Foote and Wilson (1970): 272–73.

41. Mann (1957): 66 and Härke (1990): 34.

42. Powicke (1962): 56, 86, 92.

43. Loomis and Loomis (1957): 324–89. See also Herben (1937): 483.

44. See the many examples in Nicolle (1988).

45. Nicolle (1988): #876, 919, 992, 1003–5, 1021–22, 1035, 1055, 1067–68, 1098, 1110–12, 1125, 1145, 1458, 1479, 1506–7, 1526–29.

46. Oakeshott (1980): 72–74.

47. Barbour (1997), II: 284–86.

48. Tacitus (1970): 105. See also E. Thompson (1958): 3.

49. See, for example, Sidonius Apollinaris', Procopius', and Agathias' descriptions of Frankish warriors found in B. Bachrach (1970b): 436–38 and Davis (1970): 108–9.

50. Contamine (1984): 12, 177–78; and Bruhn de Hoffmeyer (1972): 78–86.

51. Contamine (1984): 19–20. See also Bruhn de Hoffmeyer (1972): 78–86.

52. Ellis Davidson (1962). The quotation is found on page 211. This work has since been supplemented by Wilson (1965), who provides an additional catalog of Anglo-Saxon swords.

53. In addition to Ellis Davidson (1962), on the sword in relation to the status of the Anglo-Saxon warrior see N. Brooks (1978): 82–87, and on swords found in Anglo-Saxon gravesites see Härke (1990).

54. See Ellis Davidson (1962), in particular Appendix I, pp. 217–24; Engstrom, Lankton, and Lesher-Engstrom (1990); Fino (1964): 47–66; Peirce (1986): 154–55; and Williams (1977).

55. Coupland (1990): 42–46; Oakeshott (1964): 25–37; and Ganshof (1968): 65.

56. Pedersen (2002): 28–29; Brønsted (1960): 119–22; and Contamine (1984): 28. A fairly complete catalog of Viking swords, with the exception of those in Eastern Europe, is Peirce (2002).

57. Bruhn de Hoffmeyer (1961): 46–50.

58. Mann (1957): 65–66 and Peirce (1986): 154–55, 162–64.

59. For Spain see Bruhn de Hoffmeyer (1972): 119–25, 160–68; and Powers (1988): 131. For the Crusades see Smail (1956): 112–14.

60. Beeler (1971): 26.

61. Oakeshott (1964): 25–55 and Bruhn de Hoffmeyer (1963): 5–18. See also the large number of swords from this period illustrated in Nicolle (1988).

62. Oakeshott (1964): 56–79.

63. Oakeshott (1964): 80–138 and the numerous illustrations in Nicolle (1988).

64. Mann (1958): 318–19 and Ascherl (1988): 273.

65. Oakeshott (1964): 56–79 and Bruhn de Hoffmeyer (1963): 18–25.

66. The most complete study of the transition between the medieval and early-modern periods is Anglo (2000). Examples of late-medieval manuals are Talhoffer (2000) and Forgeng (2003).

67. Bruhn de Hoffmeyer (1972): 77.

68. Beeler (1971): 14.

69. Härke (1989): 144–48 and Brønsted (1960): 123.

70. Justinian (1987): 55, 145.

71. See Härke (1989); Brønsted (1960): 123; and Stork (1990): #61.

72. Capwell (2009): 26–27.

73. Herben (1937): 483–84.

74. Capwell (2009): 28.

75. Capwell (2009): 28–29.

76. Capwell (2009): 31.

77. Capwell (2009): 30.

78. Capwell (2009): 35.

79. Capwell (2009): 34.

80. Capwell (2009): 27.

81. The latest and best study of all the staff weapons noted here is Waldman (2005).

82. Bruhn de Hoffmeyer (1972): 170.

83. Nicolle (1988): #707.

84. Nicolle (1988): #686, 819, 676, 1416, 788. See also Troso (1988) and Waldman (2005).

85. DeVries (1996a).

86. Oakeshott (1980): 47–48; Deuchler (1963): 341–42; and Waldman (2005): 17–79.

87. Oakeshott (1980): 51–56 and Waldman (2005).

88. Waldman (2005): 146–47.

89. Waldman (2005): 155–59.

90. E. Thompson (1958): 5 and Thorne (1982): 50.

91. Mann (1957): 66 and Thorne (1982).

92. Nicolle (1988): #918, 1122–23, 1446, 1480, 1510, 1516, 1536.

93. See the numerous examples in Nicolle (1988).

94. Herben (1937): 483.

95. Juliet Barker (1986): 179–80.

96. See, for example, Ashdown (1925): 127–28.

97. This is the thesis behind Thorne's article (1982). See also Oakeshott (1980): 62–64 and Mann (1958): 66.

98. Oakeshott (1980): 69–72.

99. Mann (1962): 456–57 (#A975 and A976).

100. Oakeshott (1980): 69–70.

101. Bruhn de Hoffmeyer (1972): 105.

102. Justinian (1987): 55, 145.

103. Stork (1990): #74. This seems to be the case, as the manuscript copier, or someone nearly contemporary with him, has written the gloss *goliam* above the word *tyrannum* in the riddle.

104. Herben (1937): 486.

105. Nicolle (1988): #671, 696, 1212, 1423.

106. Nicolle (1988): #1606.

107. Biringuccio (1959): 434–35.

108. See Rogers (1993): 248–51.

109. See Strickland and Hardy (2005).

110. Bruhn de Hoffmeyer (1972): 72.

111. Ferrill (1986): 145.

112. On the Franks see E. Thompson (1958): 11; B. Bachrach (1970b): 438; and Coupland
(1990): 49. On the Ostrogoths see E. Thompson (1958): 9.

113. Härke (1990): 34.

114. Crossley-Holland (1979): #23.

115. Pedersen (2002): 32 and Brønsted (1960): 123

116. Pedersen (2002): 32.

117. Coupland (1990): 48–50; Ganshof (1968): 65; and Beeler (1971): 14.

118. Bruhn de Hoffmeyer (1972): 131–33 and Powers (1988): 75, 131.

119. Mann (1957): 67–68.

120. Contamine (1984): 55.

121. Bradbury (1985): 39–57; Beeler (1966): 89, 91, 140, 274; and Powicke (1962): 44, 88–89.

122. On the adoption of the longbow see Bradbury (1985): 71–90 and Powicke (1962): 119. On
the range of the longbow see McKisack (1959): 241 and Prestwich (1980): 70.

123. Strickland and Hardy (2005): 182–86.

124. See McGuffie (1955); Bradbury (1985): 91–138; and Prestwich (1980): 59, 70, 173, 197.

125. Keegan (1978): 78–116 and Gaier (1978).

126. For the traditional image of the longbow, see Rogers (1993, 1998).

127. Strickland and Hardy (2005): 182–86 and DeVries (1996a, 1997).

128. See Strickland and Hardy (2005) for a good selection of images of the bow from the
medieval period.

129. Strickland and Hardy (2005): 42. See also Prestwich (1980): 70.

130. Prestwich (1980): 192 and Allmand (1988): 101.

131. Powicke (1962): 244 and Allmand (1988): 52.

132. See Esper (1965).

133. Bradbury (1985): 8, 147–48; and Nickel (1982): 353. For good survey of the different types of
crossbow see Alm (1994).

134. Bradbury (1985): 8.

135. Alm (1994): 6–7.

136. Comnena (1969): 316–17. See also Bradbury (1985): 8–10 and Contamine (1984): 71.

137. Contamine (1984): 71–72, 274.

138. See Contamine (1984): 72; Allmand (1988): 61; and Bradbury (1985): 45, 76–77.

139. Bradbury (1985): 146–47; Foley, Palmer and Soedel (1985): 105–7; Alm (1994): 35; and D. Bachrach (2004a): 107–9

140. The interpretation of "one-foot" and "two-foot" crossbows has still not been resolved. For the latest scholarship, see G. Wilson (2007): 300–325.

141. D. Bachrach (2004): 109–17.

142. D. Bachrach (2006): 87.

143. Bradbury (1985): 150; Foley, Palmer, and Soedel (1985): 107–9; and Vale (1981): 113.

144. Harmuth (1979).

145. Bradbury (1985): 148–49 and Alm (1994). See also the illustrations in Nicolle (1988): #654, 656, 772, 833, 945, 1247, 1259.

146. Jessop (1996).

147. R. Burns (2004).

148. Bradbury (1985): 149–50.

149. Contamine (1984): 110.

150. Lane (1969–70).

151. Contamine (1984): 71.

152. Contamine (1984): 202, 274; and Bradbury (1985): 143.

CHAPTER 2

ARMOR

IT IS HIGHLY PROBABLE THAT AS SOON AS PREHISTORIC MAN INVENTED
weapons for use in battle, he also invented protective garments to defend himself against attack. Nothing, of course, survives from this early period, but cave
paintings indicate that some sort of armor may have been worn, most particularly by archers. Although it is difficult to determine specific details from such
a medium, some of the garments seem to have a protective use and are possibly
made out of bark or leather covering the breast, legs, and genitals.[1]

While this evidence of early armor is much disputed—some historians and
anthropologists regard it as nothing more than shoulder capes, loincloths,
and knee-bands—what is indisputable is that by the time of the Babylonian
and Egyptian civilizations, soldiers were wearing armor to protect themselves.
It is clear that they covered their torsos, heads, legs, and sometimes their arms
with metal, i.e., bronze, armor. In addition, most soldiers carried a shield, generally made of wood and leather, that was used not only by the regular, front-
line troops, who added its protection to their other armor, but also by the aux-
iliary soldiers, who often carried it as their only means of defense.

The ancient Greeks placed a particular importance on their armor. Both
elite soldiers and those raised from the city militias went into battle wearing:
a bronze helmet, covering the head, most of the neck, the cheeks and the nose,
and topped by a plume denoting rank; bronze greaves covering the shins and

calves; a cuirass, the armor for both the front and back of the torso which connected at the shoulder and sides; and, most importantly, a large shield.[2]

The shield, *hoplon*, from which the name of the Greek soldier, *hoplite*, derives, was made from wood, often in several layers. It was round and concave, measuring about one meter in diameter, although the size varied depending on the length and strength of the bearer's arm. Initially, it was rimmed with a bronze strip around the outer edge as reinforcement. By the fifth century BCE the front of the shield was often entirely covered with a thin sheet of bronze, upon which could be emblazoned the insignia of the bearer's military unit. While it is not known what wood was used to construct the ancient Greek shield, it is generally thought that it was a hardwood, as the shield was quite heavy, perhaps weighing as much as 7.3 kilograms. It was fitted with straps on the inside, into which the arm was inserted, and a handgrip, thereby distributing the weight along the entire left arm instead of concentrating it on the hand or wrist alone, although this meant that it was difficult to remove the shield in the midst of battle.[3]

The ancient Greeks prized their bronze armor, not only for its protective capabilities, but also for the skill involved in its construction and its artistic beauty. The best armor was said to have been made by the god Hephaestus at a forge fired by the volcanoes inside Mount Olympus, and included designs that promised the gods' favor. Such is the description of Agamemnon's armor at the siege of Troy:

> Atreides [Agamemnon] in a loud voice gave his troops the
> order to prepare for battle, and himself put on his gleaming
> bronze. He began by tying round his legs a pair of splendid
> greaves which were fitted with silver clips for the ankles.
> Next he put on his breast the cuirass.... It was made of
> parallel strips, ten of dark blue enamel, twelve of gold, and
> twenty of tin. On either side three snakes rose up in coils
> toward the opening for the neck. Their iridescent enamel
> made them look like the rainbow that the Son of Cronus
> [Zeus] hangs on a cloud as a portent to mankind below ....
> Then he took up his manly and man-covering shield, a
> nobly decorated piece, with its concentric rings of bronze,
> and twenty knobs of tin making a white circle round the
> dark enamel boss. The central figure on it was a grim Gorgon's head with awe-compelling eyes, and on either side

of her, Panic and Rout were depicted. It was fitted with a
silver baldric, round which a writhing snake of blue enamel
twisted the three heads that grew from its single neck. On
his head, Agamemnon put his helmet, with its four plates,
its double crest and its horsehair plume nodding defiantly
above   Beams from the bronze he wore flashed into the distant sky, and Athene and Here thundered in answer by way
of salutation to the King of Golden Mycenae.[4]

Defeat in single combat meant the surrendering of one's armor to his opponent, who then either donned it himself, if it was superior to his own, or kept
it as a trophy of his victory.

The Romans, too, realized the importance of good quality armor. Julius
Caesar's legionnaires, who led the Roman army into Gaul and later fought in
a civil war against Pompey, his co-ruler in the first century BCE, wore armor
consisting of a bronze breastplate (a *lorica*); a bowl-shaped open-faced bronze
helmet, which also protected the neck; and a large rectangular shield, measuring approximately 130 by 65 centimeters (the *scutum*).

Overall, first-century BCE Roman armor was not that much different from
ancient Greek armor; only the shield differed significantly. The Roman shield
was made from three layers of wood, with strips 6 to 10 centimeters wide, the
outer pieces laid horizontally and the inner vertically, covered in canvas and calf
hide. A long wooden boss ran the entire length of the shield and, while there
was no metal reinforcement, it was relatively heavy, weighing an estimated
10 kilograms. However, the shield's shape and increased size meant that the
bearer did not have to wear greaves (armor for the lower legs) as the Greeks
had, which resulted in a greater degree of freedom of movement and, therefore, speed.[5]

By the third century CE, Roman armor had changed significantly. The solid
and rigid breast- and backplates were replaced by armor made from six or seven
horizontal strips of bronze riveted to leather straps to hold them in place, the
so-called *lorica segmentata*. The bronze strips were hinged at the back and held
together at the front either by hooks and laces or by straps and buckles. The
shoulders were similarly protected by a series of curved strips of metal secured
in the same way. This construction allowed much greater freedom of movement
than did the solid *lorica* worn by Caesar's legionaries and meant that the armor
could also be taken apart easily for transportation and repair.[6] The earlier, solid
bronze helmet was replaced by a more carefully designed helmet, made from

either bronze or iron, which was strengthened inside by an iron skull-plate. The neck was protected by plates at the rear, and the sides of the head were covered by hinged cheek-pieces. A plume was not usually worn in battle, although it could still be affixed on top for celebratory and ceremonial purposes.[7]

The third-century Roman shield was still long, but more rectangular in shape and curved to fit the body, unlike the earlier shield, which was essentially flat. It was made of layers of wood, like the earlier Roman model, usually covered in leather, on which could be fastened bronze or iron decoration, often gilded or silvered, and a metallic boss. Its edges were protected by a rim of wrought iron or bronze. Oval shields, similar to those of the Greeks, also appeared at this time but were probably used solely by the cavalry.[8]

Around the beginning of the fourth century, Roman armor changed again. Recognizing the need for different helmets for the infantry and the cavalry, Roman armorers began producing two very distinct designs. The infantry helmet was bowl-shaped, made of two halves, usually of iron, and joined together by a metal strip. It had a leather lining, not attached to the outer helmet, on which was affixed an iron neckguard and iron cheekguards. The cavalry helmet was also bowl-shaped, but instead of having an inner leather cap on which the neck and cheekguards were secured, it was constructed of four to six pieces, including a ridge, noseguard and extremely wide cheek-pieces, all of which were attached to the helmet itself by rivets or hinges. Many cavalry helmets were decorated and were often gilded or silvered. Both of these helmet styles were easier to make and cheaper to produce than earlier Roman models, and their existence may indicate a centralization of the late-Roman armor industry.[9]

By the late-Roman period, the skillfully constructed and complex *lorica segmentata* was replaced by armor that was more easily and cheaply produced. Two styles of cuirasses were prevalent. The first, the *lorica squamata*, was made of a large number of small metal scales attached to each other by wire or leather laces and affixed to a linen undergarment by linen cord. The second, the *lorica hamata*, was constructed of metal rings. These rings were made in two different ways: punched out of sheet metal, so-called solid rings, and from wire, with the ends butted together. This armor was made from alternate rows of solid and butted wire rings, the wire rings used to secure the solid rings, in an interlocking pattern of rows in which each ring was joined to four others, two in the row above it and two in the row below. Some 35,000 to 40,000 rings were needed to make a complete cuirass. Both styles covered the torso from the shoulder to at least the middle of the thigh, although some extended down to the knee and both were worn by infantry and cavalry soldiers. Neither of these styles was completely new to the Romans, and, while both were lighter than the earlier cuirasses, they were also less protective than the solid breastplate, sacrificing defense for greater maneuverability and comfort.[10]

However, it is clear that Roman soldiers did not always wear armor. Even as early as the very outset of the barbarian invasions, they sometimes took off both their helmets and their cuirasses and began to rely solely on their shields for protection.[11] How widespread this practice was cannot be determined, although there is ample evidence of it on grave *stelae* and reliefs throughout Europe. An example of a relief, at Croy Hill in Strathclyde, Scotland, shows three legionaries, none of whom is wearing any protective armaments, but who are outfitted solely with their long, rectangular shields.[12] That this had an effect on the fighting capabilities of the soldiers defending the Roman Empire against the barbarian invaders is attested to by Flavius Vegetius Renatus, perhaps the most famous late-Roman military writer. Vegetius recounts that it had always been the tradition of Roman soldiers to wear breastplates and helmets, but that this tradition had lately changed, with grievous results:

> But when, because of negligence and laziness, parade
> ground drills were abandoned, the customary armor
> began to seem heavy since the soldiers rarely ever wore
> it. Therefore, they first asked the emperor to set aside the
> breastplates and mail and then the helmets. So our soldiers
> fought the Goths without any protection for chest and head
> and were often beaten by archers. Although there were
> many disasters, which led to the loss of great cities, no one
> tried to restore breastplates and helmets to the infantry.
> Thus it happens that troops in battle, exposed to wounds
> because they have no armor, think about running and not
> about fighting.[13]

To be fair to the late Roman soldiers, the enemy they faced was not well protected either. Most Germanic warriors had neither breastplate nor helmet, and their shields were not strengthened by either metal or leather. They usually went into battle naked or with a short cloak, protected from their enemies' weaponry by only a light wooden or wicker shield. Therefore, from the very first military encounter between the two societies they were perceived to be generally inferior to the Roman soldiers, whose armor was more substantial. Such a perception built confidence in the Roman military leadership who often used it to encourage their troops to battle against the Germans.[14]

Whether this disregard for armor by barbarian tribes was due to a shortage of metal, as contended by the first-century Roman writer Tacitus, or whether they developed battlefield tactics that simply did not require the same armor as the Romans, their neglect for defensive armament continued into the fourth- and fifth-century invasions of the Empire. The Germanic tribes continued to fight without helmet or body protection, although it appears that they used more substantial shields, improved by the addition of a pointed iron boss, which could also serve as a thrusting weapon; however, they remained relatively thin and were easily smashed by Roman swords and spears. Some barbarian soldiers wore armor that they had stripped from dead Roman soldiers, but the number of armored warriors in the barbarian armies remained small and was most often confined to the nobles or chieftains.[15]

EARLY MEDIEVAL ARMOR

Beginning in the late fourth century CE, Roman armies began to suffer defeat at the hands of barbarian tribes and there was a general decline in Roman military power leading, eventually, to the collapse of the Roman Empire. However, this was not a simple process. Defeat by the barbarian tribes was due in large part to the tactics and the inability of centralized Roman military bureaucracy to react to counter new threats. Of even greater significance to the general decline in Roman power were internal conflicts among the Romans and the over-extension of the boundaries of the empire. Following the defeat and death of Emperor Valens at the battle of Adrianople in 378, the Roman Empire split into two: an Eastern Empire, based in Constantinople, and a Western Empire based in Ravenna.

By the sixth century, the eastern Romans, also known as Byzantines, were armed with helmets, cuirasses, greaves, and heavy shields. All wore armor, even horse archers. The Eastern Empire was very successful in its wars against the barbarians and was able to push them out of Asia Minor and the Balkans; even Italy was recaptured for a brief period.[16] In the west the empire crumbled, and numerous barbarian tribes took control over much of Western Europe. Each attempted to establish its supremacy over the other tribes, and there was a period of almost continual warfare as they fought one another.[17]

Although barbarian soldiers tended not to wear armor, as noted above, almost all carried a shield, known as a buckler, which was the symbol of warrior status. The soldier received it when entering military service, carrying it at all times—to lose it was seen as cowardice—and it was usually buried with him on his death. Most barbarian shields were convex, either round or elliptical, and made from strips of wood covered with leather, measuring some 80 to 90 centimeters in diameter and 80 to 120 millimeters thick. In the center was a metal boss measuring about 15 to 17 centimeters in diameter and 6 to 10 centimeters high. Some shields were highly ornate and covered with symbolic figures and other decoration.[18]

While the ordinary barbarian soldier usually wore little, if any, armor, it was not uncommon for nobles and chieftains to own helmets and body armor; however, this may have been worn less for protection than to show the status of the owner. Helmets, for example, were usually only simple iron skullcaps or a metal framework covered with leather or fabric, although some Visigothic helmets were patterned after Byzantine models. Body armor was usually mail, fashioned after the Roman *lorica hamata*, or scale, like the Roman *lorica squamata*. Barbarian armor could also sometimes be very elaborate: for example, Totila, an Ostrogothic king, is said to have possessed golden armor.[19]

Armor of the Anglo-Saxon conquerors of England did not differ much from that worn or carried by barbarian soldiers invading other parts of the Roman Empire. Shields were the same shape, size, and material as those carried by Ostrogothic, Visigothic, Frankish, or other barbarian warriors, although it appears that they were thicker than those made on the continent and were usually fitted with an iron boss and frequently decorated. Some also had a metallic rim, as the poem "The Battle of Maldon" relates when noting that Atherich's shield rim burst under the blow of his enemy's sword.[20]

Anglo-Saxon helmets were also similar to those worn by barbarian soldiers on the continent. Four helmets—Sutton Hoo, Benty Grange, Coppergate, and the Pioneer helmet—show many similar construction details. Essentially, each is made of two strips of iron, one running from the back to the front of the helmet, the other from side to side, attached to a circular band of iron shaped to fit around the head. The four triangular spaces formed by the cross pieces were then filled in, by iron plates in the case of the Coppergate and Pioneer helmets, or by plates made of horn, as in the example from Benty Grange. The nose was protected by an extension of the front-to-back band, and all have cheek-pieces covering the side of the face, hinged to the lower edge of the helmet. The back of

Fig. 2.1: Reconstruction of the Sutton Hoo helmet.

© The Trustees of the British Museum / Art Resource, NY.

the neck was protected by mail, in the case of the Coppergate helmet, or a solid plate of iron in the case of the others. The Coppergate helmet was largely plain but had a decorated nose-piece. The Pioneer helmet was found in very poor condition but was originally decorated with a boar crest on top of the helmet, as was the Benty Grange helmet. The Sutton Hoo helmet was probably similar, but the very poor state of preservation has resulted in some confusion about its construction. It has also been thought that the Sutton Hoo helmet was made from a bowl of iron onto which decorative plates had been secured, but it is more likely that it was made in the same way as the Coppergate and Pioneer helmets. The Sutton Hoo helmet was a masterpiece of workmanship, heavily decorated with embossed metal panels and an inlaid strip running over its head. All four of these helmets are of a type called a *spangenhelm*.[21]

Little is known about Anglo-Saxon armor in this period, but it is clear that mail was used to protect the torso, little different from armor of the continental barbarians, extending to the mid-thigh or to the knee with short sleeves to protect the shoulders and upper arms. It is described in the collection known as the *Exeter Riddles* as an "excellent garment"; to Beowulf it was a "tangled war-net"; and in *Aldhelm's Riddles* it is described as not fearing "arrows drawn from a long quiver."[22]

Like the Anglo-Saxons, most of the Vikings, the next invaders of England, did not wear a great deal of armor, although every soldier would have carried a shield. Nobles, however, often wore a cuirass, usually mail, with a leather or iron helmet.[23] One section of the Viking army, known as berserkers (or "without shirts"), are known to have fought without any armor or shields. In some cases, these appear to have been specific warriors, while, in others, they were more conventional soldiers who "go berserk" in the heat of battle. They would work themselves into a frenzy, a blood-lust that would have given them incredible strength and made them seemingly indifferent to blows or pain. They are often mentioned in Old Norse sagas and are always praised more highly for their fighting prowess and bravery than regular soldiers who relied on a shield for protection.[24]

It seems that there was little attempt to regulate armor among any soldiers of the early Middle Ages until the late seventh century. The first to do so was Ervig, a king of the Visigoths, who, sometime between 680 and 687, wrote a legal code demanding, among other things, of his soldiers that "some shall wear armor and most shall have bucklers...."[25] This decree was followed in 750 by a similar edict from Aistulf, a king of the Lombards, which required the richest and most powerful of his warriors to be armed with armor and a shield, as well as his offensive weapons.[26] Whether either of these laws marked a change in the armaments of barbarian armies, however, cannot be ascertained by either written or archaeological evidence, although it is unlikely. In fact, it was not until the time of Charlemagne that a verifiable transformation in armor policy can be seen.

Charlemagne recognized, very early in his reign, that if he was to defend his vast empire, or to extend its borders, he needed a highly regulated, professional army determined primarily by his cavalry. Therefore, he created an army that was systematically well armed, both for attack and defense, and, crucially, had a highly developed military organization to support it. The first extant law of Charlemagne to state this policy was the *capitulare missorum* of 792/793, which demanded that all benefice and office holders in the Carolingian realm own armor and a shield, as well as a horse and weapons.[27] This was followed in 802/803 by another capitulary charging these nobles to have their own helmets and cuirasses, known as byrnies.[28] In 805, the laws were made even more specific: Charlemagne required that anyone in his empire who held 12 *mansi* of land was to have his own armor and to serve as a horseman in his army; if he failed in his duty, both his land and his armor would be taken from him.[29] Infantry soldiers were not so well regulated, although the *Capitulary of Aachen*, proclaimed in 802/803, did require them all to carry a shield.[30]

The main armor of the Carolingian soldier was the shield. It was also the least expensive piece of armor, and all soldiers, even horse archers, were required to carry it. A shield and lance together cost one third of the cost of a helmet and one sixth that of a byrnie. Like many other early medieval shields, Carolingian shields were made of wood, were round and concave, and most were covered, probably on both sides, with leather. They were usually rimmed with metal, and metal strips were sometimes added for extra strength. A dome-shaped metal boss was set in the middle of the front of the shield with a grip running across the back attached both to the boss and to the wood. A long leather strap allowed the soldier to sling the shield across his back when not in use. Carolingian shields were usually larger than other early medieval shields, measuring between 52 and 80 centimeters in diameter, and protected more of the warrior's torso, the largest covering the body from the neck to the thighs.[31]

While the Carolingian shield appears to have been similar to other shields of the early Middle Ages, Carolingian helmets differed considerably from earlier medieval ones. Now almost always made of metal, unlike many early helmets that were made of leather or a combination of metal and other materials, the Carolingian helmet fitted the head closely, was made in two pieces joined down the center, and had a broad brim. In contemporary illustrations it is apparent that the brim was very characteristic, rising to a point at the forehead and tapering downwards, forming a pronounced neckguard at the rear of the helmet. A strengthening band descended from the top of the helmet and intersected the rim at a button or large rivet. This band also served as the helmet's crest, with some sources showing a feather attached to it. Although this form of helmet is shown prominently in illustrations, the earlier *spangenhelm* form of helmet continued to be used as well.[32]

Those Carolingian soldiers who could afford it wore the byrnie, which was possibly a new form of armor, but, if not, was certainly a new style. This was highly prized armor, not only because of its cost, but also because of the protection it afforded. As early as 779, Charlemagne had forbidden the sale of this type of armor outside the realm. In 803, he added a declaration that soldiers were forbidden even to give it to a merchant, who might sell it to a potential enemy, although even with this protection it does appear that certain Frankish merchants sold byrnies to Avars, Arabs, Bretons, and Scandinavians.[33] There has been some dispute among historians as to what exactly constituted the Carolingian byrnie, yet it is now clear that it was a mail tunic with sleeves. It was quite long, reaching below the hips and covering most of the arms.[34]

Leg-guards and greaves also appeared during the Carolingian period, though their cost probably restricted their use to the wealthiest of Charlemagne's horsemen. Armguards and gauntlets for the hands also appeared around this time, later to be common armor for cavalry. Charlemagne also forbade the sale of these armaments to foreigners.[35]

Carolingian military practices remained dominant throughout the ninth and tenth centuries. The Carolingian army continued to be primarily a well-armed, cavalry-based force, with each soldier protected by a byrnie, a wide-brimmed helmet, and a large round shield. Indeed, so influential were these Carolingian practices that they stimulated change in military traditions well beyond the borders of Charlemagne's empire. Carolingian-style armor became the standard in Spain, Scandinavia, Eastern Europe, and England.[36]

The byrnie, now called by different names, continued to remain the primary body armor into the later Middle Ages. However, the shield and helmet changed in design some time during the late tenth and early eleventh centuries, although the reasons for these changes are unclear due to the lack of evidence. The round shield did not cover the whole body of the horseman, leaving his legs unprotected from enemy attack while its large size made it unwieldy for a cavalry soldier to easily maneuver during battle. These problems were solved by making the shield narrower and longer, hence the so-called kite-shaped shield.

By the beginning of the eleventh century the wide-brimmed helmet was largely superseded by a much simpler design. Just why this occurred is unclear, although it may just be that it was easier to make and subsequently cheaper. At any rate, the wide-brimmed Carolingian helmet gave way to a simple conical helmet, made in one piece, which fitted closely to the head with an extension down the front to protect the nose.[37] (Other explanations include the possibility that iron was now cheaper, or that construction techniques had developed sufficiently for the armorer to make the helmet from one piece of iron, technically quite a complex procedure.) Carolingian helmets and shields continued to be used until the twelfth century, but only infrequently and, in artistic sources at least, they are shown worn most often by non-Western European armies, such as Romans and Muslims or, by that special iconographic figure of military evil, Goliath.[38]

ARMOR IN THE BAYEUX TAPESTRY

The Bayeux Tapestry—not in fact a tapestry but an embroidery—was made some time before the end of the eleventh century to celebrate the conquest of England in 1066 by William of Normandy. Not only is it a unique survival, but it also provides a wonderfully clear snapshot of the arms and armor used in Western Europe in the second half of the eleventh century; among many other things, it depicts over 200 armed men, of whom 79 are wearing body armor. Although there are certain shortcomings in using the Bayeux Tapestry as a source for the study of armor during this period (its small scale and the fact that embroidery as a medium is fairly inexact), there is a consistency within it that gives us a great deal of confidence in the historical accuracy of the embroiderers' work.[39]

Almost all the soldiers are wearing mail armor, essentially the Carolingian byrnie, which, by the eleventh century, was called a hauberk. Worn by both cavalry and infantry, the hauberk was a mail shirt reaching to the knees with short sleeves made all in one piece, as indicated by the portrayal along the tapestry's border of dead soldiers being stripped of their armor by pulling it over their heads—an indication of the continued value of this armor. The hauberk was probably worn over, but not attached to, a heavy, quilted undergarment, the haubergeon, which added to the defensive capability of the armor, although this is not depicted in the tapestry.

Most hauberks in the Bayeux Tapestry are shown descending to the knees and divided down the front and back to allow greater freedom of movement and comfort, especially on horseback. One figure is depicted with a long-sleeved hauberk, but most have short, wide sleeves that leave the forearms bare. Colored bands along the edges of the sleeves and skirt may mean that cloth was sewn onto these to soften the roughness of the metal and to guard against irritation. One horseman is also depicted with additional protection for the forearms, although most are shown with no further protection for the arms or hands. Similarly, very few soldiers wear armor on their legs, although some leaders and other important soldiers, including both William the Conqueror and Harold Godwinson, have mail leggings (or *chausses*) but no armor on the feet. Other figures, again mostly leaders or important soldiers, are shown wearing a mail hood or coif over which their helmet fits. Whether this was connected to the hauberk or was an additional piece of mail, like the *chausses*, is unclear.

Finally, several soldiers, all Norman horsemen, including William the Conqueror, have colored rectangles on the breasts of their hauberks. This

Fig. 2.2: Bayeux Tapestry: William the Conqueror leading cavalry against Anglo-Saxon troops.
The Bridgeman Art Library International / With special authorization of the city of Bayeux.

feature, found elsewhere only in an eleventh-century Catalan manuscript illumination, has been the subject of debate for many modern commentators. Some, including James Mann and Ian Peirce, believe this to represent the addition of metal plates under the hauberk, and perhaps attached to it, to further protect the vulnerable chest. Others, most notably David C. Nicolle, claim instead that this merely depicts a mail *ventail* (the face covering of a mail coif), which has been unlaced for comfort when not in battle. In either case, and an answer is impossible to arrive at based on the Bayeux Tapestry alone, this would have been a characteristic of armor not previously seen, nor seen elsewhere.[40]

All the helmets shown in the tapestry, those worn by both Anglo-Saxon and Norman troops, are of the same pattern: a close-fitting conical helmet with a somewhat pointed apex and a wide, flat nasal guard attached to the brim and descending down over the nose. While not shown in the Bayeux Tapestry, other artistic sources from the period show that these helmets were secured in place with a leather strap tied under the chin.[41] From close examination all of the helmets appear to have been made from a single piece of iron forged into shape, although it is possible that some were made of several pieces of iron attached together as in the *spangenhelms* described above. All have a nose-guard, which would also have protected the face to some extent, but no cheek-pieces are shown. Just how well these helmets protected the face is open to some doubt, as one Anglo-Saxon soldier, most likely King Harold Godwinson, is shown pierced through the eye by a Norman arrow, unimpeded by his helmet's nasal guard.[42]

Almost all the shields depicted on the Bayeux Tapestry, whether carried by infantry or cavalry, are kite shields, long and narrow, rounded over the top and coming to a point at the bottom. Some appear to curve slightly, although it cannot be determined by how much, or whether all kite shields had this characteristic. No kite shields are known to have survived, but it is likely that, as with almost all shields, they were constructed in a manner similar to their Carolingian predecessors: wood covered with leather, a metal boss, and perhaps a metal rim, although this latter characteristic is impossible to ascertain from the Bayeux Tapestry alone.

The shields are shown held in a variety of ways by leather straps (or *enarmes*) riveted onto their inner faces. The most frequent of these shows a loose strap draped around the soldier's neck, with a shorter strap grasped in his hand. Horsemen carry their shields consistently on the left side, the lance carried by the right hand; infantry also carry their shields in the left hand.

The advantages of the kite shield for cavalry soldiers have been described above, but this shape was also good for the infantry soldier. The kite shield allowed foot-soldiers to plant the sharper bottom edge into the ground and, by overlapping the wider upper part of each shield, form a rudimentary and temporary battlefield fortification known as a "shield-wall." So effective was this infantry tactic that it became the favorite defensive maneuver of infantry against the cavalry charge during the central Middle Ages.

The shield was also frequently decorated, although there seems to be no consistency, or heraldry, in their patterns. Among the designs that appear are birds, dragons, wavy crosses, diagonal lines, and saltires, with the boss and rivets also sometimes incorporated into the pattern. Some of the English infantry carry round shields, and there is a single rectangular shield, also carried by an Anglo-Saxon foot-soldier.[43]

TWELFTH-CENTURY ARMOR

The types of armor portrayed in the Bayeux Tapestry were common throughout the eleventh and twelfth centuries across Western Europe: in France, Germany, and England as well as in Italy, Spain, Poland, Hungary, and Scandinavia. It was also these types of body armor, helmets, and shields that were worn by the Crusaders on their first two crusades into the Holy Land, and by the Christian Spaniards fighting to recover their lands from the Muslims.[44] Their armor also showed to those they faced that they were serious soldiers, with a wealth of professionalism that should not be faced unless those opposing them were willing to risk their lives for their lords or causes. That twelfth-century knights carried pride with them as they donned and wore their armor was clear, writes Ralph Niger in 1187:

> It is custom for the knights of this world firstly to fix their spurs to their shoes, and then to protect their feet, legs and groin with mail leggings. After that they throw their hauberks over the rest of their body and arrange it around their bodies and limbs with a belt. After that they put on their helmets and lace them up to their hauberks and their heads, and finally belt on their swords. After that they take up their lances and shields....[45]

The kite shield continued to be used by all troops, infantry and cavalry, until the end of the twelfth and beginning of the thirteenth centuries. Although its size, shape, and manufacture remained largely unchanged, the top edge became less rounded. Depictions of shields at this period also show that some were curved to fit more closely around the soldier's body.[46] Round shields, like those used earlier, are also shown in twelfth-century illustrations, but they continue to be shown most often as symbols of "evil." By the end of the century, however, they begin to appear in the hands of Sicilian and Spanish soldiers, perhaps due to Muslim.[47]

Helmets shown in artistic sources of the 150 years following the battle of Hastings also differ little from those depicted on the Bayeux Tapestry. Almost all are conical and made either in one piece or of segmented construction and most, but not all, have a nasal guard.[48] Surviving helmets from this period (and perhaps earlier, as these are difficult to date) are rare, but examples of both types of construction exist. Two are made of a single piece of metal hammered into shape and are very close to those shown in the Bayeux Tapestry. The first, said to be the helmet of St. Wenceslaus, is in the Cathedral Treasury of Prague, while the other is in the collections of the Imperial Armoury in Vienna.[49] The other examples are made of several pieces of iron riveted to a circular rim. Some of these have nasal guards, the others having possibly lost theirs, and at least two examples have evidence of mail attached to the lower edge. Some also have indications of gilded decoration.[50] Artistic sources sometimes show a slightly different form of helmet, in which the apex, instead of rising straight up to a point, curves forward, although if these did exist and are not simply artistic flourishes—they are again primarily associated with "evil"—they were rare.[51]

Fig. 2.3: Mail armor—German, mid-fourteenth century.

© Board of Trustees of the Armouries.

Twelfth-century body armor, still fundamentally the mail hauberk, was very similar to that shown in the Bayeux Tapestry, although the length varied somewhat from just below the waist to as low as the knees. (Some historians have suggested that the length of the hauberk was dictated by climate—in northern Europe it was longer while soldiers fighting in the Holy Land used a shorter version—but this is not borne out by artistic evidence.) In general, the hauberk hung loose and was sometimes gathered at the waist with a belt. Over the course of the twelfth century the sleeves of the hauberk were lengthened until, by the end of the century, they extended to cover the backs of the hands. These hand-protectors, today called mufflers, just covered the backs of the hands, the palms protected by cloth or leather. Only in rare examples are separate fingers shown, and in one source, an illumination of the prophet Joshua from a Winchester Bible made in 1160–70, mail mittens can be seen. However, these do not completely cover the hand, but instead leave the thumb and fingers

Fig. 2.4: Kneeling knight, from the *Westminster Psalter*, c. 1250.

free.[52] Cords or thongs at the wrist were commonly used to hold the sleeves tightly in place.[53] All hauberks continued to be worn over quilted haubergeons, which provided added protection.

Around the middle of the twelfth century a long textile garment, called a surcoat or coat armor, started to be worn. A loose sleeveless garment with a deeply slit skirt reaching to around the mid-calf, the surcoat, it has been suggested, was adopted to display the heraldry of the wearer. But this is now discredited, as surcoats bearing arms do not appear until much later. Whatever its use, surcoats became common by the end of the century and sometimes, unfortunately, obscure the details of the armor beneath them.[54]

Mail *chausses*, like those worn by the military leaders of the Norman and Anglo-Saxon armies in the Bayeux Tapestry, also continue to be depicted in late-twelfth-century artistic sources. Occasionally *chausses* are shown extending down to cover the feet, sometimes with the addition of spurs attached to the heel.[55] Most soldiers also wore a mail coif to protect the head, but whether these were separate pieces of armor or part of the hauberk is unclear, and it is probable that they could be either.[56]

Scale armor (also known as lamellar armor) was also being made and used, as is shown in several artistic renderings of medieval warfare. This armor was, however, rare, and mail was, by far, the commonest form of armor during this period. Like round shields, they too are most often seen on "enemies."[57]

SHIELDS, HELMETS, AND HERALDRY IN THE THIRTEENTH CENTURY

Important changes in the development of armor came at the end of the twelfth and beginning of the thirteenth centuries, in particular changes to the size and shape of the shield, the development of new types of helmet, the introduction of horse armor, and the beginnings of heraldry.[58]

The kite shield, the predominant form for nearly two centuries, was superseded by a smaller, lighter shield that was shorter, wider, and more triangular in shape, the so-called "heater" shield. This change probably reflects the adoption of leg armor, making the long kite shape unnecessary. The new shield was also less cumbersome and more maneuverable, especially on horseback. The kite shield continued to be used by the infantry, but eventually they also switched to the newer design.[59]

ARMS AND ARMOR

Although the ubiquitous conical helmet with a nasal guard depicted in the Bayeux Tapestry continued to be used well into the thirteenth century, a slightly more rounded form of helmet appears toward the end of the twelfth century and began to be used side by side with the older style of helmet. Another form of helmet, called a *cervellière* or, later, a *bascinet*, developed in the early thirteenth century. A very simple, rounded, skull-like helmet, it was often worn under the mail coif. From the early years of the thirteenth century an additional plate was sometimes fitted to the front of the *cervellière* to cover the face. Later on this was extended around the back of the head, leading to the development of the helm or great helm.

When fully developed, the great helm had a simple cylindrical form, with a flat top and sight, and openings for breathing cut into its front. It was worn over a mail coif and required the addition of an extra quilted arming cap on top of the head and under the helmet to hold it firmly on the middle of the wearer's head.[60] At times, however, this did not suffice to keep the great helm in place. Once, the helm of the great jouster William Marshal turned around during a joust so that his vision and breathing were cut off; only with difficulty was he able to pull the helmet off in time to save his life.[61] The small sight holes also meant that the vision of the warrior was impaired, but this obstacle could be overcome by practice and familiarization; anything larger would have significantly lessened the helm's defensibility. The great helm was quickly adopted by the mounted soldier, who needed the added protection it provided, and it soon became the predominant armor for the head throughout Europe. But it was often simply too cumbersome, too heavy, too restrictive, and too expensive for many infantry soldiers to wear.[62]

Another new type of helmet, the so-called kettle hat, consisting of a close-fitting bowl with a wide, flat brim, was also introduced in this period. Although this style of helmet had been common in the classical world and was, in fact, very similar to that used by the Carolingians, it had since fallen out of use in Europe and was not re-introduced until the end of the twelfth century. It then had a very long life, with similar shaped helmets still being made and used in seventeenth-century Europe. The early examples, at least until well into the fourteenth century, were constructed like the *spangenhelm*, an iron framework in which the spaces were filled with separate triangular-shaped plates, while later examples were made from either a single piece of iron, or from two plates joined by a central ridge. The kettle hat was, like the *spangenhelm*, relatively easy and cheap to produce and was the helmet used most often by the common soldier, although it was also sometimes worn by cavalry and knights. It

Fig. 2.5: Great helm—English, c. 1370.

was secured on the head by a leather chin-strap, and was worn either over or without a mail coif.[63]

Alongside the use of mail armor there developed, from the second half of the twelfth century, various quilted textile defenses, the *pourpoint*, the *aketon* and the *gambeson*, although just what each was and their exact purpose and use are somewhat difficult to differentiate. All of these terms seem to have been used for garments worn both over and under the hauberk. However, it is likely that the *gambeson* refers to a garment worn over the mail, rather like the surcoat, while the *aketon* was a plain, quilted coat worn underneath mail armor, although it could also be worn by the common soldier as their only defense. The *pourpoint* was probably the more generic name used for all types of soft, quilted defenses. Unfortunately, none of these garments survives, and all our information on them is derived from written sources, which are often difficult to interpret, or from illustrations, sculptures or brasses. They are also not a very prominent form of armor, as they were worn beneath other defenses, so only glimpses of them can be seen. Finally, mention must be made of *gamboised cuisses*, essentially padded thigh defenses, which started to appear in the later thirteenth century.[64]

No horse armor is shown in the Bayeux Tapestry, and it would appear that horses were not protected by armor until the later twelfth century, although the early evidence is rather confusing. After this time, however, it became common to cover the horse in a large flowing cloth, called a caparison, which, especially later on, was emblazoned with the rider's colors or arms. Defenses in the form of a mail trapper, which covered the horse from the head to its knees, appear

ARMS AND ARMOR

in artistic sources from around the middle of the thirteenth century, although the caparison often obscures it in contemporary illustrations.[65]

Throughout this period and later, armor was frequently decorated in some way. The whole range of decorative techniques—for example, embossing, gilding, etching, and engraving—was used to enliven surfaces as well as display the wealth and status of the wearer. Sometimes, too, painted and decorated surfaces were common for armor, especially shields. Indeed, if we are to believe Homer, shield decoration, sometimes with lavish and symbolic art work, was especially favored by both the Greeks and the Trojans during their wars. Roman soldiers decorated their armor and shields, and the shields of warriors depicted on the Bayeux Tapestry are painted with animals and other designs. In the Middle Ages, symbolic, religious, and secular designs were extensively used. This may have originated for Christianity with Constantine the Great, who had the "chi-rho" monogram first painted on his shields and banners at the battle of Milvian Bridge in 312, as a symbol of his acceptance of Christianity. The Crusaders traveling to the Holy Land also painted their shields, surcoats, and helmets with the cross to designate their devotion to the sacred calling of gaining the Holy Land for Christians.[66]

Much of this decoration was probably very personal and, outside of a small circle, for example a military unit or family, may not have been generally recognizable. By the first half of the twelfth century, some noble families had begun to use a variety of symbols to reflect their status. Although the exact origins and motivations of heraldry—as it came to be known—are obscure, it is clear that some form of easy recognition, especially of nobility, was very desirable. The practice became very popular and was widely adopted very quickly across Europe.[67] By the end of the thirteenth century all noble families of any rank had their own heraldic emblems. These symbols were often chosen to represent the traits of the family: a lion might represent courage, a dragon strength, a fox cunning, and so on. When families intermarried, their emblems reflected this by combining the two heraldries.[68] Very quickly there developed a whole "language" and art of heraldry leading ultimately to heraldic organizations, for example, in England where the College of Heralds was instituted in 1484 by King Richard III to regulate and administer it.[69]

As armor developed, and more and more of a warrior became covered, the use of heraldic devices as a means of identification gained in popularity. While this occurred especially on armor for parade or tournament use, and was not primarily meant to be used in combat, it did appear on some battlefield armor. The shield, of course, continued to be the primary surface for the display of heraldic symbols, but it was also used to decorate other pieces of equipment: surcoats, banners (carried by squires) warhorse caparisons, and even helmet crests.[70]

FOURTEENTH-CENTURY BODY ARMOR

Mail continued to be used and favored by soldiers in the fourteenth century.[71] However, improvements in crossbows and the introduction of longbows led to an increase in the range and power of archers, so that they were increasingly able to smash open the rings and penetrate mail armor, leading to the need for a more effective defense.[72] This led to the next, and probably most significant, development in body armor: full plate armor, essentially armor made from large pieces of iron held together by internal and external leather straps. This change started in the late thirteenth century and was completed by around 1400.

Using large plates of metal as body armor was not completely new: the Greeks had worn breastplates and backplates made from single pieces of bronze; the Romans used larger pieces of bronze and, later, iron fastened together with internal leathers; and, although not common, lamellar and scale armor existed throughout the Middle Ages. However, most medieval soldiers before the end of the thirteenth century preferred mail armor for their battle-field protection.[73]

Possibly the earliest reference to plate armor comes from *Topographica Hibernica et expugnatio Hibernica* (*The Topography and Conquest of Ireland*), written at the end of the twelfth century by Gerald of Wales, in which it is said that in a Danish attack on Dublin in 1171, the Danes were clad in long hauberks made of both mail and "plates of iron stitched together skillfully." This might refer to plate armor, but as there is no corroborating evidence even from contemporary Danish sources, it may also be simply a reference to scale armor.[74]

More certain evidence of the early development of plate armor does not appear until the early to mid-thirteenth century. Both artistic and written sources show the introduction of this new design of armor at the time. For example, one early thirteenth-century chronicler, Guillaume le Breton, writes about a fight between Richard the Lionheart of England (at the time only Count of Poitou) and William des Barres in 1191, with each combatant wearing "molded iron plates" as an extra protective garment under the mail hauberk.[75]

What is clear is that the development of plate armor started with the addition of plates to cover and protect the joints, especially the elbows and knees. These plates were, at first, made from a variety of materials, including copper alloy, horn, bone, *cuir bouilli* (shaped and hardened rawhide), as well as iron, which, of course, became the standard material for armor until its demise in the seventeenth century.[76] This is probably what is referred to in the combat between Richard and William des Barres and might also be the case with a manifesto written from the German emperor Frederick II to King Henry III of England in 1241, which mentions leather armor strengthened by iron plates sewn onto it.[77]

In about 1250, pieces of armor to cover the front and sides of the knees, called poleyns, appear in illustrations, and disc-shaped couters, i.e., armor to protect the elbows, followed about a decade after. Plate armor covering the shins also developed at around the same time, but was not common until the early decades of the fourteenth century.[78] The development of plate armor for the torso is more difficult to determine with certainty as written sources are almost non-existent, and artistic sources, including effigies, are of little more assistance since early plate armor was generally hidden under the surcoat until the middle of the fourteenth century. Indeed, there is some indication that initially metal plates may even have been attached to the surcoat itself, producing a coat of plates or brigandine, which was worn over the mail hauberk.[79]

CLOTH-COVERED ARMOR FROM THE BATTLEFIELD OF VISBY

Fortunately, 25 examples of this type of armor have been excavated from mass graves found at the site of the battle of Visby, fought on the island of Gotland on 27 July 1361.[80] Although there are six different styles of armor found at Visby, all 25 suits have the same basic characteristics: they are sleeveless and consist of overlapping iron plates which had once been riveted or laced onto the inside of a leather garment. Only two armors have plates that would have been riveted to the outside of the covering, and in both cases these were only small shoulder-plates.

The number and size of the iron plates vary considerably in number, from 8 to almost 600, and in size, from 15 by 50 centimeters to less than 2 by 10 centimeters. On some, the plates are placed vertically; on others they are placed both horizontally and vertically. Most cover the torso with a skirt to the hips, while others are more tight-fitting and extend only to the waist; extra shoulder-plates appear to have been added to some, if not all. Most cover the entire torso, front and back, although at least five may have covered only the front and sides of the torso, leaving the back without protection. Almost all opened at the back, with

Fig. 2.6: Armor from the Battlefield of Visby excavations.
Statens historiska museum.

two opening on one side, two on both sides and one in the front. Finally, some armors were decorated, either with other iron plates in scutiform, scallop, and semicircular shapes, or with bronze mountings in the shape of heraldic shields, fleur-de-lis or shells. These decorations probably showed on top of the leather covering, as they are raised from the rest of the armor.[81]

Other armors were also found at Visby, including mail hauberks, mail and plate gauntlets, arm- and leg-guards made of plate, plate *sabatons*, and almost 200 mail coifs. Interestingly, these coifs probably would have been used under helmets or iron caps, but no traces of these were found, and this may indicate that the soldiers here, almost entirely infantry, did not always wear head protection over the coif, although these helmets, being more portable, could also more easily have been removed from the battlefield.[82]

LATER FOURTEENTH-CENTURY ARMOR DEVELOPMENTS

By around 1350 the coat of plates was replaced by a larger and independent breastplate made in a single piece covering the chest to the top of the diaphragm.

At first, the lower torso—stomach, waist, and hips—were protected by a flexible horizontal coat of plate hoops (waist-lames) riveted to a fabric cover. Around 1370, these were replaced by a metallic hoop skirt which covered the same area. At first, this skirt, called a fauld, was attached to the breastplate; however, later in the century the breastplate was separated entirely from any waist or hip armor. The development of the backplate is very difficult to trace, but it was probably very similar to that of the breastplate.[83]

By the end of the fourteenth century, the solid plate cuirass, the breastplate and backplate connected together by leather straps or hooks and eyelets, was being widely used by both the cavalry and infantry soldiers, if they could afford it. For the soldier on horseback, two features were added to the breastplate to make this armor even more useful. First, a bracket, sometimes hinged, was attached to the upper right side of the chest, and served to help support and maneuver a couched lance. Second, a V-shaped bar was riveted to the armor just below the neck, designed to prevent an opponent's weapon from sliding up along the slippery plate surface into the throat. These innovations, known as a lance-rest and a stop-rib respectively, became prominent features of the knight's breastplate throughout the fifteenth and sixteenth centuries.[84]

Plate armor to cover the shins, called greaves, developed around the same time but was not common until the early decades of the fourteenth century. *Sabatons* were developed in the second decade of the fourteenth century to protect the feet. Made from a series of narrow overlapping plates held together by internal leathers, they were shaped like a pointed shoe to cover the top of the foot, and a shoe or boot was also worn. *Sabatons* could also be fitted with spurs. Sometimes, however, a knight might not wear *sabatons*, choosing instead to wear a more comfortable mail or leather shoe.[85] To protect the front of the upper legs and thighs, plate *cuisses* were developed in the early decades of the fourteenth century and were also initially constructed of a series of overlapping plates riveted together. By about 1370, however, it was more common for the *cuisse* to be made from a single metal plate fashioned to the shape of the upper leg, a style that persisted until about 1500, to which the *poleyn* was attached.[86]

Plate armor for the arms and hands also developed in the late thirteenth and early fourteenth centuries. The earliest plate gauntlet appeared in the last quarter of the thirteenth century and was probably made in a manner similar to the *sabatons*: narrow metal plates secured together with internal leathers and rivets and attached to a leather glove. This method of constructing gauntlets continued until the end of the fourteenth century, although the plates became fewer in number and began to get larger. Eventually, the gauntlet consisted of only a single plate to protect the back and sides of the hand, molded to the shape of the knuckles and the base of the thumb, and separate, smaller plates to protect the fingers and the thumb. All the plates continued to be attached by rivets to a leather glove. While earlier gauntlets had a loose, flared cuff, the later fourteenth-century cuff became more close-fitting (the so-called "hour-glass" gauntlet). Sometimes the gauntlet was also decorated with iron or copper alloy spikes or the heraldic symbols of the knight, attached to the knuckle piece, called gadlings.[87]

Plate defenses for the arms, beyond the couter mentioned above, do not appear until about 1330, a little later than plate armor for legs and hands. They consisted of two gutter-shaped plates, for the upper and lower arms, and a central cup-shaped couter, over the elbow, all strapped over the sleeve of the hauberk. Besagews, i.e., small disc-shaped plates, were sometimes fastened with laces at the shoulder, to protect the armpit.[88]

During the period from around 1275 to about 1350, plates, known as *ailettes*, were sometimes attached to the top of the shoulders and projected up on either side of the head. They probably had no defensive purpose but were used for ornamental or heraldic devices. After 1350 they ceased to appear on suits of plate armor, although why they were discarded remains a mystery.[89]

Finally, in the last decade of the thirteenth century plate armor was also developed for the chin and the neck. Up to this time, a mail coif had generally been used to protect these very vulnerable parts of the body, but this was replaced by a metal collar, known as a *gorget* or *bevor*, made of overlapping plates of metal and formed to cover the neck from the shoulders to the chin. However, the *gorget* appears to have been little used, with many soldiers choosing to continue wearing mail collars.[90]

PLATE ARMOR

From around 1330 armor made from plate came to dominate the battlefield and tournament ground and, by the middle of the fourteenth century, mail had largely been superseded except for covering those parts of the body which were difficult to protect with solid plate, for example, the armpits and the insides of the elbows and knees. Plate armor offered a number of advantages. First and foremost, of course, it offered the best protection against the weapons of the day, especially the crossbow, longbow, and early gunpowder weapons. It was also favored by knights who preferred the brilliant shine of the plate, often referred to in contemporary sources as "shining like the sun," and the added status that ownership of this very expensive armor could bring in parades or tournaments. Plate armor continued to be used until armor finally went out of use in the seventeenth century.[91]

Initially at least, a full suit of armor included all of the pieces mentioned above: a cuirass consisting of a breast- and backplate; a *gorget*, *vambraces*, and gauntlets for the arms and hands; *cuisses* and greaves for the legs; and *sabatons* for the feet. Over this, the soldier usually wore a surcoat, which added no extra protection but did serve a heraldic purpose if needed.[92] However, plate armor continued to develop throughout the fourteenth and indeed into the fifteenth centuries both technologically and stylistically with a number of national and regional styles. Large armor industries were established with centers located in every kingdom, although the regions of Northern Italy (especially Lombardy) and Southern Germany (especially along the Meuse River) were generally recognized as producing the best plate armor.[93]

By about the early fifteenth century, specific plate-armor styles were established, and armor industries everywhere in Europe were producing excellent and, usually, very expensive "suits" of plate armor to meet the demands of the wealthy, noble, and aristocratic soldiers or jousters.[94] Each center produced its own distinctive style, allowing the informed observer to determine the maker of a suit of armor and the social status of the wearer. During the fifteenth century two styles of armor predominated: the Italian and the German, although Italian-style plate armor was not always made in Italy, nor was German-style plate armor always made in Germany. As well, both styles were worn throughout Europe, with Italian-style armor also worn in Germany and German-style armor in Italy.[95]

Also, new carburizing processes and the use of the blast furnace allowed steel to become the principal metal for armor construction. Not only were the defensive capabilities of the plate armor thus improved, but steel could be polished to a high shine that impressed both the wearer and those who saw him. The shine was so brilliant, in fact, that plate armor became known as "white armor" in contemporary sources. This was further emphasized at the beginning of the fifteenth century by the removal of the surcoat worn by knights, leaving the bare, brilliant armor to be viewed by all.[96]

The cuirass was the primary part of any suit of armor, the foundation of which was a strong, well-designed breastplate. Two styles of breastplate were present in the fifteenth century. The Italian style was rounded in shape, covering the front and sides of the torso, and was cut off at the waist. The German

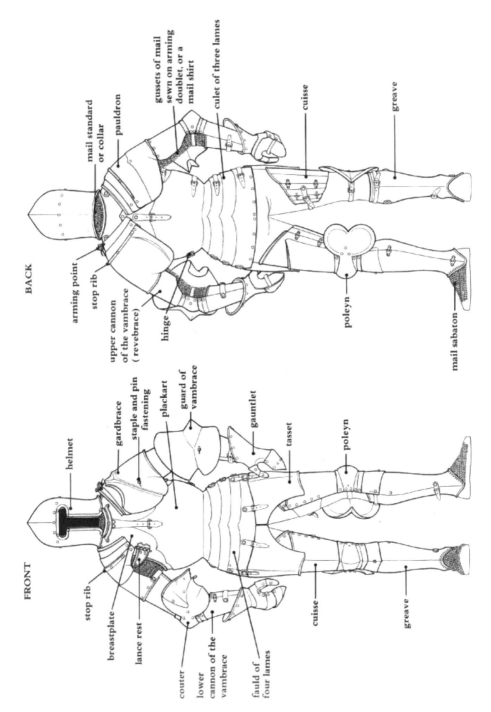

BACK

mail standard
or collar

pauldron

gussets of mail
sewn on arming
doublet, or a
mail shirt

culet of three lames

arming point

stop rib

upper cannon
of the vambrace
(revebrace)

hinge

cuisse

greave

poleyn

mail sabaton

FRONT

helmet

gardbrace

staple and pin
fastening

plackart

guard of
vambrace

gauntlet

tasset

poleyn

stop rib

breastplate

lance rest

couter

lower
cannon of the
vambrace

fauld of
four lames

cuisse

greave

Fig. 2.7: Chart of plate armor terms.

Edge and Paddock (1996): 113.

ARMS AND ARMOR

style was more box-like in shape, with the waist protected by a narrower lower breastplate (known as a plackart), which overlapped the main breastplate and was attached to it by a leather strap and buckles. Most plackarts also supported a fauld, made of a various number of waist-lames, which were joined to it by rivets and straps. Later in the century, rectangular-shaped plates, the tassets, were attached to the fauld to protect the upper leg and groin area, and a backplate completed the torso defense. It was constructed like the breastplate, with an upper plate overlapped by a lower plate to which a fauld was affixed (although generally containing fewer waist-lames). The backplate was attached to the breastplate by shoulder straps and a waist-belt.[97]

The shoulders were protected by pauldrons in the fifteenth century. These were made in various styles, although the most common type in the early part of the century was a large square-shaped plate on the left shoulder and a smaller, similarly shaped one on the right shoulder, the latter smaller to allow ease of movement when carrying a lance or wielding a sword. As the century continued, pauldrons became less angular and more spread out at the back, forming what looked like an overlapping set of "wings." Occasionally, attached to the pauldrons were additional, reinforcing plates that stood up on each side of the head, sometimes as high as the ears. Sometimes pauldrons were decorated with inscriptions, such as the invocations *Ave Maria* and *Ave Domini*.[98]

Very few changes were made to plate arm defenses, the *vambraces*, in the fifteenth century. Alterations were merely stylistic, varying generally between German and Italian designs. For example, Italian-style armors had larger upper cannons, the part of the *vambrace* covering the upper arm, while the German style preferred larger lower cannons. German-style armorers also made their *vambraces* fluted and more decorative than did Italian-style armorers, who preferred smooth, undecorated surfaces of plate armor.[99]

While the main parts of the *vambrace* remained relatively unchanged between the fourteenth and fifteenth centuries, the couter changed significantly. What had been merely an elbow-guard was greatly enlarged with a large and distinctive side-wing. This was especially large on the right elbow, part of the arm that carried the lance and thus did not have the benefit of a large protective pauldron, although the left side-wing was also quite large. In general, the Italian-style couter was larger than the German-style one, although again the German-style armorers preferred more decoration.[100]

The gauntlet changed only after about 1430, from a relatively simple cover for the top of the hand to a mitten which encompassed the entire hand. This was achieved by surrounding the entire hand with armor and by extending the

Fig. 2.8: Federigo da Montefeltro in plate armor and his son Guidobaldo, by Joos van Gent (fl.1460–75).

The Bridgeman Art Library International / Palazzo Barberini, Rome, Italy.

ARMS AND ARMOR

metacarpal plates to the tips of the fingers. The number of plates depended on the flexibility desired—the more plates the better the flexibility—although the right gauntlet, which covered the weapon-wielding hand, was always more flexible than the left. At the same time, the "hour-glass" shape of the cuffs fell out of fashion, and the cuff now extended further up the lower arm, overlapping the lower cannon.[101]

Early fifteenth-century leg defenses (*legharnesses*) also differed little from their fourteenth-century predecessors. Only two significant changes were made to the *legharness* and both came about 1430. The first was the addition of side-wings to the *poleyns*, much like those on the couters, which were made larger and more decorative in design as the century progressed. Again, as with the couter, the German-style was smaller and more decorated than the Italian-style. The second change was the addition of an articulated plate to the top of the cuisse, which protected the space between the main *cuisse* plate and the groin.[102]

The shape of the *sabatons* changed in response to fashion, but they were made much the same way as before, from narrow plates of iron. Some extended only to the end of the foot and were rounded, while others had sometimes detachable extensions, which were pointed and stretched several inches beyond the end of the foot.[103]

The *gorget*, too, changed little in the fifteenth century, although it did increase in popularity among German-style armorers after about 1430. During the fifteenth century the *gorget* was made from two main plates, at the front and rear, which enclosed the base of the neck and extended upwards. The two *gorget* plates were hinged together on one side and secured by a pin on the other.[104] At times the *gorget* was disregarded, sometimes to the detriment of those who should have worn it. The absence of the *gorget* may have caused the throat wound of the count of Burgundy, Charles the Bold, at the battle of Montlhéry in 1465, when contemporary chroniclers report that his throat-guard had fallen off, and he had not bothered to replace it.[105]

The defensive strength of plate armor precluded the need to wear a heavily quilted haubergeon under the armor for added defense, as had been the custom with mail. Still, there was a need to wear something under the armor to protect the wearer against the discomfort of the metal, so the haubergeon continued to be worn in the late Middle Ages although it was made smaller, extending only to the hips and elbows, and thinner. Eventually it was replaced by the arming doublet, a thinly padded garment with mail attached in places not covered by the plate armor: the neck (even if a *gorget* was worn), the armpits, the elbow-joints, and the tops of the thighs and groin. The Italian-style arming doublet had a relatively long, loose skirt, while the German-style arming doublet included a short, tight-fitting pair of mail breeches that contained a genital-protecting codpiece. A quilted arming cap, like those used earlier, continued to be worn under the helmet, sometimes extending around the cheeks and chin to keep the skin there from being irritated, although the late medieval helmet was generally lined.[106]

The weight of a suit of plate armor was considerable, but it was distributed over much of the body. It has been estimated that a complete suit of plate armor for use on the battlefield (including helmet and shield) weighed between 23 and 28 kilograms, while a suit of plate armor for the joust, made heavier because of the need to protect the participants, weighed between 41 and 46 kilograms.[107]

Although much is made in the popular histories about the weight of armor, it was not that heavy at all and the idea of a knight having to be winched onto his horse is completely wrong. Modern experiments with full-scale replica armor show that a knight would have been able to move quite freely and even turn a somersault should the need arise. Lost were the extremes of movement, but this was the same for all knights so that none was at a disadvantage. In fact, it is likely that plate armor was easier to wear than mail because of its even distribution of weight; the weight of mail was unevenly distributed, with most of the weight carried on the shoulders. The chief discomfort of plate armor may not have come from its weight but from the lack of ventilation, and from the fact that it was hot to wear for long periods in the summer and very cold in the winter.

Plate armor was also more difficult and time-consuming to put on, and the assistance of at least one servant or page was necessary. Geoffrey Chaucer, describing the arming of Sir Topaz, writes:

> They covered next his ivory flank
> With cloth spun of the finest hank,
> With breeches and a shirt,
> And over that (in case it fail)
> A tunic, then a coat of mail,
> For fear he might be hurt,
> And over that contrived to jerk
> A hauberk (finest Jewish work
> and strong in every plate)
> And over that his coat of arms,
> White as a lily-flower's charms,
> In which he must debate.[108]

ARMS AND ARMOR

With the rise of more powerful weapons in the later Middle Ages, wearing plate armor was essential for the front-line troops, the men-at-arms, in battle. Good plate armor was capable of withstanding penetration by crossbow bolts, longbow arrows, and handgun shots, not to mention the spears, halberds, swords, and other weapons used at the time. Failure to wear good armor could cost a soldier his life, the most prominent example of this being John Talbot, the earl of Shrewsbury, who was slain when dressed only in a brigandine at the battle of Castillon in July 1453.[109]

LATE MEDIEVAL INFANTRY ARMOR

Full plate armor was worn principally by noble or aristocratic soldiers who commonly fought on horseback, often misidentified as knights. (All knights were cavalry, but not all cavalry were knights, the knight needing to have "earned his spurs" and be dubbed a knight.) The expense of plate armor made its use by infantry soldiers rare, although in the fourteenth and fifteenth centuries a few wealthy foot-soldiers did venture to clothe themselves in this armor.[110]

For those who could afford it, especially those recruited from towns, urban militias, and mercenaries, mail shirts and helmets were worn, sometimes with the addition of a breastplate. For the very poorest, armor might be nothing more than a quilted jacket perhaps with a simple helmet and a shield.

Increasingly though, the armor that began to be adopted by the infantry during the late Middle Ages was made of a combination of cloth and metal plates of which there were two types: the brigandine and the jack of plates. The brigandine was made of small rectangular plates of iron riveted to a sleeveless fabric jacket that fastened up the front or on one side, providing continuous but flexible protection. The plates overlapped one another to provide good protection, especially against sword thrusts. Surviving examples show just how well the armorers of the time understood the problems posed by those wearing this type of armor. The iron plates of brigandines, very prone to rusting especially from the sweat produced in the extremes of battle, were coated with a protective layer, applied by dipping the plates in a molten bath of a lead and tin mixture very similar to modern solder. Although mostly used by the poorer soldiers, expensive, luxurious brigandines for the wealthy and noble were also produced, made using costly silks and brocades.

The jack was very similar to the brigandine, but made from small square plates of iron, each with a hole through its center and laced between two layers of fabric with cord, giving this type of armor a quilted appearance. Non-military clothing and hats were made in the same way. Jacks also seem to have been only made from cheap, coarse materials, and only for the common soldier.[111]

Both the jack and the brigandine were especially popular in the fifteenth century, but they were in use before then and were still being used by the light infantry, with mail sleeves and a pike, in the late sixteenth and early seventeenth centuries. However, after about 1500, it became more usual for the infantry, and also the light cavalry, to wear a corselet, consisting of a collar, breastplate, backplate, tassets, *vambraces* and gauntlets with an open helmet.

LATE MEDIEVAL HELMETS

The great helm remained the primary form of cavalry soldiers' helmet up to about 1350 and continued to be used in the joust into the sixteenth century. It remained relatively unchanged in shape, but by the end of the thirteenth century it

Fig. 2.9: An English infantry soldier as armored in the fifteenth century in a brigandine, sallet, and mail sleeves and collar.

© Board of Trustees of the Armouries.

had lost its traditional "can" shape and began to taper more. The crown resembled the earlier conical helmets, truncated at the top and sometimes ending in a slight point. It was also lengthened to rest on the wearer's shoulders and chest and was attached to the armor there. By the end of the fourteenth century, the helm became higher in the skull, with the lower edge slightly curved forward to form a pair of lips; the lower lip was longer than the upper lip, with an eye-slit open in between. This in turn developed into a form, known as "frog-mouthed," in the early fifteenth century and became extremely popular for use on the battlefield and in tournaments for the next hundred years.[112]

Throughout the late Middle Ages, crests were often mounted on top of the helm and were sometimes quite ornate, especially for parade and tournament armors—horns, plumes of feathers, crowns (for royalty) and heraldic symbols were all common. All seem to have been made of wood or *cuir bouilli* and attached to the helmets by laces. Crests remained in use until the middle of the sixteenth century.[113]

After the end of the thirteenth century the helm was often fitted with guard-chains, which attached it to the surcoat, but after c.1300 by rivets or staples to the breast- and backplates. Initially, they were probably used to keep the helmet attached during battle, but, as confirmed in contemporary artwork, they also allowed the soldier to carry the helmet slung over a shoulder by the chain.[114]

Infantry soldiers continued to wear the simple kettle-hat, which, like the helm, varied little in style. After about 1300 it was usually made from a single piece of iron instead of many pieces riveted together. The brim also grew wider and flared out away the head more. The kettle-hat, and its minor variations, including the *morion*, what would become the archetypal helmet of the Spanish conquistadors, remained in use for much of the time that armor was worn.[115]

After about 1300 the *cervellière*, the simple dome-shaped helmet, was supplanted by the *bascinet*, a type of helmet that was to become very common down to about 1450 and, although rarer afterwards, did not completely disappear until the middle of the sixteenth century. There were three types of *bascinet*: a small globular form covering the sides and rear of the head, often with a visor; a deep conical helmet arched over the face and extending down almost to the shoulders at the sides and back, and also fitted with a visor; and a tall conical helmet with a straight horizontal lower edge cut off at the level of the ears, not always fitted with a visor. Before about 1330 the *bascinet* extended down to the base of the neck and forward to cover the rear of the cheeks. After that date it was usually fitted with an *aventail*, a mail extension covering the

Fig. 2.10: *Bascinet*—Northern Italian, late fourteenth century.

© Board of Trustees of the Armouries.

neck and shoulders, secured to the helmet by *vervelles*, i.e., iron pegs with a transverse hole.

The visor with which the *bascinet* was fitted, called a *Klappvisier*, was rounded and pivoted at the sides of the skull at first, although later it would be attached to the center of the top of the face opening. The tall form of the *bascinet*, with a point at the rear and a visor pivoted at the sides, became very common throughout Europe after about 1380. It is sometimes called a "pig-faced *bascinet*" by modern scholars, although the term visored *bascinet* was more common at the time. A variation of the *bascinet*, fitted with plates resembling the *aventail*, and called a great *bascinet*, was used primarily for jousting.[116]

Three further late medieval helmet designs evolved from the *bascinet*. The first was known as the *barbuta* (also known early on as the *celata*), which appeared initially in mid-fourteenth-century Italy. The *barbuta* consisted of a visored helmet made from a single piece of metal. Like the *bascinet*, the *barbuta* was rounded and curved to the shape of the head and neck, but it stood very upright, like an ancient Corinthian Greek helmet; in fact, that prototype may have inspired it in the true Renaissance spirit.[117] The opening at the front was very narrow, essentially just a vertical slit that opened out at the top for the eyes.

From the barbuta evolved the *sallet* (or *salade*), which appeared in Italy early in the fifteenth century, becoming especially popular after about 1430. The *sallet* was somewhat of a combination of the *barbuta* and the kettle-hat: it was rounded like the *barbuta* with the lower edge flared out like the kettle-hat. Indeed, sometimes the brim was so exaggerated, especially among late-fifteenth-century German-style armorers, that it extended out to the rear to form a lengthy downward-sloping tail. It was held in place on the head by a chinstrap of leather, and its openness allowed for more flexibility of movement as well as greater air circulation and communication. As with other late-medieval helmets, the *sallet* was often visored, the eye-slit formed between the top of the visor and the lower edge of the helmet bowl. Otherwise extremely protective for the soldier, the *sallet* afforded little protection to the front of the neck and often a *bevor* was worn covering the neck and extending upwards to protect the chin. Although popular at first among Italian-style armorers, by the late fifteenth century, German-style armorers also made *sallets* frequently; they were used by both cavalry and infantry soldiers.[118]

The final late medieval helmet style to grow out of the *bascinet* was the *armet*. It, too, originated in the fifteenth century and was similar to other close-fitting helmets, and like the *barbuta* and *sallet* was conceived and produced first by Italian-style armorers, not becoming popular among German-style armorers until the sixteenth century. The *armet* comprised a skull cap of one piece that reached only to the level of the tops of the ears, except at the back where it extended down to the neck. Cheek-pieces were attached to each side by hinges, opening upwards and overlapping the back strip. The front opening was closed by a bluntly pointed visor pivoted on either side and overlapping the cheek-pieces. On some examples a metal *rondel* was attached, extending out from the rear of the helmet, although the reason for this is difficult to ascertain. The *armet* was usually worn with a *bevor* to protect the neck.[119]

LATE MEDIEVAL SHIELDS AND BARDING

The flat or slightly curved, triangular shield of moderate size, popular from the thirteenth century, continued to be used through the fourteenth and fifteenth centuries, but, it seems, only among cavalry soldiers. However, in using these, the placing of the lance in the couched position on top of the shield generally meant that it was too low in the charge or joust to provide much defense for the soldier holding it. To correct this problem, at the end of the fourteenth century the right-hand top corner of the shield often had a notch cut into it to support the couched lance without substantially affecting the shield's defense.

Around the same time, the triangular cavalry shield began to be supplanted by shields in a variety of shapes and sizes. The most common of these was oblong, either rounded or pointed on the lower edge, and often bent forward at the top and bottom. Leaf-shaped and round shields were also known. All cavalry shields of any shape were usually made of metal, and sometimes, if used exclusively in tournaments, they were reinforced by extra metal plates. However, in the early fifteenth century, all shields of any shape and size began to fall into disfavor among the cavalry, already well protected by plate armor. This trend continued until after about 1450, when the shield continued to be used only in jousts.[120]

Infantry soldiers also rejected triangular shields, returning some time in the early fourteenth century to the round shield not seen in regular use in Western Europe since before the Norman Conquest of England. Three further styles of late medieval infantry shields were also used: the target or *targe*, which was fairly large, flat, and equipped with a number of *enarmes* by which it was held along the forearm and hand; the buckler, which was small, often concave, held by a handle across the inside that was anchored through the shield by a hollow metal boss; and the *pavise*, which was a large oblong shield that, if relatively small and light, could be held in the hand, or, if longer and heavier, was generally propped up by a wooden brace to provide protection to archers, crossbowmen, and handgunners. Most infantry shields continued to be made of wood covered by leather, and all styles were used well into the sixteenth century.[121]

Finally, the late Middle Ages also saw significant changes in armor for horses. In the middle of the thirteenth century horse armor was nothing more than quilted fabric or a leather bard, used infrequently, which covered almost the entire horse but offered little protection against attack. While this style continued into the fourteenth century, its defensive ineffectiveness was recognized as an obvious problem. The development of a plate bard, made in metal or *cuir bouilli*, appeared initially in the last decade of the thirteenth century. A metal coat of plates, made similar to a human jack of plates, also developed and served as an intermediary step in the construction of metal plate armor for the entire horse, which came at the end of the fourteenth century, although most surviving examples date from the fifteenth and sixteenth centuries. When complete—and horses were not always clothed in their complete armor, especially on the battlefield where their free mobility was essential—the bard included a *shaffron*, which covered the head; a *crinet* formed of transverse plates, which protected the neck; the *peytral* to protect the chest; a crupper to protect the rear of the horse; and the *flanchards*, rectangular plates suspended on each side of the horse from the lower edge of the saddle. The *shaffron* was at first made of a

Fig. 2.11: Richard Beauchamp, earl of Warwick, fighting with Henry IV against Henry Percy at the Battle of Shrewsbury, 1403, showing *pavises*, longbows, brigandines, and other weapons.

Fig. 2.12: Gothic plate and horse armor—German, late fifteenth century.

ARMS AND ARMOR

single piece of iron shaped to fit the horse's head, but later it was usually made from several pieces that were hinged and carefully formed to fit the horse's head, with holes for the eyes, ears, and nose. All the pieces of the bard were separate and held together by leather straps and buckles. There were attempts at various times during the fifteenth and sixteenth centuries to increase the length of the bard, almost down to the hooves, but as this made the horse slower and less maneuverable, it was never put into general use.[122]

There is also a curious late medieval reference to dog armor. On 18 October 1371, the duchess of Burgundy ordered armor made for six of her dogs. However, what this armor might have been, if it was ever made, or whether it was to be used in a military enterprise or only for parade, cannot be determined by this single reference.[124]

Plate armor continued to be made in the sixteenth and, to a limited extent, in the seventeenth centuries.[125] However, its "heyday" clearly was the late Middle Ages, when chivalry reigned, tournaments were fought, knights in shining armor were revered (and feared), and gunpowder weapons had not yet effected a change in military attitudes.

Notes

1. Ferrill (1985): 22.
2. P. Hunt (2007): 113–15.
3. Hanson (1990): 55–88 and P. Hunt (2007): 113.
4. Homer (1950): 197–98.
5. Bishop and Coulston (1989): 19–20 and Robinson (1975): 11–25, 147–52.
6. Bishop and Coulston (1989): 55; Robinson (1975): 174–86; and Webster (1985): 122–25.
7. Bishop and Coulston (1989): 55–57; Robinson (1975): 125–26; and Robinson (1975): 26–107.
8. Bishop and Coulston (1989): 57–61, 67–68; and Webster (1985): 126–27.
9. Bishop and Coulston (1989): 66–67.
10. Bishop and Coulston (1989): 65 and Robinson (1975): 153–73.
11. Intriguingly, the same happened in Europe in the late sixteenth and seventeenth centuries when soldiers began to discard plate armor, especially that for the arms and legs.
12. Coulston (1988): 1–15.
13. Ferrill (1986): 128–29.
14. E. Thompson (1958): 3–4.
15. E. Thompson (1958): 4–8; Bruhn de Hoffmeyer (1972): 89–90; Ferrill (1986): 144–45; and B. Bachrach (1970): 436–37.
16. E. Thompson (1958): 8.

17. E. Thompson (1958): 11–12. There are several good books that have been published recently on the fall of Rome. While they may differ on some interpretations of what happened to Rome during this period, they all contain good histories of the barbarian invasions. See, for example, Heather (2005), Halsall (2007), and Goldsworthy (2009).

18. Contamine (1984): 178; Bruhn de Hoffmeyer (1972): 93; and Enlart (1916): 447.

19. Contamine (1984): 178; Bruhn de Hoffmeyer (1972): 90–93; and Burns (1984): 185.

20. Stork (1990): #87; Crossly-Holland (1979): #5; and Hamer (1970): 48–69. See also N. Brooks (1978): 82–92. The best overall study of Anglo-Saxon shields is Dickinson, Härke, and Härke (1992).

21. Bruce-Mitford (1974a: 198–209; 1974b: 223–52); Addyman, Pearson, and Tweddle (1982): 189–94; Tweddle (1984, 1992); N. Brooks (1978): 93–94; and Crossley-Holland (1979): #61. The Pioneer helm was relatively recently excavated and has yet to receive much analysis.

22. N. Brooks (1978): 94–96; Mann (1958): 316; Stork (1990): #32; and Crossley-Holland (1979): #35.

23. Pedersen (2002): 32–33.

24. Brønsted (1960): 123–25; DeVries (1999b): 205–6.

25. Contamine (1984): 19–20.

26. Contamine (1984): 19.

27. Coupland (1990): 30.

28. Coupland (1990): 38–39.

29. Ganshof (1968): 66 and B. Bachrach (1974): 29.

30. Coupland (1990): 30.

31. Coupland (1990): 35–38 and Enlart (1916): 450–51.

32. Coupland (1990): 31–34.

33. Coupland (1990): 39 and Ganshof (1968): 66.

34. Coupland (1990): 38–41. See also Ganshof (1968): 52 and Enlart (1916): 448–49.

35. Coupland (1990): 41–42 and Enlart (1916): 450.

36. Mann (1933): 286.

37. Other possible explanations include the possibility that iron was now cheaper or that construction techniques had developed sufficiently for the armorer to make the helmet from one piece of iron—a technically quite complex procedure.

38. Nicolle (1988): #722 and 742 for helmets, and #618, 687, 715, 726, 727, 729, 737, 743, 1120, 1393, 1417, 1418 for shields.

39. Mann (1957): 56–58.

40. Mann (1957): 60–63; Peirce (1986): 155–59; Blair (1958): 23–24; Enlart (1912): 451–53; and Nicolle (1988): I: 344–45.

41. Nicolle (1988): #742.

42. Mann (1957): 58–60; Peirce (1986): 159–60; Blair (1958): 25–27; and Nicolle (1988): I: 344.

43. Mann (1957): 63–65; Peirce (1986): 160; and Nicolle (1988): I: 344.

44. Contamine (1984): 67, 73, 88, 188–89.

45. As quoted in Crouch (2005): 141.

46. See the large number of illustrations of kite shields in Nicolle (1988). For Spain, see also Bruhn de Hoffmeyer (1972): 138–40, 179–85.

47. Nicolle (1988): #618, 687, 715, 726, 729, 743, 1387, 1393, 1396, 1397, 1399, 1417. 1418; and Bruhn de Hoffmeyer (1972): 138–39.

48. See the large number of helmets illustrated in Nicolle (1988). See also Bruhn de Hoffmeyer (1972): 170–72 and Enlart (1912): 457–60.

49. Peirce (1986): 159–60.

50. Nicolle (1988): #1094, 1095, 1107, 1108, 1109, 1144; and Peirce (1986): 159. Another helmet, now in the collection of the Metropolitan Museum of Art, was also made in a similar manner to these helmets and may also date from this period. However, its date and provenance have yet to be determined. See Peirce (1986): 159.

51. Nicolle (1988): 715, 752, 887, 888, 1149, 1280, 1299, 1300, 1301, 1304, 1309.

52. Nicolle (1988): #905. See also Blair (1958): 29.

53. Enlart (1912): 453–57; Mann (1933): 286–87; and Bruhn de Hoffmeyer (1972): 172–79. See also the numerous examples of the mail hauberk from this period in Nicolle (1988).

54. See, for example, Nicolle (1988): #747. See also Blair (1958): 28–29.

55. Nicolle (1988): #747, 906, 1161, 1163, 1165.

56. See illustrations in Nicolle (1988). See also Blair (1958): 32–36; Bruhn de Hoffmeyer (1972): 172–79; Enlart (1912): 453–57; and Mann (1933): 286–87.

57. Nicolle (1988): #715, 716, 758, 1154, 1404, 1409, 1412, 1417. See also Contamine (1984): 187.

58. Contamine (1984): 67, 89.

59. See Mann (1957): 65 and the numerous heater shields depicted in Nicolle (1988).

60. Blair (1958): 30 and Enlart (1912): 472. A large number of illustrations in Nicolle (1988) depict the helm. There are a number of extant helms, from both the thirteenth and the fourteenth centuries. See Nicolle (1988): #761, 1179, 1219, 1220, 1222, 1223, 1225, 1318. For illustrations of the arming cap, see Nicolle (1988): #926, 933, 934, 1187, 1321.

61. Juliet Barker (1986): 164.

62. Blair (1958): 29–30 and Enlart (1912): 471–73. See also the illustrations in Nicolle (1988): #759, 827, 829, 901, 1166, 1203, which all show evolutionary steps in the creation of the great helm.

63. Blair (1958): 31–32 and Enlart (1912): 474–75. For the artistic sources of the kettle-hat see Nicolle (1988): #772, 833, 834, 835, 837, 840, 955, 956, 1193, 1213, 1214, 1313, 1325.

64. Blair (1958): 33–35.

65. Blair (1958): 184; Bruhn de Hoffmeyer (1972): 187; and Nicolle (1988): #1197, 1198, 1335.

66. Contamine (1984): 190.

67. Crouch (2005): 29–35.

68. Keen (1984): 125–31.

69. A translation of the document instituting the College of Heralds is in Myers (1996): 1135.

70. Blair (1958): 30–31; Enlart (1912): 473–75; Juliet Barker (1986): 164–65, 180–86; and Nicolle (1988): #831, 1196, 1197, 1198, 1200, 1201, 1202, 1208, 1322, 1323, 1335.

71. See, for example, Mann (1933): 288–90 and Nicolle (1988): #613, 664, 697, 700, 703, 1217.

72. Richardson (1997) and Vale (1981): 104–5.

73. Blair (1958): 37.

74. Blair (1958): 37.

75. Blair (1958): 37–38.

76. Blair (1958): 41 and Nicolle (1988): #1352, 1430, 1431. A recent PhD dissertation by Eddie Cheshire at the University of Reading has established medieval *cuir boilli* as rawhide and not leather.

77. Thordeman (1939): I: 289–92. See also Blair (1958): 38–39.

78. Blair (1958): 42–43, 62–63; Mann (1933): 288–89; and Nicolle (1988): #958, 962, 964, 968, 980, 982, 983, 1238, 1240, 1241, 1242, 1352, 1357, 1376.

79. Blair (1958): 39–41; Ashdown (1925): 81–82; and Nicolle (1988): #1244, 1373, 1626.

80. Thordeman (1939); Blair (1958): 55–56; and Nicolle (1988): #1063–1066. The best study of the battle is Thordeman (1944).

81. Thordeman (1939): 245–84.

82. Thordeman (1939): 93–117.

83. Blair (1958): 56–58, 61; Juliet Barker (1986): 169–70; Brun (1951): 219–20; and Nicolle (1988): #1372. Nicolle (2002) provides an intriguing, but rather complicated, "line of development" for medieval cloth-covered armors.

84. Blair (1958): 58–61.

85. Blair (1958): 43–44, 62; and Nicolle (1988): #979, 980, 981, 1242, 1244, 1576, 1590.

86. Blair (1958): 43, 64–65; Juliet Barker (1986): 171; Brun (1951): 221–22; and Nicolle (1988): #979, 980, 981, 982, 1241, 1242, 1244, 1346, 1431, 1576, 1590.

87. Blair (1958): 41–42, 66–67; Enlart (1912): 484–87; Thordeman (1939): 230–44; Brun (1951): 222–23; and Nicolle (1988): #799, 962, 1243, 1576.

88. Blair (1958): 44–45. 64–66; Mann (1933): 288–91; Juliet Barker (1986): 170–71; Brun (1951): 221–22; and Nicolle (1988): #962, 1238, 1576.

89. Blair (1958): 45–46; Enlart (1912): 476–79; Juliet Barker (1986): 181–82; and Nicolle (1988): #978, 1237, 1615.

90. Blair (1958): 42 and Brun (1951): 221.

91. Blair (1958): 53–112.

92. Blair (1958): 53 and Enlart (1912): 479–83.

93. Blair (1958): 53–54; Vale (1981): 120–21; Nicholas (1987): 268–70. For specialized studies on the armor industry and trade see ffoulkes (1912); Gaier (1973); Larsen (1940); and Brun (1951).

94. For the cost of this armor see Contamine (1984): 95, 116–17; Vale (1981): 125–26; and Gaier (1973): 67–69, 73, 89, 343–52.

95. Blair (1958): 77–107.

96. Williams (2003); Blair (1958): 77–78; and Enlart (1912): 503. For a discussion of the technological processes of making plate see Williams (2003); Williams (1980); Vale (1981): 105–7; and Gaier (1973): 189–98, 254–79. And for tables listing the metallurgical analysis and strength of plate armor see the appendices in Williams (2003).

97. Blair (1958): 80–82, 92–96 (illustrated pp. 218–21); Oakeshott (1980): 85, 88–96; Enlart (1912): 503–8; Vale (1981): 109–12, 119–20; and Mann (1933): 293–305.

98. Blair (1958): 80–83 (illustrated pp. 210–11); Ashdown (1925): 146–51; Oakeshott (1980): 87; and Vale (1981): 110.

99. Blair (1958): 83–84, 98–99 (illustrated pp. 210–13).

100. Blair (1958): 96–99 (illustrated pp. 210–11) and Oakeshott (1980): 86.

101. Blair (1958): 84, 99–100 (illustrated pp. 206–9); Oakeshott (1980): 87; and Enlart (1912): 509.

102. Blair (1958): 83–85, 92, 99–102 (illustrated pp. 202–6, 216, 218–23).

103. Blair (1958): 81, 84–85, 100–102 (illustrated pp. 214–17); Oakeshott (1980): 87; and Enlart (1912): 508–9.

104. Blair (1958): 96 and Oakeshott (1980): 87.

105. Vale (1981): 76.

106. Blair (1958): 74–79; Juliet Barker (1986): 166–68; and Herben (1937): 479–81.

107. See the charts of armor weights in Vale (1981): 184–85; Blair (1958): 191–92; and ffoulkes (1912): 119.

108. Chaucer (1951): 199. See also Herben (1937): 479.

109. Vale (1981): 76.

110. See Contamine (1984): 132.

111. Eaves (1989). Despite the title of this article, it is the best study of both jacks and brigandines.

112. Blair (1958): 47–48, 73; Enlart (1912): 489–91; and Nicolle (1988): #611, 970, 1222, 1223, 1225, 1276.

113. Blair (1958): 48, 74 (illustrated pp. 196–97); Enlart (1912): 493–98; Juliet Barker (1986): 164–66; Herben (1937): 478; and Nicolle (1988): #847, 976, 1251, 1257, 1272, 1273, 1353, 1358, 1359, 1362, 1371, 1615.

114. Blair (1958): 48 and Nicolle (1988): #1359.

115. Blair (1958): 52, 70, 91, 105, 110–11 (illustrated pp. 198–99); Mann (1933): 296; and Nicolle (1988): #661, 976, 1074, 1075, 1245, 1274, 1276.

116. Blair (1958): 51–52, 67–70, 102–5, 109 (illustrated pp. 194–95); Oakeshott (1980): 117; Enlart (1912): 491–93; and Mann (1933): 291–92. See also the numerous archaeological and artistic sources illustrated in Nicolle (1988).

117. Blair (1958): 73–74, 85; Oakeshott (1980): 109–11; Enlart (1912): 513; and Mann (1933): 296–97.

118. Blair (1958): 85–86, 105–7, 110 (illustrated pp. 200–201); Oakeshott (1980): 111–16; Enlart (1912): 513–15.

119. Blair (1958): 86–91, 105 (illustrated pp. 202–3) and Oakeshott (1980): 118–23.

120. Blair (1958): 181–82 (illustrated pp. 224–25); Enlart (1912): 519–20; Juliet Barker (1986): 176–77; and Nicolle (1988): #979–82, 1237–44, 1274, 1371, 1372, 1590.

121. Blair (1958): 182; Enlart (1912): 499–500; Herben (1937): 484; Deuchler (1963): 332–34; and Nicolle (1988): #660, 1363. On *pavises* see DeVries (2007) and Richardson (2007).

122. Blair (1958): 184–87; Juliet Barker (1986): 175–76; Gaier (1973): 365–67; Herben (1937): 484–85; and Deuchler (1963): 338–40.

123. Gaier (1973): 87, 367. Armor was also used to protect dogs when hunting.

124. For a survey of post-medieval armor see Blair (1958): 112–55; Enlart (1912): 521–26; and Oakeshott (1980).

CHAPTER 3

THE STIRRUP, MOUNTED SHOCK COMBAT, CHIVALRY, AND FEUDALISM

PERHAPS ONE OF THE MOST IMPORTANT DEBATES OF THE LAST CENTURY among scholars of medieval history focused on the socio-economic system known as feudalism. Not only do modern historians argue about what constituted feudalism and about what its origins were, but some even question the historical validity of the system itself. These historians choose to see it as a "tyrannical construct," to use the words of Elizabeth A.R. Brown, that "must be declared once and for all deposed and its influence over students of the Middle Ages finally ended."[1]

However, for the sake of completeness, and for a review of the role of military technology in the debate, it is necessary to look at the idea of feudalism as a system defining the society, economy, and polity of the medieval world. In its basic form, feudalism, a word derived from the Latin *feodum* (meaning fief), describes the structure of medieval society in which the king was the "owner" of all the lands of his kingdom, including the peasants who lived on those lands. The peasants served the king by working his lands and gave him a portion of the produce derived from the work. The king promised to protect the peasants from invasion. Between the king and the peasants was a group of individuals who "administered" the king's lands and the peasants inhabiting them. They were the holders of fiefs, and their names varied from area to area; they were, for lack of a better general term, landlords (or lords for short).

On one level, the feudal structure was quite simple. The kings gave the fiefs to the lords, who then served as his vassals, providing an administrative organization and watching over the economic yields of the kingdom. The lords derived their own livelihood from the fiefs by taking a proportion of the yields produced by their vassals, the peasants. In return, the lords promised the king that they would deliver a certain amount of the produce of their fiefs for his maintenance, as well as to provide him with security, in the form of an army, to protect his combined landholdings. Naturally, this system did much to benefit those individuals who, for whatever reason, gained the fiefs; and it also served the king by providing a system of administration and security. The peasants, too, derived some benefits from the system, although these were far fewer than either those of the lords or the king. In return for working the lands, the peasants received a promise of peace and security from their landlords.

But the ideal was rarely reached in the Middle Ages. Invasions, for example by Vikings, Hungarians, and Muslims, as well as constant European warfare, meant that few lords were able at all times to protect their peasants. And, while strong kings had little difficulty in holding the loyalty of their lords, weak kings, who proved far more numerous, frequently faced noble insurrections or indifference. There was also a constant struggle among the lords to increase their fiefs, often at the expense of their neighbors, which increased the turmoil of feudal society.[2]

Why the lords were there, how they came to gain their status, and what their responsibilities were regarding the king and the peasants are the questions most asked in the feudalism debate. The answers vary. To Marc Bloch, they are socially determined. Feudalism was constituted by

> a subject peasantry; widespread use of the service tenement
> (i.e. the fief) instead of a salary, which was out of the ques-
> tion; the supremacy of a class of specialized warriors; ties
> of obedience and protection which bind man to man and,
> within the warrior class, assume the distinctive form called
> vassalage; fragmentation of authority—leading inevitably
> to disorder; and, in the midst of all this, the survival of other
> forms of association, family and State....[3]

To François Ganshof, the answers are political. Feudalism was

> a body of institutions creating and regulating the obliga-
> tions of obedience and service—mainly military service—

on the part of a free man (the vassal) towards another free man (the lord), and the obligations of protection and maintenance on the part of the lord with regard to his vassal. The obligation of maintenance had usually as one of its effects the grant by the lord to his vassal of a unit of real property known as a fief.[4]

To Joseph Strayer, the answers are jurisdictional. Feudalism was "a fragmentation of political authority, public power in private hands, and a military system in which an essential part of the armed forces is secured by private contracts."[5] And, finally, to Georges Duby, the answers to these questions can be reached only by considering the psychology of the Middle Ages. To him, feudalism was

> a psychological complex formed in the small world of warriors who little by little became the nobles. A consciousness of the superiority of a status characterized by military specialization, one that presupposes respect for certain moral precepts, the practice of certain virtues; the associated idea that social relations are organized as a function of companionship in combat; notions of homage, of personal dependence, now in the foreground, replacing all previous forms of political association.[6]

One of the earliest and most constant explanations for feudalism is that it was created for military purposes, and that it survived as long as the king had no other option to acquire a military force. This theory was expressed if not first, then certainly with the most impact, in 1887 by Heinrich Brunner. In an article entitled "Der Reiterdienst und die Anfänge des Lehnwesens" ("Knights' Service and the Origin of Feudalism"), Brunner claimed that feudalism began as a military organization, a socio-economic structure for producing and supporting a cavalry-based force.[7] He explained that while the barbarian tribes had had a history of fighting on horseback, by the time they invaded the Roman Empire, because their economy had shifted from a herding emphasis to an agricultural one, cavalry warfare was almost non-existent. These tribes, the Franks, who later came to dominate most of Western Europe, had little use for the horse; their chief weapon, the *francisca*, was efficient only when used by infantry.

The Franks encountered numerous enemies in the early Middle Ages, most of whom were defeated by this infantry force. Chief among these were the Muslim armies that invaded the Frankish lands until 732, when Charles Martel defeated them at the battle of Poitiers and later pushed them below the Pyrenees. The Muslims fought on horseback, and although defeated, Brunner contends, put up such a virulent opposition to the Franks that it forever changed the latter's military strategy. So quick and decisive was this change that when chroniclers describe the Frankish army at the battle of the Dyle, fought in 891, they report that "the Franks are unused to fighting on foot."

Brunner thus determined that between these two battles a shift in military tactics occurred. Working through a number of sources, he judged that the change could be dated from the mid-eighth century, principally during the reigns of Charles Martel (who ruled as Mayor of the Palace until 742) and his son, Pepin III (who ruled as King of the Franks from 751 to 768). Among other evidence, Brunner discovered that in 755, Pepin had changed the time of the Marchfield, the traditional Frankish mustering of the army, from March to May, when forage was more readily available to horses. He further found that, in 758, Pepin had replaced the Saxon tribute of payment in cattle to payment in horses. Most important, he showed that Charles Martel seized a large number of church lands after the battle of Poitiers and distributed them to retainers in exchange for military service.

Why would Charles have done this unless it was to provide his retainers with the ability to gain extra income? And why would they need this extra income if it was not to supplement their military might by adding expensive warhorses to their military equipment? Evidently, Charles gave fiefs of church lands to his retainers so that they might serve him as a force of horsed warriors. Failure to do military service meant the forfeiture of these lands and the added income they might bring. Feudalism was born.

Brunner's article was almost immediately attacked. Many military historians argued that the German scholar had no basis for his thesis because his facts were wrong. Some claimed that cavalry was known among barbarians, especially among the Visigoths, before the time of Charles Martel, and therefore that the institution of a Carolingian cavalry-based force had not created feudalism; others contended that Frankish armies, even as late as the reign of Charlemagne, were not composed of a large, nor even a primary, body of cavalry—that horsed troops were in fact far fewer in number and importance than the infantry. Therefore, if cavalry was the basis for feudalism, feudalism could not be considered a Carolingian innovation.[8]

Brunner's thesis outlived these criticisms; there was simply no reliable evidence to rebut his argument that the Frankish army during the eighth century had transformed from an infantry-based force to a cavalry-based one. Nor could it be proven that cavalry warfare had been conventional among earlier barbarian armies. Finally, while a number of scholars stated that Brunner was wrong in naming such a late date for the origin of feudalism, contending instead that the union of fief and vassal was much older than the eighth century, these scholars found it extremely difficult to counter Brunner's evidence of the seizure of church lands, the first datable grant of lands for use as benefices.[9]

WHITE'S THESIS

In 1962, in a chapter entitled "Stirrup, Mounted Shock Combat, Feudalism, and Chivalry" in his important study *Medieval Technology and Social Change*, Lynn White, Jr., challenged Brunner's thesis.[10] He did not, however, level his critical barrage on the conclusions of Brunner's argument, as other historians had done. Indeed, White agreed with the nineteenth-century German historian's view that feudalism originated out of military necessity. What White disagreed with was Brunner's contention that it was the Muslim invasion of Francia, and in particular the battle of Poitiers, that caused Charles Martel to change his military strategy by instituting a cavalry-based force and, with it, feudalism. For one thing, White found little supporting evidence for the claim that the Muslim invasion had been such a crisis for the Franks. Charles Martel "turned his attention to Islam only after he had consolidated his realm," and in fact "made little effort for several years to follow up his victory."[11] White also questioned the use by Spanish Muslims of cavalry in their attacks on the Franks, citing other studies which showed that the Muslim armies did not fight with large numbers of cavalry until the second half of the eighth century, perhaps responding to their encounters with the Frankish armies and not the other way around.[12]

Most importantly, White added, the date of the battle of Poitiers, which Brunner had placed in 732, had recently (in 1955) been discovered to have been in fact in 733. This in itself was of little consequence to the thesis, except for the fact that Brunner had placed so much emphasis on the seizure of church lands as evidence of the importance of the Poitiers battle, an action that occurred in the earlier year:

> Poitiers, therefore, cannot have inspired Charles's policy of confiscations for the improvement of his cavalry. His military reforms had begun a year earlier, although doubtless

they had not yet greatly modified the structure of the Frankish forces when he met the Muslim invaders.[13]

Still, White could not find any other reason why these lands had been confiscated except to establish a cavalry-based force, and thus he was unwilling
to completely discount Brunner's military rationale for feudalism. But if the
Muslim invasions of Charles Martel's realm had not prompted this change in
military strategy, what had? White contended that the cause was not a strategic
change, but was instead a technological one: the invention of the stirrup.

On a horse the stirrups seem small and insignificant, yet they may be the
most important invention for the military use of a horse. A cavalry soldier
might be uncomfortable without a saddle, but he could still ride; and he might
find guiding the horse difficult without reins, but by grasping the horse's mane
he could still maneuver it. However, without stirrups, the rider could only use
his mount as little more than a mode of transportation or a mobile missile-
launching platform. If he tried to mount a charge against an enemy without
them, the force of his blow would just as likely unseat him from his steed as
deliver the desired impact to his opponent.

Yet, despite their importance, stirrups were a relatively late invention. With
the exception of an isolated illustration of stirrups from the ninth-century BCE
Assyrian Empire, there is no ancient tradition of stirrups. And even though
they were well known in China, India, Korea, and Japan during the early
Middle Ages,[14] they seem not to have diffused to Europe or the Middle East
until at least the seventh or even the early eighth century. It was at that time that
the stirrup first appeared in Persia and from there was carried to other Muslim
lands.[15] From there the stirrup spread almost immediately to Byzantium and
then, either from the Byzantines or by direct diffusion, to the Franks. Using
this thesis, together with archaeological, linguistic, and, to a lesser extent,
artistic evidence, enabled White to place the use of the stirrup among the
Franks in the early eighth century.

He also found that, at the same time, there was a change in weapons policy among the Franks that led them to discard their battle axes (*francisca*) and
barbed spears (*angon*), both of which were only infantry weapons, and adopt
longswords (*spatha*) and heavier, longer wing-spears or lances, the most distinct
feature of which was their prominent cross-piece that prevented impaling an
enemy so deeply that the weapon would get stuck. The purpose of this could
only have been to allow the horsed warrior the ability to couch his lance under

his arm during the charge, adding the momentum of the horse's movement to the lance's thrust, a tactic that White called "mounted shock combat."

These changes in military tactics could have been due only to the use of the stirrup by the Franks. When Charles Martel realized the true military worth of the stirrup, and he alone did so, he began to insist on its use by his soldiers. The effect was quickly seen and Charles's conclusions verified; a cavalry force was demanded, one that was expensive to initiate and maintain. Therefore, changes in the structure of society were needed and put into effect: the result was feudalism.[16]

Cavalry-based forces are much more costly than an infantry army. Warhorses were extremely expensive to buy, more than one horse was usually needed by each soldier, and their maintenance was costly. Expensive, too, were the new arms and armor needed to fight upon that horse. A great deal of training and expertise was also required both to control the horse and to effectively use the lance from horseback, training that usually began at puberty. This meant that the soldier was unable to work in the fields or elsewhere. Thus, while the soldiers initially chosen to form this new cavalry core of the Frankish army may have been so selected because of their inherent wealth or bravery in battle, their continued presence necessitated some endowment which would extend their ability to afford the weapons and training time needed to be an effective cavalry soldier. They became the owners of fiefs: the feudal elite, nobles, knights, and the chivalric class (which, after all, derives its name from being wealthy enough to fight on horseback).[17]

If Charles Martel began feudalism, his son, Pepin III, and grandson, Charlemagne, spread it across Europe. Italy accepted the new military and socio-economic reforms with the defeat of the Lombards, as did Eastern Europe with the conquest and defeat of the Saxons and Avars. A century later, the Byzantines, in constant contact with the Carolingians, adopted feudalism, and two centuries later it was taken by the Normans to England and Sicily and by the Crusaders to the Holy Land and Spain.[18] Lynn White concludes his article thus:

> Few inventions have been so simple as the stirrup, but few
> have had so catalytic an influence on history. The require-
> ments of the new mode of warfare which it made possible
> found expression in a new form of western European
> society dominated by an aristocracy of warriors endowed

with land so that they might fight in a new and highly specialized way. Inevitably this nobility developed cultural
forms and patterns of thought and emotion in harmony
with its style of mounted shock combat and its social pos-
ture; as [N.] Denholm-Young has said: "it is impossible to
be chivalrous without a horse." The Man on Horseback, as
we have known him during the past millennium, was made
possible by the stirrup, which joined man and steed into
fighting organism. Antiquity imagined the Centaur; the
early Middle Ages made him the master of Europe.[19]

CRITICISM OF WHITE'S THESIS

Although initially praised by reviewers for its insight and novelty, Lynn White's
thesis was not allowed to stand without criticism for long. His use of military
technology as the determining factor in the origin and rise of feudalism almost
immediately produced a stir among those historians who believed in an economic, social, political or psychological cause. Several criticisms were quickly
written. The first was published in 1963 in the prestigious journal *Past and
Present*. Written by P.H. Sawyer (and combined in a "review article" with criticism of another of White's chapters in *Medieval Technology and Social Change*, on
the invention of the plough, by R.H. Hilton), the article, entitled "Technical
Determinism: The Stirrup and the Plough," condemned White's use of technology to determine anything in social history, especially feudalism.[20] The
criticism was harsh:

> The technical determinism of Professor Lynn White, Jr.,
> however, is peculiar in that, instead of building new and
> provocative theories about general historical development
> on the basis of technical studies, he gives a misleadingly
> adventurist cast to old-fashioned platitudes by supporting
> them with a chain of obscure and dubious deductions from
> scanty evidence about the progress of technology.[21]

In particular, Sawyer argued that White had not produced enough evidence to
prove that the introduction of the stirrup could have made such radical social
changes as those of feudalism. He also attacked White's conclusion that it was

Charles Martel's genius that allowed the stirrup to be exploited by the Frankish army, while being ignored elsewhere, namely in Anglo-Saxon England. And he argued that White had not sufficiently traced the diffusion of the stirrup from China, something that was needed before going further in his hypothesis.[22]

But it was at White's sources that Sawyer leveled his severest criticism. He contended that archaeological remains, because of the meagerness of finds, the problems in dating, and the fact that it was impossible to use evidence from graves farther to the east as evidence for Frankish customs, could not be used as conclusive evidence for either the dating or the significance of stirrups in early Carolingian military strategy. The artistic and linguistic sources were also suspect. Most of the artistic sources cited by White, Sawyer claimed, were made at least a century later, and the written work also dated from a later period. Finally, Sawyer criticized White's discussion of the Frankish movement from infantry to cavalry arms and armor, arguing that, again, the dating was imprecise and there was a lack of significant change as seen in later sources (in particular the Bayeux Tapestry, which shows a number of horsed soldiers using non-wing-spears as cavalry lances).[23] Sawyer went on to criticize White's contention that mounted shock combat tactics were adopted by the Franks in the eighth century and by others within a century or two: "There is no evidence to support this claim and there is much against it." And he criticized White's understanding of the expense of mounted warfare.[24]

Sawyer's article was written quickly and with much, sometimes undue, emotion, and while it asked some very important questions of White's thesis, it did not offer sufficient evidence to show that White was wrong in his conjectures. Indeed, Sawyer, too, often answered White's generalizations with equally sparse arguments. Furthermore, despite not saying so directly, it was impossible not to read in the harsh tone taken by the author his obvious dislike of the military explanation of the origin of feudalism defended by White, a point that tended to decrease his objectivity.

Yet another criticism of White's thesis appeared three years later in a relatively obscure publication, *The University of Colorado Studies: Series in Language and Literature*. Written by literary historian J.D.A. Ogilvy, the article "The Stirrup and Feudalism" was, in many regards, an embarrassment of historical criticism that probably should not have been published.[25] Ogilvy approached White's thesis on two levels: criticism of White's understanding of military matters and criticism of his linguistic evidence. In the latter, Ogilvy was competent, showing where White made mistakes in his discussion of the linguistic changes in describing the mounting of horses. But none of these linguistic criticisms was new, and, in fact, all Ogilvy's examples had been pointed out by Sawyer. Of his criticisms of White's understanding of military history, however, Ogilvy fell into the trap of having perhaps too much zeal with too little knowledge. Deriving most of his material from Sir Charles Oman's *A History of the Art of War in the Middle Ages*, written in the early twentieth century, Ogilvy began by stating, without any corroboration, his belief that stirrups did nothing more for a horseman than allow him a more convenient means of mounting his steed and of remaining in the saddle; certainly, he claimed, they were not necessary for effective couched lance warfare. In this he followed Oman's statement that the Byzantine *cataphract* and the Tamberlaine horse-archer were far more formidable than the lancer and that the Frankish lancer gained his reputation only because of the lack of first-class infantry to oppose him. Then, again largely following Oman, Ogilvy tried to show that victory in medieval warfare was not won by the adept use of mounted shock troops, but rather by the leaders of these victorious armies or the ineptitude of the opposing force. However, almost all of the battles he chose as examples—Hastings, Falkirk, Louden Hill, Bannockburn, Crécy, Poitiers, Rosebeek, Agincourt, Joan of Arc's battles, and the fifteenth-century Swiss battles—took place in the fourteenth and fifteenth centuries, some 600 years after White's date for the rise of mounted shock combat.

Finally, Ogilvy questioned the date of the invention of the winged spear (an illustration in the *Utrecht Psalter* shows a winged spear being used by an infantry soldier); the date of the appearance of mounted shock combat troops (they had occurred earlier, used by Alexander the Great, Hannibal, Caesar, and the Visigoths at Adrianople); and the belief that the stirrup was somehow more important in the formation of heavy cavalry than heavy armor. In the last criticism, Ogilvy held that it was the necessity for heavy, expensive armor that brought about the land endowments given by Charles Martel to his military elite. Whereas cavalry had no advantages in sieges, armor did, and armor also defended a knight from horse archers when a horse was of little help. Since these were the manner of the battles and the opponents facing Charles Martel, Ogilvy could only conclude that cavalry at the time was merely an adjunct to infantry, that mounted shock combat occurred before the eighth century, and that the stirrup played only a minor role in warfare and none at all in the origins of feudalism. Ogilvy's use of Oman, whose classical work on medieval military history is constantly being reworked by military historians, showed his inherent lack of understanding of the field, a criticism that he hypocritically directed at White. Had he done any research, he would have recognized his flaws and rewritten (or perhaps withdrawn) his article. Even if his linguistic criticisms were valid, placed as they were next to his many military historical errors, they too looked suspect.

Thus it seemed that White's article met, at least, the initial onslaught of criticism and passed these tests, suffering only a modicum of historical bruises. Then came the publication of two articles in 1970, both of which seriously criticized and weakened White's thesis. The first was only a small part of a larger article written by D.A. Bullough and published in the *English Historical Review*. Entitled "*Europae Pater*: Charlemagne and His Achievement in the Light of Recent Scholarship," it reviewed current studies on Charlemagne and the Carolingians.[26] Although the article was relatively short, Bullough's criticisms cast significant doubt on three of White's primary arguments: the change of the army muster from March to May in 755 (or 756 as Bullough contended the date should have been); the evidence for Carolingian cavalry successes in narrative sources; and the absence of stirrups from pre-eighth-century Frankish graves and their presence in later graves.

Bullough dismissed moving the month of Marchfield as unimportant, both because there was little evidence to support the idea that armies in the Frankish world had always been mustered in March—*Campus martius* means "field of war" not "field of March"—and because in 755 (or 756) the explanation for a late muster was that the snows blocking the Alpine passes had not yet melted.[27] He dismissed Carolingian cavalry successes because he found no evidence in the narrative sources that the armies of Charles Martel, Pepin, Carloman, or even Charlemagne succeeded against their enemies because of their mounted shock combat tactics. Bullough contended that they succeeded because they were able to fight in a number of different ways, adapting their strategy and tactics to whatever military need presented itself.[28] Finally, on the presence or absence of stirrups in Frankish grave-finds, Bullough first agreed with White that there had been no stirrups found in pre-eighth-century warriors' graves, but at the same time he demonstrated that there had also been no stirrup finds in any eighth-century grave. Furthermore, Bullough showed that the only artistic source used by White to support his claim of eighth-century stirrups, the illuminations found in the *Valenciennes Apocalypse*, was actually misdated, the correct date being post-800.[29]

Bernard S. Bachrach's lengthy article "Charles Martel, Mounted Shock Combat, The Stirrup, and Feudalism" was also published in 1970 in *Studies in Medieval and Renaissance History*.[30] Bachrach, a military historian, approached his criticism of White's argument in a manner similar to Bullough, although in much greater depth. He preferred to criticize point by point the evidence on which White built his thesis, thereby destroying its foundations. He also preferred to attack these points not by using generalizations or secondary sources, but by using what he believed was superior, or at least contradictory, primary evidence. At the same time, he also sought to refute Brunner's theory, which he saw as irrevocably intertwined with White's, in both their basic arguments and their flaws.

After almost cavalier mention, in a footnote, of new evidence from Arabic sources confirming the date of the battle of Poitiers as 732, destroying perhaps the most central attack of White on Brunner,[31] Bachrach began by criticizing three pieces of literary evidence that both authors used to date their theses to the mid-eighth century: Pepin's changing of the Saxon tribute from cattle to horses in 758; the shifting of the Marchfield to May in 755 (also criticized by Bullough); and the fact that, at the battle of the Dyle in 891, the Franks fought on horseback.

With each of these issues Bachrach questioned the evidence used by the authors as well as the logic that led them to their conclusions. In all three cases he showed that other conclusions were equally possible, if not preferable. The Saxon tribute of 758, which had been in cattle in 748, nearly a decade and a half after the purported switch was made to cavalry, was so low that it may in fact have been merely "a mayor or king who needed horses only for his household." The Marchfield, which several scholars and one contemporary writer, Hincmar of Reims, claimed meant simply the "field of Mars," might have been a "general muster for war which might be held at any time of the year." And the Latin linguistic evidence used by Brunner and White to show that at the Dyle the Franks were "unused to fighting *on foot*," might just as easily have meant that the Franks were "unused to fighting *step by step*," indicating that they were not used to advancing on an enemy as slowly as they had to on the swampy terrain of the Dyle battlefield.[32] Taken alone, the problems that Bachrach pointed to in these pieces of evidence might not detract from the earlier theses, but they did show that these authors' conclusions were built on rather weak foundations.

From these smaller issues, Bachrach next moved to a more significant question (and one also raised by Bullough): Were there horsemen in Charles Martel's armies? This he answered as follows: "A detailed review of Charles Martel's post-733 military campaigns suggests serious reservations as to whether heavily armed horsemen engaging in mounted shock combat were in fact the decisive element of his armies." Most of the military engagements were sieges, naval expeditions, or campaigns with too little tactical information to substantiate the claim that cavalry was a main factor in their outcome.[33] If Charles Martel's armies were not cavalry-based, what then about those of his sons, Pepin and Carloman? Again Bachrach answered: "A detailed review of the campaigns of Pepin and Carloman show them to have been very like those of their father, Charles." Most were either sieges or expeditions for which too little tactical information was known to substantiate Brunner's and White's theses.[34] Bachrach concluded:

> From the many campaigns of Charles, Pepin, and Carlo-
> man described by contemporaries and near contemporaries
> there is not a shred of evidence to suggest that heavily
> armed horsemen engaging in mounted shock combat were
> the decisive element of their armies.[35]

In addition, Bachrach looked at White's contention that changes in weapons by the Franks, with the adoption of the longsword and the winged spear, signified a move away from an infantry-based army to a cavalry-based one. In both cases Bachrach could not find archaeological evidence to substantiate White's dating of these changes to the eighth century; both, he concluded, date from much earlier.[36]

Having shown that the eighth-century Carolingian armies were not cavalry-based, Bachrach next shifted his focus to the existence of stirrups among the few horsed warriors who did fight with these armies. First, he established that the linguistic arguments for a mid-eighth-century date for stirrups were inaccurate, for the same philological evidence used to prove White's date also appeared in the sixth century. Second, the earliest artistic depiction of stirrups could not be dated until sometime between 863 and 883, and even after this time there was an inconsistency in the artistic sources, some showing stirrups, others not. Third, stirrups were also absent from inventories of military equipment found in historical documents, literary sources, military manuals, and descriptions of Charlemagne's military regalia.[37] If nothing else, stirrups failed to impress Carolingian artists and authors.

Finally, Bachrach questioned White's archaeological evidence for the prominence of stirrups in the Carolingian world. Archaeological evidence did substantiate the existence of stirrups in the late seventh or early eighth centuries, but, Bachrach contended, at the same time it did not show "that the use of the stirrup was common among horsemen or that it helped bring about the development of mounted shock combat." This could be proven by citing the archaeological excavations of 704 Frankish warriors dating from the seventh to the ninth centuries. Of these 704, 135 can be identified as possible cavalry soldiers (85 sure identifications and 50 likely identifications), and of these 135 only 13 had stirrups buried with them. Not only did this show that stirrups were not common among Frankish horsemen, but it also established the fact that horsemen did not make up a significant proportion of the fighting troops of the Frankish armies.[38]

With White's and Brunner's theses effectively denounced, Bachrach attempted to provide his own theory about the reasons for Charles Martel's seizures of church lands. To Bachrach, the occurrence of these seizures was undeniable, although it was not solely church lands that were confiscated, but also the lands and moveable wealth of laymen. All were then given away in return for the service and support of military retainers. However, Bachrach explained this, not as the origin of feudalism, but simply as the existence of military *honores*, nothing more than gifts given to armed retainers to reward their service. They did not originate with Charles Martel—in fact they had been a tradition among Frankish leaders at least since the time of Clovis (481–511) and probably before—nor did they represent the purchase of "mercenaries" or feudal warriors.[39] With all of this evidence, Bachrach concluded:

> ... some doubt has been cast upon the allegedly creative or innovative genius of Charles Martel. He did not grasp the importance of the stirrup, he did not make heavily armed horsemen using mounted shock combat the decisive arm of his military forces, nor did he even make cavalry the decisive arm of his military forces, and he did not provide for the explosive development of a new or little used technique for the securing of armed support called feudalism by some. In both military tactics and military organization Charles essentially continued to use techniques which were prevalent under his predecessors.[40]

Bullough's and Bachrach's criticisms were not answered by Lynn White, nor has any other historian risen to White's defense. Evidence of this can be seen by the fact that in a 1985 article entitled "Animals and Warfare in Early Medieval Europe," Bachrach repeated most of his criticisms against White, although no one had rebutted them in the 15 years since his first attack.[41] These arguments, principally those put forward by Bachrach, cast so much doubt on the credibility of White's evidence that his thesis on the stirrup causing feudalism, at least for the moment, seems to be dead. General histories of medieval warfare or military technology written since Bachrach's critical article either have chosen to mention the invention of the stirrup without linking it to the rise of feudalism,[42] or have supplied summaries both of White's thesis and of his critics, principally the criticisms of Bachrach.[43] Most do recognize the necessity of the stirrup for mounted shock combat, although they generally refuse to give a date for this technological development.[44] More specific studies on medieval cavalry also spend little, if any, space on the question of the stirrup and feudalism. Most focus on other aspects of White's thesis: the couching of lances for mounted shock combat, the use and breeding of warhorses, and the transformation of cavalry to knighthood and chivalry.[45]

Notes

1. E. Brown (1974): 1063–88. The quotation is from page 1088.

2. An adequate, although far from comprehensive, survey of feudalism is found in Strayer (1985). More extensive studies of the subject are Stephenson (1942), Bloch (1961), and Ganshof (1964).

3. Bloch (1961): II: 446. See also E. Brown (1974): 1071.

4. Ganshof (1964): xvi. See also E. Brown (1974): 1071.

5. Strayer (1965): 13. See also E. Brown (1974): 1073.

6. Duby (1958): 766, as quoted in and translated by E. Brown (1974): 1074.

7. Brunner (1887).

8. See L. White (1962): 5.

9. See L. White (1962): 6–11.

10. L. White (1962): 1–38.

11. L. White (1962): 11.

12. L. White (1962): 12–13.

13. L. White (1962): 12.

14. See Littauer (1981): 99–105.

15. L. White (1962): 14–20. On the impact of stirrups on the Middle East see Kennedy (2006).

16. L. White (1962): 25–28.

17. L. White (1962): 28–33.

18. L. White (1962): 33–38.

19. L. White (1962): 38.

20. Hilton and Sawyer (1963): 90–100.

21. Hilton and Sawyer (1963): 90.

22. Hilton and Sawyer (1963): 90–92.

23. Hilton and Sawyer (1963): 92–94.

24. Hilton and Sawyer (1963): 94–95.

25. Ogilvy (1966): 1–13.

26. Bullough (1970): 84–90.

27. Bullough (1970): 85–86.

28. Bullough (1970): 88–90.

29. Bullough (1970): 86–87.

30. B. Bachrach (1970a): 47–75.

31. B. Bachrach (1970a): 50n2.

32. B. Bachrach (1970a): 50–53; italics in the original.

33. B. Bachrach (1970a): 53–54.

34. B. Bachrach (1970a): 54–57.

35. B. Bachrach (1970a): 57.

36. B. Bachrach (1970a): 57–58.

37. B. Bachrach (1970a): 58–62.

38. B. Bachrach (1970a): 62–66.

39. B. Bachrach (1970a): 66–72.

40. B. Bachrach (1970a): 72.

41. B. Bachrach (1985): 737–42.

42. See, for example, McNeill (1982): 20; van Creveld (1989): 18; Beeler (1971): 9–10; and Keen (1984): 23.

43. See Contamine (1984): 179–84; O'Connell (1989): 86–87; and Gillmor (1982): 201–2.

44. See Davis (1989): 51.

45. For works discussing the couching of the lance see Ross (1963); Buttin (1965); V. Cirlot (1985); and Flori (1988). For works on the medieval warhorse see B. Bachrach (1969, 1985); Bautier (1976); and Davis (1983, 1989). And, for works on the rise of chivalry from cavalry see Verbruggen (1947); Duby (1980); T. Hunt (1981); Barber (1982); Keen (1984); Mortimer (1986); Lyon (1987); and Nelson (1989).

PART II

Artillery

PERSONAL ARMS AND ARMOR WERE IMPORTANT IN BATTLEFIELD WARFARE, but most military engagements were not fought on the battlefield, but instead were intended to attack and take castles or fortified towns. Without the means to capture these fortifications, the conquest of foreign lands was impossible. There was, therefore, a need for weapons that could breach fortifications. Swords, spears and other hand weapons could do no damage against them; nor could the most powerful bowman firing the heaviest bow destroy even the most basic fortification. Starvation could be and was used frequently, often with success, depending on the abundance of food supplies in the besieged fortress and on the availability of relief troops. But the procedure of driving a town or castle into starvation—known customarily as a "siege"—was protracted, often requiring as much as a year, or even longer, to gain victory. The ten-year siege of Troy was not created by Homer simply as a literary metaphor; it reflected ancient reality. Even after ten years it required a ruse, the Trojan Horse, to take the heavily fortified city and end the siege.[1]

Other ancient methods of conquering fortifications were also, often, inadequate. Chief among these was mining. An attacking force would tunnel under the fortification's walls and then collapse the tunnels in order to bring down a section of the walls above. In some instances mining was successful, but the defenders could often countermine the attackers' mines, and it was not always possible to dig mines—especially in rock.

The tactic of direct assault, using scaling ladders and battering rams, was also nearly always ineffective—the attack could be relatively easily countered by the defenders inside the fortress. Sometimes the terrain on which the fortification was built could not be easily surmounted, such as the Judean fortress at Masada, which, in the first century CE, held out for nearly three years before the Roman attackers constructed an earthen ramp, 114 meters high, to scale its walls.[2]

Very early, the need for heavy weapons, artillery pieces, with enough power to breach the gates and walls of fortresses was recognized. From these a missile—a stone or bolt—could be launched with enough force either to break down the wall or to weaken a part of it so that continual impact would eventually cause a collapse. In this way, the fortress would eventually yield to the attacker. Later it was found that these weapons, although their main targets were walls and fortifications, could also be used on the battlefield as long-range anti-personnel weapons.

The following three chapters will deal with the technology of medieval artillery. The first describes non-gunpowder artillery pieces: traction catapults, torsion trebuchets, counterweight trebuchets, and the incendiary compound known as Greek Fire. The second chapter discusses the invention and early use of gunpowder artillery, while the third chapter describes non-artillery siege machines, i.e., battering rams, siege towers, and so on.

Notes

1. There are many different editions and translations of Homer's *Iliad* and *Odyssey*, the earliest literary works on the Trojan War. For a modern interpretation of the war see Wood (1985) and Strauss (2006). On the fortifications see Fields (2004).

2. The account of Yigael Yadin's excavations of the site is found in a number of books, including Yadin (1969).

CHAPTER 4

NON-GUNPOWDER ARTILLERY

TORSION CATAPULTS

THE WORD CATAPULT IS A GENERIC TERM USED TO DESCRIBE ALL ANCIENT and medieval non-gunpowder propelled missile-throwing artillery. The first catapult may have been invented in the early fourth century BCE. In 399 in Syracuse, King Dionysius I, threatened by the Carthaginians and other enemies, assembled a large group of engineers to create an arsenal of weapons. Among these was the first non-torsion artillery piece, the *gastraphetes*. In essence the *gastraphetes* (which in Greek means "belly-bow") was little more than a large, powerful, and flexible bow. The flexibility of the weapon came from the material of the bow itself, which was a composite of wood, horn, and animal sinew: a wood core covered by a tension layer of sinew in front and a compression layer of horn in the back. This, using a sinew bowstring, supplied the propulsive force to the missile.

It was, in fact, not much different, although larger, from the handheld composite bow, which by the fourth century BCE had been known for several centuries. However, the difference between the handheld weapon and the *gastraphetes* was its power, supplied by the latter's elaborate stock apparatus. It consisted of a heavy stock, made in two sections. The lower section, the case, was fixed solidly to the bow. The upper section (or slider), of approximately the same dimensions as the case, fitted into a dove-tailed groove in the case and was able to slide freely back and forth. On each side of the case was a straight ratchet with two curved bars, or pawls, fitted into the ratchets and attached to a claw-like trigger mechanism. At the end of the stock was a concave rest that the operator placed against his stomach and, with the front of the bow fixed on the ground, allowed him to withdraw the slider, attach the string to the trigger, load a missile, and discharge it. A man could thus draw the bowstring and discharge a missile with much greater power than was possible with the traditional hand-drawn bowstring. The *gastraphetes* had a range of between 50 and 100 meters greater than the hand-drawn composite bow, which has been estimated to have had a maximum range of 500 meters. More importantly, the missile was launched at greater velocity so that few pieces of armor could withstand it, although it was probably still too weak to breach the walls of even earth-and-wood fortifications.[1]

Non-torsion artillery technology spread quickly throughout the ancient world, and soon improvements were made to the design of the original *gastraphetes*. By about 360 BCE, winches had been added to the stock, allowing for easier and greater drawing power; this ultimately brought increased force, and therefore velocity, to the missile. A base was also added, increasing both the stability and size of the weapon.[2] Still, non-torsion artillery continued to be limited in force and power, both of which remained dependent on the strength and flexibility of the bow. If these were exceeded the bow simply broke. While some *gastraphetes* were equipped to fire stone balls, most fired only heavy, arrow-shaped bolts that also limited the force of impact.

To increase the velocity of the projectile, making the *gastraphetes* more powerful, it was necessary to change both the bow and the size and type of missile fired. Increasing the power of the bow was achieved by replacing the single, flexible bow of the earlier weapon with two non-flexible arms set in "springs" made from sinew. The users of the *gastraphetes* were probably aware that it was the sinew in the bow's composition that gave it its power, so by using the sinew to form tightly twisted "springs," the power of the artillery could be increased.[3] Apart from this development, the rest of the torsion catapult remained little altered from its non-torsion predecessor, with a heavy sinew string, slider, winch, ratchet apparatus, and trigger mechanism. The springs were the only significant change in technology, and this allowed for much more powerful devices firing missiles, now almost always stone, weighing from 13 to 26 kilograms, although stones as large as 162 kilograms are known to have been fired. When the bowstring was drawn back on a torsion catapult, the force was transferred to the sinew springs which, when the trigger was pulled, made the bow arms spring forward, discharging the missile. The short, stout arms were able to withstand a much greater force than the flexible bow of earlier devices and together with the use of stone balls as ammunition meant that this weapon was capable of breaching the walls of fortifications and towns.[4]

It is believed that the first torsion-spring catapults were made by Macedonian engineers between 353 and 341 BCE and used afterwards by Philip II in his conquest of Greece.[5] The technology then passed to Philip's son, Alexander the Great, who used it in his conquest of Persia, the Middle East, Egypt, and India. Alexander seemed to have been particularly impressed by his catapults' power and used them successfully to take towns, such as Tyre in 332 BCE, which would have been nearly impossible to conquer by other siege methods.

After Alexander's death, torsion artillery technology, which had by then clearly supplanted non-torsion pieces, passed to his successors and from them to Carthage, Rome, and other lands. Over time, improvements to the mechanism were made to increase its flexibility, power, and range. Most important among these was the addition of washers to the springs, which meant that the distance that the arms of the catapult could be drawn back was easily adjusted. In this way the amount of force delivered to the missile at discharge could be varied: a close target could be struck by a looser tension on the springs, while a more distant target needed a tighter tension. The springs could also be loosed when not being used in military campaign, to keep from weakening the sinew from the constant stress of being tightly wound.[6] Other important innovations were the addition of bronze coverings over the springs, which kept them dry during rain or river crossings, and tripod swivel mounts, which allowed for a rapid change of direction in discharging missiles.[7] Improvements were also made in the operation of torsion catapults. Training and thorough practice in their use developed and actively encouraged by competitions between catapult operators. Training schools, especially those at Samnos, Ceos, and Cyanae, also resulted in increased skill in their use. Rhodian operators were particularly highly prized for their proficiency in catapult firing, and they were frequently employed by both Greece and Rome as mercenary artillery operators.[8]

In the ancient world the most sophisticated artillery was made at Alexandria under the Ptolemies, and their machines were much sought after. It is highly plausible that both Carthage and Rome, during the First and Second Punic Wars, faced each other using Alexandrian catapults. This gave Alexandria the impetus to construct some highly experimental catapult models. One of the most curious examples was a chain-driven repeating catapult described by Philon in the last part of the third century BCE. In this machine, bolts were fed one at a time from a magazine into the slider trough by means of a revolving drum. The chain-link drive, operated by a winch, then fired the bolt and recocked the weapon by engaging the lugs on the chain links with a pentagonal gear. A trigger claw was locked and fired at the appropriate time by pegs mounted in the stock of the weapon, past which the slider moved. There were, however, many problems with this machine. First, because it was so elaborate, the need for it to be constantly repaired must have been great. Second, it fired only along fixed lines, and thus would have been useful only against fixed targets, like a fortification wall. There is, in fact, no indication that this weapon was ever constructed, and it may indeed have been only an engineer's dream design.[9]

The Romans made two important alterations to the traditional torsion catapult—which they called a *ballista*. First, they made it smaller and more portable. Known as the *cheiroballistra*, this variation of the older torsion model contained all of the former's parts and was probably not too much lighter. It was, however, more compact, easier to assemble, and easier to transport. In addition, the springs were set farther apart, giving a wider field of view, which made aiming easier. The bow arms seem to have been capable of greater range than larger torsion artillery. Clearly, this weapon was meant to be used on the battlefield, or at sea, rather than against fortifications.[10]

The second alteration to the traditional ancient torsion catapult was more extreme. Rather than simulating a bow using two vertical sinew springs with two arms swinging horizontally, the *onager* used only one horizontal spring and one arm swinging upwards. There was no bowstring; at the end of the single arm was a sling in which a missile, presumably a stone ball, could be placed for launching. The trigger was a piece of rope used to anchor the arm for loading. The arm was mounted on two large, heavy main horizontal beams held apart by a number of crossbeams. The *onager* was much more like our modern perception of a catapult than other ancient models. However, it should be noted that this weapon was infrequently used by the Romans, who continued to prefer traditional torsion artillery. Apparently, it appeared only at the end of the Empire and is mentioned only by one author, Ammianus Marcellinus (330–390 CE).[11]

That torsion catapults were effective in sieges and on the battlefield is without question. Although their range seems not to have differed much from non-torsion catapults or even from strong bowmen without a substantial decrease in accuracy—most stone-throwing artillery needed to be within 150 meters of a fortification to be effective[12]—the force of impact of a missile fired from one of these weapons was astonishing. At the siege of Gaza, Alexander the Great was wounded in the neck by a catapult bolt that pierced both his shield and his breastplate. A skull unearthed at Maiden Castle in Dorset was pierced by a catapult bolt moving at such a high velocity that it did not smash it; had the missile been an arrow from a handheld bow, the skull would surely have shattered.[13] Perhaps the most vivid picture of the awe-inspiring power of these weapons comes from the pen of Josephus, the Jewish historian of the first-century Roman conquest of rebellious Judea, who details their use by the Romans at the siege of Jotapata in 67 CE:

> The force with which these weapons threw stones and
> darts was such that a single projectile ran through a row
> of men, and the momentum of the stones hurled by the
> engine carried away battlements and knocked off corners
> of towers. There is in fact no body of men so strong that it
> cannot be laid low to the last rank by the impact of these
> huge stones.... Getting in the line of fire, one of the men
> standing near Josephus [the commander of Jotapata, not
> the historian] on the rampart had his head knocked off by a
> stone, his skull being flung like a pebble from a sling more
> than 600 meters; and when a pregnant woman on leaving
> her house at daybreak was struck in the belly, the unborn
> child was carried away 100 meters.[14]

When the barbarian tribes invaded the Roman Empire in the fourth and fifth centuries, they were met by an enemy using artillery—*ballistae*, *cheiroballistae*, and *onagers*. Indeed, the Romans might have had catapults to defend nearly every fortification besieged by the invaders, and it is reported that several arms factories continued to supply artillery pieces for military use during the early invasions.[15] It is similarly recorded that in some engagements these catapults were successful in thwarting barbarian attacks. For example, Ammianus Marcellinus describes how one attack by the Goths was halted when a single large stone fired from an *onager*, despite hitting no one, caused such mass confusion that the attackers were routed.[16] And Procopius, writing about the defense of Rome in 537–38, provides a colorful witness to catapult destruction:

> ... at the Salerian Gate a Goth of goodly stature and a
> capable warrior, wearing a corselet and having a helmet on

his head, a man who was of no mean station in the Gothic nation...was hit by a missile from an engine which was on a tower at his left. And passing through the corselet and the body of the man, the missile sank more than half its length into the tree, and pinning him to the spot where it entered the tree, it suspended him there a corpse.[17]

Ultimately, however, even with the use of catapults, the Roman armies could not withstand the barbarian invaders. Indeed, it seems likely that there were many problems with their technology and use. First, many towns and fortifications probably did not have a large arsenal of catapults at the beginning of the barbarian invasions. After all, most western imperial towns had been very secure for a long time and had rarely, if ever, been threatened. Second, at this time many military detachments seem to have been unfamiliar with catapults and untrained in their use, a fact attested to by many contemporary authors. Finally, many of these machines were probably not in good working order. It has been estimated that the life of sinew springs was no more than eight to ten years, and many of the existing artillery pieces undoubtedly had strings that did not function properly.[18]

TRACTION TREBUCHETS

Following their victory over the Roman Empire, barbarian tribes do not seem to have acquired catapult technology from their conquered foes. Why this was the case has been the subject of debate among modern historians. Some, led by Kalvero Huuri, E.A. Thompson, and Lynn White, Jr., have contended that barbarians were simply unable either to use or to continue to construct Roman-style catapults.[19] They argue that, although there is some evidence of early barbarian use of artillery, at the siege of Thessaloniki by the Goths in 269 and at Tours by the Alemanni or Franks a century later, the use of artillery failed to prove significant, as the defenders were able to burn the catapults by hurling blazing missiles at them.[20] By the sixth century there is no further mention of them. Whether this was, as Thompson surmises, "owing to the low technical level of their [barbarian] society generally,"[21] or whether they simply did not feel the need for the use of artillery against fortifications that fell relatively easily to them by other means, cannot be known. For whatever reason, these historians contend, catapult technology seems to have passed into obscurity.

However, this thesis has also been questioned by a number of historians, namely David Hill, Carroll M. Gillmor, and Paul E. Chevedden, who argue that the reason for the barbarians' rejection of Roman catapult technology is that they had accepted an alternative: the trebuchet.[22] It is well established that trebuchets originated in China between the fifth and third centuries BCE, and from there diffused westward to Islamic lands by the end of the seventh century CE, where they continued to be used until the fifteenth century.[23] The earliest of these artillery pieces were large and had a long, tapering rotating beam supported on a wooden tower and base. The beam was positioned unevenly on the fulcrum—at a ratio of between 5:1 and 6:1 for a light trebuchet and between 2:1 and 3:1 for a heavy trebuchet. Attached to the longer, thinner end of the rotating beam was a sling in which projectiles, generally stone boulders, would be placed. On the opposite, thicker short section of the beam were secured 40 to 125 ropes that were pulled by a team of men—estimated to number between 40 and 250. By pulling in unison, the team generated enough force to discharge a projectile weighing between 1 and 59 kilograms in a relatively flat arc for a distance of up to about 150 meters.[24] It is this source of power that gives the artillery piece its modern name: the traction trebuchet.

None of these points is questioned by the historians mentioned above. However, the first group maintains that the traction trebuchet was not introduced to Western Europe until it was seen by the Crusaders when they attacked the Muslims on the First Crusade. The second group contends that trebuchets were known and used by Western Europeans as early as the sixth century. As evidence, they point to an eyewitness account of the siege of Thessaloniki by the Avaro-Slavs in 597 written by John, the Archbishop of Thessaloniki. In this account, John describes some siege machines of the Avaro-Slavs (known to him as *petroboles* or "rock throwers"), a description that seems to indicate that they were traction trebuchets:

> These *petroboles* were tetragonal and rested on broader
> bases, tapering to narrow extremities. Attached to them
> were thick cylinders well clad in iron at the ends, and there
> were nailed to them timbers like beams from a large house.
> These timbers had the slings from the back and from the
> front strong ropes, by which, pulling down and releasing
> the sling, they propel the stones up high and with a loud
> noise. And on being fired they sent up many great stones so
> that neither earth nor human constructions could bear the

impacts. They also covered those tetragonal *petroboles* with boards on three sides only, so that those inside firing them might not be wounded with arrows by those on the walls. And since one of these, with its boards, had been burned to a char by a flaming arrow, they returned, carrying away the machines. On the following day they again brought these *petroboles* covered with freshly skinned hides and with the boards, and placing them closer to the walls, shooting, they hurled mountains and hills against us. For what else might one term these extremely large stones?[25]

These weapons had been transferred to the Avaro-Slavs by a captured Byzantine soldier named Bousas, a decade before the siege of Thessaloniki.[26]

Other references to siege machines appear frequently among the chronicles of the early Middle Ages, which perhaps indicates a continual use of the trebuchet,[27] including two riddles in the Old English *Exeter Riddle Book* that have been interpreted as describing catapults.[28] However, none of these references is descriptive enough to allow the validation of a more secure claim that traction trebuchets were being used, until perhaps the siege of Paris by the Vikings,

Fig. 4.1: Traction trebuchet at the Middelaltercentret, Nykøbing, Denmark.
Photo by the author.

in 885–886. At this siege, according to the historical poem *De bello Parisiaco* (*The Attack on Paris*) by Abbo of Saint-Germain-des-Prés, the defending Franks deployed a type of defensive apparatus known as a *manganum* or *mangonel*, the mechanics of which were similar to the traction trebuchet—a rotating beam engine throwing huge stones against the opposing Vikings:

> The Franks prepared some heavy pieces of wood each
> with an iron tooth at the end, so as to damage the Danish
> machines more quickly. With coupled beams of the same
> length they built what are commonly called *mangonels*,
> machines for throwing vast stones, which could blast the
> lowly race of barbarians often blowing out their brains,
> crushing crowds of them and their shields. Not one shield
> that was hit did not break; not one unfortunate who was hit
> did not die.[29]

Yet the lack of corroborative evidence (despite the large number of sources on this siege, only Abbo's poem makes reference to the presence of *mangonels*), the lack of an elaborate description (there is no reference either to the shooter holding the sling or to a team pulling on ropes to discharge the stone), and the lack of a definitive conduit for the diffusion of this artillery technology from either the Avaro-Slavs or the Muslims (although some historians suggest that Charlemagne's forces may have learned it from their numerous attacks against the Spanish Muslims or from the Byzantines in Sicily) all undermine the credibility of this reference. More importantly, despite the possibility of similar weapons appearing again at the siege of Angers in 873, they seem to disappear from Western Europe until the twelfth century. Therefore, if these were indeed traction trebuchets, they may not have had an enduring influence on European military strategy.[30]

In 1147, two traction trebuchets were reportedly used by the Crusaders to capture Muslim Lisbon. They were operated by crews organized in shifts of 100 pullers who fired 5,000 stones in 10 hours—that is 250 shots per hour or one shot every 14½ seconds.[31] After this, traction trebuchets appear at sieges throughout Western Europe, being noted both in numerous narrative references as well as in a large number of diverse artistic sources. For example, traction trebuchets are depicted in a relief carving of the late twelfth to early thirteenth century in the church of St. Nazaire in Carcassonne (which seems to show a crew of women operating the traction trebuchet) and in illuminations found in the *Maciejowski Bible* (Paris c.1250), the *Le chevalier du cygne* (French c.1200), a *Histoire du Outremer* (French c.1300), another *Histoire d'Outremer* (Jerusalem c.1280), the *Liber ad honorem* of Peter of Eboli (Sicily or southern Italy c.1200–20), and the *Skylitzes Chronicle* (Sicilian or Byzantine, twelfth to early fourteenth century).[32] There is also the famous story of the death of Simon de Montfort, the leader of the Crusaders waging war against the Albigensians in Southern France. In 1218, while besieging the well-fortified city of Toulouse, ironically using several of his own army's trebuchets to batter the walls, he was hit and killed by a stone cast by one of the traction trebuchets defending the city. According to *The Song of the Cathar Wars*, this machine was operated by "noblewomen, … little girls and men's wives."[33]

COUNTERWEIGHT TREBUCHETS

However, traction trebuchets had one fundamental flaw—they were inconsisten. Primarily, this was because the force exerted by the team of pullers was not consistent—depending, as it had to, on the strength and unity of a team of pullers. When a team was well trained it is likely that the force pulled was relatively constant from shot to shot. However, when a team of pullers was not well trained or had suffered losses in numbers, the force exerted would be very variable, resulting in a lack of consistency. Consequently, there was a need for an alternative power source, the counterweight trebuchet.

The counterweight trebuchet differed from its technological cousin in the substitution for the pulling ropes for a fixed counterweight, usually a box filled with stones, sand or some other heavy material, which provided the power to discharge the missile.[34] Not only did the counterweight allow for a more consistent discharge, i.e., each time it was discharged the force was the same, but it was also likely that it was more powerful than the traction trebuchet. The weight of the counterbalance depended, of course, on the size of the machine, but it is estimated that they varied from about 4,500 to about 13,600 kilograms and it is likely that they could propel projectiles, weighing between 45 and 90 kilograms, up to 300 meters. Larger projectiles might also have been used— what are thought to be fourteenth-century trebuchet balls made of marble and excavated at Tlemcen measured 2 meters in circumference (roughly 65 centimeters in diameter) and weighed 230 kilograms.[35]

The counterweight trebuchet first appeared around the middle of the twelfth century in the eastern and southern Mediterranean area, then spread

Fig. 4.2: Counterweight trebuchets from the Middelaltercentret, Nykøbing, Denmark. Photo by the author.

into northern Europe, the Middle East, and North Africa. It may have had a Byzantine provenance, as the earliest secure recorded use of the counterweight trebuchet was at the Byzantine siege of Zevgiminon in 1165, but the Byzantines may have learned the technology from elsewhere, as it is possible that both the Muslims and Crusaders were using the technology prior to this.[36] (It is also possible that a "hybrid trebuchet," which combined the elements of the traction and counterweight trebuchets, was also developed, although this theory is disputed.[37]) The Muslims seem to have especially favored this weapon, and they used it frequently against the Christians in the Holy Land, including against the strongholds of Hims in 1248–49 and Acre in 1291, where it is reported that they had 92 counterweight trebuchets.[38]

After this time the counterweight trebuchet appears throughout Western Europe and may have been used in conjunction with the traction trebuchet. The weapon appeared right across Europe—for example, in Flanders, where a counterweight trebuchet is depicted in an early fourteenth-century illumination of the *Roman de Saint Graal*; in England where it was known to have been used in Northumberland in 1244; and in Scotland, where it is found in a Carlisle charter illustration of 1316.[39] So prevalent did counterweight trebuchets become in Europe that they formed the basis, in thirteenth-century England, of a Royal Artillery arsenal, which served the military needs of kings John, Henry III, and Edward III (1199–1307).[40]

As Lynn White, Jr., contends, the counterweight trebuchet was "the first important mechanical utilization of the force of weight."[41] As such, it was of great interest to many technical writers and draftsmen of the late Middle

Ages and the Renaissance, leading to detailed descriptions and drawings of the mechanism by such eminent authors as Villard de Honnecourt and Giles of Rome in the thirteenth century; Conrad Kyeser, Marino Taccola, Roberto Valturio, and the "Anonymous of the Hussite Wars" in the fifteenth century; and Leonard da Vinci and Agostino Ramelli in the sixteenth century.[42]

Both traction and counterweight trebuchets seem to have been effective siege weapons. Although they were never used in large numbers—the 92 counterweight trebuchets at Acre in 1291 being an exception—they often brought a quicker resolution to a siege, although not always by breaching the walls. For example, at the siege of the abbey of Holyrood near Edinburgh in 1296, Edward I had three trebuchets that fired 158 stones in three days leading to its surrender, and in 1304, at the siege of Stirling, the same king used 13 trebuchets that fired 600 stones and within days breached the walls of the castle.[43] However, the best description of the destructive capabilities of these catapults can be found in the *Chanson de la croisade albigenoise*, which discusses the siege of Castelnaudry by the Occitans in September 1211:

> The besiegers set up their trebuchet on a road but all around they could only find stones which would have fragmented under the impact of firing. In the end they found three which they brought from a good league away. With their first shot they knocked down a tower. With their next, in everyone's sight, they destroyed a chamber. With the third shot they fired the stone disintegrated but not before causing great injury to those who were inside the town. Following this display of force, the town surrendered.[44]

Trebuchets were used not only to breach fortification walls, but also to intimidate and destroy the morale of the besieged. For example, stone missiles were sometimes replaced by incendiaries, the carcasses of putrefying and diseased animals, or even the bodies or body parts of captured enemies. At the siege of Schwanau in 1332, the besiegers from Strassbourg massacred 48 prisoners and placed their bodies in barrels that were then catapulted into the castle in an effort to frighten the besieged inhabitants.[45]

Although the trebuchet was the primary siege weapon for the next two-and-a-half centuries, by the mid-fourteenth century gunpowder weapons were beginning to make their presence felt on the battlefield and by the end of the century were making an impact in siege warfare. As gunpowder weapons became more effective and more powerful, the use of trebuchets declined, although they were present at almost all of the early sieges of the Hundred Years' War.[46] Indeed, it is clear that the two technologies, counterweight trebuchets and gunpowder weapons, were used side by side in both attacking and defending fortifications right down to the eventual demise of the trebuchet. They were present with gunpowder weapons in 1373 at the defense of Queenborough Castle.[47] And as late as Charles V's reign (1364–80), the French continued to build counterweight trebuchets and produce trebuchet balls while at the same time increasing their supply of gunpowder weapons.[48] A manuscript illumination from the Bodleian Library (ms 264), dated to the end of the fourteenth century, shows a counterweight trebuchet next to a cannon at the siege of a fortified city, although it is perhaps telling that the trebuchet stands loaded but unused while a gunner aims the cannon at the walls.[49]

Even with the advances in gunpowder artillery, trebuchets continued to be used into the fifteenth century: at the siege of Mortagne in 1405, at St. Omer in 1406, in Saint-Pol in 1419–20, in Touraine in 1421, at Paris in 1421–22 and in Picardy in 1422. Although trebuchets continued to appear in inventories until the 1460s and 1470s, it is clear that the use of this artillery technology was becoming more infrequent and sporadic—indeed it is likely that they were just in store at this time and not used.[50] Trebuchets were replaced by the new, and ultimately more powerful, gunpowder artillery.

GREEK FIRE

Of all the weapons and machines developed in the medieval period, perhaps the most mysterious is the substance called Greek Fire.[51] Although we know very little today about what Greek Fire was, it appears that we can divide it into three distinct weapons: an early liquid weapon pumped out of a nozzle; a liquid weapon that was put into small ceramic grenades; and a later solid incendiary probably based on gunpowder. The first two were used exclusively by the Byzantines and Muslims, while the third was used in Western Europe.

Although there is a great deal of uncertainty about precisely where Greek Fire originated, what it was or how it was discharged, all the evidence indicates that it was an incendiary weapon. The currently accepted account is that it was a weapon that spouted fire from ships and was invented by a man called Kallinikos of Heliopolis, who mounted them on ships of the Byzantine fleet to be used against Arab attacks on Constantinople from 671 to 678 CE. [52]

But just what it was, what made it work, or exactly what it was made from, are all still hotly debated. What is reasonably certain is that Greek Fire was a liquid that was pumped out under pressure through the nozzle of some form of pump or siphon, and set alight producing a jet of flame, that it burned even on the surface of the sea, and that it made a loud roaring noise and a lot of smoke. It was also apparently very effective. For sailors on wooden ships, fire was always a great fear, as they had nowhere to go—they either burned to death or drowned, as most sailors could not swim. As such, Greek Fire is often seen as decisive in engagements where it was used, its reputation growing far more than its use perhaps warranted. In fact, it could be said that the stories about its terrifying effects grew at the expense of knowledge about what it actually was and the secret of its composition became gradually forgotten.[53] Maybe it is for this reason that since the nineteenth century Greek Fire has exerted such a fascination on historians, researchers, and some military men who have dreamed of rediscovering its forgotten secrets.[54]

So just what can be determined about this early Greek Fire? Historians writing in the late nineteenth and early twentieth centuries thought that it was some sort of flammable liquid that was mixed with saltpeter as an oxidizing agent—something that when combined provided oxygen to assist in the burning process.[55] In contrast, J.R. Partington, in his very influential and still vitally important A History of Greek Fire and Gunpowder, published originally in 1960, suggested that Greek Fire was made from a distilled natural petroleum, a liquid similar to gasoline—from beds on the northern shores of the Black Sea—that when pumped out under pressure over a flame performed very much like a modern flame thrower, and that it did not contain any saltpeter.[56] However, whether the contemporary makers of Greek Fire could distill natural petroleum to use in this way is uncertain. It has also been suggested that an early use of saltpeter in China was as the igniter for similar highly flammable liquid weapons.[57] But this cannot be the whole story either—if saltpeter was used in the earliest Greek Fire, where did it come from? With so little detailed and reliable evidence to go on, it is almost impossible to be sure just what Greek Fire was—and the controversy will probably continue.

The use of this type of Greek Fire was rare and primarily in naval conflicts. For example, the Byzantines are recorded to have used Greek Fire to destroy an Arab fleet in 718 CE. An account of this action, attributed to Emperor Leo VI, but written more than one hundred years later, has perhaps the best description of the apparatus used by the Byzantines for Greek Fire:

Nothing required for the outfitting of the dromon should be
omitted, and there should be two of each of them . . . . By all
means, it should have a siphon, bound in bronze, and placed
up front on the prow, as is customary, so that it can project
the prepared fire against the enemy. Above this particular
siphon there should be a platform made of planks and
walled around by planks.[58]

Other recorded naval uses include Emperor Leo III's defeat of the fleets of
rebellious Hellas and the Cyclades in 726; the usurper Artabasdos' unsuccessful
attack on Constantine V's allied fleet of *Kibyrrhaiotai* outside of Constantinople
in 743; the Arab capture of a Byzantine vessel carrying the apparatus to use the
weapon in 827; the Byzantine annihilation of a fleet of Russian ships attacking
across the Black Sea from Kiev in 941; the naval defense of Constantinople
against Rus ships in 1043; the Byzantine attack of a Pisan fleet near Rhodes,
causing it to flee, in 1103; the preparation for an attack of a Norman fleet off the
coast of Sicily in 1147; the use against a Venetian ship outside of Constantinople
in 1171; and the destruction of the fleet of the rebel Alexios Branas in 1187.[59]
Surprisingly, though, Greek Fire does not seem to have been used by the
Byzantines to defend Constantinople against the Fourth Crusaders in 1203.[60]
In addition, in 812 the Bulgar Khan Krum captured the fortress of Develtos on
the Black Sea, where he found in its arsenal a substantial amount of Greek Fire
and a number of weapons to use it. These were presumably for use against ships
approaching the harbor and not against attackers from the land side, a conclusion that is presumed as the fortress's defenders had not used the weapons
against Krum.[61] Two citations in Arabic sources, dating to 904 and 941–994,
may also indicate the use of this type of Greek Fire on Muslim ships, but the
evidence is far from conclusive.[62] Perhaps the rarity of use resulted from the
fact that although the weapon was tremendously effective against enemy ships,
with their inflammable hulls, sails, and rigging, it was no doubt also a danger
to the ship on which the weapon was mounted.

This type of early Greek Fire also appears mounted on the prow of a
Byzantine ship in an illumination in the *Skylitzes Chronicle* manuscript of the
Biblioteca Nacional in Madrid, dating from between the twelfth and the early
fourteenth centuries.[63] A second illustration, in the eleventh-century treatise
on *poliocetics* (siege warfare) said to have been written by the ancient Greek
engineer Heron of Byzantium, may show a handheld Greek Fire weapon being

Fig. 4.3: Greek Fire fired from a Byzantine ship as depicted in the *Skylitzes Chronicle*,
eleventh century.

The Bridgeman Art Library International / Madrid, Prado, *Biblioteca Nacional de España*, MS Graecus Vitr.
26–2, f. 34v.

used against the walls of a fortification by a soldier standing atop a siege tower.
Other land uses of Greek Fire are recorded, but this use was even rarer than in
naval conflicts.[64]

The second type of Greek Fire also appears to have been a liquid and may be
the same as, or similar to, the substance used by the Byzantines, although later
recipes appear to also add a mixture of resin, oil, asphalt, and lime. However,
instead of being pumped out over a flame, small vessels were filled with the
substance and these were thrown by hand, like a grenade, or by some form
of catapult. This type of incendiary was a specialty of Muslims and seems to
have come as quite a surprise to the Crusaders when they came up against it for
the first time in the twelfth century. That it was being used very extensively in
the Middle East is evident from a large number of written sources, including
a report, in 1168, that 20,000 barrels of a flammable liquid were used to burn
down the city of Cairo to prevent its capture by the Crusaders.[65]

Although most of the references to this form of Greek Fire are to its use and
effects, there are also numerous examples of the containers into which it was
packed. These have been found all over the Middle East and Western Asia, from
as far afield as Syria, Palestine, Egypt, Tashkent, and Samarkand. These are
quite small, most fitting into a large man's hand, made of glass or ceramic, and
usually either spherical or spheroconic in shape, the latter essentially a sphere
that has been pulled out to a point on one side. Although evidence for what
went inside them is very scarce, in the 1930s archaeologists working in the cita-
del of the Syrian town of Hama made an intriguing discovery. Here they found

not only what they believed to be a workshop to produce ceramic grenades for Greek Fire, but in one particular area of the excavation were some very large ceramic vessels, possibly used for distillation, in a room that appeared to have specialized ventilation: one wall had large circular openings just half a meter from the ground. Pieces of a burnt material were also found and identified as asphalt, which in later medieval recipes is known to have been used in the production of Greek Fire together with resin or oil and lime. Although there is still some doubt, it has been strongly suggested that this part of the workshop was for making Greek Fire to fill the small spheroconic vessels found throughout the site. The workshop dates to the first half of the thirteenth century, probably before Hama was largely destroyed by the Timurid Mongols in 1259.[66]

In the fourteenth century, incendiary weapons, often also called Greek Fire, started to appear in Europe, and these are referred to and illustrated in early sources, particularly the so-called *Firework Books* dating from the early fifteenth century. Whether these were the same as the earlier types of Greek Fire is unclear, but it seems more likely that the term was transferred from the older Byzantine or Arabic weapons to newer ones that acted largely in the same way but were now based mainly on the newly introduced explosive, gunpowder.

A question that is often asked is why Europeans failed to adopt the new technology at an earlier stage. The most likely explanation is that they lacked the materials to make the earlier types of Greek Fire—the petroleum-like materials were available only from areas that were, to Western Europeans, inaccessible. Europeans had certainly heard of it, and, after all, they had encountered it during the Crusades. What seems likely is that they were unable to make it due to the unavailability of the raw materials, but when gunpowder was introduced and new forms of incendiary were possible the term was transferred to the new weapon. The difficulties in our understanding can be very well summed up in an instance, in 1340 at the siege of Tournai. After a lengthy and fruitless campaign against the town by Edward III's English and Low Countries forces, the situation had become so dire that the *Chronique des Pays-Bas* reports that Edward called on an expert in siege artillery to discuss tactics to be used against the fortifications of the town. Among other things that this man proposed was a "dragon" made of wood that would spew out Greek Fire. The dragon was then built, "using magic," and was in fact successful in destroying some of Tournai by fire (how this happened is left vague, although it seems it was not by Greek Fire). The English king then paid the engineer a large sum of money to build more of these machines, but, incapable of fulfilling his promises, he fled and, despite a fervent search for him by the army, he was never seen again. The anonymous chronicler does assure us, however, that the engineer died "an evil death" for his sins.[67]

Whatever the importance of incendiaries elsewhere, they never really gained a serious place in the medieval arsenal, and it was the advent of gunpowder that heralded a new chapter in the history of medieval military technology.

Notes

1. Marsden (1969): 5–12 and Landels (1978): 99–104. The only ancient writer to describe this catapult is Heron (c350–270 BCE). See Marsden (1971): 17–60.

2. Marsden (1969): 13–16.

3. Marsden (1969): 16.

4. Marsden (1969): 16–47 and Landels (1978): 104–30. A number of ancient writers describe these torsion catapults. See Marsden (1971).

5. Marsden (1969): 58–61.

6. Marsden (1969): 29–33; Landels (1978): 112–15; Baatz (1978): 1–17; and Soedel and Foley (1979): 153.

7. Landels (1978): 119 and Baatz (1978): 1–17.

8. Marsden (1969): 73–76.

9. Landels (1978): 123–26; Soedel and Foley (1979): 155–56. For Philon's description of this catapult see Marsden (1971): 146–53.

10. Landels (1978): 130; Marsden (1971): 206–32; and Marsden (1969): 189–90. Heron's description of the *cheiroballistra* is found in Marsden (1971): 215–27. For a description of the use of catapults on the battlefield and at sea see Marsden (1969): 164–73.

11. Landels (1978): 130–32; Marsden (1969): 190–91; and Marsden (1971): 249–65. Ammianus Marcellinus' description of the *onager* can be found in Marsden (1971): 250–54.

12. On the ranges and accuracy of these weapons see Marsden (1969): 86–95.

13. Marsden (1969): 95–98 and Soedel and Foley (1969): 153.

14. As quoted in Hacker (1968): 45.

15. Marsden (1971): 234–48.

16. Lander (1984): 259.

17. As quoted in Hacker (1968): 45–46. See also Wolfram (1988): 345.

18. S. Johnson (1983): 79 and Lander (1984): 259.

19. Huuri (1941); E.A. Thompson (1958): 13–17; and L. White (1962): 102–3. For a more complete list of other authors who agree with this contention see Gillmor (1981): 1 n.1.

20. E.A. Thompson (1958): 13–17 and S. Johnson (1983): 78.

21. E.A. Thompson (1958): 13.

22. Donald Hill (1973); Gillmor (1981); and Cheveddan (1995).

23. On the Chinese origin of the trebuchet see Needham (1976). On the diffusion to and use of these weapons in Islam see Donald Hill (1973): 100 and Chevedden (1990): 20–27.

24. Szwejkowski (1990) and Donald Hill (1973): 102–3. More recent discussions of the traction trebuchet are Cheveddan, Eigenbrod, Foley, and Soedel (1995) and Cheveddan, Shiller, Gilbert, and Kagay (2000).

25. Cheveddan (1990): 10–11 and Vyronis (1981): 384.

26. Cheveddan (1990): 12–13.

27. See David Hill (1979): 112–13.

28. Crossley-Holland (1979): #17 and 53. See also David Hill (1979): 116–17. These have also been interpreted as describing fortresses, ovens, and battering rams.

29. David Hill (1979): 113–15; Gillmor (1981): 2–5; and Fino (1972): 27–28.

30. Gillmor (1981) and Cheveddan (1995) believe that the *mangonels* at the siege of Paris were traction trebuchets, while Donald Hill (1973) and L. White (1962) contend that the introduction of the traction trebuchet comes later.

31. Donald Hill (1971): 102; Cheveddan (1990): 16–17; and L. White (1962): 102–3.

32. Nicolle (1988): #723, 772, 774, 787, 830, 1423, and 1427.

33. Tudela (1996): 172. See also France (1999): 124.

34. Donald Hill (1973): 105.

35. Donald Hill (1973): 105–6; Payne-Gallwey (1903): 309; and L. White (1962): 103. On the dynamics of trebuchets see Donald Hill (1973): 106–14.

36. Cheveddan (2000).

37. Cheveddan (1998) proposes this idea, but it has been disputed by Basista (2007).

38. On the Muslim use of the counterweight trebuchet and the number of Muslim technical treatises describing the weapon see Cheveddan (2000): 87–98.

39. Fino (1972): 25, 35–41; Donald Hill (1973): 104; Nicolle (1988): #977 and 1261; and Contamine (1984): 104–5.

40. D. Bachrach (2004b, 2006b).

41. L. White (1962): 103.

42. On Villard de Honnecourt see Contamine (1984): 103–4 and Nicolle (1988): #798, 1587. On Giles of Rome see Giles of Rome (1968): 357v-358r and Fino (1972): 29. On the "Renaissance" engineers see Gille (1966), Prager and Scaglia (1972) and B. Hall (1979).

43. Contamine (1984): 104–5.

44. As quoted in Contamine (1984): 104.

45. Contamine (1984): 104.

46. Contamine (1984): 194.

47. Brown, Colvin, and Taylor (1963): II: 801–2.

48. Contamine (1984): 194.

49. Norman (1975).

50. Contamine (1984): 195.

51. The name Greek Fire certainly dates back to the later medieval period, but just how far back it goes is unclear.

52. The contemporary historians Theophanes and Cedrenus reported that the Byzantine emperor Constantine VII was so concerned with the safety of his capital that he ordered a number of fireships to be equipped with siphons of Greek Fire. Ellis Davidson (1973): 62; Forbes (1955): 102; Partington (1960): 12–15; and Pryor and Jeffreys (2006): 607–8.

53. Roland (1992).

54. See, for example, Long and Roland (1994).

55. See, for example, Berthelot (1891).

56. Partington (1999): 28–32. This book was reprinted in 1999, and the references here are to this printing.

57. Needham (1986): 82.

58. Leo VI (2010): 504–5. See also Partington (1960): 18, although he admits that his is a loose translation and does take some liberties with the original text.

59. Pryor and Jeffreys (2010): 608–10, 630; Ellis Davidson (1973): 62–64; Forbes (1955): 103; and Partington (1960): 18–20.

60. On this curiosity see Pryor and Jeffreys (2010): 630–31.

61. Pryor and Jeffreys (2010): 609.

62. Pryor and Jeffreys (2010): 611–12.

63. Madrid, Biblioteca Nacional, Vitr. 26–2, f. 34v. See the discussion of this illustration in Bruhn de Hoffmeyer (1966): 140–52; Pryor and Jeffreys (2010): 612–13; and Nicolle (1988): #1427.

64. Pryor and Jeffreys (2010): 618–21.

65. Partington (1960): 21–28.

66. Pentz (1988).

67. *Chronique des Pays-Bas* (1856): 153–54.

CHAPTER 5

GUNPOWDER ARTILLERY

PERHAPS THE GREATEST AND CERTAINLY THE MOST ENDURING OF ALL THE innovations of the later medieval period were the introduction of gunpowder and the development of firearms. Invented in China, gunpowder was probably discovered and developed in the period between the sixth and ninth centuries CE. Just when its military potential was recognized is unclear, but gunpowder was being used as an incendiary by the tenth century, and by the twelfth century a range of devices, bombs, grenades, fire lances, rockets, and fireworks, were in use. (There is also some evidence that gunpowder was known in India in the early twelfth century.[1]) However, exactly when the Chinese developed firearms is not known. Needham in his seminal work on Chinese military technology suggests that they did not develop guns until the late thirteenth century. However, this dating has recently been challenged, with an earlier date suggested, although precisely when is still unclear, but certainly by the middle of the thirteenth century and probably earlier.[2]

By the second half of the thirteenth century, gunpowder, or at least the knowledge of gunpowder, had made its way to Western Europe, although by a means yet to be ascertained. The most likely conduit was through Islamic lands to Byzantium or to Spain and then on to Western Europe.[3] However, just when gunpowder first reached Europe is still very controversial. The first widely accepted reference to gunpowder is to be found in the work *Opus tertium* of about 1267 by Roger Bacon:

> By the flash and combustion of fires, and by the horror
> of sounds, wonders can be wrought, and at any distance
> that we wish–so that a man can hardly protect himself or
> endure it. There is a child's toy of sound and fire made in
> various parts of the world with powder of saltpeter, sulphur
> and charcoal of hazelwood. This powder is enclosed in an
> instrument of parchment the size of a finger, and since this
> can make such a noise that it seriously distresses the ears of
> men . . . . If the instrument were made of solid material the
> violence of the explosion would be much greater.[4]

A number of works, including Albert the Great's *De mirabilibus mundi* (*Concerning the Wonders of the World*) of c.1275, and Marcus Graecus' *Liber ignium ad comburendos hostes* (*Book of Fires for the Burning of Enemies*) of c.1300, also refer to gunpowder recipes containing saltpeter, sulfur, and charcoal in a mixture that when lit combusted with a forceful explosion.[5] Still, none of these authors describes a weapon that could use their gunpowder mixture.

―――――

EARLY HISTORY OF EUROPEAN GUNPOWDER WEAPONS

It is difficult to determine when the first cannon was used or made in Europe. Written evidence from the early fourteenth century is scarce and often disputed. References to guns appearing at the defense of Forlì in 1284 and in the armory of Ghent in 1313 are suspect and unsubstantiated.[6] More trustworthy are references to guns at the siege of Metz in 1324, in a Florentine armory in 1326, and at the siege of Cividale (Friuli) in 1331, although even these references have been questioned.[7] Less controversial are two artistic sources, an illumination found in Walter de Milemete's *De nobilitatibus, sapientiis et prudentiis regum* (*Concerning the Majesty, Wisdom and Prudence of Kings*), made in London in 1326, and a second illumination, obviously inspired by the first, found in a companion volume to the Walter de Milemete treatise known as the *De secretis secretorum Aristotelis* (*The Secrets of Secrets of Aristotle*), also made in London in 1326. Both depict a large vase-shaped cannon lying on its side. In the first, a soldier, dressed in

Fig. 5.1: Early gun depicted in the *De Nobilitatibus, Sapientiis et Prudentiis Regum*, by Walter de Milemete, 1326.

The Bridgeman Art Library International / Peter Newark Pictures.

armor, is firing the gun, with a lit match held in iron tongs, although this is not entirely clear, through a hole in the breech of the weapon. A large arrow-shaped bolt is shown protruding from the muzzle of the piece, which is aimed at what appears to be a fortification.[8] The second illustration, similar to the first in the shape and mount of the cannon and in the missile it fires, differs in that the cannon appears to be larger, no target is shown, and there are four armored soldiers with the gun.[9] After the late 1330s and 1340s, references to gunpowder weaponry increase markedly. For example, guns were included in armories in Lille, Lucca, Aachen, Deventer, London, Siena, and St. Omer, and they were used at the sieges of Tournai in 1340 and of Calais in 1346–47, and almost certainly, although disputed, at the battle of Crécy in 1346.[10]

Although the beginnings of gunpowder weapons were quite modest, their developmental progress was spectacular. Over the next 150 years a whole arsenal of cannon and firearms was developed—from handheld guns to monster cannon weighing 10 tonnes or more. The way that guns were made also changed and developed, and the industries making them expanded to be able to manufacture huge quantities of cannon and firearms easily and cheaply. Transportation methods, metallurgy, and powder chemistry were subjected to experiment and continually improved. More importantly, gunpowder weaponry led to significant changes on the battlefield and at sieges. It was, in the words of William McNeill, "an arms race," which affected every kingdom and principality.[11]

SIEGE, BATTLEFIELD, AND NAVAL APPLICATIONS

The first and most enduring impact of gunpowder weapons was on siege warfare. From about 1375, large artillery pieces with large calibers firing heavy stone projectiles appear in ever-increasing quantity.[12] Guns like this were ideal for this type of conflict, as the heavy shot could do severe damage to castles and fortifications, such that almost every siege thereafter was accompanied by a gunpowder artillery bombardment. By the end of the century, cannon began to have an effect on the outcome of sieges. One of the first instances we have is in 1377, when, at the siege of Odruik, Philip the Bold, Duke of Burgundy, used cannon that fired large bolts to penetrate the walls. Contemporary chronicler Jean Froissart tells the story:

The castle of Odruik was situated on a motte, surrounded
by a ditch filled with very large spikes, which was not easy
to defeat.... Then the duke of Burgundy set up his cannons
and fired maybe five or six quarrels in order to provoke a surrender. These quarrels were such that, because of the power
of the discharge, they penetrated the walls. When those in
the castle saw the strength of the artillery which the duke
had, they doubted themselves more than ever before... and
the duke fired from his cannons two hundred quarrels in
number, which penetrated the walls... [and those defending
Odruik] surrendered the fortress, to save their lives, and they
were led by the duke of Burgundy all the way to Calais.[13]

Froissart also records that in 1379, at the siege of Oudenaarde, the rebellious
Ghentenaars, led by Philip van Artevelde, "fired their cannons against those in
the town." Not only did this greatly damage the walls of the city, but many of
the projectiles also passed over the walls, so that the inhabitants of Oudenaarde
had to cover their houses with dirt to protect their roofs from fire. Louis de
Male, the count of Flanders against whom the Ghentenaars were rebelling, was
forced to sue for peace.[14]

In siege warfare during the fifteenth century, gunpowder weaponry continued to be significant, although not always decisive. For example, in 1412,
at the siege of Bourges, the Duke of Berry, defending the city, was forced to
vacate his residence no fewer than seven times to avoid the persistent and
accurate gunfire of the Burgundian cannon, primarily from a large bombard
called *Griette*.[15] At Harfleur, in 1415, Henry V used his guns to bring down the
walls of the town when his mines were continually countermined. Eventually
he moved his guns next to the walls of the town before the siege was effective.[16]
Fortepice was flattened in 1433 by a single great bombard, the *Bourgoigne*,[17] and
the town of Bouvignes fell in 1466, when, as chronicler Philippe de Commynes
states, "two bombards and other large pieces of artillery, [shattered] the houses
of the town... and [forced] the poor people to take refuge in their cellars and to
remain there."[18] And, in August 1466, the town of Dinant, which had resisted
17 sieges during the Middle Ages, fell to Charles the Bold, the duke of Burgundy,
after only a week of gunpowder artillery bombardment.[19]

Sometimes a long and heavy bombardment was used in an attempt to defeat
a fortification: at the siege of Maastricht from November 24, 1407, to January 7,

1408, the town was hit by as many as 1,514 large bombard balls, an average of 30 per day (although they did not bring its submission); at the siege of Lagny in 1431, 412 stone cannonballs were fired into the town in a single day; at Dinant in 1466, 502 large and 1,200 smaller cannonballs were fired; and at the siege of Rhodes in 1480 over 3,500 balls were shot into the town.[20] Sometimes, simply the presence of large gunpowder weapons among the besieging army intimidated the inhabitants of a town or castle. An example of this was the siege of Bourg, in June 1451, which Charles VII captured in just six days after his heavy artillery was brought up to the walls of the castle, although they never fired a shot.[21] At the siege of Ham in 1411, only three shots were fired from the bombard known as *Griette*. The first passed over the town's castle and fell into the Somme; the second hit the ground in front of the castle but still had enough power that it began to destroy a tower and two adjacent walls; and the third shot, which also struck the ground, made a breach in the wall itself. Before a fourth shot could be fired, the town capitulated.[22]

For medieval commanders, the quicker the surrender of a medieval fortification, the quicker they could move onto other campaign goals. So King Henry V of England moved rapidly across Normandy and Maine in 1417–20, prominently displaying his gunpowder artillery train at each location before offering the garrison terms: should the French king not show up with a relief force within three weeks, they would surrender the castle or town to him, and in return they would be allowed to leave with their possessions and, perhaps more importantly, avoid being bombarded. Using this strategy, fortress after fortress fell without any actual fighting. In the end only Caen and Rouen, the two largest Norman towns, required a siege of any significant length, allowing the English king to capture the most territory more quickly than any commander during the Hundred Years' War.[23] In June 1429, Joan of Arc negotiated a similar surrender of the garrison of Beaugency after several days of firing against the walls of the city and the twelfth-century castle that stood just inside them, into which many of the soldiers had retreated. After promising not to fight against the French for a period of three months, the English troops retreated toward Paris, with their possessions and arms, and Joan was able to get on with her more pressing mission: the crowning of the dauphin as King Charles VII at Reims.[24]

However, having gunpowder artillery to lay siege did not always guarantee success. Sometimes commanders may not have been able to recognize the capabilities of these new weapons and were thus unable to use them effectively. Sometimes the supply of gunpowder and projectiles was a problem. This seems

Fig. 5.2: Besieging a fortification with cannon and fire-arrows, from the *Feuerwerkbuch*, Royal Armouries. © Board of Trustees of the Armouries.

to have been the case, even as late as 1472, when the duke of Burgundy, Charles the Bold, besieged Beauvais. Philippe de Commynes reported:

> [He] had two cannons which were fired only twice
> through the gate and made a large hole in it. If he
> had had more stones to continue firing he would
> have certainly taken the town. However, he had
> not come with the intention of performing such an
> exploit and was therefore not well provided.[25]

Other examples of besieged fortifications not falling even after very intensive gunpowder artillery bombardment include Maastricht in 1409–10, Orléans in 1428–29, Compiègne in 1430, Calais in 1435, Belgrade in 1469, Neuss in 1474–75, and Rhodes in 1480, among many other examples.[26]

The misuse of guns by inexperienced gunners also occasionally caused problems. Early gunpowder weapons were not always reliable, and they sometimes exploded. Occasionally bizarre accidents occurred. At the siege of Poeke in July 1453, the relieving army of Ghentenaars, when facing the Burgundian besiegers, broke ranks and fled because one of their gunners allowed a spark to fly into an open sack of gunpowder that subsequently burst into flames. All the nearby gunners panicked and ran, and when the rest of the army saw this, they also took flight.[27]

Gunpowder weapons had less impact on the late medieval battlefield. We know that guns were used at the battle of Crécy in 1346, but there are only infrequent references to gunpowder weapons on the battlefield throughout the rest of the fourteenth century, and even then rarely did they play a role in the outcome of the battle. One example, however, stands out: the battle of Beverhoutsveld, fought outside the walls of the town of Bruges in 1382, as guns may have decided the outcome. Here, gunpowder weapons brought by the Ghentenaars to besiege the town were turned against the attacking Brugeois militia, which had ventured outside of the protective walls of the town to fend off a Ghentenaar onslaught. As the anonymous author of the *Chronique de Flandre* describes the scene, "The Ghentenaars moved themselves and their artillery forward. This artillery fired a blast with such furor that it seemed to bring the [Brugeois] line directly to a halt."[28] Guns were also used at the battles of Aljubarrota in 1385 and Castagnaro in 1387.[29]

By the closing decade of the fourteenth and the beginning of the fifteenth centuries a wide range of gunpowder artillery had developed, from small handguns and large battlefield pieces to huge siege guns. Indeed, the destructive capabilities of guns by the early fifteenth century have led M.G.A. Vale to state that it was "patently obvious that the gun could not only batter down fortifications, but could kill, and kill selectively, from afar."[30] Guns began to appear more frequently on the battlefield: at Tongeren and Othée in 1408, at Agincourt in 1415, at Cravant in 1423, at the battle of the Herrings in 1429, at Bulgneville in 1431, at Formigny in 1450, at Castillon and Gavere in 1453, at Blore Heath and Ludford Bridge in 1459, at St. Albans in 1461, at Montlhéry in 1465, at Brusthem in 1467, at Grandson and Murten in 1476, at Nancy in 1477, and at Bosworth in 1485, among many others.[31]

As in siege warfare, sometimes these guns were quite effective. For example, at the battle of Castillon, a letter written to "my beloved friends" by an anonymous author describes the destruction: "Girault the cannoneer and his assistants and companions directed their artillery against the enemy. And it was very sorrowful, for each ball hit five or six men, killing them all."[32] More often, however, battlefield gunfire was extremely ineffective. At Othée, for example, the guns fired too slowly to have any effect.[33] At Montlhéry, the Burgundian cannon were well positioned on the field but were unable to fire more than 10 salvos at the French army.[34] At Brusthem it is reported that:

> The battle began with an artillery duel. The Burgundians . . .
> advanced their pieces up to the dikes at four or five spots
> and from there fired at the Liégeois. Moreover, they man-
> aged to unleash a considerable bombardment (the Burgun-
> dians are said to have fired seventy rounds). But the trees
> and hedges impeded their line of fire.[35]

And at Grandson the Swiss army, anticipated by Charles the Bold to follow the "clear" path around Lake Neuchâtel, instead filtered through the woods to the north of an earthen rampart built especially to mount the Burgundian gunpowder artillery, "large and small," according to the *Légende Bourguignonne*, and attacked their opponents' flank. By the time Charles recognized what was happening it was too late to move his guns and, without them, the battle was quickly over.[36]

Exactly when the portable, handheld firearm first appeared is uncertain, but the suggestion that they were used at the battle of Este in 1334 put forward by some historians is doubtful.[37] They were certainly being used by the turn of the fourteenth century, however, as shown by an illustration in Conrad Kyeser's

Bellifortis of about 1400. It depicts a gunner firing a weapon supported at the front by a tripod and at the rear by his hand.[38]

From the 1420s, handguns were being ordered in large quantities and must have been used extensively on the battlefield, although again there are few written sources, and only rare glimpses of them in the chronicles of the period. Therefore, it is difficult to know their tactical use. Presumably they augmented the archers and crossbowmen and were maybe used in much the same way. However, whether they were more effective than longbows or crossbows is not an easy question to answer. While the longbow needed long years of practice and considerable skill to shoot, the crossbow was a relatively easy weapon to master, and both could be shot considerably more quickly and were more accurate than the early handgun. The fact that these early handguns had to be loaded by the muzzle was not the only reason for the slow rate of fire; they also had to be loaded with propellant and projectile, while the bow had to be loaded with only a projectile. Some recent experimental work has, however, indicated that the velocity of a bullet was considerably greater than either the crossbow's bolt or the longbow's arrow.[39] Handguns, therefore, offered a greater range and firepower, offsetting their inaccuracy and low rate of fire.

By the middle of the fifteenth century, most battlefield engagements included handheld gunpowder weapons. So conventional had they become, in fact, that in January 1456, when Philip the Good, Duke of Burgundy, was planning a crusade against the Turks, he included 500–600 gunners armed with handheld gunpowder weapons under the command of a master of artillery.[40] By the 1460s and 1470s, Philip's successor, Charles the Bold, had forces equipped with haquebusses "without number," guns that he continually used in his military engagements against the French, Germans, and Swiss. For example, at the siege of Neuss in 1474–75, one eyewitness reports, "It was pitiful how culverins [handguns] were fired at [the people of Neuss] thicker than rain...."[41] They were also used at the battles of Grandson, Murten, and Nancy. At Nancy the Burgundians were defeated and Charles the Bold killed by primarily Lorraine forces equally well equipped with handheld gunpowder weapons.[42]

Gunpowder weaponry also began appearing on board ships in the fifteenth century. While small gunpowder weapons may have been added to ships shortly after they began to be used on land, the infrequent references to gunpowder artillery as arms on board ships before the last four decades of the fourteenth century are questionable.[43] After the beginning of the fifteenth century, however, it seems that few ships left port without carrying gunpowder weapons. They were probably used by English, French, and Iberian ships at the battles of

La Rochelle in 1372, of Dunkirk in 1387, and of Harfleur and the Seine in 1416, and they were certainly found on board Italian ships in the Lombard Wars of the 1420s and 1430s.[44] In 1410, Christine de Pisan, in her *Le livre fais d'armes et de chevalerie* (*The Book of the Feats of Arms and Chivalry*), advocated "greeting" attacking ships with shot from bombards when encountering them.[45]

Although we have little evidence of the types of weapon being used at sea, by the middle of the fifteenth century shipboard guns seem to have been more standardized and were capable of being loaded from the rear—i.e., breech loading—with separate powder chambers that were interchangeable with one another.[46] However, it is clear that the artillery carried on ships was not used primarily for the attack of enemy ships but as anti-personnel weapons—the usual naval tactic was to come alongside and board and capture an enemy vessel. The first documentary evidence for the sinking of a ship by another ship is in 1499 during the Battle of Zonchio, when an Ottoman ship sank a Venetian one by gunfire, but this may have been an isolated case and was not the usual naval tactic at the time.[47] It was not until well into the sixteenth century that ships were armed with sufficient numbers of large cannon to regularly attack ships with the intention of sinking them. It is worth noting that sinking an enemy ship was not always a good tactic—capturing it by defeating the crew was almost always the desired outcome, as the captured ship was worth a great amount of money to the victors, while once sunk it was worthless.[48]

TYPES AND MANUFACTURING OF GUNPOWDER, GUNPOWDER WEAPONS, AND PROJECTILES

The earliest gunpowder weapons were known simply as cannon, and it is uncertain what they looked like or how they were made. Indeed, for much of the fourteenth century the only images of guns are those to be found in the two manuscripts noted above, but there is no way of knowing if this was the normal form of artillery. The two guns both appear to be made from bronze that would have been poured molten into a mold—like the casting of bells—a technology that was already well known by the beginning of the fourteenth century. Once cool the finished casting was removed from the mold and cleaned up to be ready for use.[49]

Three types of metal were used for gunpowder weapons in the fourteenth and fifteenth centuries (and indeed right down to the nineteenth century):

bronze, forged iron, and cast iron. Bronze was not only the first but also probably the favored metal from which to make cannon; however, its high cost limited its use in some armies, with the result that there were probably many more iron cannon than bronze ones made during this period.[50] Iron was a more plentiful and less expensive metal for making gunpowder weapons.[51] However, it has a very high melting point, so for much of the medieval period it was produced in a semi-solid process, a material called wrought iron. Iron in the molten state could be produced only as an alloy with carbon—i.e., cast iron.

Wrought iron can be worked very easily, and pieces of it can be joined one with another by the relatively simple process of heating them to white heat and then hammering them together: the blows of the hammer simply force the two pieces together to form a single forging. Wrought iron had been used throughout the medieval period for a good deal of arms and armor, as well as for a number of other domestic and religious purposes, and smiths quickly adapted the technique to make cannon. What they developed was a method of making cannon that today is called hoop and stave construction. Long strips of iron were laid edge to edge to form the barrel, and these were bound together by iron hoops, which were made slightly smaller than needed; heating to white heat meant that these expanded slightly so that they could be forced over the tube of staves, and when they cooled and shrank they bound the whole together, something similar to the way in which wooden barrels were made. Through this technique cannon of all shapes and sizes could be assembled relatively easily and cheaply. Hoop and stave construction was used for all types of cannon in great numbers from at least the later fourteenth until the eighteenth century, although in later times only for small swivel guns.[52]

Before it was perfected in the 1540s, cast iron was a very brittle material— unlike wrought iron, which was very ductile and tough, and easily shattered when dealt a heavy blow, so it was not usually a suitable material for making cannon.[53] Intriguingly, however, there are references to small cast-iron cannon from the early decades of the fifteenth century, although only in small numbers. Just how effective they were is impossible to ascertain.[54]

Making cannon from wrought iron, using the hoop and stave method, has been greatly misinterpreted in the past by historians of artillery. It has often been labeled a poor technique, the method of construction primitive, and the maintenance of gas-tight joins problematic. Many historians have stated that, to overcome this latter problem, the staves were welded together or soldered in some way. Recent work has, however, proved these assumptions to be incorrect and shown that wrought iron and the hoop and stave construction were perfectly adequate for making cannon. In fact, these construction techniques were highly sophisticated. The staves did not need to be—in fact could not have been—joined or welded together. When the outer layer of hoops shrank on cooling, they forced the staves together so tightly that there was no problem of gas leakage.[55] What is probably true to say, though, is that wrought-iron cannon were unable to contain the forces of the new gunpowder and iron balls introduced in the late fifteenth century and were used after that date only for specialist pieces.

The detailed study of early cannon and firearms is made particularly difficult by the fact that there is no way to understand just what a contemporary scribe meant when he used a particular name for a gun. Although from the sixteenth century on the names of cannon were fairly well fixed and were dictated by the size of the bore of the piece, in the fourteenth and fifteenth centuries names of guns do not appear to follow any easily identifiable system. Pieces of widely differing size, bore, length, and weight frequently have the same name in original sources. This means that it is difficult, if not impossible, to be sure of what is being referred to, and this has hindered an understanding of the development of guns in this period. Before about 1420 there are few names for artillery. In the Burgundian sources, for example, which are particularly rich and have been well studied, only two names for artillery are used in the fourteenth century: bombard and canon. During the fifteenth century other names occur, including *coulovrine*, *veuglaire*, *crappadeau*, *courtau*, *serpentine*, *mortar*, and *hacquebus*, leading to the assumption that different types of gun were developed, probably for different purposes.[56]

The largest, best known, and most impressive of all of these weapons were the bombards. There was no standard size for a bombard, and they ranged in size greatly: they could measure from just a meter or two up to 5.2 meters in length, weigh from just a few hundred kilograms to as much as 20 tonnes and have calibers as large as 71 centimeters. The bombard developed in the fourteenth century, and during the first half of the fifteenth century it became a major feature of most siege trains. Although most were large and heavy, weighing up to 15 or even 20 tonnes, they were not, as most modern historians state, difficult to the point of impossible to move around. Late medieval armies of 10,000–20,000 men were not that mobile, with a rate of movement normally in the region of 12–20 kilometers a day, and much the same as has been calculated for some of the largest bombards in the fifteenth century.[57] These large guns were moved around on specially reinforced carts capable of taking their enormous weight, and on campaign they were escorted by pioneers

Fig. 5.3: The bombard, *Dulle Griete*, in Ghent.

Photo by the author.

who ensured that roads were suitable and that bridges would take the weight, although accidents occasionally happened. Once at the siege they were taken off their carts by means of cranes, called *gins* in the French sources, and were then mounted within large reinforced frames of wood for firing. Ranges were, on the whole, very short, perhaps in the region of less than 180 meters. To protect the artillerymen working the piece from attack, wooden hoardings and walls, pre-fabricated and transported to the siege or made up on the spot, were set up in front and around the gun position.[58]

Whether bombards made a difference to the outcome of sieges is hard to ascertain, although their continual use and transport to siege operations certainly strongly suggest that they were seen as important, even vital, weapons. The larger guns always fired stone shot that, in modern tests, has been shown to be very effective against almost all defenses.[59] However, evidence for their use and effectiveness on the battlefield is, for the early period at least, circumstantial. They were stockpiled by rulers and kings and taken on campaigns, but written sources state neither what they were capable of nor whether they made a difference to the outcomes. They certainly impressed medieval eyewitnesses with their sounds, "like devils out of hell," and the destruction they caused. This is seen clearly in a contemporary account of the siege of Bourges in 1412:

> [The besiegers] . . . caused a cannon called *Griette*, which was
> bigger than the others, to be mounted opposite the main

gate. It shot stones of enormous weight at the cost of large
quantities of gunpowder and much hard and dangerous
work on the part of its expert crew. Nearly twenty men were
required to handle it. When it was fired the thunderous
noise could be heard four miles away and terrorized the
local inhabitants as if it were some reverberation from hell.
On the first day, the foundations of one of the towers were
partly demolished by a direct hit. On the next day this cannon fired twelve stones, two of which penetrated the tower,
thus exposing many of the buildings and their inhabitants.
At the same time, other batteries at the siege were also making breaches in other parts of the wall.[60]

Intriguingly, bombards were frequently named, unlike most other gunpowder weapons. Often these names indicated the city of their construction or
ownership, e.g., the *Brucelles, Dijon, Paris, Montereau, Valexon*, etc., while others denoted their regional origins: *Cambray, Artois, Bourgoigne, St. Pol, Brabant,
Luxembourg*, etc. Some were give the names of classical heroes, such as *Jason*
and *Medea*, or of contemporary military leaders; for example, the French had
La Hire, Barbazin, and *Flavy*, while the English christened theirs *Bedford, Robin
Clement, Brisebarre*, and *Herr Johan*. Other bombards seem to have had feminine
names such as *Katherine, Griette*, and *La Petite Liete*. Some, however—such as
Prusse, Ath, Bergier, Bergière, Le Damp or *La plus du Monde*—are more enigmatic.
Pope Pius II named his gunpowder weapons after himself, *Enea* and *Silvia*, and
after his mother, *Vittoria*.[61] Bombards continued to be used through most of
the fifteenth century but then gradually disappear from the records. The reasons for this have often been attributed, by modern authors, to their large size
and the problems in transport. However, as will be seen below, by about 1475
there was a revolution in both gunpowder and cannon technology that seems
to have made them redundant.

From the 1420s, other types of gunpowder weapons are noted in accounts
and inventories. In the Burgundian sources, for example, *veuglaires* seem to
have been a shorter gun with a large bore, while *crappadeaux* and *serpentines* were
long and thin. This mirrors the development at the end of the fifteenth and the
beginning of the sixteenth centuries of the two classes of guns that went on to
dominate artillery in the subsequent three centuries: the cannon and the *cul-
verin*. The former was a shorter large-caliber weapon used for battering walls

and fortifications, while the latter was used for longer-range fire. Both fired iron shot and were, from the beginning of the sixteenth century, cast from bronze.[62]

Most cannon in the late Middle Ages had removable powder chambers to hold the gunpowder. The removable chamber fitted into the rear of the barrel and was held tightly in place by a wedge inserted between it and the wooden or iron stock, which acted as a mount. Having several chambers, either two or three, for each artillery piece, allowed for a rapid rate of fire. This innovation in gunmaking was known as early as 1342, when an account of a St. Omer bailiff lists gunpowder weapons with separate chambers at the castle of Rihoult in Artois. After this date, and indeed well into the sixteenth century, many cannon had separate, removable chambers.[63]

While gunpowder weapons themselves varied in weight, length, and caliber, and whether they had removable chambers or not, what went inside these weapons—projectiles and gunpowder—varied little until the last decades of the fifteenth century, when they underwent a very dramatic change. Gunpowder consists of three ingredients—saltpeter, sulfur, and charcoal—the best proportions being approximately 75% saltpeter, 10% sulfur, and 15% charcoal. In the past, historians and writers on artillery have tended to concentrate on the proportions of the three ingredients and the way in which they changed over the decades. However, modern analysis has shown that its composition is not the only important factor in the way that gunpowder behaves. The purity of the ingredients, the size of the grains of gunpowder used, and, especially, the degree to which the gunpowder was compacted within the gun barrel prior to firing are all equally as important.

For the first 50 years or so after their introduction at the beginning of the fourteenth century it seems that guns were, on the whole, relatively small. A possible reason for this was the scarcity of saltpeter to make gunpowder: it is likely that supplies had to be imported from the east, making it expensive. However, from about 1375 the technique to make saltpeter was mastered, prices fell considerably, and there was a marked increase in the size and quantity of guns thereafter.[64]

The purity of the saltpeter used to make gunpowder was (and is), of course, vital to the explosive power, and it appears that in the fourteenth and fifteenth centuries there was a considerable amount of "cheating" and adulteration. The number of tests that can be carried out to check its purity listed in the *Firework Book (Das Feuerwerkbuch)* surely attests to that.[65] Sometimes other, cheaper, substances, particularly common salt, were added to make the expensive saltpeter (potassium nitrate) go further.[66]

The size of the grain of the gunpowder mixture was also important. Gunpowder was made by grinding the three ingredients into a very fine powder, either individually or together, or, as was probably most often the case, first individually and then together. The result would certainly work but tended to be inconsistent and possibly not as powerful as when the powder was "corned." Corning was the process whereby the fine gunpowder mixture was wetted, with alcohol or water (brandy, vinegar, or the urine of a "wine-drinking man" are all mentioned in texts), and formed into small balls, i.e., corns, and then dried. This altered the characteristics of gunpowder in a number of ways. First, it seems to have made the mixture easier to ignite; second, it made it more consistent in its action; third, and most important, it probably made the gunpowder more powerful. What corns also do is slow down the rate of burning of gunpowder: instead of burning extremely quickly, producing all its propulsive force and exhaust gases fast, corned powder burned more slowly. As the powder burned, the pressure in the barrel increased and the ball started to move down the barrel, increasing the volume available for the gases produced by the explosion and thereby lessening the pressure these gases exerted on the walls of the barrel, making it less liable to burst. However, because it took a long time, in relation to the speed of the explosion, for the ball to travel down the barrel, the velocity of the ball coming out of the muzzle of the gun was little affected. Corning was introduced in the first two or three decades of the fifteenth century, but whether it was adopted everywhere at the same time is difficult to ascertain.[67]

However, the most important factor in the behavior of gunpowder may be the degree of compaction, meaning just how tightly the powder is confined prior to being fired. Loosely confined gunpowder burns relatively slowly—indeed, an open pile of powder burns with a whoosh rather than a bang—while if the powder is "stoppered," like a wine bottle, it burns much faster and more intensely.[68]

The projectiles fired by gunpowder weapons changed somewhat during the fourteenth and fifteenth centuries. In the early period cannon balls of stone and the cannon arrow or bolt, the *garro*, shown in the early illustrations, were used in cannon. Arrows were used, perhaps, because that was the traditional ammunition of the longbow and crossbow, and would continue to be used for a few decades, although, by the end of the fourteenth century, they had disappeared. Stone balls remained the main ammunition for cannon throughout the fifteenth and sixteenth centuries. The first reference to the use of metal, possibly wrought iron, cannonballs was in 1325–26, but they do not seem to have been frequently used until the early fifteenth century when references to cast-iron shot as ammunition appear frequently, although not in large quantities. Lead balls were used for the smaller gunpowder weapons, including handguns.[69]

There was a significant change in artillery in the last decades of the fifteenth century. Cannon barrels underwent a change in the 1470s, or thereabouts, from parallel-sided large-caliber barrels with a smaller-diameter powder chamber to barrels that were much smaller in diameter, with smaller caliber, and a taper from rear to front. At much the same time there was a rise in the use of cast-iron ammunition. These changes were related to a change in casting technology. Earlier, bronze cannon were cast with the muzzle of the gun down and the breech uppermost; in the 1470s this changed so that cannon were cast muzzle up and the breech down. This was significant because when pouring the molten metal the best casting was at the bottom of the mold and the worst, full of air holes and impurities, at the top. This change to muzzle-up casting, with the important addition of an extension of the mold, the gun head, in which the impurities and flaws could collect and then be removed from the casting, meant that cannon were now able to withstand a much greater explosive force. The result was that the amount of gunpowder, in proportion to the weight of the cast-iron cannonball, increased significantly, as did the velocity of the ball leaving the barrel. The increase of both velocity and ball weight—cast iron is roughly three times heavier than stone—meant that as much damage could be inflicted with smaller cannon firing iron balls as with the large bombards firing huge stone balls at much lower velocity.[70]

There is also some evidence for the existence of incendiary cannonballs in the fourteenth and fifteenth centuries. They are recorded to have been at the sieges of Breteuil in 1356, Oudenaarde in 1379, and both Beaulieu and Dinant in 1465.[71] They are also in the French armory inventory of the Bastille in 1428.[72] The incendiary mixture in these cannonballs was probably based on gunpowder and not Greek Fire and would no doubt have caused much havoc when used against towns and ships. Yet exploding cannonballs, or shells, while intriguing several late medieval engineers,[73] are never mentioned in fourteenth- and fifteenth-century narratives, not appearing regularly until the beginning of the sixteenth century. Interestingly, though, in May 1475 at the siege of Neuss, a cannonball appears to have been used in a very unusual manner, as a messenger to the besieged inhabitants delivering letters reporting that a German relief army was on its way.[74]

In the fourteenth and the first half of the fifteenth centuries, gunpowder artillery was transported to the site of a siege or battle on carts. Large pieces, the bombards were, when possible, transported by water. The guns were then placed on mounts either transported with the guns or constructed on site by carpenters who always accompanied artillery trains.[75] By the middle of the fifteenth century, however, this had changed. Cannon were mounted permanently on wheeled carriages that sometimes also carried their ammunition and gunpowder, although these could also be carried separately. Protection for the gunners while operating the guns—mantles, shields, and palisades—were also taken to the site of the battle or siege, although again they could be constructed on site as needed.[76]

Even with these improvements, the easy movement of guns to and on the battlefield or at a siege was not fully achieved until the middle of the fifteenth century. Until then, the strategic and tactical agility of these weapons was not fully realized. Sometimes gunpowder weapons, despite their wheeled carriages, were too heavy to transport across existing bridges and roads. Such was the situation in 1411, when the large bombard *Griette* fell through a bridge in Flanders and landed in the ditch below, and in 1436 at Châtillon in Burgundy, when the passage of heavy cannon en route to the siege of Calais badly damaged a bridge on the main road.[77] At other times, again despite their wheeled carriages, cannon were unable to maneuver on the battlefield. At the siege of Neuss, on May 23, 1475, the Burgundians under Charles the Bold were able to pass around the German artillery set up along the river Rhine because of its inability to quickly change its direction.[78]

Bombards and other large gunpowder weapons were mounted alone, but small and medium-sized cannon were frequently mounted together as a battery of artillery on the same carriage. Artillery batteries as large as five guns were known, and sometimes two different types of gunpowder weapons were mounted on the same carriage.[79] The mount also set the aim of a cannon. This could be accomplished in a number of ways: first, by placing a fixed mount on terrain angled to provide the correct aim; second, by mounting the cannon on a fixed axle to provide its aim; third, by using the terrain and axle together to aim the weapon; fourth, by using a wall or rock under the carriage to move the aiming angle; and fifth, by adding a calibrated aiming device to the mount to change the aiming angle.[80] Although these methods seem simple in comparison with modern techniques, medieval gunners were adept at the aiming of their weapons. Philippe de Commynes reports an incident in 1465 near Paris which shows that sometimes they were able to shoot great distances with accuracy: "The king [Charles VII] had a train of artillery mounted on the walls of Paris, and they fired several shots which reached as far as our [the Burgundian] army;

this is no small distance, for it consists of two leagues; but I believe that their muzzles were raised very high."[81] And when Ottoman Sultan Mehmed II, "the Conqueror (I)" who besieged and captured Constantinople in 1453, found that ships fighting at the entrance of the city's harbor were outside of the range of his cannon on shore he sought to reach those distances. Kritovoulos, the Sultan's contemporary biographer, describes what Mehmed did:

> He then showed [his cannon makers] another way of doing this by a new form of cannon. For, he said, if they were willing, it was possible to construct a different sort of gun with a slightly changed design that could fire the stone to a great height, so that when it came down it would hit the ships amidships and sink them. He said that they must first aim it and level it, getting the measures by mathematical calculation and then fire on the ships. Thus he explained his plan.

These artisans responded by constructing a cannon and "leveling it by special design" so that it "shot the stone up to a great height." The first shot fired missed, but the second shot struck a ship "in the center," sinking it. Seeing this other vessels fighting for the Byzantines withdrew, never to return.[82]

SOCIETAL IMPACTS AND ADMINISTRATIVE CHANGES

The invention of gunpowder weapons had an impact not only on warfare, but on society and the state as well. Most knights, nobles, and princes seem not to have welcomed the introduction of gunpowder weapons. Traditional medieval warfare respected their social status, leading frequently to ransom rather than death following capture. But gunpowder weapons had no such respect for class, and nobles risked death as much from gunshot as did non-noble soldiers. Eventually, they too began to be wounded and killed by cannonball: in 1383, at the siege of Ypres, Louis Lin, described by a contemporary as a "very brave English esquire," was killed by a cannon shot; in 1414, the Bastard of Bourbon was killed by gunshot at Soisson; in 1428, Thomas Montagu, Earl of Salisbury and leader of the English forces in France, was killed at Orléans when a stone cannonball fired from a bombard shattered a metal windowsill that fatally struck him in the face; in 1438, Don Pedro, the brother of the King of Castile, was decapitated by a cannonball during the siege of Capuana; four years later, in 1442, John Payntour, an English squire, was killed by a *coulovrine* shot at La Reole; in 1450, two prominent French military leaders, Pregent de Coëtivy, Lord of Rais and Admiral of France, and Tudal le Bourgeois, Bailiff of Troyes, were killed at the siege of Cherbourg; in 1453, two more prominent individuals lost their lives by gunshot: John Talbot, Earl of Shrewsbury, was killed at the battle of Castillon in July, and Jacques de Lalaing, called "le bon chevalier" in a contemporary chronicle, was killed that same month at the siege of Poeke; and in 1460, King James II of Scotland died when one of his large cannon exploded next to him.[83] These deaths did not, however, keep nobles from using the weapons, and by the end of the fifteenth century, nearly every military leader, no matter his status, had introduced gunpowder weapons into his armies.[84] One, Jean Bureau, who was not a noble but had served for many years as King Charles VII's Master of Artillery, commanded the French army at the battle of Castillon in 1453, the final battle in the Hundred Years' War, which was won, perhaps unsurprisingly given its leader, using a large number of gunpowder weapons.[85]

At first, common soldiers too were reluctant to accept these weapons. Their sounds were thunderous, and the ground shook when they fired. Such weapons could not have come from God, despite a tradition which developed that they were invented by a German monk named Berthold Schwarz.[86] John of Mirfield, an English surgeon in the late fourteenth century, described guns as "that diabolic instrument of war," and the title page of a 1489 Basel edition of St. Augustine's *De civitate dei* (*The City of God*) shows two towns, one guarded by angels and the other by devils, one of the latter armed with a gun.[87]

However, this was not the image of gunpowder weapons generally held by the Catholic Church. The same church that had banned the use of the crossbow at the Second Ecumenical Lateran Council in 1139 did not seem to hold a similar dislike for guns, especially since it became apparent even before the beginning of the fifteenth century that the Ottoman Turks showed no hesitation in using them against Christian armies. If the Islamic God had given guns to His people, the Christian God would also want His people to defend themselves with the same powerful weapons.[88] Indeed, in Christian Europe, gunpowder weapons were seen to provide justice. A bombard made in 1404 for Sigismund of Austria was so inscribed: "I am Katerine. Beware of what I hold. I punish injustice."[89] And Pope Pius II was so impressed by the weapons that not only did he encourage the rulers of Europe to acquire guns, but he even possessed his own.[90] Early in the history of gunpowder weapons the Church also furnished gunners with their own patron saint, Saint Barbara. She was a fitting patron for those who operated gunpowder artillery, for at her martyrdom, her father, who had denounced her Christianity, was struck down by a clap of thunder and a lightning bolt. Icons of Saint Barbara were painted on guns, and her name was invoked by gunners in battle, as they believed that she would protect them from death.[91]

Kings and princes quickly became interested in the use and procurement of gunpowder weapons. Edward III of England (1328–77) may have been the first sovereign to see the future uses of guns, as he stockpiled a small number of the relatively new weapons at the Tower of London and used them both at the battle of Crécy and at the siege of Calais, as well as other conflicts.[92] Similarly, the dukes of Burgundy, Philip the Bold (1363–1404), John the Fearless (1404–19), Philip the Good (1419–67), and Charles the Bold (1467–77), took a great interest in artillery and gunpowder. They amassed large quantities of gunpowder weapons and used them on almost all of their many military expeditions. They also refused to allow their gunpowder technology to remain stagnant and experimented with sizes of weapons, methods of manufacture, modes of transportation, metallurgy, and powder chemistry.[93]

It was during the reign of these dukes that gunpowder and artillery became an official part of their military organization. Philip the Bold supervised the construction and testing of guns, and he organized their use in war under the leadership of a Ducal Cannoneer.[94] John the Fearless further increased the number and quality of the Burgundian gunpowder weapons, appointing Germain de Givery as the first Ducal Master of Artillery, ordering him to bring all the gunpowder weapons of the duchy "which were not actually in use in his castles" together at a special arsenal in Dijon, the duchy's capital. During John's reign gunners were even given separate uniforms, including a blue hat, for use in ducal processions.[95]

Philip the Good continued the artillery program of his father and grandfather and added many more gunpowder weapons to the Burgundian artillery stores. Philip fought against the French, English, and Germans, and he was also involved in putting down several insurrections in his ducal holdings, principally in the southern Low Countries. In all of these campaigns he used his large and elaborate artillery train. He also recognized the threat of an enemy's artillery and is reported to have kept a spy in England solely for the purpose of assessing the strength of the English gunpowder artillery holdings.[96]

However, Philip's son, Charles the Bold, possessed none of the military or diplomatic skills of his forebears, nor was he able to successfully add on to the lands he inherited. He was, however, interested in continuing the now traditional Burgundian gunpowder artillery plan. Charles even imported a particularly experienced cannoneer from Nuremburg, known as Master Hans, paying the gunner's wife to watch his children during his absence (October–November 1467). But Charles's enemies, the Germans, Swiss, French, and Lorrainers, had also increased their artillery holdings, equaling the quality if not completely the quantity of the Burgundian gunpowder weapons. Eventually they were able, using these weapons as part of their tactics, to defeat the Burgundian forces and to end Burgundian power.[97]

The French under Charles VII (1422–61) also established a "modern" artillery train. Charles increased the royal budget to obtain ever larger numbers of new guns, and he increased taxes to pay for it. He also took a special interest in the construction of new, and often unworkable, inventions related to his gunpowder weapons. An example of this is recorded in 1449/50 when Charles requested the design of a new carriage for his artillery, the object of which "was to create a gun-carriage which was not drawn by horses...."[98]

But perhaps the most important feature of Charles VII's gunpowder artillery train was its intricate organization and superior leadership. Under his Masters of Artillery, Jean and Gaspard Bureau, French guns grew in number and efficiency. The duties of gunners were established, officers were appointed, competency was improved, and pay increased. This allowed Charles to take his artillery on nearly every military expedition, and its use contributed to the eventual French victory over the English in the Hundred Years' War.[99] Moreover, after Charles VII's death, the French artillery holdings were enlarged by both Louis XI and Charles VIII, the latter using it to invade and easily conquer Italy in 1494.[100]

By the end of the fifteenth century and the beginning of the early modern era, gunpowder weaponry had become a feature of everyday life. Guns had become so conventional that they began to be used in celebrations, in fashion, and in crime. Ultimately, guns even became virility symbols.[101] A musical instrument took the name "bombard" because of its shape and sound, both of which resembled the gunpowder weapon of that name. Engineers became interested in guns and designed new ones.[102] And new surgical techniques were developed to heal the new wounds created by gunshot.[103]

Perhaps no other weapon in the history of man has had the impact of gunpowder weapons. Even before the end of the sixteenth century Francis Bacon recognized them as one of the three inventions that had changed the medieval into the modern world—the other two being the compass and the printing press. From their meager beginnings in the fourteenth century, gunpowder weapons developed to affect every aspect of warfare, from battles to campaigns, from fortifications to ships, and from armor to the longbow.

Notes

1. Needham (1986): 67–69 and Gwei-Djen, Needham, and Chi-Hsing (1988).
2. Needham (1986): 276–341 and Smith (2010): 81–84.
3. A number of ways have been suggested—see Smith (2010): 88–90 for a brief discussion of the probable routes.
4. Bacon (1912): 51; as translated in Partington (1960): 77–78.
5. Partington (1960): 42–81; Needham (1986): 39–50; and DeVries (1996a): 123–25.
6. Contamine (1984): 139; Partington (1960): 97–98; and Clephan (1911): 55–56.
7. Contamine (1984): 139; Clephan (1911): 56–57; Partington (1960): 100; and Carman (1955): 18–19.
8. James (1913): 140. See also Nicolle (1988): #976; Contamine (1984): 139; Needham (1986): Figure 82; Clephan (1911): 57; Partington (1960): 98–100; and Carman (1955): 17–18.
9. James (1913): 181. See also Needham (1986): Figure 83. A debate on the historical validity of these illustrations has recently appeared in successive *Journal of Ordnance Society* issues. See DeVries (2003); Blair (2004); and Tittman (2005).
10. On the disputed reports of cannon at Crécy see Burne (1955): 192–202.
11. McNeill (1982): 80.
12. Vale (1975): 59.
13. Froissart (1888): 249. See also Smith and DeVries (2005): 13–14.
14. Froissart (1888): 196–201. See also Smith and DeVries (2005): 59–62.
15. Smith and DeVries (2005): 80–81 and Vaughan (1966): 150–51.
16. Burne (1956): 42–46.
17. Garnier (1895): 98–99 and Smith and DeVries (2005): 106
18. de Commynes (1969): 149 and Smith and DeVries (2005): 152–54.
19. Smith and DeVries (2005): 154–56 and Vaughan (1970): 397.
20. Contamine (1984): 200–201. On the sieges of Maastricht, Lagny, and Dinant see Smith and DeVries (2005): 76, 79, 106, 152–56; and on the 1480 siege of Rhodes see Smith and DeVries (2011).
21. Vale (1981): 138.
22. *Livre des trahisons* (1873): 96. See also Smith and DeVries (2005): 79–80.
23. Burne (1956): 126–27; Newhall (1924): 71–72, 92–97; and Jacob (1947): 129–30.
24. DeVries (1999a): 113–14.
25. de Commynes (1969): 236.
26. DeVries (2005b, 2009).

27. Vaughan (1970): 34 and Smith and DeVries (2005): 130–33.

28. DeVries (1998b), with quotation on p. 300. See also Smith and DeVries (2005): 60–62.

29. Contamine (1984): 199.

30. Vale (1975): 64 (author's translation).

31. Burne (1956): 235, 319, 333–41; Goodman (1981): 28, 30, 47, 93, 121; Vaughan (1966: 60; 1970: 26, 328–30, 385; 1973: 20–22, 223, 376–77, 387–88, 423–24); Smith and DeVries (2005): 76–78, 91–93, 105, 132–34, 142–46, 158–61, 188, 201; DeVries (2001b); and *Livre des trahisons* (1873): 169–70.

32. "Lettre" (1846–47): 246 (translation ours).

33. Contamine (1984): 199 and Smith and DeVries (2005): 76–78.

34. Vaughan (1970): 387–89.

35. As quoted in Contamine (1984): 199. See also Gaier (1968), 345–46 and Smith and DeVries (2005): 158–61.

36. Smith and DeVries (2005): 188–92.

37. Brusten (1953): 108.

38. Gille (1966): 61 and Fino (1974): 24.

39. Krenn (1989) and Krenn, Kalaus, and Hall (1995).

40. Vaughan (1970): 361; Smith and DeVries (2005): 122–24; and DeVries (2004).

41. As quoted in Vaughan (1973): 322–23. On the siege of Neuss see Smith and DeVries (2005): 174–89 and the articles in Neuss (1975).

42. Deuchler (1963): 302–3 and Smith and DeVries (2005): 188–201.

43. DeVries (1990a: 818–21; 1998a: 390).

44. DeVries (1990a: 821–22; 1998a: 390–91).

45. Christine de Pisan (1932): 182. See also DeVries (1998a): 391.

46. DeVries (1990a, 1998); Smith and DeVries (2005): 259–60; 343–44.

47. DeVries (1998a): 393 and Lane (1973): 155.

48. Sicking (2010).

49. Smith (1999).

50. Cipolla (1965): 24–25 and Smith and DeVries (2005): 239–40.

51. Gaier (1973): 195–99.

52. Smith (2000) and Smith and DeVries (2005): 238–39.

53. Awty (2003): 19–27

54. Smith and DeVries (2005): 240–41.

55. Smith (2000).

56. Smith and DeVries (2005): 204–36.

57. Sommé (1991).

58. Smith and Brown (1989) and Smith and DeVries (2005): 204–11.

59. N. Hall (1998).

60. *Religieux de Saint-Denis*: IV:652 (translation ours).

61. Vale (1981): 145.

62. Smith and DeVries (2005): 214–36.

63. DeVries and Smith (2006).

64. B. Hall (1997): 58–59.

65. Kramer (2001).

66. Smith (2010): 61–62.

67. B. Hall (1997): 69–77 and Smith (2010): 65–69.

68. Smith (2010): 69–70.

69. Smith and DeVries (2005): 248–54.

70. The importance of this is shown by the equation $E = \frac{1}{2}mv^2$, where E is the energy of the ball, m is its mass and v its velocity. Increasing the mass is important, but increasing the velocity is far more important, as the energy, E, rises by the velocity squared. Increasing the amount of powder increased the velocity, making these new cannon very effective weapons. See Smith (2010): 111–12.

71. Fino (1974): 26; Vaughan (1962): 70; and Brusten (1953): 113.

72. [Inventaire] (1855): 333.

73. See, for example, Kyeser (1967): f.110v.

74. Vaughan (1973): 330–31; Smith and DeVries (2005): 179; and Kuphal (1957).

75. Smith and DeVries (2005): 256–58.

76. Brusten (1953): 109 and Gaier (1973): 200.

77. Vaughan (1970): 79.

78. Vaughan (11973): 200–201.

79. Garnier (1895): 129.

80. Brusten (1953): 110 and Smith and DeVries (2005): 258–59.

81. de Commynes (1969): I:133.

82. DeVries (1996b): 360, quoting Kritovoulos (1954).

83. DeVries (1991): 131–46. See also Contamine (1984): 206 and Vale (1981): 136–37.

84. Hale (1966): 123–24.

85. Dubled (1976) and "Lettre" (1846–47).

86. Tittmann (1983).

87. Contamine (1984): 138 and Hale (1966): 18–19.

88. Hale (1966): 125–26.

89. Hale (1966): 117.

90. Vale (1981): 145.

91. Hale (1966): 126; de Lombares (1984): 29–30; and Cipolla (1965): 23.

92. DeVries (1998c): 139–40.

93. DeVries (1998c): 133–39 and Smith and DeVries (2005).

94. Smith and DeVries (2005): 55–70.

95. Smith and DeVries (2005): 71–84; Vaughan (1966): 151, 168; and Brusten (1953): 108.

96. Smith and DeVries (2005): 85–136 and Thielmans (1966): 71.

97. Smith and DeVries (2005): 137–202 and Vaughan (1973): 16.

98. Vale (1974): 127, 141.

99. Dubled (1976) and Contamine (1972): 230, 238–39, 311–17, 534.

100. Pepper (1995).

101. Hale (1966): 131–33 and Contamine (1984): 206–7.

102. See Gille (1966).

103. DeVries (1991).

CHAPTER 6

SIEGE
MACHINES

ATTACKING THE WALLS OF A FORTIFICATION BY ARTILLERY UNTIL A BREACH
was made was not the only means of entering a medieval fortification. Even
if a besieged site did not surrender from starvation or treachery, or if the
besieger did not have artillery sufficient or strong enough to breach the walls
or to frighten the inhabitants into submission, a fortification might still be
taken by other forceful means. These generally included a wide variety of siege
machines. Ladders, mining, battering rams, and siege towers were all used during the Middle Ages to capture castles and fortified towns. Indeed, contemporary sources indicate that their use was far more widespread and enduring than
either non-gunpowder or gunpowder artillery during the pre-modern period.

Unfortunately for the study of non-artillery siege machines in the Middle
Ages, the number of technological sources is meager. Surprisingly, both written and artistic sources are far less numerous in the medieval period than they
are in either the ancient or early modern periods. Why this is the case is not
known. Clearly, siege warfare held the same importance for medieval military
leaders, especially those who were forced to endure the desperation and depri-
vation of one of the extremely large number of sieges that were fought between
the end of the fourth and beginning of the sixteenth centuries. Siege warfare,
then, as it had been in the ancient world and would be in the early modern, was
the most prominent form of armed conflict and, it should also be pointed out,

the most fruitful.[1] Battles, again like their ancient predecessors and early modern descendants, always interest modern historians more, no doubt because of their action, but they rarely decided anything. For every battle of Hastings (1066) fought, where Anglo-Saxon England became in an afternoon Anglo-Norman England, or the battle of Bouvines (1214), which cemented the loss of English lands in northern and central France, changed the imperial leadership of the Holy Roman Empire, and quelled the desire for sovereignty in several Low Countries principalities, or battle of Castillon (1453), which ultimately led to the English losing the Hundred Years' War, and almost all of their French holdings, there were at least ten battles which, whether one side was victorious or not, decided nothing. Even what appeared to be major victories at the time—for example, the battles of Legnano (1176), where northern Italians led by Milan defeated the forces of Emperor Frederick Barbarossa; Courtrai (1203), where the Flemings defeated the French army of King Philip IV (the Fair); Bannockburn (1314), where the Scots defeated the English army of Edward II; Crécy (1346); Poitiers (1356); and even Agincourt (1415), where the English defeated the French armies of Philip VI, Jean II, and Charles VI— meant very little in the longer term: by 1185 the northern Italians were back under German control, by 1204 the Flemings were back under French control, by 1347 the Scots were back under English control, and by 1453 the English had lost almost all they acquired during the Hundred Years' War and earlier, except Calais, despite all those victories on the battlefield.[2]

But sieges often did change the landscape and determine at least the fate of the besieged town or castle. It is Calais that serves as a good example of what could be an endless list. After his victory at the battle of Crécy, Edward III sought to take advantage of a defeated, leaderless, and demoralized French army by advancing on the port town, one that he felt could serve both as a beachhead for further military conquests into northern France and as a safe place to send his wool exports for European trading, and thereby avoid paying the exorbitant import duties charged by the Flemings, Brabantese, and Dutch. He judged Calais to be the best location for this, so, marching immediately there from Crécy, he laid siege to the town. Despite the state of the French army, his victory there was far from assured. The same king had followed his victory at the naval battle of Sluys in 1340 with a siege of Tournai that had turned out to be a military fiasco with dire results: the bankrupting of his kingdom, the widening of the division between himself and his Parliament, and the severing of all his alliances with leaders of the Low Countries (the duke of Brabant, the count of Hainault and Holland, and the governor of Flanders) and the Holy

Roman Emperor.³ No doubt there was a great deal of worry when a French relief force, led by the French king, showed up midway through the siege. But Philip VI chose not to attack, which one might suggest was understandable after his loss at Crécy only months before, although the immediate reason for his departure without at least trying to raise the siege is not provided by the sources; after his withdrawal to Paris, and just under a year after the siege had begun, in 1347, Calais fell.⁴ It would stay in English hands until 1558, weathering the loss of the Hundred Years' War and the English civil war that followed, known as the Wars of the Roses, which destroyed much of the English military potential and ended two dynasties, the Lancastrian and Yorkist, descendants of that same Edward III who had initially taken the city. Only with Mary on the throne, and following numerous losses by the English to the French in the mid-sixteenth century was Calais lost, a defeat for which Mary was to have said, allegedly, on her deathbed that the word Calais "would be found written on my heart."⁵ An even more decisive example might be Constantinople, which after its 1453 defeat by the Ottoman Turkish army under Sultan Mehmed II "the Conqueror" never again fell back into European or Christian hands.⁶

So what military technologies, other than artillery, assisted in the sieges and conquests of medieval fortifications?

LADDERS

There is little question that the first "siege machine," in its broadest definition, was a simple ladder. Its use extends back to the earliest attempts to climb the walls of a fortification, i.e., to the Bronze if not the Stone Age, and forward well into relatively modern times, at least to the Napoleonic and American Civil Wars. Made at the very beginning pretty much as it has been made for the many centuries since, the ladder consisted of two vertical pieces of wood—their length varying depending on the height of the wall that had to be ascended, and when leaned against that wall preferably measured at least half a meter above it—between which a number of horizontal pieces of wood are attached, determined by the height of the vertical pieces of wood, and spaced no less apart than the distance between the knee and foot when the leg is bent. While correct height may seem to be an obvious statement, the ancient Roman writer Polybius felt the need to mention it twice in his writings, while the late Roman Vegetius also emphasized the point, recommending two methods of determining the height of a wall: fastening a string to an arrow to be shot over the wall or measuring the length of the wall from the shadow it cast at sunrise or sunset. Both, of course, have their obvious problems, namely the variable distance over the wall an arrow might fall and the fact that the besieged wall might not face either south or north and therefore not cast a shadow that could be correctly measured. Still, the fact that Vegetius gave these directions clearly shows that it was a problem that needed solving.[7] So it was for the English besiegers of Boulogne in 1351, when they were forced to raise their siege when their ladders proved to be too short to give them access to the top of the town walls.[8]

The type and quality of the wood varied depending on what was available nearby, although later in the Middle Ages ladders were often made at a central, and well stocked, location in the homeland of the besieger and brought to the siege. As long as the wood, and the bindings that secured the pieces together, could hold the weight of the man (or men) ascending it, what kind and how good the wood was made little difference. Rope could also be used for scaling ladders, but this was infrequent.[9]

Ladders are frequently seen in ancient artistic depictions of sieges, thus clearly showing the frequency with which they were used. They also appear in numerous depictions of siege warfare during the Middle Ages, although comparatively fewer than in ancient depictions. They are not often mentioned in accounts of the various medieval sieges, but this absence should not be taken as proof that ladders were not widely used in medieval sieges. In fact, this lack of proof can just as easily be seen as evidence that ladders were so common that they needed no mention—that only when there was something "out of the ordinary" did ladders seem to catch the attention of medieval writers. That the ladders were too short to use at the English siege of Boulogne mentioned above is a perfect example of the unusual meriting comment. But there are many more, such as the mention by William of Tyre of Bohemond's ladder at the siege of Antioch in 1097–98, described because of its features, which were clearly different from other, simpler ladders: it was made of hemp rope with hooks at both ends, to secure the ladder both to the top of the wall and to the ground.[10] At Jerusalem in 1099, military leaders of the First Crusade had one ladder built for every two soldiers, although as one of their difficulties was a lack of wood in the surrounding countryside it is hard to know how this was accomplished.[11] At the siege of Llanstephen, in 1146, one of the ladders of King Stephen's English attackers was pushed away, which forced those on it to fall into the moat.[12] At the siege of Tortona, in 1155, one of Frederick

ARTILLERY

Barbarossa's soldiers did not have a ladder, but he nevertheless climbed the wall using notches cut into it by an axe (his climbing speed was no doubt affected by this).[13] At the siege of Constantinople, in 1204, the Venetians were quite adept at using rope ladders to climb from their ships to the top of the seaward walls.[14] At the siege of Pontorson, in 1361, a ladder was pushed away from the walls by French military hero Bertrand Guesclin's sister, Julienne, a nun.[15] At the siege of Smyrna, in 1415, the chronicler Ducas reports that his grandfather was climbing up a ladder when he paused to take off his helmet, presumably to catch his breath, only to be hit at that moment between the eyes by a crossbow bolt fired from above.[16] At the siege of Constantinople in 1453, more than 2,000 ladders were made ready for the Turkish troops to assault the powerful walls, although whether they were used to reach the breach made by Mehmed's gunpowder artillery is not mentioned.[17]

Then there are the exploits of Boucicault, a French marshal at the end of the fourteenth and beginning of the fifteenth century. His anonymous biographer recounts that, in demonstrating his prowess and strength, even while wearing armor, after performing a somersault (although without his *bascinet*, which might have fallen off), dancing, leaping onto his horse without using the stirrups, jumping from the ground onto a "strong man's shoulders mounted on a horse," leaping over a horse, grabbing the saddle pommel and the horses neck below its ears, and between two walls placed close enough to allow him to climb unaided to the top, Boucicault "ascended the underside of a great ladder placed against a wall to the top without using his feet, simply jumping with both hands from rung to rung and, then, taking off this coat, he did this with one hand until he was unable to ascend any higher."[18]

Sometimes modifications were made to the ladder, as in the case of Bohemond's at Antioch. One of the more interesting of these modifications was suggested by an anonymous Byzantine tactician (known, without much creativity, as the Anonymous Byzantine) around the tenth century. He describes a ladder mounted on wheels with a platform affixed to the top, obviously meant to bridge a gap between it and the wall. The rungs hung out past the sides with holes drilled into them so that a rope could be threaded through them, presumably to give more stability to the structure, and also attached to the platform, so that it could be lowered from the ground. The whole was also wide enough to let three to five men climb it at the same time, and it was covered in hides that could be wetted to keep it safe from fire. The Anonymous Byzantine does not say whether this contraption actually worked.[19]

SIEGE TOWERS

But ladders, even with their modifications, had one serious drawback in siege warfare: those climbing them were completely unprotected from attack from the walls above. The ideal, then, if possible, was to protect the soldiers using the ladders with some defensive cover. The result was the siege tower. Again, it is difficult to say exactly when the first siege tower was invented or used. Wall carvings of the Assyrians show them using towers, as well as towers and battering rams fitted together in the same structure. Alexander the Great's Greeks also used them in their sieges, as did the Carthaginians and Romans. Indeed, one of the best descriptions of a siege tower from any time is that given by Vitruvius in the first century BCE, who ascribes their invention to Polydus, a Thessalian, who made them for Alexander the Great, although the date of the Assyrian portrayals, ninth to seventh century BCE, places their invention several centuries earlier. Many ancient and medieval towers sometimes covered rams as well as ladders, but the purpose of both types was to protect the besiegers inside them.[20]

Both the Assyrian carvings and Vitruvius' description are of fairly elaborate siege towers. But the earliest recorded medieval siege towers were far less so, although they could be called "simple" only in comparison to ancient ones. The goal of the makers of siege towers was to protect the attackers from the defenders, and while that was far from an easy task, it also did not need to be as complicated as ancient military engineers had made it. Medieval siege towers appear always to be wheeled, have several levels, and to be protected from fire by hides, usually of oxen, which would absorb enough water essentially to be fireproof for, it was hoped, the short time it took for the tower to be put in place and the men inside or on the ground to climb it. That did not always happen, however, as will be seen.

Most of the chroniclers who describe siege towers—and chronicles are essentially the only sources—give additional details, especially if the towers were somewhat unusual. Abbo, with one of the earliest accounts of their use, at the siege of Paris in 885–886, reports that the towers built by the Vikings were roofed, made of oak, rode on 16 wheels, and covered with deerskins. Some towers covered rams, tipped with metal and handled with chains and ropes, and others ladders. Sixty men were assigned to their use, although Abbo reports, feeling some justice, that two of these Vikings were killed by catapults, thus suffering "the same fate they had prepared for us."[21] (The siege of Paris was not the earliest medieval use of siege towers, as they were used also by the Ostrogoths at Rome in 537 and the Avaro-Slavs at Thessaloniki in 597.[22])

They were also used by the late Carolingian king, Lothar, at the siege of Verdun in 985. The chronicler Richer reports that oak was again used for the construction, cut into beams. Four of these beams, measuring approximately 10 meters in length, were used for the base and many others for straight and traverse ties to strengthen it. Planks, also of oak, were laid between these. A smaller platform of similar construction was placed on top. There were a number of levels in the tower, with the lowest one holding a ram, which could be swung back and forth with ropes. The sides were covered not with hides but with iron, which might suggest a huge weight for the overall structure, far greater than its three wheels could carry. But Richer says that the tower was quite maneuverable and moved right to the walls of the town.[23]

Finally, James I of Aragon provides a very descriptive account of a tower built for his army during his conquest of the island of Majorca in 1229. He reports in his autobiography, written about 40 years after the conquest, that it was constructed with two supports on each side, with two beams to steady them. Platforms were built halfway up and on the top, from which slings and crossbowmen could shoot at the defenders. The tower was mounted on wheels, without a number specified, and was pushed along with poles. It was also covered with three layers of wooden hurdles; the roof had an added covering of earth. Apparently this tower had no hides for fire-proofing, or at least James does not mention them in his account, although the earth might have protected the roof from fire.[24]

Several other medieval accounts have equally detailed descriptions of the siege towers their authors saw or heard about. Their size seemed to especially impress those who saw them. Their height: the five-story tower at Tyre in 1124 or those at Acre in 1191, 40, 50, and 60 cubits high (although how large the author's "cubit" was is not indicated); and the seven-story tower at Damietta in 1218–19. Their breadth: the tower at Ma'arrat in 1098 had several knights standing on its top platform as it was pushed toward the wall, one, Everard the Huntsman, blowing a horn to announce their approach; the tower at Lisbon in 1147 had a priest preaching a sermon to the archers and crossbowmen on board and more than 100 other soldiers who pushed and protected it (perhaps this was why the tower only moved about 30 meters a day); and the French tower at Breteuil in 1356, which was said to have been capable of holding 200 men—specified as knights and squires—on each of its three stories (although the chronicler who reported the details of this machine, Froissart, was somewhat prone to exaggeration).

Also of great interest to chroniclers was how these siege towers were covered: the oxhides with the tails still attached mounted on top of an English tower at the siege of Lisbon in 1147, which, when wetted by water, the tails would distribute evenly around the vulnerable parts of the structure, as well as collision mats made of osiers that also covered its surface; the oxhides on a tower at the siege of Acre in 1191, which were soaked with vinegar and mud; the belfries covered with iron placed atop Frederick Barbarossa's towers during his numerous sieges of Italian cities in the twelfth century; the leather covering the tower of Breteuil in 1356; and the Ottoman towers at the siege of Constantinople in 1453, which were protected both inside and out by earth and by bullock and camel hides, and also inside and out of the turrets and barricades at their top, presumably to cushion them against the force of gunfire.[25]

Fire remained the best way to defend a fortification against siege towers. One of the two siege towers used by the Crusaders at Jerusalem in 1099 was burned to the ground, as was one of the two at Lisbon, although in both cases the other tower proved to be sufficient to capture the town. Stones and other missiles could be shot at them from trebuchets and *ballistae*, or dropped on them from towers above. The latter happened at Nicaea in 1097 and at Arsuf in 1102. The besieged inhabitants could also sortie out through sally ports or gates, attach hooks to the tower, and pull it back and forth, knocking men out of it, which sounds rather cinematic but actually happened at Verdun in 985. At other times, siege towers simply collapsed from the weakness of their manufacture, difficulty of terrain, or shoddy construction, such as at Montboyau in 1026, when Odo I's siege tower collapsed as it was being pushed to the wall of the fortification, to the delight of those being besieged, who quickly rushed out and set fire to the remains so that the wood could not be used to construct another machine.[26]

But for the attackers who wished to build and use a siege tower, there were more pressing logistical problems than the worry about its being successfully attacked. One was the acquisition of the large amount of good wood to build a tower. As most towers were built on-site, the wood had to be found or brought to the siege. The acquisition of wood was rarely an easy undertaking. Sometimes it had to be acquired a long distance away, because everything around it had been destroyed or previously used. At Jerusalem in 1099, for example, after the Crusaders had scavenged all around the nearby countryside to find wood, and had even dismantled houses to provide it, only to find that it was still insufficient for their construction plans, they were forced to transport it on the backs of camels and in wagons from more than 15 kilometers away, and then when even that did not work out, dismantled two ships that had brought them supplies, forcing the need to bring wood from even farther away. Ships were also dismantled at Tyre in 1124, where particularly the mast and rudders were useful for building the towers. In 1167 at Alexandria, Amaury I, king of Jerusalem, also used masts to build his tower. Some military leaders planned ahead of time, bringing the wood for their siege towers with them on the campaign. Richard the Lionheart did this for his siege of Acre in 1191, although Arab commentator Ibn al-Athir added the distance that the Third Crusaders—including even the king himself, evidently—had still to carry the wood, more than two kilometers, and this was done "not without perspiration." Louis IX (St. Louis) of France transported the wood for his towers over seven kilometers on more than 1,600 carts for his campaigns against English king Henry III in 1242. And Edward I, in 1303, had to transport his wood and hides first to Bothwell, where he constructed the towers, and then the completed towers to his siege of Stirling Castle, a distance of more than 50 kilometers.[27]

But these movement problems seem minor compared with the difficulties of actually pushing siege towers those final meters to the actual walls, especially as the defenders were trying to do whatever they could to keep them away. Lisbon's 30 meters a day seems awfully slow, but it was probably average for men who used poles, ropes, wheels, and their own strength to propel these heavy machines forward. James I of Aragon's engineers added grease both to the wheels of the towers on Majorca and to the tracks of wood they laid in front of them in an attempt to flatten the ground. The terrain was always an issue, for it was never the ideal, flat ground leading straight up to the walls. One of the towers at Jerusalem in 1099 fell into a ditch, and this happened also at Acre almost a century later, in 1191. At Laon in 986–987 and at Damietta in 1218–19, towers could not be pulled up the incline leading to the walls and were simply abandoned. And at Carlisle in 1318 the ground proved to be so marshy that the tower became bogged down and had to be hauled out.

If there was a moat surrounding the fortification, as there frequently was, it had to be filled in. Stones, trees, branches, sticks, earth—almost anything that could be used to fill in the moat would be used. At Jerusalem, the Crusader leaders offered a penny for every three stones thrown into the moat, and at Acre, a woman who was fatally injured while working to fill in the moat asked that her body also be thrown into it after she had finally died. At Pujol in 1343, even the knights, sergeants, and burgesses, who had come to the siege from allied towns, carried bundles of sticks on their backs to be thrown into the ditch. Only after the besieged at Troyes in 1429 saw that Joan of Arc's army had sufficient material to fill in the moats near their walls did they open their gates and surrender. The Byzantines in 1453, not offered the same option, held out even after the Turks had filled in and moved their towers across the moat in front of the walls outside of Constantinople. The same thing happened at Rhodes in 1522; although the citizens were initially able to keep up with the besiegers by removing at night the stones that had been placed in the moat during the day, eventually they simply could not continue doing so and the moat, 30–50 meters wide, was filled in. At Constantinople the city was then taken by force, while at Rhodes the Knights Hospitaller were granted a conditional surrender; in both the result was the same: the Ottoman Turks captured the city.[28]

The last few moments before a siege tower hit the walls must have been terrifying; however, with this massive construction slowly making its way forward until its platform was close enough to the walls to be lowered on top of them, the fear and anticipation of those inside the tower must have been equal to the fear and anticipation of those inside the fortification they were attacking. Some of this emotion can be seen in William of Tyre's account of the siege of Banyas in 1140:

> Soon an engine of great height towered aloft, from whose top the entire city could be surveyed. From this vantage point, arrows and missiles of every sort could be sent, while stones hurled by hand would also help to keep the defenders back. As soon as the tower was ready, the ground between it and the walls was leveled off and the machine was brought up to the ramparts. There, as it looked down upon the whole city, it seemed as if a tower had suddenly been erected in the midst of the place. Now for the first time the situation of the besieged became intolerable; they were driven to the last extremity, for it was impossible to devise any remedy against the downpour of stones and missiles which fell without intermission from the moveable tower.... The weapons and modes of assault used by those fighting below could be considered little or nothing in comparison with the manifold dangers to which they were exposed from the fighters in the tower. In fact, it seems to be rather a war with gods than with men.[29]

ARTILLERY

The soldiers fighting from the machines, and those defending the walls, are almost always nameless in the historical narratives, but their bravery in response to what must have been equal feelings of fear and anticipation cannot be doubted. More is known about the builders of these machines. At Nicaea in 1097, the engineer is merely described as a "Lombard specialist," but elsewhere names are given: King James I of Aragon had Nicoloso, Holy Roman Emperor Frederick II had Calamandrinus, and St. Louis had Jean de Mézos. The names of English engineers are almost always provided: Master Urric for King John; Master Bertram for Kings Henry III and Edward I; Master Richard, John de la Dolyve, Robert de Woodhouse, and Reginald also for Edward I. In fact, Master Bertram became so famous during his time that almost his entire career can be followed as he supervised the building of siege machines at virtually every English siege between 1276 and 1284 and, when not fighting, acquired the material for siege machines to be stored in the Tower of London.[30]

Master Bertram was well paid for his artisanal and organizational skills, and this, too, seems characteristic of those who could create military technologies that were well made and desired. For example, the engineers at the siege of Carcassonne in 1226 were paid a comparatively impressive 21 livres a day for their skills and service. But perhaps the greatest honor came to Jean de Mézos when he was knighted by St. Louis in 1254 for his achievements in siege technology.[31]

BATTERING RAMS AND MINING DEVICES

As mentioned, some siege towers included battering rams at their lowest level. As the soldiers climbed the ladders within the towers and went across the platforms and bridges between them and the walls, others were swinging away at the walls with a large battering ram below them. Battering rams seem to have been used at many sieges, especially when it, or a siege tower, could be placed against the gate. A wooden gate, no matter how thick, and even a portcullis were vulnerable, but regardless of its size a battering ram was unlikely to make much of a dent on stone walls that were two or three meters thick.

As with all other siege technologies, including non-gunpowder artillery, the battering ram originated in ancient times. In the ninth- to seventh-century BCE the Assyrians frequently depict battering rams in wall carvings celebrating their victorious sieges. So numerous and so clear are these carvings that the details of the rams they depict can be easily determined. They were wheeled battering rams covered with wicker mats so that they often looked like animals. The mats would be wetted to keep fire from burning the ram, while the wooden structure on which the mats were mounted kept missiles from hitting those operating the ram. It was a slow process to breach a wall or gate but, judging from the Assyrian successes, these battering rams were effective at doing so. In fact, they were so effective, and as they too appeared in the guise of animals, that some historians wonder if this is not the origin of the Trojan Horse myth—after all, the Trojan Horse led the Trojans to dismantle their gates and destroy the walls next to them so that they could bring it inside the city.[32] Vitruvius and Vegetius both give clear descriptions of a battering ram that would be used by the Romans in their conquests: a large tree suspended by ropes from a structure that was moved into position on rollers. Other ropes would then be used to swing the ram back and forth so that it could hit the door with an enormous amount of force. (Vegetius also describes how to defend against one.)[33]

Unfortunately, for the Middle Ages the only depiction is from the Anonymous Byzantine's illustrations,[34] and they are far from clear. Otherwise, only the use of rams is indicated in medieval sources. From these few citations it can be determined that Attila's Huns used battering rams against Orléans in 451; that the Sabirs surprised their Byzantine allies when they built rams at Petra in 550; that Merovingian Franks used some against Leudegisel in 585; that Anglo-Saxons invading England had them in 711; and that First Crusaders used them at Jerusalem and Tyre, Second Crusaders at Lisbon, Third Crusaders at Acre, and Albigensian Crusaders at Beaucaire.[35]

It is likely that these battering rams were simply large trees suspended from ropes or chains tied to some sort of a structure. At least that is the assumption. When details are indicated, as is the case with ladders (see above) they seem to point at the unusual, for example at Acre in 1191, where the battering ram end is encased in iron.[36] At other times, it is when there is an effective defense made against them, such as at Tyre in 1102, when the defenders were able to catch the head of the ram with hooks dangling from ropes and, lifting the ropes up, turn it over, or at Beaucaire in 1216, when the defenders also caught the head of the ram, this time with a rope noose, and pulled it over.[37]

However, the best defense was attack from above, by archery or the casting of stones and other heavy objects on people. (Boiling oil, while apparently loved by moviemakers, considering the number of times it is shown in films depicting medieval sieges, was not dumped on those attacking the walls, or at least there are no accounts of this happening in any medieval narratives.) Those operating the rams clearly had difficulty fighting off these attacks while their intent was to keep hitting the walls or gates over and over again at the same spot. So sometimes battering rams were also covered with roofs, fixed or mobile structures, which were sometimes called by the names of animals: cat, mouse, weasel or sow, although, strangely, not a tortoise, which was the animal most often used by the Romans to describe their similar machines.[38]

Roofed defenses were also often used to protect miners, or sappers, attempting to dig under the fortifications in an effort to weaken the foundation and thereby cause a collapse or breach in the wall above. Mining was, after all, perhaps the most frequent siege activity—it was always easier, it seems, to go under the walls rather than through or over them. In simple terms, miners would dig a large mine under a besieged fortification's wall, support that mine with wood, preferably green wood, and having dug directly under where the wall stood, "fire" the mine, meaning setting the wooden supports on fire, and retreat out of it. It would take some time for the wood inside the mine to burn, especially if it was green, so the miners had plenty of time to exit from it and to watch as it caved in, hoping that it would also bring the wall down above it.

Mining was probably the most ancient means of defeating a fortification. Archaeologists have shown that Jericho's fall in 1250 BCE came as a result of mining, a lot of mining, which sheds new light on the story in the Bible about Joshua's siege of the city (Joshua 6:1–27). Joshua had his people walk seven times around the city (perhaps to weaken the earth above the many mines they had dug), and then, with a blowing of rams' horns (perhaps to signal the firing of the mines), the walls came tumbling down (perhaps with the mines collapsing below the walls).[39] The Assyrians, Persians, Greeks, and Romans were all adept at mining fortifications, which assisted them in their numerous, and usually successful, conquests.[40]

There would be no end to a list of medieval sieges where mines were dug. It would probably be far easier, in fact, to list the sieges where mines were *not* dug, but even then the lack of mention in the sources might simply be because mining was so prevalent that it needed no mention. Of course, beyond the indication of mines being dug at a siege, little more is said about them by the chroniclers recording what happened. The tools miners used, assumed to be picks, shovels, spades, and so on, are likewise not mentioned in the sources, again no doubt because of their commonality.

What does get mentioned, however, is when roofed structures or other devices are used to protect the miners. These begin quite early in the Middle Ages, although not early enough to suggest a link to ancient precursors. But they do indicate how widely across Europe they were used. For example, the Vikings used fixed roofs to protect their miners at Chester in 918, which they later covered in hides when the defenders began to drop fire onto them. At Nicaea in 1097, a steep roofed structure, with a device inside that somehow attached itself to the wall, was made for the Crusaders by the "Lombard expert" mentioned above. At Lisbon in 1147, a roofed structure, called a "Welsh cat" by the English eyewitness who reports its use—a term that might not have been understood outside the British Isles—was attached to one of the siege towers, covered with osiers. At Toulouse in 1218 a very large "cat" was built out of wood, iron, and steel that was sufficient enough to protect not only miners, but also 400 soldiers and 150 archers. And at Lisbon in 1147 and Berwick in 1307, roofed structures referred to as "sows" protected miners.[41] At times, however, such elaborate machines did not need to be used to protect miners. At Rhodes in 1522, Suleyman the Magnificent merely placed planks of wood and doors over the mines to protect those inside; more often than not these performed their purpose adequately.[42]

Often mining was successful, but sometimes it was not. There were, of course, means of defeating the mining of a fortification. Most often this was done by countermining, i.e., digging a mine to try to connect with the besiegers' mines. When underground, miners were almost completely defenseless, so if the defenders of a city could reach their opponents' mines before they were fired, there was a good chance they could chase away the miners, fill in the mine under the wall, usually by caving it in up to the spot of vulnerability, or protect its supports from fire. This occurred at the siege of Tortona in 1155, where a countermine of the inhabitants of the besieged town reached Frederick Barbarossa's mine before any damage to the walls could be done. This allowed them to collapse what had already been dug, killing some of the imperial miners who were still inside.[43]

At the very end of the Middle Ages besiegers began to use gunpowder to fire their mines, perhaps the final example of one of the most ancient tactics being combined with one of the most "modern" technologies. Gunpowder removed the necessity of firing the mine by directly lighting the wood, which was always risky in case it burned too fast and collapsed the mine before those inside could escape, or failed to catch fire at all, leaving the mine, and therefore the wall, unaffected. By using gunpowder the process became more secure and safe. A fuse could be placed into the gunpowder by which a more exact time of firing could be determined. In addition, the percussive force of the gunpowder added to the natural effect of the collapse of the ground underneath the walls. It became much easier to breach even the largest of walls.[44]

Nowhere was the impact of the explosive mine better witnessed than at the 1522 siege of Rhodes. To take this city only one year after ascending to the Ottoman throne, a city that had eluded his great-grandfather, Mehmed the Conqueror, in 1480, Suleyman the Magnificent employed every means at his disposal. This included some of the largest and most powerful gunpowder artillery pieces the world had ever known, and an almost endless supply of men—Suleyman would confess to the Knights Hospitaller in granting them a conditional surrender that he had lost 103,000 men in his seven-month siege, and "would gladly lose another 103,000 to take the city." It also included, as almost every siege before had, mining. But at this siege Suleyman added gunpowder to his mines. As the Knights had added almost every new anti-gunpowder innovation to their fortifications since Mehmed's 1480 siege, as well as more than doubling the size of the moat and increasing the size of the width of the walls from roughly 1.4 meters to more than 7 meters, gunpowder was probably the only means that the Turks could have used to bring down the walls above a mine. Several breaches were successful, which ultimately prompted the Hospitallers to agree to a conditional surrender.[45]

Explosive mines did not always work, though. The gunpowder might not be placed where it could do the most damage, it might be too wet, or the venting, which was always needed in any mining endeavor, but especially with explosive mines, might be the wrong size or placed in the wrong position. At other times, as with any mining—or any military technology for that matter—the unexpected simply happened. Such was the case, as reported by one Hospitaller eyewitness, Jacques de Bourbon, with one mine that was exploded by the miners about midway through the siege and which, naturally, the Turks "thought would knock the wall down to the ground, but all the mine did was to leave the wall hanging over the enemies, which was more to their disadvantage than to our damage." While the mine did lift the wall, it left it leaning into the moat, so that it became dangerous to continue to hack at or mine it from below as the Turks had been doing. Suleyman chose not to risk the lives of his men and, as the wall was badly damaged by the explosion, he pulled them back and allowed his gunpowder artillery to fire at it for a few days. Bourbon concludes, "it was broken down and there was a way and an opening into the town."[46]

Notes

1. B. Bachrach (1994); Bradbury (1992); and Purton (2010a, 2010b).

2. While numerous sources for each of these battles can be listed, for a general, but very outdated, overview of medieval battles see Oman (1924) or, for a more popular account of several of the battles mentioned, see DeVries et al. (2006).

3. DeVries (1995a).

4. DeVries (1991).

5. This is ascribed to Mary by John Foxe, whose enthusiasm for a good phrase is well known, so it might, therefore, be considered suspect. See Marshall (1993): 142–43.

6. See Runciman (1965) and Crowley (2005) for the conquest, and Freely (1998) for its subsequent history.

7. Nossov (2005): 75–76.

8. Bradbury (1992): 275 and Nossov (2005): 75.

9. Bradbury (1992): 275–76.

10. Bradbury (1992): 275.

11. This again comes from William of Tyre, though, so it is not written by a contemporary of the siege. See Bradbury (1992): 275.

12. Bradbury (1992): 85, 276.

13. Bradbury (1992): 275.

14. Bradbury (1992): 276.

15. Contamine (1984): 242 and Bradbury (1992): 276.

16. Bradbury (1992): 276.

17. Bradbury (1992): 275.

18. Contamine (1984): 216–17.

19. Nossov (2005): 76–77.

20. Kern (1999): 46–73 and Bradbury (1992): 241.

21. Bradbury (1992): 242.

22. Nossov (2005): 106 and Vyronis (1981): 384.

23. Bradbury (1992): 242.

24. Bradbury (1992): 242–43.

25. Bradbury (1992): 243–49.

26. Bradbury (1992): 248.

27. Bradbury (1992): 244–247.

28. Bradbury (1992): 247–49; Contamine (1984): 102; DeVries (1999a): 130–32; and Smith and DeVries (2011): 95–122.

29. As quoted in Nossov (2005): 113.

30. Bradbury (1992): 245–46; Taylor (1989); and D. Bachrach (2006b).

31. Bradbury (1992): 245 and Nossov (2005): 97.

32. Kern (1999): 46–53.

33. Bradbury (1992): 274.

34. Nossov (2005): 94–95.

35. Bradbury (1992): 274–75 and Nossov (2005): 96.

36. Bradbury (1992): 274.

37. Bradbury (1992): 274–75 and, for Beaucaire, Sumption (1978): 186.

38. Bradbury (1992): 274–75.

39. Ferrill (1985): 28–30.

40. Anglim et al. (2002): 182–83, 217–20; and Bradbury (1992): 270.

41. Contamine (1984): 102–3 and Bradbury (1992): 271–72.

42. Smith and DeVries (2011): 110–11.

43. Bradbury (1992): 270.

44. Bury (1982).

45. Smith and DeVries (2011): 117–18.

46. As quoted in Smith and DeVries (2011).

PART III

Fortifications

MEDIEVAL MILITARY TECHNOLOGY SERVED NOT ONLY TO PROTECT (OR TO harm) the individual, but also to protect the masses. The desire to defend one's lands, family, and possessions may be an innate trait. Throughout history humans have defended themselves through aggression, flight, the protective strength of specialized members or castes whose function is to guard it, alliances or confederations—diplomacy—with their enemies, and the construction of fortifications.[1] As can be seen in the large number of their remains, the last of these, fortifications, have proven to be very effective. In fact, it is the number of early fortified sites that has convinced some anthropologists that Neolithic man was deeply involved in warfare, perhaps more than any other activity, and that warfare, or at least the defense against attack, may have been the reason for the foundation of most Neolithic villages, especially those built around the eastern Mediterranean between 8000 and 4000 BCE.[2]

The purpose of these early fortifications was to keep an enemy out of villages and homes. This usually meant that the builders had to choose a site that was in the first place geographically and physically difficult to reach and then increasing the defensibility of it with the addition of barriers made of earth, wood, stone, or brick. The size of these barriers was often impressive. For example, the fortifications of Jericho, built between 8350 and 7350 BCE, consisted of an earth and stone wall 3 meters thick, 4 or more meters high, and 700 meters long, surrounding an area of 10 acres. A large solid tower inside the wall was 10 meters in diameter and 8.5 meters high, with a stairway through the center and access through a door at the bottom. There may also have been other towers. This fortification protected a population estimated at 2,000, with 500 to 600 fighters capable of defending the walls with archery. That these walls provided substantial security for Jericho's inhabitants is evident from the fact that the town itself did not fall until 1250 BCE, more than 6,000 years after its walls were constructed.[3]

While it is difficult to compare most medieval fortifications to those of Jericho, the motives for building them were mostly the same. However, during much of the Middle Ages there was also an implicit contract made by nobles to protect the peasants living on and farming their lands, even if they were not living there themselves. When the nobles were unable to provide this protection, the medieval socio-economic system broke down.

The following chapters will discuss the history of medieval fortifications. They will determine where, why, and how they were built, and, ultimately, if warranted, how they were taken. For ease of study a chronological approach will be followed, with chapters devoted to early medieval fortifications, motte-and-bailey castles, stone castles, urban fortifications, and fortified residences.

However, before doing so it is important to note that one generalization of fortification study, "castellogie" as it is sometimes called, is not pertinent when discussing the Middle Ages. Historically during times of peace, fortifications have fallen into disuse and ruin, as they were deemed unnecessary. Yet, sometimes this "peace dividend" backfired on the civilizations who promoted it, as the weakened defenses allowed later attacking armies easy access to the land and people behind them. This has been given as an explanation for the fall of both the Old and Middle Kingdoms of Ancient Egypt, Sparta-controlled Ancient Greece, and perhaps even Troy, if one wishes to discount Virgil's romantic story of the Trojan Horse.[4] But for the Middle Ages, except for a brief period during and shortly after the reign of Charlemagne, there was simply not enough peace to allow civilization to neglect its fortifications. Consequently, a large number of fortifications still exist that are in marvelous condition, although they now serve more as tourist attractions than as protective deterrents against attacking forces.

Notes

1. Wright (1964): 27.
2. Ferrill (1985): 26–28.

3. Ferrill (1985): 28–30.

4. See Ferrill (1985): 44–53, 170–75 for discussions on the fortification problems of Egypt and Greece. See Wood (1985): 114–18 for a discussion of the destruction of Troy VIIa, believed by many historians and archaeologists to be the Troy of Homeric legend. See Virgil (2006): 26–34.

CHAPTER 7

EARLY
MEDIEVAL
FORTIFICATIONS

LATE ROMAN AND BARBARIAN

ALTHOUGH IT WAS THE ARMY THAT BUILT THE ROMAN EMPIRE, CONTINUED peace and stability depended on its defenses. This was a fact well understood by Rome's leaders, and perhaps no other civilization has ever devoted so much effort or money to the construction and upkeep of its defenses. By the time of Emperor Hadrian (117–28 CE) the very extensive Roman Empire was nearly surrounded by fortifications. Stone fortifications comprising Hadrian's Wall divided the Roman-controlled province of Britannia from Pict-controlled Scotland. In Germany, between the natural boundaries of the Rhine and Danube Rivers, lay a series of trenches and wooden palisades that separated the empire from a number of barbarian tribes, generically called the Germans by contemporary Roman historians. Between the Danube and the Black Sea a stone wall was built, also to keep out barbarian invaders. In North Africa, a trench-and-earthen wall system known as the *fossatum Africae* ran over a distance of more than 750 kilometers separating the province of Numidia from the Bedouin tribes living in the Sahara desert. Finally, a double ditch, 24 kilometers long, separated Roman-held northern Mesopotamia from Sassanid Persia between the Khyber River and the Jebel Sinjar mountains. These fortifications, together with their nearby natural barriers, which were also lined with fortresses, formed the Roman *limes,* or defended borders. Within these borders walled towns and fortified garrisons were built throughout the empire. These fortifications all fitted into a defensive strategy of the Roman Empire that had by this time become less interested in outside conquest than in preserving internal peace and prosperity.[1]

The most complex and elaborate of these border fortifications and also the one that shows how earnest the Romans were about fortification construction was Hadrian's Wall. Built between 122 and 125 CE, Hadrian's Wall crossed Britain for 117 kilometers between Bowness in the west and Newcastle in the east. It was not the first set of fortifications built along this route, but it roughly followed the system of wooden stockades and trenches built in 81 CE by Agricola, the famous governor of Britain. While Agricola's fortresses were only temporary barriers against the Picts, Hadrian's Wall was meant to be a permanent frontier, consisting not only of the wall itself but also of a number of watchtowers, fortresses, signal towers, and outpost forts.

For most of the wall's length it was 2.3 meters thick, except for a 37-kilometer portion, crossing between North Tyne and Newcastle, where it measured nearly 3 meters in thickness. It was constructed of stone with a rubble and mortar core. It is estimated that Hadrian's Wall stood 5 to 6 meters high, although this varied with the terrain. It had a rampart walk at a height of 4 to 4.5 meters. In front of the wall, for most of its length, was a V-shaped ditch, 8–9 meters wide and at least 3 meters deep.

At intervals of approximately 494 meters along the wall, raised turrets, made to hold only a few men, were constructed to serve as watchtowers. At every Roman mile (1,480 meters) along the wall, a small fortress, known as a milecastle, was built, 80 in total. Erected in stone and earth, these rectangular fortresses measured 21.3 by 18.3 meters. Inside were two barracks made to hold approximately 50 soldiers. A larger fortress, known as a homestead, was built every 5 Roman miles along the wall. The 16 homesteads were enclosed on three sides by a stone wall, 1.5 meters thick, supported by an earthen rampart 4.5 meters thick; the fourth side was Hadrian's Wall itself. Square towers were placed on each of the homesteads' angles and along their walls. The homestead was built in the traditional garrison manner enclosing several barracks, meant to hold perhaps 600 men, and a number of official military buildings. Only four gates, each guarded by two towers, allowed access into these fortresses. Finally, within 240 kilometers of Hadrian's Wall were two fortified legionary garrisons, at York and Chester. These could quickly come to the aid of the wall garrisons, if needed, as a series of signal towers linked them to the Wall.[2]

Other Roman border defenses were not so sophisticated, the German wall simply a wooden palisade 3.7 to 4 meters high, and the *fossatum Africae* only a ditch, 4 to 6 meters wide and 2.3 to 3.4 meters deep, in front of an earthen wall, 2 to 2.5 meters high.[3] But, when combined with the natural protection provided by rivers, mountains, and deserts, all of which were also lined by fortresses, these too could impede any invasion of the imperial lands, at least until Roman soldiers from neighboring garrisons could arrive to put an end to the assault.

If invaders were able to break through these border defenses, though, they still had other fortifications to breach before sacking the major, prosperous cities of the empire: walls surrounded most large urban areas. The city of Rome was first enclosed by a wall, a defensive structure of earth and later stone, as early as the fifth and fourth centuries BCE, and this system was added to and rebuilt several times over the next 700 years. This early Roman wall was massive, measuring 3.6 meters wide at the base fronted by a ditch 29.6 meters wide and 9 meters deep. It was also effective, for example holding off Hannibal for more than 14 years during the Second Punic War.[4]

By the end of the second century Rome was not the only fortified city within the empire. No fewer than 54 towns in Western Europe were fortified by walls, 17 alone in Britain. Most enclosed large areas, some as big as 200 hectares, and many took on the shape of the towns (or *urbs*) they surrounded at the time of construction, often needing to be enlarged to encompass later expansions (the *suburbs*). Surviving and excavated walls show that they were built in stone, usually did not exceed 10 meters in height, and had a width of between 1.5 and 2.5 meters. An earthen rampart on which a single soldier could stand was often banked against it, with stone wall-walks built on the inside of other town walls. Round, semicircular, polygonal, trapezoidal, or rectangular towers were constructed along the walls at wide intervals, some measuring as large as 9 meters in diameter. Large ditches almost always surrounded the walls. At Cologne, for example, the ditch measured 8 to 12 meters wide and 5 meters deep and stood nearly 4 meters from the walls.[5]

Roman walls were built with great technological sophistication. They were freestanding, built throughout with very precisely measured small blocks, mixed occasionally with patches of *opus reticulatum* and mosaic work. The towers contained windows facing out from the walls, the lower register narrow slits and the upper levels larger keyhole types. The gateways, usually flanked by towers, were built to emphasize their monumental aspects. They allowed passage for at least one vehicle, sometimes with flanking passageways allowing pedestrian traffic as well. In many instances these monumental gateways were also decorated with ornamented cornices, moldings, architraves, and pilasters, and contained inscriptions celebrating the historical deeds of those from the town.[6]

The peace of the second century was to be short lived, however, as the third century brought invasions from outside and civil war from inside the empire. A neglect of earlier fortifications and the complacency in the building of new ones certainly exacerbated some of these problems. There had been a lull in the construction of new fortifications, especially town walls, after the death of Hadrian because of the sense of security that attended the peace,[7] and new fortifications were built in a far less sophisticated manner, without the durability of earlier fortifications. An example of the latter was the Antonine Wall—an earth-and-timber structure, much narrower and shorter than Hadrian's Wall, with fewer attached fortresses—constructed 160 kilometers north of Hadrian's Wall in 139–43 CE. Less than 20 years after its construction the Antonine Wall was abandoned, with later attempts to re-garrison it failing after only short periods.[8]

No doubt, though, it is the large number of civil wars that must be blamed for the weakened defenses of the empire during the third century. Between the reign of the "five good emperors" that ended in 180, and the reign of Constantine, which began in 312, there were 36 Roman emperors, many of whom reigned for less than a year. Frequently, one army and its candidate for emperor opposed another, which generally meant that the two contending armies would leave their posts garrisoning fortifications that guarded the imperial borders to fight each other elsewhere inside the empire.

Weakened and ungarrisoned fortifications led to invading forces pushing against the *limes* of the empire. In 249, the Goths broke through the Danube River fortifications and invaded the Balkans. This was followed in 256 by the Franks, who broke through the Lower Rhine River fortifications into Gaul. At the same time, the Saxons ventured across the English Channel and raided Britain. Sometimes the Romans defeated these invasions, but as their number increased, the number of Roman victories decreased. By 262, the Goths had completely overrun Greece and reached Athens, although they were eventually driven back before they could sack the city. Six years later, another German tribe, the Heruli, followed the Goths, and this time did sack Athens. Outside Europe, boundary fortifications also failed. In 256, the Borani, a tribe living in southern Russia, raided the Black Sea coast, in the same year that the Sassanid Persians, from Mesopotamia, overran Syria and even captured and imprisoned the inept Emperor Valerian who, after a year of being used as a step-stool by the Persian king, Shapur I, to climb onto his horse, died in captivity.

After 269, Rome began to regain its military strength: the Sassanid Persians were pushed behind the borders of Syria, the Goths driven across the Danube, and the Franks across the Rhine. Fortresses along all those borders were also rebuilt or replaced. Finally, Diocletian, who took over the imperial throne in 284 (and reigned until 305), recognized that border fortifications were neither too few nor too weak. They had never been built to withstand invasions, but merely to impede the progress of invading armies until the legions garrisoned behind them could respond. When these support armies became too involved in selecting and defeating opposing emperors instead of guarding the borders, then the empire could easily be invaded. So Diocletian first rebuilt the army by dividing his soldiers into two branches: those who garrisoned border fortifications and those who served in field armies meant to aid the garrisons should they be threatened. He then re-established the old, effective border fortifications, especially along the Rhine and Danube Rivers and in Syria.[9]

Diocletian also built new fortifications in areas which were vulnerable to new invasions. One of these was on the coast of Britain between the Isle of Wight and Norfolk, which during the third century had been frequently raided by Saxons. The result was what became known as the "Saxon Shore" forts, a series of high fortifications (exceeding 7 meters in height), with thick walls (measuring on average 4.3 meters) and covering a large area (between 1.5 and 4 hectares). Most were the traditional rectangular shape, but others, such as those at Pevensey and Sussex, were different—Sussex, for example, was oval—and almost all were supported by large D- or U-shaped towers designed to support Roman artillery. Each fort had two large main gates on opposite sides, with two smaller gates on the remaining two sides. Eleven of these fortifications still exist, several in excellent condition, although two more may also have been built.[10]

Finally, Diocletian encouraged the fortification (or refortification in some cases) of the towns and cities of the empire with walls. During the third century, towns that were not defended by walls or had not kept up their walls were pillaged and looted, and the Emperor was determined not to allow this to happen again. The result was incredible. While only 54 walled towns can be identified in Europe from the second century and earlier, more than that number were built in the province of Gaul alone between 286 and 306. In total, several hundred European towns constructed walls during this period. Rome itself completed the new walls that had been under construction since the reign of Aurelian, with a circumference of 18 kilometers, a thickness of 4 meters, and a height of 6 meters; 381 gates and towers were also built and equipped with artillery.[11]

Roman imperial fortifications are important to a study of medieval military technology for two reasons. First, these were the fortifications that ultimately failed to keep the barbarian invaders from overrunning the empire during the fourth and fifth centuries. Second, these fortifications would remain the primary defensive strongholds of Europe during the early Middle Ages.

Diocletian's reorganization of the Roman army and construction of new fortifications provided some security for the empire against outside invaders. The possibility of invasion remained, however, especially after yet another civil war, this one to decide Diocletian's successor, again depleted the numbers of soldiers along the empire's borders. With this in mind, Constantine's decision to move the imperial capital from Italy to Constantinople in 330 can be seen as a retreat from the sparsely populated and poorer western part of the empire, with its long, vulnerable border to the more populous and wealthier east, with a shorter, more easily defended border. If he, or his successors, were able to defend only one part of the empire from invaders, it was far more important to protect the eastern part.

That the later Romans were aware of potential invasion is reflected in several written sources of the fourth century. In an angry letter written in June 365, Emperor Valentinian I urges the military commander of the *limes* of *Dacia Ripensis* to "not only restore the fortifications which are crumbling, but also [to] build each year further towers in suitable locations."[12] And the anonymous author of the late fourth or early fifth century *De rebus bellicis* urged that there be "a continuous line of forts constructed at intervals of one mile with firm walls and very powerful towers . . . so that the peaceful provinces may be surrounded by a belt of defenses, and so remain unimpaired and at peace."[13]

Yet, despite the awareness of potential problems with the fortresses on their borders, the Romans built very few new fortifications after Diocletian's reign. This can be seen, for example, in the *Notitia dignitatum et administrationum omnium tam civilium quam militarium in partibus Orientis et Occidentis (Register of All Dignitaries and Administrators, both Civil and Military, in Eastern and Western Districts)*, an early-fifth-century administrative list of fortresses and garrisons in the empire, which records few fortifications built after Diocletian.[14] Even the city of Constantinople did not receive its walls until 413, long after the barbarian invasions had begun.[15] The lack of soldiers to garrison the border fortifications continued to be a problem for the late Romans, as can be seen from the complaint of the fifth-century writer Zosimus, an eyewitness to the barbarian invasions, that Constantine "withdrew from the frontier the great majority of soldiers to install them in towns which had no need for protection."[16]

Although some historians may disagree, the barbarian invasions began in 376 when the Visigoths, with the Huns encroaching on all sides of their territory, asked Emperor Valens to allow them to cross the Danube River and to cultivate the wastelands of Thrace as *foederati*, or confederates of the empire. Valens agreed to their request as he felt that not to do so would likely mean that the Visigoths would cross over the Danube anyway, and it would be far better for them to do so as allies than as enemies. A Visigothic presence in Thrace would provide the Romans with a defensive deterrent in that unpopulated region. What Valens did not realize, however, was how many Visigoths actually wanted to enter into the empire. When an estimated 200,000 Visigoths crossed over the Danube River, Valens found that he could not feed them, and the Visigoths were forced to challenge the Roman army, defeating it at the battle of Adrianople in 378. From then on the imperial borders began to crumble as barbarian tribes began to cross into the empire from all directions.

The fall of the western Roman Empire took very little time. By 406 the Alans, Suevi, and Vandals had crossed the Rhine River and entered Gaul. Three years later they crossed the Pyrenees into Spain. By 410 the Visigoths had moved into Italy and sacked Rome, moving two years later into Gaul and finally, two years after that, into Spain. By 416 they had crushed the Alans and Vandals there and set up their Visigothic kingdom. By 428 the Vandals had conquered Africa.

In the mid-fifth century another wave of barbarian invaders entered the empire, again because of the Hunnic threat to their security. By 436 the Burgundians had invaded the region around Geneva and by 449 the Angles, Jutes, and Saxons had raided and settled in Britain. By 451 the Franks, Ostrogoths, and Alemanni had entered Gaul, the Ostrogoths eventually moving into Italy. The western part of the Roman Empire remained so only in name, and even that was lost in 476 when the last western Roman emperor, Romulus Augustulus, was removed by Odovacar the Ostrogoth.[17]

Because the result of the barbarian invasions of the fourth and fifth centuries was so decisive, with the western Roman Empire failing, it might be assumed that the empire's fortifications had also failed. But this does not seem to have happened. As was often the situation throughout the Middle Ages, when the people behind the walls wanted to hold on against the barbarians they generally did. Despite possessing what should have been adequate siege technology to defeat the Roman fortifications, invading armies suffered some spectacular failures in their attempts to take the walled towns of the empire. For example, the Visigoths were unable to capitalize on their victory at Adrianople in 378 by advancing on the major towns of the empire. Although they were able to conquer the largely unfortified towns of Greece—Piraeus, Corinth, Argos, and Sparta—they could not take the walled town of Thebes. Even the small, but ably fortified, town of Tegea defended itself successfully against the Visigoths.[18] Similar problems with walled towns accompanied the Visigoths' attack on Italy in 401–410. Although they were able to conquer and sack Rome, they could not take Asti, Pollenzo, or Ravenna.[19] In 441, Palermo successfully defended itself against a siege by the Vandals.[20] In 451, Attila's Huns were unable to take Orléans.[21] In 501, Avignon withstood the siege and attacks of the Frankish Merovingian king, Clovis, and six years later, in 507, Arles did the same, also against Clovis.[22]

Clovis's sons and grandsons faced similar problems in taking towns fortified by walls. In 532, Theuderic was unable to take the town of Vitry; in 542, Saragossa withstood the attacks of Chlotar and Childebert; in 581, Chilperic failed to take Bourges, and that same year Guntram Boso was unable to take Avignon; and, in 585, Childebert was unable to take Bellinzona, Pavia, or any other fortified Italian town.[23] In the sixth century, the Ostrogothic king, Witigis, had difficulty capturing fortified towns, failing first in 536 to take Rome and then in 537–38 to take Arminium.[24] Even as late as the eighth century, would-be conquerors still faced problems capturing towns fortified during the late Roman Empire, as evidenced by the Spanish Muslim general Al-Samh ibn Malik al-Khawlani's inability to take Toulouse in 721 and the Frankish general Charles Martel's failure to take Narbonne in 737.[25]

The frustration of these failed conquests can be seen no better than at Arles in 568. In that year the Merovingian Frankish king, Chlotar, died, leaving the town of Arles divided between his two sons, Sigibert and Guntram, who immediately began to fight over it. Ultimately, Sigibert was able to enter Arles unopposed, but when Guntram heard of his brother's occupation, he sent his own forces to besiege it. As the siege progressed Sigibert became convinced that Arles could not hold out for long against a siege, so he tried to surprise Guntram's army by advancing out of the gates in an early morning attempt to break the siege. This attack failed, however, but when Sigibert tried to return to Arles he discovered that the gates of the town were locked and the inhabitants turned against him. To save their lives, Sigibert and his remaining soldiers abandoned their equipment and swam across the Rhone River to safety.[26]

Eventually, the fortified towns of the late Roman Empire fell to the barbarians, some by surprise attacks, some by treason, some by negotiation, and some by prolonged siege leading to starvation. The fifth-century siege of Rome by Alaric and the Visigoths provides an example of why sometimes even the best fortifications could be captured. Despite having perhaps the finest fortifications of any city in the late Roman Empire, Rome finally fell in 410 after several attacks and a siege of nearly two years. The richest prize in the Western Empire, the imperial capital had been a target of conquest by the Visigoths from their first attacks on Italy in 401. But after two defeats at the hands of the Roman general Stilicho, Alaric had not even reached the outskirts of the city before 408. However, that year the Roman political leadership turned against Stilicho and he was killed, leaving his armies in disarray and the road to Rome open for Alaric and the Visigoths. Recognizing his inability to breach the city's fortifications, Alaric besieged it by blockading all land and river routes into the city. For two years the Roman inhabitants held out against the Visigoths, until finally hunger and disease drove the inhabitants to surrender. With their walls still intact, but without hope of a relieving army or food and water, on 24 August 410 the Romans opened their gates to their besiegers—though this is disputed by several contemporary sources which claim that the city would have held out even longer against the Visigoths had a gate not been opened by "traitors" hoping to buy leniency from their besiegers.[27] Rome would again be sacked in 455, this time by the Vandals, and in 537–538 by the Ostrogoths. In both of these attacks, the Romans allowed the barbarians into the city without defending it, in the hopes of being granted mercy.[28]

No doubt because of their experiences facing them, most barbarian leaders refused to destroy the walls of a captured town unless they feared that the walls might harbor later resistance against them.[29] They added few new fortifications of their own,[30] but they did seem to keep the older ones in fairly good condition. This can be seen in the description of the mid-sixth-century Dijon walls by the contemporary Gregory of Tours, which describes fortifications not much changed from their construction three centuries earlier:

> It is a fortress girded round with mighty walls and set in the center of a pleasant plain.... The four entrances of the town are placed at the four quarters of the compass, and thirty-three towers adorn the circuit of the walls which are made of squared stones rising to a height of twenty feet, with smaller stones placed above to reach in all some thirty feet, the whole being fifteen feet thick.[31]

Even as late as 890 towns fortified during the third century were praised. Chartres, for one, is described in the *Cartulaire de Saint Père* as being "famous for the thickness of its walls."[32]

What the barbarian conquerors of the Western Roman Empire added instead of new town walls were rural fortifications, precursors of the later medieval castle. Little is known about these early castles, however, as few archaeological remains survive, although there are some written references to how many there were, who inhabited them, what purpose they served, and even, to a certain extent, how they were constructed.[33] From these several general traits can be determined.

First, they seem to have been a strictly barbarian structure with no Roman precursors. Some even appeared early in the barbarian invasions (at least as early as the late fifth century) and were so numerous, particularly in the regions of Western Europe dominated by the Franks, that this style of fortification may actually have preceded the invasions themselves, at least in the Frankish regions. Certainly by the early sixth century there were so many of these fortifications that their numbers impressed several contemporary writers, among them Sidonius Apollinaris, Sulpicius Severus, and Gregory of Tours.

Second, they did not rely primarily on walls or towers for their defense, but rather on their inaccessibility. Most were built on high places, some on rocky promontories or isolated buttes. Sometimes, such as in the fortresses of Grèze, Chastel-Marlhac, and Ronzières, this provided their only security, while at other places a wall or rampart was added to increase the site's defensibility. Only rarely was this a stone wall; more frequently it was an earthen rampart, often with stones or wood placed on top of the walls. In two places, at Piègu and Nicet, the castles themselves were actually built on top of an earthen rampart.[34]

These castles were built away from urban areas already defended by town walls, making them often in effect the sole protection for the rural areas of Western Europe. Several were constructed to protect agricultural and economic centers, serving as refuges for farmers and other agricultural workers during times of war. Others were sanctuaries or ecclesiastical centers. Yet many castles were also built and controlled by wealthy individuals, in these cases serving both as residences for these "nobles" and as defenses for the people who worked on the nearby agricultural lands. For example, Sidonius Apollinaris' wealthy friend, Pontius Leontius, owned the fortification at Arvernie, at the confluence of the Garonne and Dordogne Rivers, an area of prime agricultural land, likely using this castle for the same purposes as those built by later medieval lords.[35]

To the early medieval writers who mention them, these fortifications appeared formidable. Sidonius Apollinaris was so impressed with the castle at Avernie, built on a jagged rock promontory and nearly surrounded by water, that he was "fain to keep silence about it."[36] Gregory of Tours was another contemporary fan. Describing the fortress of Chastel-Marlhac, he writes:

> The people of Chastel-Marlhac were besieged, but they retained their liberty, for they bribed the invaders not to take them captive. It was only because of their own stupidity that they had to pay anything at all. The place was a natural fortress, for it was surrounded not by man-made walls, but by cliffs which rose sheer for a hundred feet or more.[37]

CAROLINGIAN

These rural fortifications were built and used, together with the Roman town walls, as a means of defense for the people of Francia during the turbulent and unstable Merovingian era (c.450–751). They even took on an official and legal status in some areas. They were still providing defense for the Franks as late as the mid-eighth-century attempts of Pepin III "the Short" to unite the realm under his Carolingian rule. Pepin was forced to subdue a large number of these fortresses, and frequently, because of their superb natural defenses, this was a difficult task, so difficult, in fact, that he was forced to impose sanctions on anyone who participated in their defense, sanctions still in effect nearly 100 years later.[38]

Pepin died in 768, leaving the Carolingian realm to his son, Charlemagne. The father had made a kingdom; the son would make the kingdom an empire. In almost every one of his 42 years of rule, Charlemagne summoned his army for conquest outside of the kingdom's borders. By 814 this included the whole of modern France, Belgium, Holland, and Switzerland, most of Germany, and a large part of Italy and northern Spain. He defeated the Avars in the east, the Lombards in Italy, the Frisians in the north, the Saxons in the northeast, the Muslims in northern Spain, and the Danes in southern Denmark.

Yet there is some dispute over whether Charlemagne built fortifications. Certainly he knew their worth, for on a number of occasions the people he defeated were lodged behind their walls and fortresses, and their subjugation sometimes took a very long time. Two towns in particular, the

Lombard-controlled Pavia and the Muslim-controlled Barcelona, both defended by strong Roman fortifications, necessitated sieges of longer than a year before they fell to him. Charlemagne also had to capture Avar and Saxon fortresses.[39]

Still, it is uncertain whether Charlemagne added many castles and town walls to his realm. Scholars argue both sides of the debate. On one side, Bernard S. Bachrach and Charles Bowlus maintain that Charlemagne built many fortifications during his reign. Bachrach insists that Charlemagne "did appreciate the significance of fortifications and utilized them as a basic element in the military organization in several parts of his kingdom, including Saxony and the Spanish March." He notes that in many instances after Charlemagne captured a fortress or a walled town, he repaired the existing defenses and then garrisoned a number of troops inside them. He also built several new fortifications, although most of these were small rural fortresses or castles. In particular, Saxony and Aquitaine were filled with fortifications built under Charlemagne's direction.[40] Bowlus agrees with these conclusions, noting in his specific study of the eastern frontier of the Carolingian Empire that "by the end of the ninth century the entire frontier region was studded with fortifications," many of which had been built during Charlemagne's reign.[41]

On the other side of the debate, Gabriel Fournier and Rosamond McKitterick claim that Charlemagne did not construct many fortifications. Neither denies that some were built in Saxony, Aquitaine, or on the Ostmark, as claimed by Bachrach and Bowlus. However, they do not agree that these were significant in number, size, or defensive capabilities. Fournier insists instead that at best these fortifications were but transitional measures and used only to garrison troops in the years immediately following the conquests of these lands. He claims that on campaign Charlemagne neither used existing fortifications nor built new ones. Charlemagne also neglected town walls, Fournier contends, although he is uncertain whether this was a deliberate act or done simply because the Roman walls were still in good repair. Instead, he preferred to use other means to provide military security: the isolation of hostile lands, hostage taking, the creation of large dependencies, local noble administration, Christianization, and the installation of solid religious foundations.[42] With all of this McKitterick agrees. She writes:

> It seems that once an area with fortified sites had been subdued, the Carolingians retained only a limited interest in this form of military organization .... Town walls were not

repaired or rebuilt; indeed, they were often destroyed for
the sake of the masonry.[43]

THE VIKING INVASIONS
AND REACTIONS

There may be no answer to this dispute, and for Charlemagne's rule it was not especially important. His lands were never invaded, and he in fact lost few battles. It became more important, though, within 100 years of Charlemagne's death when the Holy Roman Empire that he had established and which had been divided into several parts by his grandsons, was invaded numerous times by both the Vikings and the Hungarians. The ease with which these "new barbarian" invaders sacked towns leaves the historian searching for reasons.

The first and perhaps most ruthless of these invaders were the Vikings. Their initial attack was in 787, when they landed and pillaged the southern coast of England. Six years later they returned and sacked the wealthy Lindisfarne Abbey. These successes led to further, larger raids. By 834 they had swept through both England and Ireland and turned their wrath on the continent. By 840 they had raided the Low Country towns of Noirmoutiers, Rhé, Dorestad (four times), Utrecht, and Antwerp. In 843 they wintered for the first time in Gaul, capturing Nantes and ravaging the valleys of the Loire and Garonne Rivers; they even threatened the Muslim towns of Lisbon and Cadiz. In 845 they sailed up the Seine with an estimated 120 ships and destroyed Paris. In the following 30 years they raided up the Rhine, the Meuse, the Scheldt, the Somme, the Seine, the Marne, the Loire, the Charente, the Dordogne, the Lot, and the Garonne Rivers. One expedition even sailed through the Straits of Gibraltar and raided Nekur in Morocco, the Mercian coast of Spain, the Balearic Islands, and Rousillon. These Vikings then wintered on the Rhone delta and the following year raided upstream as far as Valence, sacking Pisa and Luna (which they mistook for Rome) before returning to Brittany. In 879 the Vikings sacked Ghent. A year later they destroyed Courtrai and numerous towns in Saxony. In 881 they sacked Elsloo and Aachen, where they raided Charlemagne's palace; in 882, Condé; in 883, Amiens; in 884, Louvain; and in 885–886 they besieged Paris but were bought off by King Louis the Fat, who paid them 700 pounds of silver and gave them permission to spend the summer sacking Burgundy, an area that he did not control. Generally avoiding combat, only twice were the Vikings defeated in battle: in 878 at Edington by Alfred the Great, and in 891 at the Dyle by Arnulf, king of the East Franks. By the second decade of the tenth century, the number and ferocity of the Viking raids began to decline, although they did not completely disappear until the end of the eleventh century.[44]

The Hungarian raids lasted a shorter time and were perhaps less destructive. They were, however, still devastating to late Carolingian Europe. These raiders were first used as mercenaries by Arnulf against the Moravians in 892. Enticed perhaps by the booty they acquired during this fighting, they returned to raid the west in 899, when they advanced south into Italy and attacked Pavia. The following year, they moved to Bavaria and in 901 to Carinthia. From 906 to 909 they raided Saxony, Carinthia, Bavaria, and Thuringia. The attacks then stopped until 917, when the Hungarians reappeared in the eastern Carolingian empire and proceeded for the next seven years to raid Basle, Alsace, Burgundy, Saxony, Lombardy, and Provence. After 924 their power waned, although they continued to remain a menace to central and southern Europe until Otto the Great defeated them at the battle of Lechfeld in 955 and pushed them out of the Holy Roman Empire back into Hungary.[45]

While some of the details of these raids are disputed, such as the number of participants and ships and the military organization of the forces, one characteristic that is generally agreed on is that the raiders successfully sacked many supposedly fortified towns and palaces. Both continental Europe and England appear to have been unprepared for the Viking and Hungarian onslaughts and suffered significantly. The question that must be asked then is what happened to the fortifications that were supposed to protect their inhabitants from this very thing?

In the Carolingian Empire, it appears, not only was there so little fortification construction in the ninth century that chroniclers of the period describe such building as "novel"—not even the emperor's palace at Aachen had been fortified[46]—but some previously constructed fortresses were actually being dismantled. For example, in 814, Louis the Pious, Charlemagne's son, gave permission to the Bishop of Langres to destroy the walls of the town so that he might use the masonry to construct a church. This was repeated a number of times: in 817–825, when Ebbo, Archbishop of Rheims, was allowed to demolish the town gates and walls of Rheims to build the cathedral; in 859 at Melun, when the Archbishop of Sens, Wenilo, was given permission to use the town walls to build a church there; and finally in Charles the Bald's *Edict of Pitres*, proclaimed on 25 June 864, in which he commanded that all fortresses that had not been built with the permission of the king be taken down. Thus, even though the Vikings were already raiding the countryside, some fortifications that should have been used by the people for their protection were being destroyed.[47] Other fortifications had been so neglected that they were easily overrun.[48]

However, by 900 the Viking and Hungarian raids had forced almost all of Western Europe threatened by continual invasion to build new fortifications. These were usually built quickly, and therefore they were often not elaborate constructions, tending to be less technologically sophisticated than simply utilitarian. They were also built to protect the more urban regions of a kingdom as these were often the chief targets of the raiders and were primarily projects funded and supported by kings rather than by their barons.

In England there is no written record of any new defensive construction taking place after the fall of the Roman Empire until the reign of Alfred the Great in the ninth century. Roman fortifications, mostly town walls, had been built more than 600 years previously, and these appear to have been poorly maintained; many of the stones had also been mined and reused to construct houses and religious buildings. What was left provided little protection to their inhabitants and other potential refugees. This is no better expressed than in an Old English poem entitled "The Ruin," written during the Viking invasions:

> Splendid this rampart is, though fate destroyed it,
> The city buildings fell apart, the works
> Of giants crumble. Tumbled are the towers,
> Ruined the roofs, and broken the barred gate
> ... Often this wall
> Stained red and grey with lichen has stood by
> Surviving storms while kingdoms rose and fell.
> And now the high curved wall itself has fallen.[49]

England was the earliest land hit by the Viking invaders, and it also had to endure their attacks the longest. In their late-eighth- and early-ninth-century invasions the Vikings had to contend with very few fortifications, even around the most populated towns. At the same time, the disunity and small size of the Anglo-Saxon kingdoms resulted in a very slow defensive response. Even London was easily conquered, falling into the Vikings' hands without much resistance in 872. It was not until the late ninth century when Alfred the Great, the king of Wessex, began to unite the kingdoms of England that the Vikings started to encounter organized opposition. In 878 Alfred defeated what became known as the "Great Danish Army" at the battle of Edington, and in 886 he freed London from Viking control. In response to these military feats, much of the rest of England recognized his rule.[50]

But the defeat of the Vikings at Edington and in London was not the limit of Alfred's military exploits. He also recognized that the failure to withstand invasions was a result not only of the disunity of English political entities, but also of the lack of fortifications. Therefore, after uniting his neighboring kingdoms and also momentarily halting the invasions, Alfred began to improve the fortifications of England. This meant repairing the old Roman walls and also building new ditch and earthen rampart fortresses known in Old English as *burhs*.

Alfred was not the first to construct a *burh*. They may instead have originated in Mercia during the reign of King Offa (758–796). As well as Offa's Dyke, a 103 to 192-kilometer-long ditch and rampart dug between Wales and Mercia—the difference in distance depends on which modern scholar is determining where the dyke begins and ends[51]—he constructed a small number of these fortifications to house his own residences. Only two of these Mercian *burhs* have been excavated, but they are very similar to those of Alfred and may have provided the archetype.[52]

Due to the survival of an early-tenth-century list of Alfred's *burhs*, known as the *Burghal Hidage*, which delineated their administrative and economic role in the kingdom, much is known about the locations and responsibilities of these fortifications.[53] This, coupled with the large number of archaeological excavations of the sites, has provided a unique opportunity to understand what these structures were and how they were used.[54]

Alfred built thirty of these fortifications. They were distributed widely throughout his kingdom and evenly placed so that no more than a single day's march separated one fortress from the next. They were constructed mostly along the kingdom's routes of communication—roads, navigable rivers, and trackways—and in several instances reused the sites of earlier Roman or Iron Age fortifications. They were also frequently constructed near the king's fortified residences and permitted him better military control over his kingdom.[55]

Although the *burhs* had some administrative and economic functions, ultimately their most important purpose was as a refuge to give military protection for the inhabitants of the kingdom against the Viking invaders, including, if needed, the necessary supplies to withstand a prolonged siege. Second, they were to provide an offensive threat to the Vikings by housing a large garrison of troops. These troops could be summoned to encounter any invading army or band and perhaps thwart attempts at raiding the kingdom.[56]

The *burhs* were quite large. Estimates from the *Burghal Hidage* indicate that the garrison in each fortress could number nearly 900, with refugees increasing the number that needed to be housed.[57] This is confirmed by their archaeological remains. The Wareham *burh*, a rectangular fortress, measured roughly 700 by 610 meters, and the Wallingford *burh*, also rectangular, measured 760 by 550 meters. Even the smallest *burhs* excavated, such as that at Crickdale, measured 412 square meters. The area enclosed was between 20 and 40 hectares.[58]

Their defenses were relatively simple. *Burhs* were what have been called "ring works," not too different in construction from the Iron Age hill forts that cover England. They were surrounded by a large ditch, sometimes 34 meters wide and between 5 and 8 meters deep. They were also protected by a 3-meter-high wedge-shaped earthen rampart, with a timber facing or revetment at the front. Above this rampart was a stone wall at least 1.5 meters in height.[59]

Their construction was expensive, both initially and in their maintenance. These expenses were covered by the king and other landowners of the kingdom, who naturally profited from the physical and economic protection these fortresses provided against the Viking invaders. They also appeared to have been fully manned, as early charters place the garrisoning of *burhs* alongside bridge building as the most important obligations of Alfred's subjects.[60]

But the expense seems to have been worth it. The *burhs* were relatively effective in halting the Viking raids of the period. Although some raiders were able to go around them to attack the interior of the island, this was always a risky plan, as it meant that a large number of armed troops would be positioned between the Vikings and their ships, which threatened any force returning to or left at the ships. Both in 893 and 914 this strategy failed when the Vikings, having initially bypassed the Anglo-Saxon *burhs*, were attacked and defeated as they tried to return to their vessels. The Vikings seem also to have been unable to take the *burhs* by attack or starvation. On a number of occasions—at Pilton in 893, Chichester in 894, and Bedford and Wingamere in 917—Viking attacks on the *burhs* failed; in only one instance, in 892 at Lympne, were the Vikings able to capture the fortress, and it has been suggested that this was because of its poor construction and small number of defenders.[61]

The building of *burhs* continued after Alfred's death in 899, especially during the reign of his son, Edward the Elder (899–924), who maintained the *burhs* built during the reign of his father and added several more himself. It was also during his reign that the *Burghal Hidage* was written. However, after his death, the number of newly constructed *burhs* declined, as did the maintenance of older *burhs*, and they ceased to be garrisoned. Ironically, it is during this period that the Vikings, who clearly knew the value of these fortifications, began to seize Alfred's *burhs* as bases from which to raid against the populations they once protected. These defensive fortifications had become offensive threats, still being used by Danish Vikings when, in 1013, they eventually gained control of all England.[62]

The fortifications constructed on the Continent to check the Viking and Hungarian raids were neither as extensive nor as well planned and organized as Alfred's *burhs* in England, although they have not been studied as thoroughly. For example, there is some evidence that a fairly large number of fortifications were built in the Carolingian Ostmark (today's lower Austria and Carinthia), primarily as a defense against the Hungarians. But so few archaeological excavations have been done and so little written evidence survives that very little can be determined about them, including whether they might be described as the "program" of fortification construction that Charles Bowlus proposes. Those that have been excavated, at Freisach and Mosaburg, show that they were constructed of earth and timber and were situated in rather harsh terrain—Freisach in a marshy area near a river and Mosaburg in an impenetrable swamp—which also provided natural protection. In addition, because of their location, near communities of peasant farmers, they seem to have been built as refuges, although their small size would have precluded a very large refugee population.[63]

The situation in Italy may have been similar to that of the Ostmark, although again very little is known about the fortifications constructed there between the ninth and eleventh centuries. The major urban areas certainly still relied on their old Roman walls for protection against raiders and armies, walls that some documentary evidence suggests they struggled to repair and rebuild, some with the addition of new towers. A few written sources, several early-tenth-century charters, describe several new fortifications being constructed. These fortresses were supposed to have been elaborate structures, made of stone and incorporating elevated platforms, apertures for archery, defensive towers, and ditches; this would indicate that castle building in late Carolingian Italy had far surpassed any other in Europe during this period. But archaeological excavations have yet to confirm this.[64]

In France and Germany following the deaths of Charlemagne and Louis the Pious, the number of new fortifications built depended largely on peace between the various kings and nobles, regardless of the intensity of Viking or Hungarian invasions. So, during the period from about 830 to 862–864, when wars between the sons of Louis the Pious were fought throughout the Carolingian lands, and despite an extremely large number of Viking and Hungarian raids, only one new fortress is recorded in the documents, built in 830 by the abbot of the Monastery of St. Philibert de Noirmoutiers. During the relatively peaceful years that followed, 862–879, the opposite occurred, with an extensive, royally supported program of fortification construction, which ultimately saw a number of different defensive structures built against the northern raiders. Then between 879 and 887 there was little new fortification construction, as the Carolingian kingdoms were filled with dynastic quarrels and civil war, in addition to an increased number of Viking raids. Even the maintenance of older fortifications was neglected. Finally, from 887 into the eleventh century, the number of new fortifications once again increased, although these were financed largely by the lords whose political and economic power had increased during the struggles of 879–887.[65]

Most of the fortifications constructed during these centuries were town walls or rural earth-and-timber fortifications—including those at Le Mans, Orléans, Tours, and Saint-Denis built by Charles the Bald, king of the West Franks, and meant to provide security to many in the Parisian and Loire regions of France[66]—although at least one stone fortification was ordered to be built by Charles: a fortified palace for himself at Compiègne.[67] But there were also what have been described as fortified bridges. The construction of fortified bridges was a very logical strategy: if the Vikings were traveling upstream to raid the towns of France, including Paris, why not try to stop them on the rivers before they reached those towns? But no one had ever tried to fortify a bridge before, so when Charles the Bald ordered two fortified bridges built in 862, one at Pîtres on the Seine River and a second at Treix on the Marne, the success of this strategy had yet to be proved.

The bridge at Pîtres, the most extensively excavated, was chosen because of its particularly favorable strategic location. It was situated at the confluence of the Seine and two of its tributaries, the Andelle and the Eure; this removed the possibility of portaging from the Seine to one of its tributaries and thereby avoiding the fortification. It took between 6 and 15 years to complete and consisted of two stone bridgeheads, large enough to garrison troops, with a wooden span extending across the 400-meter width of the river. Surrounding the bridgeheads on each bank were earthen fortresses, which measured 600 meters in perimeter and probably served as refuges for the nearby population.

The size of the bridgeheads is not known but has been estimated to have covered an area measuring 25 by 5 meters and to have been at least 3.5 meters high and 1.3 meters thick.[68] What little of the bridge at Treix has been excavated shows a similar construction.

Later fortified bridges were planned on the Seine at Charenton, on the Oise near Pontoise, and on the Loire at Les Ponts de Cé, but there is no evidence that they were completed. Charles the Bald may also have constructed a fortified bridge in Paris, but this too is uncertain.[69]

These two fortified bridges seem to have been remarkably effective in their defense of the Seine and Marne. No Viking fleets are recorded to have passed beyond the bridge at Treix after its construction, and between 879 and 885 no ships sailed up the Seine past the bridge at Pîtres. Moreover, although the Vikings did successfully row up the Seine to besiege Paris in 885, the four months it took them to reach their destination, a distance of only 234 kilometers, indicates a continued strong defense against them by the troops garrisoned at Pîtres. Perhaps the greatest measure of success can be seen when the Vikings were forced, contrary to their usual custom, to besiege the uncompleted fortified bridge at Pontoise, also in 885. Although the garrisoned troops at the bridge fortress did eventually surrender, they had hindered the Viking advance along that river toward Paris for several weeks, allowing the Parisians more time to strengthen their own defenses.[70]

One particular characteristic of late Carolingian fortification construction needs to be highlighted: the transformation from royal to noble financing. After the civil wars that followed the deaths of the last of Charlemagne's grandsons, Louis the German in Germany in 876 and Charles the Bald in France a year later, and a series of inept kings, lords began to take over the building of fortifications. Few generalizations can be made about these fortifications. Every lord simply became responsible for the defense of his own lands, and, as would be the case throughout the Middle Ages, the stronger and more wealthy lords built the strongest and most numerous fortifications. Powerful, wealthy lords, such as the counts of Flanders and the lords of Luxembourg-Trèves, covered their lands with fortifications, while weaker, poorer lords left their lands almost unprotected.[71]

Older fortifications were improved, and new town walls and fortified monasteries were built,[72] but the majority of the new fortifications were smaller, more rural, and used as defenses primarily for the local populations, not unlike the rural fortresses of the Merovingian kingdom. Most were constructed of earth and timber and relied, also like their Merovingian predecessors, on the harshness of the terrain as their primary defense. There were exceptions, however: the smallest fortresses throughout Flanders, averaging only 200 meters in diameter, appear to have been used less as refuges for the population and more as private noble residences and as garrisons for troops.[73]

This period of fortification construction, from the end of the ninth through the middle of the eleventh centuries, was in response to the amount of warfare then spreading across Europe. Civil wars continued, as did Viking and Hungarian raids, and most of these fortifications were used in military situations. For example, between 930 and 948 the fortress at Mouzon, built on land owned by the Archbishop of Rheims, was taken and retaken no fewer than five times; and between 938 and 945, the fortress at Montigny, built on land owned by the Abbey of Saint-Crispin at Soissons, was fought over three times and destroyed twice.[74] It was becoming obvious that earth-and-timber fortifications were no longer proving sufficient for the defensive requirements of either the nobles or their subjects. Other more defensible and stronger fortifications were needed, and by the end of the tenth century stone castles, in their traditional medieval form, began to appear throughout Europe.

Notes

1. Luttwak (1976): 55–80.
2. There are a number of good and rather lengthy descriptions of Hadrian's Wall. I have used those found in Forde-Johnston (1977): 59–64 and Toy (1955): 6–49.
3. Luttwak (1976): 68.
4. Lander (1984): 5.
5. Fino (1970): 56–63; S. Johnson (1983): 9–27; and Butler (1959): 26–27.
6. S. Johnson (1983): 13–14.
7. S. Johnson (1983): 20.
8. Forde-Johnston (1977): 65–66.
9. Luttwak (1976): 170–88; von Petrikovits (1971): 179–82; and Cary and Scullard (1975): 534.
10. Forde-Johnston (1977): 66–69 and S. Johnson (1983): 201–7.
11. Lander (1984): 168–69.
12. As quoted in Contamine (1984): 6. See also von Petrikovits (1971): 184–88.
13. E.A. Thompson (1952): 122–23.
14. Contamine (1984): 6. See also S. Johnson (1983): 245–61 and Lander (1984): 263–93.
15. Toy (1955): 52–54.
16. Zosimus is quoted in Contamine (1984): 6–7. For *De rebus bellicis* see E.A. Thompson (1952): 112–13. Only the *Notitia dignitatum* claims that the Romans had more troops along

the borders during the invasions than during Diocletian's reign, and its credibility on this calculation has been attacked rather forcefully. See Contamine (1984): 7–9.

17. On the barbarian invasions see Bury (1967); Lot (1961); E.A. Thompson (1982); Wolfram (1988); and Geary (1988).

18. Wolfram (1988): 141.

19. Wolfram (1988): 151–55.

20. Bury (1967): 127.

21. Bury (1967): 147–49.

22. B. Bachrach (1972): 9, 11–12.

23. B. Bachrach (1972): 21–22, 26, 53–54, 55, 59, 60–61.

24. E.A. Thompson (1958): 16.

25. B. Bachrach (1972): 101, 105.

26. B. Bachrach (1972): 37–38.

27. Bury (1967): 91–97; Wolfram (1988): 155–61; and Lander (1984): 293–97.

28. Contamine (1984): 12–13.

29. E.A. Thompson (1958): 16–17.

30. Wallace-Hadrill (1962): 32–33.

31. Gregory of Tours (1974): 182–83.

32. Quoted in Guillerme (1988): 23.

33. The best discussion of these rural fortifications is found in Fournier (1978): 27–34.

34. Fournier (1978): 31–32 and M. Jones (1981): 157.

35. Fournier (1978): 32–34.

36. Sidonius Apollinaris (1963): I:262–83.

37. Gregory of Tours (1974): 172–73.

38. Fournier (1974): 123–35; B. Bachrach (1974): 9–10; and McKitterick (1983): 51.

39. On the fortifications and siege of Pavia see Bullough (1965): 49–50; on the siege of Barcelona see B. Bachrach (1974): 28; on the Saxon fortifications see Fournier (1978): 36; and on the Avar fortifications see Bowlus (1978): 17.

40. B. Bachrach (1978: 23–25; 1983: 183).

41. Bowlus (1978): 22–25.

42. Fournier (1978): 36–38.

43. McKitterick (1983): 51.

44. There are several good accounts of the Viking raids. See in particular G. Jones (1968); and Sawyer (1962, 1982).

45. Macartney (1930); Musset (1965); and Leyser (1965). Bowlus's recent book (2006) is the definitive word on the battle of Lechfeld and what resulted from it.

46. Riché (1983): 42–46.

47. Fournier (1978): 38; McKitterick (1983): 233; and Vercauteren (1936): 119–20.

48. Vercauteren (1936): 120.

49. Quoted in Hamer (1970): 27.

50. On Alfred the Great see Abels (1998); Duckett (1956); and Stenton (1971): 239–76.

51. The most popular book, Hill and Worthington (2009), has the shortest length, while Fox (1955) has the longest.

52. Abels (1988): 68–69.

53. An edition and the most complete study of this text is Hill and Rumble (1996), but more concise introductions can be found in Hill (1969): 84–92 and Bachrach and Aris (1990): 1–17.

54. Hill and Rumble (1996); Abels (1988): 68–78; Bachrach and Aris (1990): 1–17; Forde-Johnston (1977): 74–76; Brown, Colvin and Taylor (1963): 8–10; Radford (1970): 83–103; and H. Turner (1971): 17–20 and *passim*.

55. Abels (1988): 69.

56. Abels (1988): 69–71.

57. Abels (1988): 74–75 and Bachrach and Aris (1990): 2–3.

58. Forde-Johnston (1977): 74–75; Radford (1970): 84–103; and Bachrach and Aris (1990): 2–4.

59. Forde-Johnston (1977): 74–75 and Bachrach and Aris (1990): 3–4.

60. Abels (1988): 76–78; Brooks (1971): 71–73; and Hollister (1962): 143.

61. Abels (1988): 71–74. An excellent discussion of the military thinking and the use of archery in the defense of these fortifications is found in Bachrach and Aris (1990): 5–17.

62. Abels (1988): 92–93 and Brooks (1979): 17–18.

63. Bowlus (1978): 24–25.

64. Drew (1964): 444–47.

65. Vercauteren (1936): 121–29.

66. Vercauteren (1936): 123–28; Fournier (1978): 38–39; and Sawyer (1982): 89–90.

67. Fournier (1978): 39.

68. Vercauteren (1936): 123–24; Gillmor (1988): 87–106; Dearden (1988): 107–12; and Boyer (1976): 21–27.

69. Boyer (1976): 23–27 and Sawyer (1982): 89.

70. Gillmor (1988): 106.

71. Fournier (1978): 39; Coulson (1976): 29–36; and Binding (1972): 23–34.

72. Vercauteren (1936): 131; Coulson (1976): 32–34; and B. Bachrach (1975): 545.

73. Fournier (1978): 51.

74. Fournier (1978): 39–40.

CHAPTER 8

THE
MOTTE-
AND-BAILEY
CASTLE

BEFORE EMBARKING ON A STUDY OF THE HISTORY OF STONE CASTLES IN THE
Middle Ages, it is necessary to consider the motte-and-bailey castle, which
were highly effective earth-and-timber fortifications of complex construction
although generally thought to be primitive. Motte-and-bailey castles were
used by William the Conqueror to conquer England after his invasion in 1066,
marking the first deliberate and organized attempt in the Middle Ages to use
fortifications in an offensive military strategy: to garrison troops as a threat
to the inhabitants of a region.

In its simplest definition, the motte part of the motte-and-bailey castle was
little more than a mound made of earth topped by a superstructure of timber.
The bailey was a yard enclosed by an earthen rampart that surrounded the
motte and was usually separated from it by a ditch. A wide and deep ditch also
usually surrounded the bailey. As such, the motte-and-bailey castle provided
protection for its inhabitants by the rampart, the size of the bailey, the depth
and width of its ditches, and the height of the mound.[1]

As with all innovations in medieval fortification construction, it is difficult
to trace the origin of this castle. Most motte-and-bailey castles were located in
the northwest regions of Europe, and some historians have argued that their
origin is geographical: they were built to raise the ground above marshlands
and floodplains.[2] Others contend that their origin is strictly military, that they

Fig. 8.1: Hen Domen motte-and-bailey castle.

Photo by the author.

were descendants of similar Roman, Merovingian, Anglo-Saxon, or Viking fortifications.[3] Both of these are merely conjectures. Remains of motte-and-bailey castles have been found in Denmark, the Low Countries, the Rhineland, Northern France, England, and, outside of northwest Europe, in Southern Italy, and most date from the late tenth and eleventh centuries, although certainly there are some in England that were built in the twelfth and possibly the thirteenth centuries.[4] Therefore, their origin might be linked to the last phase of fortification construction against the Vikings and Hungarians. Again, without better evidence, this too remains only conjecture, however chronologically logical.

Motte-and-bailey castles seem to have been particularly attractive to the most powerful lords of northern Europe, who benefitted much from the civil wars of the late Carolingian age; they are found in great numbers on the lands of the dukes of Normandy and the counts of Flanders, Brittany, Blois, and Anjou. Indeed, the best depiction of a motte-and-bailey castle is found in the early-twelfth-century writings of Walter of Therouanne who describes the castle of Merkem in Flanders:

> There was near the atrium of the church a fortress, which
> we may call a *castrum* or *municipium*, exceedingly high, built
> after the custom of that land by the lord of the town many
> years before. For it is the habit of the magnates and nobles

FORTIFICATIONS

of those parts, who spend most of their time fighting and slaughtering their enemies, in order thus to be safer from their opponents and with greater power either to vanquish their equals or suppress their inferiors, to raise a mound of earth as high as they can and surround it with a ditch as broad and deep as possible. The top of this mound they completely enclose with a palisade of hewn logs bound close together like a wall, with towers set in its circuit so far as the site permits. In the middle of the space, within the palisade, they build a residence, or, dominating everything, a keep.[5]

THE INFLUENCE OF WILLIAM
THE CONQUEROR

It is the motte-and-bailey castles in Normandy that provide the link ultimately to the later, more famous ones in England. The Norman motte-and-bailey castle can be traced to Count Fulk Nerra of Anjou. Fulk Nerra, whose

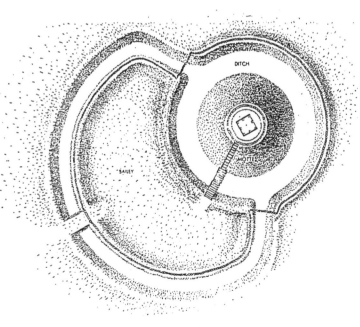

Fig. 8.2: Drawing of the Abinger motte-and-bailey castle.

Hope-Taylor (1956): 26

construction of stone castles will be discussed later, built many fortifications during his reign as the powerful count of Anjou (987–1040). As attested to by literary and archaeological evidence, many of these were motte-and-bailey castles, and they were used by both Fulk Nerra and his son, Geoffrey Martel, for the defense of their realm and the conquest of neighboring regions, including Maine and Normandy, in which, once conquered, they built several more motte-and-bailey castles.[6]

It is also from Normandy that the first motte-and-bailey came to England. In 1051 at the request of King Edward the Confessor, several Norman nobles entered England when the powerful Earl Godwin, Edward's chief counselor and father-in-law, was banished from the kingdom with his family. As Edward's new advisors, one of the first problems the Normans encountered was the continual raiding along the Welsh marches by small bands of raiders. To stop these raids, they constructed three castles along the border between England and Wales. These fortifications, known by the names Hereford, Ewyas Harold, and Richard's Castle, were all motte-and-bailey castles, and even after the return of Earl Godwin in 1052, they seem to have supported small Norman garrisons kept on apparently to assist in keeping peace along the borders.[7] (The mottes and most of the baileys of Ewyas Harold and Richard's Castle still survive.[8])

William the Conqueror, as duke of Normandy and later count of Maine, knew the value of the motte-and-bailey castle long before his conquest of England. He built a number of them, in the eastern part of his duchy, where he resided, in the western part, where he had to fight some of his nobles for power, and in the county of Maine, which he conquered in 1062.[9] In these castles William placed his most trusted lieutenants, his *vicomtes*, and in this way extended his control over the whole of Normandy.[10] Four of these motte-and-bailey castles—at Dol, Rennes, Dinan, and Bayeux—are depicted in the Bayeux Tapestry.[11]

William also used motte-and-bailey castles in his conquest of England. Between September 28, and October 22, 1066, when the Norman army defeated the English at the battle of Hastings, killing Harold Godwinson, the king of England, and destroying or dispersing the Anglo-Saxon army, William built at least three motte-and-bailey castles. His first, built shortly after landing on the southern coast of England, was at Pevensey, on the site of one of the Saxon Shore fortresses. It was followed two days later by another at Hastings, recorded on the Bayeux Tapestry, with a third constructed at Dover a few days after that. Others may also have been built but are not recorded by any contemporary source.[12] While some historians have suggested that the duke built these castles fearing that he might need to retreat to their protection, it is more likely that they were built to serve as a "beachhead" to receive reinforcements and supplies from Normandy. Never would William have believed that in a single battle he could knock out the English king, his brothers, and most of the Anglo Saxon military. He was clearly planning for a much longer campaign of conquest.

But even with his victory at Hastings William's conquest was not complete. Although their army had been soundly defeated and the potential for further defense largely gone, the English were not yet willing to embrace Norman rule, economy, and culture. William also realized the difficulty of subduing any people and the fact that he had only a few soldiers to accomplish this task. He determined that a number of fortifications would be needed to aid him in his further conquest. As he had in Normandy and on the southern coast of England prior to the battle of Hastings, William built motte-and-bailey castles, fortifications that were relatively quick and easy to build. In addition to subjugating the English, these motte-and-bailey castles would also provide protection against invading armies and control over William's own lords, whose loyalty he could not always count on, something he had learned as duke of Normandy. These castles would thus help him consolidate his rule over all of his new kingdom.[13]

It was not long before the anticipated revolts began. Having constructed several motte-and-bailey castles, William returned home to Normandy in March 1067. Almost as soon as he left, rebellions occurred in Dover and Hereford. William's administrators, Odo, Bishop of Bayeux, and William FitzOsbern, newly appointed duke of Hereford, were unable to put down these revolts, and the king was forced to return to England in December 1067.[14] His response to the growing dissatisfaction with Norman rule was to construct even more motte-and-bailey castles, and from 1068 to 1070, a large number were built.[15]

Still the revolts continued, with several following William's return. But each was quite easily put down by the Normans, with a motte-and-bailey castle often playing a role in the suppression. An example of this took place in the town of York, which, at the time of the Conquest, was undoubtedly the most important northern English town. It was the provincial capital of Northumbria and one of the two archiepiscopal sees in England. The people had supported Harold Godwinson—who had taken their side when they rebelled against the rule of his brother, Tostig, as earl in 1065, and had also freed them following Harald Hardrada's conquest of the town earlier in 1066[16]—and after his defeat continued to defy Norman rule (although their archbishop, Ealdred, had crowned William as king on Christmas Day 1066, and supported him).

Beginning in 1068, the citizens began a series of revolts against their Norman rulers. William answered the first of these by building a motte-and-bailey castle at what became known as Baile Hill. It was a particularly large fortress, with a garrison of more than 500 soldiers. Still, in early 1069, the inhabitants of York revolted once again, even attacking the castle that William had constructed to subdue them. It held until William arrived with reinforcements and the uprising was put down. William then constructed a second motte-and-bailey castle across the Ouse River from the first—what is now the motte below Clifford's Tower—building the fortification in eight days. But even this did not secure the town against rebellion. A few months later, in September 1069, the citizens of York, aided by some Danish mercenaries, again rose against Norman rule, and attacked the castles. On this occasion the York rebels prevailed, capturing and burning the wooden superstructures of both castles. William was once more forced to come north with his army, severely punished the people—part of what became known as "the harrowing of the north"—and in 1070 the two motte-and-bailey castles were rebuilt. Finally, the people submitted to their new king.[17]

The townspeople of York were unusual only in the frequency and obstinacy of their revolts, and also, perhaps, for the success of their 1069 uprising, however short-lived. But insurrections by newly conquered peoples were not the only reason for the construction of so many castles. Potentially a greater problem was the rebellions of William's nobles, which would increase if they held a large number of castles as well as armed retainers. In order to prevent these, which were costly and could potentially lead to defeat, William was forced to limit and regulate the further construction of motte-and-bailey castles. All of these were to be built only by barons, whom, like his *vicomtes* in Normandy, William had entrusted with their construction; in turn he granted them jurisdiction over the lands the castles protected. The barons were also given permission to confiscate any lands needed for the construction of these defenses, and many confiscated far more land than was required for the motte-and-bailey castle, thereby solidifying their own economic and political power.[18] As a result of involving a number of nobles in the fortification-construction process, but at the same time limiting the number and power of these fortifications, William established the politico-economic transformation—what traditionally has been called the "feudalization"—of the English people, while at the same time protecting his own rule.[19]

These regulations, designed to protect the king from baronial revolt, succeeded in doing just that until the last couple of years of his reign.

By the time of William's death in 1087 he had seen the building of a large number of motte-and-bailey castles. It is quite likely that this was the most extensive and rapid castle building program in history.[20] Unfortunately, there is no accurate means of knowing when or how many motte-and-bailey castles were built during the reign of William, or even before the end of eleventh century. The only land survey of William's realm, the *Domesday Book*, is incomplete and often in error when it mentions castles. It misses the well-known motte-and-bailey castles of Dover, Nottingham, Durham, and even the stone White Tower in London, for example.[21] Most scholars estimate, however, that between 500 and 550 were built between 1066 and 1087, although D.J. Cathcart King numbers them at 741 and R. Allen Brown claims that the number may actually have been closer to 1,000.[22]

After William's death his sons continued his policies of fortification construction, although they did so with less urgency or commitment than had their father. There had not been a foreign invasion for several years, and, more importantly, the people of England were more accepting of their Norman occupiers. Therefore, the need for new construction had diminished, while other castles, already completed, were allowed to fall into disuse. Besides, even before William died, it was becoming apparent that motte-and-bailey castles would be replaced, sometimes using the mottes as foundations, by stone castles. William himself built two of these, in London (the White Tower) and in Colchester, and more would follow during the rule of his successors.[23]

CONSTRUCTION TECHNIQUES

Despite their short period of influence, there is much known about motte-and-bailey castles because of the large number of extant English examples and because of the amount of attention paid to them by modern historians and archaeologists. There is also the rather unique portrayal of them as found in the Bayeux Tapestry, where no fewer than five motte-and-bailey castles are depicted.[24] Although there is little detail in the tapestry's depiction of them, it does provide a general picture of how motte-and-bailey castles were designed and built. When archaeological evidence from recent excavations is added to this source, the sophistication of these fortifications emerges.

The motte part of the castle structure was made of earth, which unless destroyed by later construction still remains. As a result, it is the easiest part of the castle to study in detail. But in starting such a study one must begin with the ditch around it. The simplest form of earthen defense has always been a ditch dug around an area to be protected. On a motte-and-bailey castle, when such a ditch was dug the removed earth was piled high in the center of the enclosed space. As the ditch grew deeper, it also grew wider; the greater the width and depth of the ditch, the greater the defensibility of the structure, and motte ditches were usually quite deep and wide. For example, the ditch at Baile Hill in York measured 21 meters wide and 12 meters deep.[25] As the ditch grew, the mound in the center of the ditch also grew in size and height. Some ditches were water-filled, as at Abinger and Baile Hill, but this was an infrequent addition and usually required a nearby natural water source.[26]

Mottes varied greatly in size and shape. They measured between 5 and 11 meters high and between 6 and 30 meters in diameter across the top. The larger mottes probably contained a hall and may be considered "residential mottes," while the smaller and much more common mottes contained only a tower and may have served to garrison just a few soldiers.[27] The steepness of the sides also varied considerably depending on the type of soil used in its construction. If the motte was built with a heavy clay soil, its sides would be very steep; if built with more of a sandy soil, it would have a gentler slope.[28]

While none of the wooden superstructures of mottes remains, post holes provide an idea of the size and design of these buildings. Some of these were quite large. For example, the structure on the motte at Bayeux, as depicted in the Bayeux Tapestry, is shown as a massive building with windows, a domed roof, and a forebuilding near its bridge.[29] In many other cases, as at the castle of Abinger, for example, post-holes reveal a small tower of large height. This may mean that the size of these superstructures was not as important as their height.[30] Some of the walls of these towers, especially the very tall ones, were not solid to the ground, but on stilts, as shown in the Bayeux Tapestry. This provided added defense for the inhabitants of the castle, an elevated fighting platform, and an excellent view of the surrounding countryside.[31] Adding to the defense of the structure, there may have been tiles of hide or thick bark attached to the sides of the towers. Such a protective skin appears on the motte tower at Dol in the Bayeux Tapestry.[32]

Archaeological excavations have also revealed that motte-and-bailey sub-structures, if present, varied substantially.[33] Many had no substructure; the tower was merely erected on top of the motte. This was certainly the situation when a natural knoll was used as a motte—which occurred only infrequently—but also on man-made mottes, and it may indicate a hastily built fortification not meant to provide permanent defense.[34]

At other times a substructure was built on the surface of the ground and the motte then constructed around and above it. This appears to have been the type of structure built at Hastings, for the Bayeux Tapestry shows men building the motte with the stilts of the tower already erected.[35] Some have suggested that this may indicate that the motte towers built by William before the battle of Hastings were prefabricated in Normandy and transported to England on board William's ships.[36] However, archaeological excavations have also indicated this as a frequent substructure construction after the battle of Hastings, for example at the Burgh motte-and-bailey castle in Suffolk, where the post-holes descend through the entire motte.[37]

Another type of substructure was also erected on the ground surface; however, only its exterior was buried, while the interior was retained as a cellar. These seem to have been an innovation of the early twelfth century. Examples dating to this period have been found at South Mimms, where the substructure was built in wood, and at Farnham, Ascot Doilly, and Wareham, where the substructure was constructed in stone.[38]

Finally, a third type of motte substructure, also from the early twelfth century, was a free-standing wooden tower to which an earthen mound was later added. This may indicate that the motte was not in the builder's original plan, and perhaps that the tower had a different original purpose, i.e., for whatever reason a later defensive addition was desired by the owner of the wooden tower. This must have been the case, for example, at the castle of Lydford in Devon, where the motte covers windows in the base of the tower. As such, both might represent transitional ideas in castle building, marking the end of the motte-and-bailey castle age and the beginning of stone castles.[39]

A wooden palisade was built around the top edge of the motte, as shown in the Bayeux Tapestry and by archaeological excavations. The post holes discovered during the archaeological excavations at Abinger, for example, showed that the palisade there consisted of two uprights, the outermost much taller than those inside. It is thus assumed that the palisade included a fighting platform that gave added defense and some offense to the motte. This is confirmed by the Bayeux Tapestry, where the motte palisade at Dinan is provided with two external fighting platforms.[40]

Outside the motte and separated from it by the ditch was a large bailey. Most often this was kidney-shaped, but its shape generally took advantage of the terrain of the site.[41] On the outside edge of the bailey was another palisade, probably just a simple single-log fence. Sometimes there was yet another ditch beyond the bailey palisade.[42] The bailey was fortified so that it too provided a defensive fortress, and as such it could have provided refuge to the nearby population or shelter to the horses and cattle belonging to the inhabitants of the castle. There is evidence of buildings constructed within many baileys, which, as for example at Hen Domen, seems to indicate that the bailey defended a small village, likely filled with people who served those in the castle.[43] Generally the purpose of the bailey was simply to protect the motte.[44]

The bridges from the bailey to the motte were also important in the defense of the castle. Two types seem to be most prevalent. First, except for the castle at Dol, the motte-and-bailey castles pictured in the Bayeux Tapestry all have a "flying bridge" leading directly from the bailey edge to the top of the motte. These bridges were all stepped with transverse bars of wood at regular intervals for safer passage and had gates at one end of the bridge.[45] Second, the excavations at Abinger reveal a short bridge across the motte ditch, with small steps leading up the side of the motte to get to the top. If an attack occurred, this bridge would simply have been destroyed to prevent crossing the ditch to the motte.[46]

It should be noted that there was never a "standard" motte-and-bailey castle design. Almost as many variations exist as castles themselves. For example, the mottes were square-shaped at the castles of Cabal Trump and Aughton;[47] double ditches enclosed the motte-and-bailey castles at Berhampstead, Corbets, Llanstephan, and Penrhos; two baileys were attached to a motte set midway between them at Windsor and at Arundel; and finally, two mottes were attached to one bailey at Lewes and at Lincoln.[48]

Strategically, the motte-and-bailey castles were very effective. They were quickly constructed and could be built by unskilled labor using material available at the site.[49] Frequently Englishmen were pressed into the service of building them.[50] On occasion they also seem to have played a strong role in stopping large armies.[51] However, they did have some disadvantages. For instance, timber was ill-suited for warfare: it could not withstand heavy assaults, and it needed constant repair; it was also very susceptible to fire.[52] Sometimes the castles were also constructed on sites that had been previously occupied by other dwellings: 166 houses were destroyed in Lincoln, 113 in Norwich, 27 in Cambridge, and in York one-fifth of the town was razed to build motte-and-bailey castles. Even part of the cemetery of the monastery at Ely was dug up to build the ditch of the castle there.[53] Perhaps this is the reason why motte-and-bailey castles were quite quickly replaced by stone structures throughout England and on the continent.

Notes

1. Higham and Barker (1995), which is informed by their excavations of Hen Domen castle: Higham and Barker (2000).
2. See de Bouard (1964): 19–26.
3. Fournier (1978): 67, 72–74; Fino (1970): 103; Hope-Taylor (1956): 247–48; and Renn (1973): 4.
4. Fournier (1978): 67; Renn (1973): 3; Fino (1970): 9; R. Brown (1976): 34; King (1988: 38; 1972: 101).
5. Quoted in R. Brown (1976): 60.
6. Fournier (1978): 68–69; Renn (1973): 4; Platt (1982): 3–4; and Le Patourel (1976): 304.
7. Brown, Colvin, and Taylor (1963): I: 19 and R. Brown (1989d): 84.
8. On Ewyas Castle see Boucher (2007), and for Richard's Castle see Pike (2009). Only slight traces of Hereford Castle survive.
9. Fournier (1978): 67; Le Patourel (1976): 204–5, 305–6; and Douglas (1964): 42, 140–41.
10. Douglas (1964): 140–41.
11. R. Brown (1989a): 222–25 and Stenton (1957): pl. 23–26, 28.
12. R. Brown (1976): 50; Renn (1973): 27–28; and Stenton (1957): pl. 51.
13. Le Patourel (1976): 303–5; Platt (1982): 2; and Stenton (1961): 197–200.
14. Beeler (1966): 36–37.
15. Beeler (1966): 37.
16. DeVries (1999b).
17. Brown, Colvin, and Taylor (1963): I: 21; Beeler (1956): 585–86; and Addyman (1972): 7–12.
18. Beeler (1956): 598 and Le Patourel (1976): 305.
19. Brown, Colvin, and Taylor (1963): I: 23–26; Beeler (1966): 51–53; Le Patourel (1976): 309–15; R. Brown (1989d): 83–84; Douglas (1964): 216–17; and Barrow (1956): 47–48.
20. R. Brown (1976): 50–51 and Beeler (1956): 584–86.
21. Ellis (1833): I: 223–24.
22. Beeler (1956): 586; Painter (1935): 322; King (1972): 102; and R. Brown (1989b): 65–66.
23. Brown, Colvin, and Taylor (1963): I: 29–32 and R. Brown (1989b): 74.
24. Stenton (1957): pls. 23, 24, 25–26, 28, and 51; R. Brown (1989a): 222–25.
25. Addyman (1972): 9.
26. Hope-Taylor (1956): 224–25 and Addyman (1972): 9.
27. R. Brown (1976): 55–56; Kenyon (1990): 9–12; Hope-Taylor (1956): 226; and King (1972): 101–12.
28. Hope-Taylor (1956): 226.

29. R. Brown (1989a): 223–24 and Stenton (1957): pl. 28.

30. Abinger's tower was only 3.7 square meters in area. See Hope-Taylor (1956): 237. See also R. Brown (1976): 34–35 and M.W. Thompson (1960): 89–90.

31. Kenyon (1990): 13–23; Brown, Colvin, and Taylor (1963): I: 23 and Stenton (1957): pl. 26.

32. Stenton (1957): pl. 23.

33. M.W. Thompson (1961): 305–6.

34. Hope-Taylor (1956): 225.

35. Stenton (1957): pl. 26.

36. Hope-Taylor (1956): 248.

37. M.W. Thompson (1961: 306; 1960: 88).

38. M.W. Thompson (1961): 306; R. Brown (1976): 34; and Davison (1967): 206–7.

39. M.W. Thompson (1961): 306.

40. Hope-Taylor (1956): 236–37; R. Brown (1989a): 223; and Stenton (1957): pls. 25–26.

41. R. Brown (1976): 56–57; Brown, Colvin, and Taylor (1963): I: 23; and Hope-Taylor (1956): 226.

42. R. Brown (1976): 58–59; Kenyon (1990): 31–38; and Hope-Taylor (1956): 226–27.

43. Higham and Barker (2000). It is their excavation of Hen Domen that led to their seminal work on wooden castles, Higham and Barker (1995).

44. R. Brown (1976): 61 and Brown, Colvin, and Taylor (1963): I: 23–24.

45. R. Brown (1976): 61 and Stenton (1957): pls. 24–26, 28, 51.

46. R. Brown (1976): 61.

47. King (1972): 196–97.

48. R. Brown (1976: 57–58; 1989b: 70–72); and Taylor (1958): 103.

49. Taylor (1958): 103.

50. R. Brown (1976): 51–52.

51. Lindsay (1974): 152.

52. Hope-Taylor (1956): 233–34 and Taylor (1958): 104.

53. R. Brown (1976): 51 and Brown, Colvin, and Taylor (1963): I: 24.

CHAPTER 9

STONE CASTLES

THE ORIGIN OF STONE CASTLES

EARTH-AND-TIMBER FORTIFICATIONS PROVED ENTIRELY INADEQUATE TO protect Western Europeans from the Viking and Hungarian incursions of the ninth and tenth centuries. Although motte-and-bailey castles were successfully used by William of Normandy to conquer and subdue England in the late eleventh century, construction of stone castles in London and Colchester seems to indicate that he recognized that these earth-and-timber structures were but temporary defenses for his kingdom. More permanent fortifications, made of masonry, were needed to defend the lands of Europe and their inhabitants from foreign attacks and domestic rebellions.

Yet, despite the obvious need for stone castles and the fact that by the end of the twelfth century they dotted the landscape of every medieval principality, one of the most difficult dates to determine in the history of medieval military technology is when they began to be built in Europe. Unless the historian of fortifications is willing to accept the early-tenth-century Italian charters for stone castles discussed in the first chapter of this section, which are without archaeological confirmation, there are neither written sources nor archaeological evidence to prove the existence of a stone castle before the late tenth century.

This was a period of instability and lack of strong central government throughout all of Europe, a condition that seems to have led to experimentation in fortification construction, experimentation that probably produced stone castles. As in the case of the motte-and-bailey castle, the late-tenth- and early-eleventh-century count of Anjou, Fulk Nerra, may be credited as the initiator of this new defensive construction.

Fulk was faced with almost continual conflict throughout his reign, from both outside and inside his territory, and he countered by building fortifications. Fulk fortified all of his borders with castles, at least 30 major strongholds in all. Frequently, these became the targets of his enemies, but rarely did they fall. Moreover, Fulk's own offensive forces, quartered in these fortifications, were able to make extensive attacks into his enemies' lands, ultimately giving him much more territory at the expense of his neighbors.[1]

Most of Fulk Nerra's fortifications were constructed using earth and timber, and some of them were motte-and-bailey castles. However, at least two, at Langeais and at Montbazon, seemed to have been constructed in stone. Both of these castles played important roles in Fulk Nerra's castle-building strategy. Langeais was built on the Loire River, and together with the fortress at Amboise, which had been constructed upstream by Fulk's father, Geoffrey Greymantle, controlled the entire region. Montbazon was built to the east of Langeais, on the Indre River, and provided defense for a southern route of communication with the fortresses of Amboise, Langeais, and Loches.[2]

It has been suggested that the stone ruins at both sites date from Fulk's reign. The ruins of Langeais reveal a tower keep (also called a *donjon*) originally 15 to 16 meters high with an outer rectangular perimeter measuring 17.5 by 10 meters. The walls were built on a shallow crushed-rock foundation that in places is only 70 centimeters below the surface. The walls were made of ashlar, and measured between 1.2 and 1.7 meters thick. The fill between the ashlar frame was composed of limestone and mortar. It was built not on a man-made motte, but on a natural rise of relatively low height. No wooden elements survive, but it is apparent that the tower was divided by wooden floors into three levels and that access was gained by a wooden door and staircase.[3]

That these are the ruins of Fulk Nerra's castles is disputed. Fulk's castle at Langeais is first mentioned in documents dating to 993/994, and three historians, J. F. Verbruggen, Marcel Deyres, and Gabriel Fournier, claim that what is mentioned there was nothing more than a wooden fortress. The stone keep, in ruins today, did not replace it until the late eleventh century and then was not built as a military structure but as a domicile.[4] Disputing their conclusions are

Pierre Héliot, J.F. Fino, Bernard S. Bachrach, and Philippe Contamine, who contend that the stone tower at Langeais was indeed Fulk Nerra's late-tenth-century fortress and that it was constructed for defensive purposes. As proof, they claim that the extensive and unsuccessful siege operation that Odo I, count of Blois, undertook there in 996 could only have occurred if the structure was a stone fortress.[5]

The dating of the stone fortress at Montbazon to Fulk's reign is also disputed. Although built in a similar rectangular pattern to Langeais, the keep at Montbazon was much larger. It measured 19.65 by 13.75 meters at the base and stood between 28 and 30 meters high. The walls were also thicker than at Langeais, measuring between 2 and 2.4 meters. There may also have been an exterior (or curtain) wall with a tower built on its northeast corner.[6]

Fulk Nerra's Montbazon castle dates to the early eleventh century, as a written reference of 1005/6 attests to its completion by that time. Again it is Héliot's and Bachrach's contentions that the stone castle that now lies in ruin there today is Fulk Nerra's, while Deyres claims that it should be dated after 1050, although even he admits that stylistically it could have been built earlier.[7]

The dispute is perhaps inconclusive, but what may ultimately shift the argument in the favor of those who wish to date the stone castles of Langeais and Montbazon to Fulk Nerra's reign is the large number of stone ruins on sites of other Fulk Nerra castles. Most of these have not been examined as well as the keeps at Langeais and Montbazon, but at least some appear to date from the late tenth or early eleventh century and may have actually been built by Fulk Nerra himself or by his retainers. These include the castles at Loudun, Argenton-sur-Creuse, Melle, and Brosse.[8] Other unexamined stone castles in lands adjacent to Fulk Nerra's also seem to date from the early eleventh century and may have been influenced by the Angevin count's building strategy (or perhaps by the stone castles on his borders). Odo II of Blois, William II of Angoulême, Odo of Déols, Boso the Old of La Marche, and even King Robert II of France may have built stone castles. Dating is still imprecise, but archaeological evidence supports these as early stone constructions, as does the fact that many of these fortifications successfully withstood lengthy and harsh sieges during the late tenth and early eleventh centuries, sieges that could only have been endured if the castles were built of stone.[9]

Another possible site for the origin of medieval European stone castles is Catalonia. Since the invasion of southwestern Francia by Muslim armies across the Pyrenees Mountains in the third decade of the eighth century, the area had been contested between Frankish and Muslim Spanish armies.

Charles Martel halted the initial Muslim invasion at the battle of Poitiers in 732, but a large number of Iberian soldiers and settlers remained in the region until, at the end of the eighth century, Charlemagne pushed them below the Pyrenees and captured Barcelona. To protect the lands of Provence and Aquitaine from further Muslim conquests, Charlemagne established a royal province along the Spanish March, although it would not acquire the name Catalonia until the twelfth century. After 809, when offensive action by the Franks against the Muslims ceased, this province became a defensive "buffer zone" between Carolingian France and Muslim Spain.

By the middle of the tenth century the situation in Catalonia had changed dramatically. The counts of the province, who had initially been drawn from the Carolingian nobility and military and were tied directly to the Carolingian throne, had gained the same freedoms from central rule that other Frankish nobles enjoyed. Perhaps more importantly, the various Muslim principalities in Iberia began to fight what would become the first of many wars against each other, wars that quickly destroyed the unity of the Muslim Umayyad dynasty in the Iberian peninsula. This allowed the Christian Visigoths in the northeast to establish their own kingdom, León, and to build up their own military strength. By 911 the Christians had conquered one-fifth of Iberia, and although the more populous and powerful southern portions remained in Muslim hands, the call for *Reconquista* (reconquest) spread throughout the rest of Europe.[10]

Catalonia was to play a major role both offensively and defensively in the early years of the *Reconquista*. To do so, the counts of the region first had to increase their military strength and then had to build permanent barracks to hold these soldiers. By the end of the tenth century, a large number of castles were built throughout Catalonia. They performed a dual purpose: they provided a defensive formation against any Muslim attacks, and by harboring soldiers, they also provided an offensive threat to the Muslim principalities on the other side of the Pyrenees.[11]

It is not known exactly when these castles began to be built of stone. It seems that initially they were built of earth and wood, although they were clearly not motte-and-bailey castles. By the beginning of the eleventh century (or maybe even earlier), most of these fortifications were built or rebuilt in stone. They were keeps, similar, it appears, in purpose to the castles of Fulk Nerra, but rather than being rectangular in shape, most were circular. They were also massive structures, and in fact dwarfed most castles built at around the same time in France. For example, the tower of Vallferosa was 38 meters in circumference and more than 30 meters high. Most also contained at least three and some-times as many as five stories with round and elliptical windows.[12]

Whether Fulk Nerra (or one of his neighbors) or the counts of Catalonia first originated the stone castle is not important. Of far greater historical sig-nificance is that by the end of the eleventh century stone castles had begun to be built everywhere in Europe. In France, the increase in the number of fortifications was incredible. In Poitou, for example, the number of castles increased from 3 at the beginning of the eleventh century to 39 by its end, and in Touraine, the increase was from 9 to 26 during the same period. In other regions, even more stone castles were built in even less time. For example, in Auvergne the number of castles grew from 8 to 34 between 1000 and 1050, and in Maine the number increased from 11 to 62 between 1050 and 1100.

By the end of the twelfth century the total number of castles that had been or were being built reached a very impressive total. In France, during the reign of Philip Augustus (1180–1223), the king alone held more than 100 castles, with his nobles holding several hundred more, and in England, at the beginning of the reign of Henry II, in 1154, there were an estimated 274 castles held by the king and his barons. While this number cannot compare with the 500–1,000 motte-and-bailey castles built during the reign of William the Conqueror, con-sidering the more sophisticated and elaborate building technology, the need for materials not easily accessible, and the greater expense required to construct stone castles, the number is quite impressive.[13]

––––––

ELEVENTH- AND TWELFTH-CENTURY STONE CASTLES

During the eleventh and twelfth centuries, the stone castle was seen in medi-eval society as a representation of power, strength, and defense. Even popu-lar literature began to use the castle as a metaphor both for aristocratic and noble strength, and, to a lesser extent, for the oppression of the poor and of the church.[14] Still, the castles themselves had changed little in style and function by the end of the eleventh century from those built earlier. They remained simple keeps built to garrison troops for defensive and offensive military operations.

However, at the end of the eleventh and beginning of the twelfth centu-ries the function of castles began to change, and changes in style soon fol-lowed. Instead of being just fortified barracks for soldiers, they began to be built and used as royal and noble residences. No longer would the simple keep, a tower built more for its size than for its comfort, satisfy the needs of its owner. Apartments, halls, chapels, kitchens, storage chambers, and latrines had to be incorporated into the new castle structure, and all these changes had to meet the station and comfort of a royal or noble inhabitant and his family. At the same time, the primary function of the fortress, providing protection to the lands and population surrounding it, necessitated that a continued military strength be present. Often this led to a compromise between the comfort of the residents and the defensibility of the structure.

Although this move to castle residency occurred everywhere throughout Europe in the late eleventh and early twelfth centuries, it is nicely exemplified by the stone castles of the Norman kings of England and their barons from 1077 to 1154. The motte-and-bailey castles built by William the Conqueror had performed their function well. Anti-Norman revolts were quelled throughout the kingdom, and by 1077 had nearly disappeared, with few, ineffectual invasions, all quite small in size. This success would mean that motte-and-bailey castles continued to be built for the conquest and subjugation of Wales, Scotland, and Ireland; but in England proper they were no longer needed.[15]

Rather than building what were essentially tall stone barracks, like those on the Continent, what replaced the motte-and-bailey castles in late-eleventh-century England were stone residential castles. In some ways these new castles were merely an extension of William the Conqueror's castle-building strategy, replacing the earth-and-wood motte-and-bailey castles with stone ones. For one thing, their military functions were the same, providing both defense against outside invasion and domestic stability. At the same time, with the English kingdom now effectively subject to Norman rule, it was time to replace the obviously weaker motte-and-bailey castle with stronger stone fortifications. Therefore, while some motte-and-bailey castles continued solely as earth-and-wood constructions—one of the York castles remained a wooden fortress until the end of the thirteenth century[16]—new stone castles were often built on top of the mottes, replacing wooden structures.

New castles built in England were of two distinct styles. The first style has been characterized by R. Allen Brown simply as the "keep-and-bailey castle." These were the easiest and probably the most economical castles to construct, for they made very few alterations to the old motte-and-bailey castle design: the bailey remained relatively intact, with a stone keep added to replace the old wooden fortress on top of the motte. The keep was the strongest and most important part of this castle. Called a shell-keep, because of its usual circular shape, it was constructed on top of the motte, if large enough, or around it, if the motte was small. In the latter case, the motte was usually leveled or hollowed out, although in a few cases it was actually incorporated into the shell-keep structure.

The keep contained the lord's living quarters and sometimes also a hall, chambers, and a chapel. Other residential buildings—kitchens, storehouses, stables, barracks, and, if not included in the keep, the hall and chapel—were built in the bailey enclosure. This meant that the bailey almost always needed more than ditches and wooden palisades to protect its perimeter, and a stone wall would be added. Only a few keep-and-bailey castles, among them Framlingham, Helmsley, and Pickering, did not add a stone wall to their baileys, and then only because their defenses, wide double ditches, seem to have been sufficient to provide the necessary defense for the bailey buildings.[17] Large and often quite intimidating stone gatehouses and stone towers were also added to protect the bailey enclosure.[18]

A good example of a keep-and-bailey castle is the one constructed at Farnham. Built c.1138 by Henry of Blois, the Bishop of Winchester, as his residence, Farnham Castle was erected on a D-shaped motte-and-bailey castle with the motte lying slightly off-center and apart from the bailey walls. A stone motte substructure, 11.3 meters square, provided the foundation for a keep, 15.6 meters square, although whether this was a feature added at the time the keep was constructed cannot be determined, but the fact that it was significantly smaller may indicate an earlier date. The height of the keep is not known, although it could not have been very tall, judging from the width of the keep and the size difference between the substructure and the keep built on top of it. The motte and keep were further surrounded by a circular stone shell-wall entered by a wide and shallow gatehouse, along which four rectangular towers were also built. The bailey was enclosed by a stone wall, and there were at least three buildings standing in the bailey, including a large hall and a chapel.[19]

Although there are several examples, this style of Norman castle seems not to have been very popular, and its presence may in fact represent a situation in which only a little money was available for castle building, although that is mere conjecture and misses the fact that the keep-and-bailey castle continued to be built into the thirteenth century, with the most famous example being the one constructed by Henry II at Windsor.

The second style of stone castle built in England during this period was the rectangular tower keep. Rectangular tower keeps were extremely large castles, much larger than shell-keeps of the keep-and-bailey type. Many of them covered an area more than 30 meters square, with two of the largest being the White Tower in London, which measured 36.5 by 32.5 meters, and Colchester Castle, which measured 46.5 by 35 meters. They were also quite tall, having at least two or three stories and a cellar.[20] This gave ample space inside the keep for all the rooms needed for residency: the lord's apartment, halls, chambers, staircases, kitchens, chapels, fireplaces, storerooms, latrines (which at times opened directly onto the outer keep walls), and sometimes even a dungeon, although these were probably used primarily as storerooms. The roof, sometimes pitched but most often flat, was made of wood and often contained a rampart or crenellated parapet. It also usually contained a fighting gallery, which opened to the outside through arrow slits, and one or more watchtowers. Gatehouses, many equipped with drawbridges and portcullises, were also attached to the keep and sometimes had limited access to it.

The most important and technologically complex feature of these castles was their walls. Here defensive strength and stability were emphasized over comfort. They were of course thickest at the base of the structure, as they had to support the walls above them, and also because this was the place where the castle was most likely to be attacked by picks, bores, and battering rams, but their uppermost stories were also of an impressive size. The size of these walls varied between castles, although few measured less than three meters thick and some measured as much as six meters. Generally the walls were constructed of ashlar, limestone if it was available, between which was stuffed large amounts of stone rubble. Stability was brought to the structure by its substructure, its numerous buttresses, and the fact that there were few openings in the walls.

These keeps were also often built on the sites of motte-and-bailey castles. Sometimes they replaced exactly the wooden motte structure, as at Castle Acre and at Lydford, but most often they were simply too large to fit on the smaller motte. In these cases, the motte was either discarded, with the keep being built on the bailey, as at the White Tower, Colchester, and Canterbury; built on the bailey wall, as at Kenilworth and Corfe; or built on the edge of the motte, rising out of the ditch, as at Clum and Guildford. The bailey surrounding these keeps continued to serve as the outer defense of the castle and was enclosed by a stone wall, as in the keep-and-bailey castles, although enlargements beyond the old bailey often took place.

There are numerous examples of this style of castle in England, as it was the most popular of Norman castle-building designs. Perhaps the most famous of these are the two earliest constructed: the White Tower and Colchester. Both were built under the direction of William the Conqueror, and they may have been completed before his death. Both may also have been the work of the same architect: Gundulf, the Bishop of Rochester.

The White Tower, so called because it was whitewashed during the Middle Ages, was begun c.1078. It rose nearly 27.5 meters, not including the extra height of the three turrets, and enclosed two stories and a basement. Each story was divided into two large halls, the largest of which measured 28 by 11.3 meters; a further subdivision enclosed the chapel of St. John, which rose from the basement to the roof and included a crypt and sub-crypt. The first story contained the halls and chambers for conducting the kingdom's affairs, with the second story, which was later divided into two, containing the chief residential chambers. The second story was quite lofty and contained a fighting gallery built halfway up the halls. Finally, the basement, which was only partially below ground level, was divided into two separate chambers and may have served only for storage and as a prison. Spiral staircases in each of the turrets led between the stories and also gave access to the watchtowers and roof, except for the basement, which was reached only by a single staircase.

The walls of the White Tower were suitably thick, measuring between 3.5 and 4.5 meters at the base, and were constructed with ashlar dressings and a rubble core. On each side of the keep a number of flat and narrow pilaster buttresses rose from the ground nearly to the top of the castle, with the largest turret also similarly buttressed. There was only a single entrance to the keep's first story, through a forebuilding that is now missing.

It is likely that the White Tower was intended by William the Conqueror to be his primary personal residence. In contemporary writings it is rarely described simply as a castle or a tower; instead, as in the twelfth-century writings of William Fitzstephen, it is described as a "fortified palace." Still in excellent condition, it continues to be the grandest example of Norman stone castle building.[21]

Although larger, Colchester castle was built in a style similar to that of the White Tower. It stands on the ruins of an old Roman temple, which may have influenced its large size; it also seems to have reused some of the Roman masonry in its construction. Its walls were of similar size and construction as those at the White Tower, although the three turrets at Colchester were larger and more square-shaped than the White Tower's turrets, adding more stability to its immense structure. Colchester was also entered by a single entrance through a forebuilding equipped with a portcullis and a large wooden door.

Fig. 9.1: Drawing of the White Tower.

The interior was also similar to the White Tower; however, the chapel and hall were smaller than those in the London keep. Differences included the addition of a small room on the first story, the purpose of which is unknown, and only two turret staircases, the third turret containing the building's latrines. Finally, there was a third story at Colchester, although it was destroyed in 1683.

While this keep was built in the residential style, it may not have served as one. At least it seems not to have been regarded as a royal residence by William the Conqueror. Built to guard against Scandinavian invasions, Colchester appears to have been a military barracks, which explains the large latrine facilities.[22]

The Norman rectangular castle style continued in use in later fortification construction and was especially favored by Henry II in his numerous late-twelfth- and early-thirteenth-century castle-building projects. However, by the middle of the thirteenth century, its popularity had diminished, replaced by a round-shaped castle style that nevertheless retained the residential aspects introduced by earlier Norman castles.[23]

While this discussion of residential castles has focused on England in the late eleventh and early twelfth centuries, there were numerous examples of this type of fortification in continental Europe. With few exceptions, they followed the two styles in which English castles were constructed. For example, the castle at Gisors in Normandy, which was built in 1123–24, and Pfeffingen Castle in Switzerland, built later in the twelfth century, were like the keep-and-bailey castles of England,[24] while the castles built at Arques in Normandy (1125), Loches in Touraine (early twelfth century), and Ghent in Flanders (mid-twelfth century) were like the English rectangular keeps. The only difference between these continental castles and those in England was that they were smaller. For example, Loches measured only 25 by 13 meters, although it rose more than 37 meters high, while Ghent measured only 28 by 17 meters. At Ghent, the walls were also thinner than most English castles, only 1.7 meters thick.[25]

————

CRUSADER CASTLES

The next important development in medieval castle construction came with the Crusades to the Holy Land beginning at the end of the eleventh century. Called initially at the Council of Clermont on November 27, 1095, by Pope Urban II, the First Crusade attempted to regain the lands where Jesus Christ was born, lived, and died, which they called the Holy Land and which then, and for the previous five centuries, had been under Muslim control. The response to Urban's call was enthusiastic, and a large army gathered to set out on Assumption Day, 1096. After a difficult journey to the Holy Land, which saw the Crusaders fighting more against the harsh conditions of the Middle East than against the Muslims, the Crusade was successful. The first prize,

Antioch, fell on June 28, 1098, followed a year later, on July 13, 1099, by the fall of Jerusalem.

By 1101 the Crusaders had secured their presence in the Holy Land. Their initial success resulted to a large extent from a war that was being fought in the Middle East between the Seljuk Turks and other Muslim peoples, most notably the Egyptian Fatamids. This extended war had both depleted the fighting strength of the Muslims and brought disunity in the defense of their territories. For a while the Crusaders met little military reaction to their conquests. However, they soon realized that they would eventually be forced to defend their newly won territories. They would also have to do it with fewer soldiers than they had in the initial conquests, as many, perhaps as much as one-half to two-thirds of the initial force, returned to Europe following the fall of Jerusalem.[26]

Eventually four Crusader kingdoms were carved out of the captured Middle Eastern territory: Edessa, Antioch, Tripoli, and Jerusalem. Kings were elected and a European socio-political structure created. In order to ensure the security of the kingdoms against both Muslim attacks from outside and Muslim/Jewish uprisings from inside these kingdoms, two practices were instituted. First, the Crusaders negotiated with the Muslims and Jews for peace. Treaties were made, bribes paid, and alliances formed; some Muslims and Jews were even used as tax collectors and policemen. Second, numerous castles were built throughout the four kingdoms. The Crusaders realized the need for building castles, and for building them quickly, and within three decades after the fall of Jerusalem most of their castles were completed.[27] Of the two practices, the building of castles was the most effective. Treaties, alliances, and even bribes all failed to keep the peace during the century following the First Crusade. But the castles seldom failed, especially in the first hundred years of occupation, and when they did, it took a long time and necessitated a large number of men.

Of initial concern to these castle builders was the security of the Crusader kingdoms' frontiers. Three were especially vulnerable, and the Crusaders concentrated their initial castle construction in these areas. The first, and perhaps most important, was the sea coast. At the end of the First Crusade the Christians had conquered almost all of the coast from Antioch to the Sinai Desert, with the exceptions only of Tyre (not captured until 1124) and Ascalon (not captured until 1153), and it needed to be protected. The second was the frontier facing Damascus. The third was to the south and protected the kingdom of Jerusalem against incursions from Egypt. Numerous castles were built along all these frontiers. A fourth frontier, west of Antioch and facing Aleppo, would also have been filled with castles, except that negotiations between the Crusaders and the Seljuk Turks led to a "demilitarized zone" without either Muslim or Crusader fortifications.[28]

Castles were built along all major routes and in every major mountain pass, along the deserts, the mountains, the rivers, the lakes, and the sea. But protecting the frontiers was only one obligation undertaken by the Crusaders, and it was a responsibility that they could not completely fulfill. There was simply a limitation to the defensibility of the kingdoms' frontiers, especially when so few soldiers were available as reinforcements should a border or a castle be attacked.[29]

The function of many other castles built by the Crusaders was not the protection of the kingdoms' boundaries, for they were built deep inside the Crusaders' lands. These served as garrisons for soldiers who could be used to besiege nearby Muslim towns, such as Tyre and Ascalon, or to raid neighboring, unfriendly Muslim lands. Defensively they served as refuges against the attacks of strong Muslim leaders, like Saladin, until relief could come from elsewhere in the Crusaders' kingdoms or from Europe. They served as centers of authority and police posts for the governance and security of the kingdoms against domestic insurrections.[30] Finally, these castles were administrative centers and hubs of economic development and colonization.[31]

With the exception of a few castles built to defend the larger towns of the Holy Land, at Tripoli, Tortosa, Tyre, Beirut, Acre, and Jerusalem, most Crusader castles were built in the countryside. It was here that the Crusaders could use the harshness and inaccessibility of the Middle Eastern terrain to add to the defensibility of their structures. Castles were built on the summits of precipitous rocks or next to steep ravines. At two places, Tyron and Habis, the Crusaders even fortified caves. Most castles had thick walls faced with stone. Because their inhabitants anticipated long sieges that might last until reinforcements could arrive from Europe, the castles were provided with reservoirs for water supply and large cellars for food storage. For example, at the castle of Margat it is estimated that there were sufficient food and water supplies to feed a garrison of 1,000 men for 5 years.[32]

In general, two types of castles were built by the Crusaders. The first followed the style that began to be common in Europe at the end of the eleventh century: large rectangular keeps encircled by a stone wall. They were built with the same simple utilitarian character and the same solid construction as those in Europe. They were often also as large in area, but usually only two stories instead of three.[33]

Two of the best examples of this type of Crusader castle were built at Safita and Jebail and were known to the Crusaders as Chastel Blanc and Giblet. Lying in the southern coastal region of Syria, the castle at Safita was built on a rocky knoll nearly 1,000 feet above sea level. At this height and with the precipitousness of its slope, defense was secured. The keep measured 30.5 by 18.3 meters and stood more than 25 meters high. It had two stories: in the upper story was a large, vaulted room, presumably the living quarters, which filled the entire extent of the keep and was lit by only a few arrow-slits; below it was a hall, also filling the extent of the keep, which was used as chapel. The flat roof was enclosed by a crenellated parapet. Around the keep was an oval wall with a large polygonal tower at its southwest end. There may also have been a gatehouse near this tower, although it has now disappeared. On the lower slopes of the knoll was another polygonal wall with a fortified gateway, adding to the defense of the castle above. It is not certain when the castle at Safita was originally built, although it must have been before 1166–67 when the Muslim leader Nur ad-Din is said to have captured it. It was also known to have been a Templar castle, although whether that Order initiated its construction is uncertain.[34]

The castle at Jebail is a good example of a rectangular keep castle, but it is different from Safita in many ways. It was built not on a precipitous location, but at the southeast corner of a wall surrounding a town and a small harbor, the site of the ancient Phoenician seaport of Byblos. It was also much smaller, measuring only 17.7 by 22 meters, with only two stories. One of the strongest Crusader castles, the keep of Jebail Castle was built by reusing large blocks of ancient stone masonry, with old marble columns cut up and used for bonding. Enclosing this keep was a rectangular curtain wall reinforced with small corner towers. An extra tower in the center of the north face guarded the gate. Jebail Castle was constructed as early as the first decade of the twelfth century and served as a part of the fortifications of the kingdom of Tripoli.[35]

Most of the Crusaders' castles were not rectangular keeps, however. Such castles, too small in both keep size and overall size, simply could not sufficiently meet the military needs of the Christian force occupying the Holy Land. They could not house enough troops to stand in the way of an attacking force, nor could they store enough food and water for a prolonged siege. Rectangular keeps often took a long time to construct, and, as they were the focal point of a castle's defense, there was little protection until they were completed. The Crusaders needed a fortification that was larger, more quickly built, and more defensible as it was being built. Therefore, they built most of their castles in the style of older Byzantine fortresses already prominent in the Holy Land.

On their journey to Jerusalem the Crusaders had seen and been impressed by the majestic walls of Constantinople. They then besieged the Muslim-held Byzantine fortresses at Nicaea and Antioch. Throughout the Holy Land they confronted other Byzantine defensive structures, so strongly built that they had been repaired by the Muslims who had inhabited them since the seventh century. These clearly influenced the Crusaders, and they began to imitate them.[36]

This style of fortification can most easily be described as castle complexes, although they are most often called concentric castles. They did not rely on a single rectangular keep for their defense; instead, they imitated urban fortifications with large and powerful outside walls strengthened on the sides and in the corners with towers. The buildings inside the complex, none of which were like the rectangular keep castles, became less important in the defense of the castle. They were meant simply to provide housing and storage. These castles were also larger, their size determined by the extent of their outside walls, and could be more quickly constructed than rectangular keep castles.

The Crusaders built many of these castle complexes, most of which were impressive in their size and structure. Walls, sometimes double walls, surrounding a large bailey dominated each castle. As they were the primary means of defense, the walls were very tall and made of the strongest masonry. They were also protected at intervals by a number of crenellated towers. Entrance into the castle was through a single large gatehouse equipped with heavy wooden doors, portcullises, and occasionally a drawbridge. Buildings in the bailey varied in size, shape, and purpose. There were halls, barracks, kitchens, magazines, stables, baths, latrines, storehouses, and, especially in the cases of castles held by the monastic military orders, chapels and chapter houses. Most also contained large, deep wells and/or rainwater reservoirs that were meant to sustain their inhabitants if besieged for long periods until reinforcements could arrive, perhaps from Europe. In some castles there were also keeps, built as residences or barracks and meant to stand as a final line of defense should the outer walls fail.

The shape of these castles was determined by the terrain on which they were built: the harsher the terrain, the more defensible the castle. Many Crusader castle complexes were on high, precipitous hill tops or ridges. Often a deep and steep ravine or ditch, sometimes natural and sometimes hewn out of solid rock, was added. The terrain also determined that some castles, among them Saône, Beaufort, and Toprakkale, were divided into two separate baileys or fortresses accessible to each other only by means of a small drawbridge. In spite of

Fig. 9.2: Krak des Chevaliers (twelfth–thirteenth centuries), Syria.

The Bridgeman Art Library International. © Julian Chichester.

the harshness of terrain on which most of these castles were located, though, most covered quite large areas. For example, the castles at Saône and Subeibe covered an area of 5 and 6.5 hectares respectively.[37]

Perhaps the most impressive of these castles, and certainly the one most studied by modern historians and architects, was Krak des Chevaliers. It remains to this day one of the best preserved and most awe-inspiring medieval castles in the world. No less a historical figure than T. E. Lawrence (Lawrence of Arabia) was struck by its beauty and endeavored to make a study of it. He described it as "perhaps the best preserved and most wholly admirable castle in the world, [a castle which] forms a fitting commentary on any account of the Crusading buildings of Syria."[38] Built in the mountainous regions of southern Syria not far from the castle at Safita, Krak des Chevaliers was constructed using the terrain to improve its defensibility. It was erected on a hilltop over 640 meters high and surrounded on three sides by steep slopes. Yet its area measured nearly 140 by 210 meters, making it one of the largest of the Crusaders' castles.

The outer defenses consisted of a polygonal wall, which contained several defensive galleries and semicircular towers. A small gate in the northern face of this wall was guarded by two adjacent towers. Between the outer and inner defenses was a forecourt, 16 to 23 meters wide, with a deep rock-hewn ditch in the southern section serving as a reservoir. The stables, magazine, baths, and latrines were also located in the forecourt.

FORTIFICATIONS

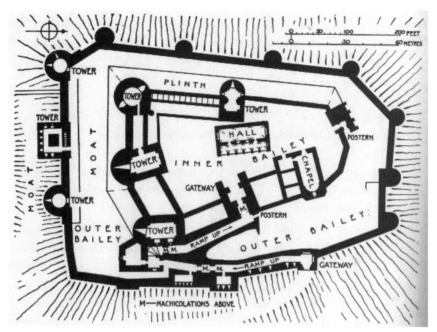

Fig. 9.3: Plan of Krak des Chevaliers.

Toy (1955): 99.

The inner stronghold of the castle lay on top of a steep revetment rising from the forecourt. It was large and spacious and contained a range of buildings serving different functions, including more water tanks and food storehouses. The inner stronghold also included a chapel, although whether this originated with the construction or was added later when the castle came under the control of the Knights Hospitaller cannot be determined.

The entrance to the castle was protected by three fortified gateways, between which are sharp-turning narrow corridors. For even more defense, on the walls were five massive towers, one on the northern, one on the western, and three more on the southern perimeters. All five towers contained many chambers in their several stories and were probably the living quarters of the knights. They were separated from each other and from the main fortress by a series of stepped bridges. All the buildings in the complex, like the outer walls, were built using the most proficient of architectural and masonic skill. The stone was solid—pierced only by arrow slits—and smoothly cut with some, albeit minor, ornamentation.

Krak des Chevaliers was built in the early twelfth century on the site of a Muslim fortress, which for the most part was dismantled, and it remained a formidable defensive stronghold during the entire Crusader occupation of the Holy Land. It also housed a large number of combatants. In 1212 Wilbrand of Oldenburg estimated that the castle held more than 2,000 soldiers, although most of these were probably Maronite or Syrian soldiers rather than Knights Hospitaller. Its location and garrison meant that it became a target of many Muslim sieges and attacks. The castle survived sieges by Alp Arslan, the Sultan of Aleppo, in 1125 and by Saladin in 1188, and withstood further Muslim attacks in 1163, 1167, 1207, 1218, 1229, 1252, 1267, and 1270. It also survived two major earthquakes during this time. Finally, after being almost completely evacuated by its inhabitants, and after an extensive siege, Mamluk Sultan Baibars captured the castle in 1271.[39]

After their initial conquests, the Crusaders had limited military success. In time, the nearby Muslim rulers began to unite and threaten the Crusader kingdoms. The first major setback for the Crusaders came in 1144, when the poorly protected kingdom of Edessa fell to Nur ad-Din, leaving the other kingdoms open to conquest. In response, the Second Crusade was immediately called by Pope Eugene III. However, it proved to be a miserable failure. Arriving in the Holy Land in late 1147, the Second Crusaders began to quarrel with the resident Crusaders, primarily over the latter's willingness to make alliances and treaties with the Muslims, and this divisiveness brought a lack of offensive military unity that ultimately led to failure at Damascus against the more unified Muslim forces.

With the failure of the Second Crusade, Nur ad-Din began to extend his power to the south: Damascus was taken in 1154 and Egypt fell in 1168. Nur ad-Din died in 1174, but he was succeeded by Saladin, the nephew of Shirkuh, Nur ad-Din's lieutenant who had conquered Egypt. Saladin proved to be an even more capable general than both his uncle and Nur ad-Din. When he succeeded to the throne he controlled almost all of the land surrounding the remaining Crusader kingdoms, and it was only a short time before he began to think about extending his power there as well. By 1187 he began to move into the Crusader lands, and on July 4, 1187, he met and defeated a large Crusader army at the battle of Hattin. The road to Jerusalem lay open to him, and the city fell on October 2, 1147. Only Tyre, the kingdom of Antioch, and the kingdom of Tripoli remained in Crusader hands.[40]

This again brought an immediate response from the papacy. Jerusalem, the gem of the Holy Land, captured by the First Crusaders, had fallen to the Muslims, and it was the responsibility of the kings and princes of Europe to retake it. The Third Crusade brought large armies from the three most powerful kingdoms of Europe: Germany, France, and England. All three armies were led by their kings. However, despite the royal and papal influence in this Crusade, it also met with failure. The German army, choosing to travel overland to the Holy Land, never reached its target. Its emperor, Frederick Barbarossa, 68 years old, drowned in the Saleph (now Göksu) River between Armenia and Antioch, and shortly thereafter much of his army, deprived of their royal leader and decimated by disease and Muslim attacks, returned to Europe. The French and English armies, traveling overseas rather than by land, did arrive at the Holy Land, but once there, the two kings, Philip Augustus of France and Richard I "the Lionheart" of England, could never agree on any military action. No major campaign was ever launched by the two together, and no battle ever fought. Acre fell in July 1191 to the Crusaders after a lengthy and uneventful siege, but then, in October 1191, Philip went back to France and began attacking Richard's territory there. Richard campaigned further up the coast toward Jerusalem, but Saladin kept him from the city and, late in 1192, Richard also returned home.[41]

With the failure of the Third Crusade came the end of defensible borders in the Holy Land; now there were only defensible areas, all of which were protected by castles.[42] One by one they too fell to Muslim armies. Further Crusades had no better success. The Fourth Crusade became diverted to Constantinople, which was conquered in 1204, but did not proceed to the Holy Land from there. Crusades also failed in 1212, 1221, 1229, 1254, 1270, and 1272. One famous Crusader, King Louis IX (St. Louis) of France, saw not only a large part of his army captured in Egypt in 1250, but his own death in Tunisia in 1270. Only King Frederick II of Germany eventually retook some of the lost Holy Land, including Jerusalem, in 1228, but by this time Muslim power had shifted with the Mamluks to Egypt, and Frederick had no better success there than any other thirteenth-century Christian general. By the middle of the thirteenth century the remaining Crusader territory and castles in the Holy Land began to fall. In 1268 the kingdom of Antioch surrendered; in 1289, Tripoli capitulated; and finally, in 1291, when Acre fell, the last vestiges of the Crusaders' conquest returned to Muslim control.

During this time, until finally forced out of the Holy Land, the Crusaders continued to build castles. But these fortifications, most of them erected in urban areas, were not nearly as elaborate or sophisticated as those constructed during the first half of the twelfth century. Indeed, there seems to have been an air of desperation in much of their construction.[43] But one feature prominent in these later fortifications is important to note. The Crusaders had discovered during their attacks on Muslim fortifications and then later in the defense of their own castles that there were many disadvantages to rectangular keeps and towers. For one thing, the straight walls of a rectangular keep were relatively easy to destroy by a battering ram or siege machine. They also presented virtually unprotected corners to attackers, with almost no potential for flanking fire. A circular or multi-angular keep or tower was more easily defended than a rectangular structure. It presented no unseen or shielded cover to the enemy and often offered no straight walls to his battering machines.[44] It would soon become an important option for European castle builders as well.

A parallel history of Crusader castle construction, both in chronology and style, is to be found in Spain. Muslim soldiers had crossed into Spain from Morocco in 711, and by 720, due both to the strength of their armies and to the disunity of the Visigothic kingdoms, had conquered most of the Iberian Peninsula. Only the kingdom of Asturias in the north successfully resisted their conquests, securing this success at the Battle of Covadonga in 722. This victory may have come because Muslim leaders had split their forces between those responsible for taking northern Iberia and those that had crossed the Pyrenees Mountains and entered France. The latter army's defeat by Charles Martel in 732 at the Battle of Tours further secured the independence of the Asturias kingdom.

An uneasy peace settled on the Iberian Peninsula for the next few centuries. Neither Christian nor Muslim Spaniards lost their religious animosity toward the other, but both the lack of funds and the lack of unity seem to have kept them away from major military incursions into the other's realms, although border clashes and raids were frequent. The disunity in the Christian lands would eventually see a division of Asturias into several separate kingdoms: Galicia and León in 910, Navarre in 987, Castille in 1035, and Aragon in 1035. Initially, this weakened Christian political and military power, prompting fears of Muslim invasion among those in kingdoms neighboring Al-Andalus, or Islamic Iberia.[45]

To calm these fears, Christian kings built a large number of fortifications. One good example was Loarre Castle, built near the large Muslim town of Huesca. Constructed by King Sancho III Garcés "the Great" in c.1020 as one of a line of fortifications he built in the lower Pyrenees, Loarre consisted initially of three tall towers tied together and able to be defended on their own if needed. In 1073 the king of Aragon, Sancho I Ramírez, grandson of Sancho III Garcés, significantly added to this castle, while at the same time exhibiting his piety, by attaching an Augustinian priory to the front of the towers, which also served

Fig. 9.4: Loarre Castle (eleventh–thirteenth centuries).

Photo by the author.

as an extended defense of the castle as a whole. Should it have been attacked, enemy soldiers would have had to fight through the crypt and nave of the church before they could even reach the central fortifications, which remained the three initial towers.[46]

Another of these strongholds was a Muslim fortress that stood 10 kilometers from Loarre Castle and was easily seen from the walls of the Aragonese fortification. Although this fortress does not survive and has not been excavated, and thus its strength is unknown, it represents a similar castle-building policy held among the Al-Andalusian leaders. They also saw the need to protect their borders from invasions and raids wherever they faced a Christian threat. But slowly the Christian kings' *Reconquista*, as it would be called later, began to cut into the Muslim realm. Coimbra was captured in 1064 by Ferdinand I of León and Toledo by Alfonso VI of Castille in 1085. Between 1073 and his death in 1094, Sancho Ramírez, using Loarre Castle as a base, captured the lands around Huesca, with the city itself falling to his successor, Peter I, in 1096. Afonso I Henriques, King of Portugal, with the help of Second Crusaders from England, Flanders, and the Rhineland, took Lisbon in 1147, with these same Crusaders and others from Catalonia, Genoa, and Pisa capturing Almeria later that year.[47]

But the *Reconquista* was interspersed with warfare between and within Christian kingdoms, as evidenced in the military adventures of the famous El Cid (Rodrigo Díaz de Vivar), who fought both for and against the Castilian king Alfonso VI in the late eleventh century.[48] Only with the Christian victory in the battle of Las Navas de Tolosa in 1212 were significant inroads into Al-Andalus made, and by 1249 all but the emirate of Granada had fallen—although it would hold out until its conquest in 1492 by King Ferdinand II of Aragon and Queen Isabella of Castile.

At each phase of the *Reconquista*, as their borders moved, Christian kings constructed new fortifications, almost always answered by new Muslim fortifications. Often these were built in sight of each other. Soon the country was covered by castles, the largest number of any medieval land. On both sides some of these fortresses were controlled by kings, some by nobles, and some also by ecclesiastics, as elsewhere throughout Europe and the Eastern Mediterranean, but, uniquely, some were also built and controlled by the common people.[49]

Perhaps no other event in medieval history had the impact on military technology, especially European fortifications, as did the Crusades. Because most Crusader and *Reconquista* castles were larger and more capable of a sustained defense than European ones, they tended to impress everyone who saw them. This, added to the fact that so many soldiers of different European kingdoms and principalities served in the Holy Land and Iberia, many of whom would authorize and control the construction of castles when they returned home, meant that the Crusader and Iberian castles greatly influenced late-twelfth- and thirteenth-century castle building throughout Europe. This would create a "golden age" of castle construction that produced perhaps the finest examples of what modern students see as the archetypical medieval castle.

THE GOLDEN AGE OF CASTLE CONSTRUCTION

While it is true that the building of rectangular keep castles continued until the end of the Middle Ages, by the beginning of the fourteenth century their numbers were being surpassed by those built in other styles. These were constructed in a style that differed radically from European castles of the late eleventh and early twelfth centuries but was very much like many Crusader castles. In particular, these new European castles were built as complexes that relied on walls and towers, and not a central keep, for their principal defense. When a keep was added, which occurred frequently, it was often not rectangular in shape, but round or multi-angular.

It was this round or multi-angular keep of the Crusader castles that made the earliest and perhaps the greatest impact on European fortifications. So overwhelmingly logical was the improved defense of this new castle style, and so little did it change the cost or technology of the construction, that it immediately began to alter all further castle building. In fact, its impact away from the Holy Land occurred so quickly that some historians have determined that this was a European innovation and not due to the influence of the Crusades.[50] Yet it is difficult to deny what must have been a strong influence on the many European Crusaders who saw the impressive Byzantine circular towers on the walls of Constantinople, or to suggest that they might not want to duplicate it in their homelands.[51]

The first multi-angular keep (or "transitional" keep, as it is sometimes, erroneously, called) may have appeared in France as early as 1130 with the construction of the keep at Houdan. There a two-story tower was built in a round shape, with walls measuring 3.5 meters thick and four projecting circular turrets or contreforts added to the outside. Inside, Houdan castle had a square-shaped plan on both stories. The bottom story served as a store-room, while the upper one was a great hall. Residential chambers were in three of the turrets, while the fourth contained a staircase to the crenellated roof. The only entrance to the castle was into the second story through the north turret (six meters above the ground).[52]

The size of the castle at Houdan—measuring only 30 meters in height and 15 meters in diameter, not including the two-meter-wide turrets—was not particularly impressive, nor were its accompanying outer defenses. But it established a style that would be followed by several later and often larger castles, including Provins, Gisors, and Etampes in France, and Orford, Conisborough, Chilham, Odiham, and Longtown in England. These castles, all built before 1200, varied little in style from Houdan. Provins and Conisborough were larger, containing four stories instead of two, and Gisors and Provins were built on top of mottes. Other differences included the shape and function of the inner residences and the number and quality of the bailey defenses. However, the chief difference at Houdan was in the turrets added to the keep. In this only Provins imitates the original. Etampes was built in a quatrefoil style, and Chilham and Odiham were octagonal; none of these had any turrets. Orford had square instead of round turrets—three of them—all taller than the keep. Gisors, Conisborough, and Longtown did not contain turrets in the functional sense but instead had three or more buttresses added to the outside of the keep.[53]

The circular shape, the crenellated roofs, and the guarded entrance to the keep all meant that the builders of these castles seemed to be emphasizing the defensibility of the structure. A further step in this defensive development of castles came in the early thirteenth century with the removal of all additions, turrets, or buttresses from the outside of newly constructed keeps, leaving the round-shaped structure alone: the multi-angular keep.

In England, the most notable example of this castle style was built at Pembroke c.1200 by the famous knight, baron, and regent of England, William Marshal. William's keep was perfectly circular and large, more than 24 meters high and 16 meters in diameter. It contained four stories, with three residential floors and a basement, and its only entrance was into the second story over a drawbridge. The walls were thick, measuring 4.6 meters, and were the same thickness throughout the entire structure. Stability was added to the keep by the lack of windows—only four were put in the building—which produced a very strong fortification, although with a very dark interior. Outside defenses were negligible, with only a thin curtain wall strengthened by a few circular towers, as it is clear that William was relying on the strength of the keep and the harsh terrain for the defensibility of the castle.[54]

In France, circular keep castles were much more popular than in England, especially as they seem to have been promoted by King Philip Augustus. The castles at Dourdan, Falaise, Rouen, Issoudun, and Villeneuve-sur-Yonne all contained large circular keeps, but perhaps the two best examples of this French castle style are found at Aigues-Mortes and Coucy.

The circular keep at Aigues-Mortes, known as the Tower of Constance, was not exceptionally large or impressive. Built in the mid-thirteenth century, it measured only 30 meters high and 22 meters in diameter, and contained just two residential stories and a small basement. But this structure clearly showed the new European emphasis on defensibility. The walls were 6 meters thick at their base, and the foundations were 18 meters deep. Access to the keep was through a single entrance guarded by machicolations and gained only by traversing a drawbridge over an encircling moat and going through two heavy wooden doors and a portcullis. Otherwise, only two small windows and a number of narrow arrow slits penetrated the walls. Initially, the keep stood alone, although perhaps surrounded by a wooden palisade, but an 11-meter-high stone curtain wall was added in 1289–1300 as extra defense.[55]

Both the Tower of Constance at Aigues-Mortes and the keep at Pembroke were dwarfed by the round tower at Coucy. This was by far the largest, strongest, and grandest of the French circular keeps. Built between 1225 and 1242 as the chief residence of Eugerrand III, the Sire of Coucy, it covered an area 31 meters in diameter and rose more than 55 meters high. Coucy also had a very secure entrance that contained all of the same defenses present at the Tower of Constance: the moat, drawbridge, machicolations, doors, and portcullises. But unlike the Tower of Constance, Coucy had a second entrance, also protected by a drawbridge, which led from the second story to the curtain wall-walk. Also unlike the Tower of Constance, Coucy included powerful outer defenses from the very beginning of its construction. A large trapezoidal bailey wall, 20 meters high and flanked by four large drum towers, surrounded the circular keep and provided further protection to the already strong castle.[56]

More important even than the circular keep, the Crusaders' castles introduced the castle complex to Europe. As with their predecessors, the European castle complexes always included extensive bailey defenses: high walls, large flanking towers, crenellated wall-walks with machicolations, and extensive, secure gateways. Most were also built on the summits of precipitous hilltops or on high man-made mottes. However, unlike the Crusader castles, the European ones almost always added a keep to the complex, sometimes using an existing keep, constructing the new fortress around it, and at other times building an entirely new keep at the time the outside walls were being constructed. When an existing keep was used it tended to be rectangular in shape, a new keep multi-angular or circular.

Although they were numerous, three of these European castle complexes should suffice as examples of this castle-building style. The first, the castle at Dover, was built by King Henry II as a defense of the vulnerable southeastern coast of England and also probably as a royal residence. (The site had been recognized previously by the Romans for its defensibility, a lighthouse built by them still extant.) Dover Castle was an extremely expensive venture for the powerful English king, who spent a recorded £6,400 on its construction, an expense that was added to later by his sons, Kings Richard and John. The initial construction, between 1181 and 1187, was of a powerful keep. Built in a rectangular style, it was very large, measuring almost 30 square meters at its base and rising to a height of 29 meters. It contained two stories and a basement. Both stories held a large hall, divided down the middle by a cross wall, a number of smaller chambers, a latrine (which emptied its contents onto the outside castle yard), a well, and a chapel. The second story, which was twice the height of the first story, also included a gallery. Two spiral staircases, located in opposite corners of the keep, gave access to the two stories and also to the roof, which was surrounded by a crenellated rampart and four crenellated square corner turrets rising another 3.7 meters. The walls were well buttressed and varied at the base between 5.2 and 6.4 meters in thickness. The keep could be entered only through a separate multi-story gatehouse, containing three long flights of stairs and strengthened by three towers. The keep was further protected by a tall wall surrounding the bailey, which was fortified by 14 square towers. There were two entrances, each guarded by two flanking towers, the largest of which was known as Constable's Gate. Each gate tower was equipped with a long outer defensive structure, known as a barbican, placed in relation to the gateway so that an attacking force was exposed to maximum flanking fire.

The defenses of Dover Castle were quickly put to the test, as it came under siege in 1216 by the French dauphin, later King Louis VIII. The castle walls held, and the keep was not threatened. However, the attack prompted the construction of a parallel outer wall, built between 1230 and 1260, which also contained a large number of towers, this time semi-circular in shape.[57]

A second example of the European castle complex can be found in the castle built at Najac in southern France. Begun in 1253 by Alphonse of Poitiers, the brother of King Louis IX, on the site of a small early-twelfth-century rectangular keep, the castle of Najac had many of the same characteristics as the castle at Dover. A new keep was constructed, circular in shape, but instead of standing alone as the previous castle had, it was incorporated into the bailey wall as its largest and most formidable tower, and thus became a functioning part of the initial defenses. This outer wall was the most important defensive feature of Najac Castle. It rose between seven and eight meters in height and had a thickness of one meter. It was also strengthened not only by the keep at its southeast corner, but by two more, smaller round towers on the northeast and northwest corners, the old rectangular keep placed on the southwest corner and two semi-circular towers guarding the two gateways. The entrances were further guarded by barbicans and ditches. Along the wall was a walk equipped with an elaborate system of stairways and passages, some visible and some hidden, capable of being isolated from the rest of the castle by barriers.

The keep at Najac, while not as elaborate or as comfortable as the keep at Dover, was nevertheless impressive. It was 11 meters in diameter, 40 meters in height, and contained three stories. Its walls were also very thick, measuring

2.2 meters in width, and were pierced only by arrow slits. The keep could be entered on the ground level from inside the castle yard, but this entry was protected by both a moat and a drawbridge. Other entrances into the second and third stories were connected to the bailey wall.

Adding to the defense of the castle, perhaps its most imposing feature in fact, was the harshness of its terrain. In imitation of the Crusader castles, Najac Castle was built on the summit of a steep hill, 200 meters high, which presented any would-be attacker with an intimidating target. As a result, there is no record of this castle ever being captured or even besieged during the Middle Ages.[58] The most successful medieval castle was the one that was never attacked.

However strong and impressive the castles at Dover and Najac might have been, one of the best examples of a European castle complex was Château-Gaillard. Built in 1196–98 in Normandy at the behest of the English king, Richard the Lionheart, who controlled the region, Château-Gaillard stood on a precipitous cliff, over 90 meters high, overlooking the Seine River. The castle consisted of three baileys, each surrounded by a large wall. The outer bailey had a triangular plan with its apex facing the valley below. Its wall was fortified by one large circular tower at the apex and three other smaller semi-circular towers, and it was completely surrounded by a moat, 17 meters wide and 15 meters deep. The middle bailey was located across the moat to the northwest of the outer bailey. Its wall was also fortified by three semi-circular towers, located on the two corners facing the outer bailey and on its northern face, and by one square tower on its southern face. The inner bailey, which was enclosed completely by the middle bailey, had no towers on the walls, but was built on a precipice rising more than 12 meters above the middle bailey. It too was surrounded by a moat. Access to the middle and inner baileys was possible only over a drawbridge connected to the outer bailey. The outer bailey in turn had only a single entrance, on its northwest corner, which was guarded by a flanking tower, and was reached only by a drawbridge.

The keep, which may have been a slightly later addition, was built on the edge of the cliff, mostly within the inner bailey, but also forming a part of the southeast face of the wall. It was circular in shape, with walls three to four meters thick, except for one thicker side that jutted out almost like a beak toward the courtyard in the direction most vulnerable to attack. The keep also had buttresses along the wall, adding further strength, with machicolations placed between the buttresses through which soldiers inside could fight those attacking directly below them. It contained two stories but seems to have been used only as a barracks for the troops garrisoned at the castle rather than as

Fig. 9.5: Château-Gaillard Castle, France (twelfth century).
Photo by the author.

a residence for a noble or castellan. The keep could be entered only by a long flight of stairs that ascended from the courtyard to a guard room in the upper story. Other courtyard buildings, constructed along the inside of the inner bailey wall, served as barracks, storehouses, and domestic structures.

Château-Gaillard was constructed very quickly, in only three years. It was also an expensive castle, costing an estimated £21,203, including the cost of materials and waste removal, transportation, and labor. Because of the conflict between Richard the Lionheart and Philip Augustus over Normandy, which began after Philip returned from the Crusades prior to Richard, Château-Gaillard was attacked less than five years after its construction. Philip besieged the castle for more than a year and eventually captured it, but not before suffering many casualties. It was also besieged several times during the Hundred Years' War: in 1418, the French lost the castle to Henry V's English force after a six-month siege; in 1420, the French regained the fortress, only to have it recaptured by the English before the end of the year; and finally, in 1449, Charles VII restored it to French control.[59]

The castle complex style was so influential in the late twelfth and thirteenth centuries that many castles built earlier were added to in order to improve their

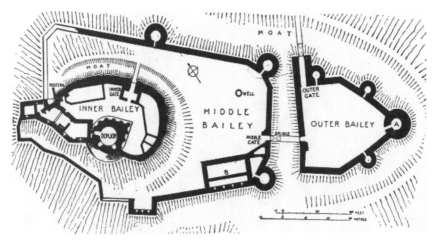

Fig. 9.6: Plan of Château-Gaillard Castle.

Toy (1955): 129.

outer defenses. Such was the case with both the White Tower in London, which
continually saw its outer defenses rebuilt and strengthened, ultimately gaining
two bailey walls, cylindrical flanking towers, a moat, a main gatehouse guarded
by a barbican, and a series of lesser gateways, and the Counts of Flanders' castle
at Ghent, to which, around 1180, was added an extensive crenellated outer wall
fortified by several towers and a gateway reinforced with a barbican and machicolations to its early-twelfth-century rectangular keep. A water-filled moat surrounding the outer walls was also added.[60]

EDWARD I'S CASTLES IN WALES

Perhaps the most extensive, and definitely the most expensive, medieval forti-
fication-building program came at the end of the thirteenth century when the
English king, Edward I, constructed a number of castles in Wales in order to
suppress rebellions there. Between 1277 and 1297, 10 new royal and four new
"lordship" castles were begun; added to these were three native Welsh castles
that underwent major reconstruction. ("Lordship" castles were held by strong
noble allies of Edward and were essentially under his control.) Edward's strategy in building these castles was certainly not new, as William the Conqueror
had previously established the policy of facing insurgency and rebellion with
fortifications. But while William's castles were the small, cheaply constructed

Fig. 9.7: Castle of the Counts of Flanders, Ghent, Belgium.
Photo by the author.

motte-and-bailey castles, Edward I's were large, expensive fortifications. They were also built in the complex style, with powerful bailey walls fortified by strong towers.[61]

Most of these castles were built in the north of Wales, including the royal castles built at Flint, Rhuddlan, Ruthin, Hope, Conwy, Caernarvon, Harlech, and Beaumaris; the four "lordship" castles at Hawarden, Denbigh, Holt, and Chirk; and two of the three reconstructed Welsh castles, at Dolwyddelan and Criccieth. Two other new castles, at Builth and Aberystwyth, and another reconstruction, at Bere, were built in the middle of Wales. Five of the castles were also integrated with urban fortifications: Aberystwyth, Flint, Rhuddlan, Conwy, and Caernarvon.

Because this was a systematic construction program, there was an attempt by Edward's architects, led by the famous Master James of St. George, to use a similar, but not exactly duplicated, concentric plan.[62] Most of these castles were built in a quadrangular shape with two bailey walls, and all, except for the castle at Flint, had no keep. The walls provided the primary defense for the castle, and these, especially the inner walls, were extremely large—Rhuddlan Castle's inner wall measured 10 meters high and 3 meters thick, for example—and was

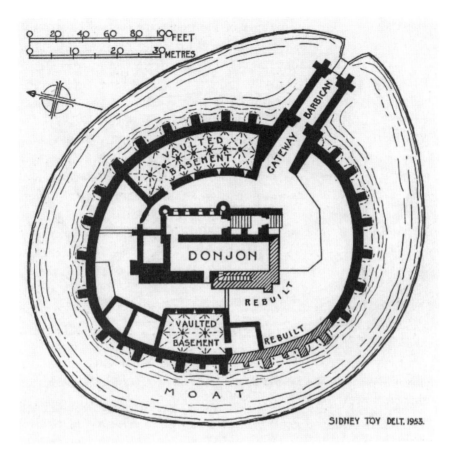

Fig. 9.8: Plan of the Castle of the Counts of Flanders.
Toy (1955): 146.

fortified by ramparts, crenellations, and machicolations. Beyond, and some-times between, the bailey walls were large moats.

To provide even further security, large circular towers, known as "drum tow-ers," were built on the four corners of the inner walls of these castles, with fur-ther towers added where the walls were perceived to be vulnerable. Towers were also used to guard the entrances to the castle, as only three castles—Harlech, Beaumaris, and Rhuddlan—contained large gatehouses. (Harlech Castle had only one gatehouse, while the castles at Beaumaris and Rhuddlan had two.) These towers also served as the chief residential dwellings and barracks, although they were often supplemented by buildings constructed within the inner bailey, functioning as halls, kitchens, latrines, and stables.

Only when the terrain warranted a less fortified structure was there a deviation in the concentric design of Edward I's Welsh castles. For example, at Flint there was no need for an outer ring of walls, as the castle was constructed near the Dee River and used its banks as a protective outer defensive curtain, while Rhuddlan Castle was built on top of a low bank next to the tidal river Clwyd and therefore needed only the protection of two bailey walls on three sides.

The two largest and most important, strategically at least, of these castles, Conwy and Caernarvon, differed quite a bit from the other fortifications constructed or reconstructed by Edward I. Both of these castles remain relatively intact and are impressive fortifications.[63] The castle at Conwy has been described by the distinguished historian J. Goronwy Edwards, who devoted much of his career to its study, as "incomparably the most magnificent of Edward I's Welsh fortresses," and Caernarvon Castle is said to have elicited from Dr. Samuel Johnson the exclamation, "I did not think that there had been such buildings." The two buildings were among the largest of English castles. Conwy Castle enclosed an area of 91.5 by 30.5 meters, with a town wall extending from the fortress for more than 1,280 meters, and Caernarvon Castle's area measured 170 by 60 meters with an additional town wall of 731 meters.

Probably because both were designed by the Master of St. George, these castles were very similar. Both were irregularly shaped castle complexes that adapted to and exploited the terrain on which they were built. The castle at Caernarvon was constructed on a low peninsula of rock projecting into the Menai Strait and situated between the Seiont and Cadnant Rivers, and Conwy Castle was erected on an isolated spur of rock lying between the Conwy River and its tributary, the Gyffin River. This latter site was judged to be of such strategic worth that the Cistercian abbey of Gwynedd, which had previously stood there, was appropriated and removed for the construction of the castle. Because of the natural defensibility of these sites, both castles did not require an outer bailey wall.

As with the other Welsh castles of Edward I, the castles at Caernarvon and Conwy relied chiefly on their high and thick walls for defense. At Caernarvon, these walls measured 4.6 meters thick and 17 meters high. The walls also had arrow slits, crenellations, and ramparts. Caernarvon Castle even had two extra levels of firing galleries built into the walls below the rampart, thus providing three ranks of fire against any attacker.

As was conventional with all thirteenth-century castle complexes, including all of Edward I's castles in Wales, huge towers lined the bailey walls of Conwy and Caernarvon. Conwy Castle contained eight massive drum towers, four on

Fig. 9.9: Caernarvon Castle, Wales (late thirteenth century).
Photo by the author.

each face, measuring 12.2 meters in diameter, with turrets added to the top of the four surrounding the inner bailey. At Caernarvon there were nine large towers. Strangely, however, these were polygonal, a style that some historians claim was influenced by the fifth-century Theodosian Wall at Constantinople.[64] The towers of both castles provided flanking fire, which succeeded in exposing all points on the bailey wall to intense crossfire.

None of these towers was more impressive than the largest one built at Caernarvon, known as the Eagle's Tower. This imposing and powerful structure guarded the most vulnerable spot on the bailey wall, at the confluence of the two rivers, and served as the keep of the castle. It had several chambers, two chapels, and a sally port through which the inhabitants of the castle could flee.

As usual in castles from this period, the entrances to these two castles were heavily fortified. At Conwy, the two gateways were each guarded by double drum towers with accompanying barbicans, and at Caernarvon two of the three entrances were guarded by elaborate gatehouses, named the King's and Queen's Gate, similar to those built at Harlech and Beaumaris. A third entry, leading from the river and known as Water Gate, did not have a gatehouse but led to a wall, four meters thick, which jutted out into the river and protected a dock leading to the gate. The interiors of both castles were divided longitudinally into two wards of unequal sizes. At Caernarvon there is no discernible reason for this division, and in fact the dividing wall is quite thin, but at Conwy the inner bailey (measuring 24.4 by 21.4 meters) separated the royal apartments from the castle's great hall and barracks.

Perhaps the only significant difference between Conwy and Caernarvon castles, besides the shape of the towers, is the time it took to construct each fortification. Conwy Castle was built quickly, in five seasons of construction between 1283 and 1287, while Caernarvon Castle took much longer, erected between 1293 and 1323. Consequently, the castle at Caernarvon, at an estimated £20,000, cost much more to complete than did the castle at Conwy, which cost an estimated £14,086.

The Welsh castles of Edward I constituted the last large castle-building project of the Middle Ages. Costing between £62,000 and £80,000 in total, the enterprise was too expensive to be repeated elsewhere in England or on the Continent. Most of the financing for these castles was supplied by the royal treasury, the *forinsec* accounts of the King's Wardrobe. It was a sum that was generally not available to the kings and nobles of Europe embroiled in the almost constant warfare of the fourteenth and fifteenth centuries.

The Welsh castles were designed and built by Savoyard artisans, including Master James of St. George, who were imported by Edward I for their expertise in castle building. They controlled a large army of English masons, carpenters, diggers, and other workmen: 1,845 diggers, 790 sawyers, and 320 masons worked on the castles of Chester and Flint in 1277; 400 masons, 200 quarrymen, and at least 2,000 laborers worked on the castle at Beaumarais in 1295.[65]

By the end of the thirteenth century, medieval society was on the brink of change. Urbanization was rapidly increasing; the new and growing cities could not be sufficiently protected by rural castles designed for the guarding of sparsely populated agricultural lands. Even the powerful castles at Conway and Caernarvon would have been unable to protect their urban populations had they not been accompanied by a large, heavily fortified town wall. With this rapid urbanization also came a new societal class, one that rose above the lower or peasant class but did not have the inherited privileges of nobility: a "middle class." Some of these people grew very wealthy and desired fortified dwellings to protect their families and possessions. However, they did not need the extra defensive structures that comprised traditional castle complexes; instead, they desired more comfort. These new castles can best be described as fortified residences. This then was the future of medieval fortifications: town walls and fortified residences.

Notes

1. B. Bachrach (1983): 538–60. B. Bachrach (1993) extends this view in a more complete biography of the count.

2. B. Bachrach (1979): 531–49.

3. B. Bachrach (1979: 534–35; 1984: 47–50).

4. Verbruggen (1950): 51, 54; Deyres (1974): 7–28; and Fournier (1978): 69.

5. Héliot (1966): 504–5; Fino (1970): 386–88; B. Bachrach (1979: 534–41; 1984: 47–62; 1993: 49–50); and Contamine (1984): 47. For a discussion of the evidence supporting this claim see the works by B. Bachrach.

6. B. Bachrach (1979): 544.

7. Héliot (1966): 505–6; B. Bachrach (1979): 541–47; and Deyres (1974): 7–28.

8. B. Bachrach (1979): 549–54.

9. B. Bachrach (1979): 554–59.

10. Lomax (1978): 31–43; Collins (1983): 253–68; and O'Callaghan (2003): 4–6. For a history of the *Reconquista*, see O'Callaghan (2003).

11. Beeler (1971): 163–64 and Araguas (1979): 205–8.

12. Araguas (1979): 208–23.

13. Contamine (1984): 46, 109.

14. See van Emden (1984): 1–11.

15. R. Brown (1954): 35.

16. R. Brown (1954): 36.

17. Platt (1982): 20.

18. R. Brown (1954): 37–43 and King (1988): 63–67.

19. Renn (1973): 187–89; Platt (1982): 22; and M.W. Thompson (1960): 81–94.

20. On the Norman rectangular keep see Renn (1973); R. Brown (1954): 35–59; Platt (1982): 7–45; Kenyon (1990): 39–54; Toy (1955): 74–85; King (1988): 67–74; Brown, Colvin, and Taylor (1963): I: 29–40.

21. There are numerous writings on the White Tower. Probably the best are two articles by R. Brown (1989f, 1989g); see also Lapper and Parnell (2000); Renn (1973): 326–30; Brown, Colvin, and Taylor (1963): I: 29–32; Platt (1982): 10; Toy (1955): 78; Forde-Johnston (1977): 84–86; and Bonde (1984): 84–91.

22. Renn (1973): 151–54; Forde-Johnston (1977): 86; and Toy (1955): 78–79.

23. R. Brown (1954): 52–54.

24. On Gisors Castle see Fino (1970): 372–76 and Toy (1955): 71; on Pfeffingen Castle see Toy (1955): 72–73.

25. On Arques Castle see Toy (1955): 80–81; on Loches Castle see Fino (1970): 399–403 and Toy (1955): 76–77; on Ghent Castle see Fino (1970): 368–71 and Héliot (1974): 218.

26. On the numerical strength of the First Crusade and early Crusaders' kingdoms see Runciman (1964): I: 336–41.

27. See Toy (1955): 86–103; Müller-Wiener (1966); Boase (1967, 1977); Lawrence (1988); and Smail (1956; 1951: 133–49).

28. Toy (1955): 93 and Prawer (1980): 104–12, 472–79.

29. Smail (1956: 60, 204–7; 1956: 135–38); Kennedy (1994): 21–97; and Ellenblum (2007): 103–86.

30. Smail (1956: 60–62, 205–14; 1956: 135–45).

31. Smail (1956: 214; 1956: 145–49); Boase (1967): 41; and Prawer (1980): 52.

32. Toy (1955): 93–94; Smail (1956): 217–18; Boase (1967: 44–45; 1977: 141–42).

33. Smail (1956): 226–30.

34. Kennedy (1994): 138–42; Müller-Weiner (1966): 51–52; Toy (1955): 101; Boase (1967: 60–61; 1977: 145).

35. Kennedy (1994): 64–67; Müller-Weiner (1966): 64–65; Boase (1967: 45; 1977: 144–45).

36. Toy (1955): 86–93; Smail (1956): 230–32; and Boase (1967): 42–43.

37. Kennedy (1994); Müller-Weiner (1966); Toy (1955): 94–101; Smail (1956): 215–16, 218–30; Boase (1967: 49–67; 1977: 145–62).

38. Lawrence (1988): 77.

39. Müller-Weiner (1966): 59–62; Toy (1955): 99–101; Smail (1956): 223–26; Boase (1967: 51–56; 1977: 152–56); and Lawrence (1988): 77–88. Kennedy (1994), who mentions Krak des Chevaliers throughout his book, also contains a number of excellent photographs of various parts of the castle on pp. 146–68.

40. Phillips (2008).

41. See Nicolle (2006), although a more lengthy study of the Third Crusade needs to be written.

42. Prawer (1980): 483.

43. Boase (1967): 63–66 and Ellenblum (2007): 275–86.

44. Toy (1955): 104.

45. Collins (1983): 222–65.

46. Guitart Aparcio (2003) and Bolea Aguaron (1983).

47. O'Callaghan (2003) is a recent account of the *Reconquista*.

48. Fletcher (1989).

49. Monreal y Tejada (1999).

50. See, for example, King (1988): 77–89.

51. Toy (1955): 86–91.

52. Toy (1955): 104–6 and Fino (1970): 377–80.

53. Toy (1955): 104–13; Platt (1982): 32–45; Lawrence (1988): 93–101; R. Brown (1954): 52–57; and Fino (1970): 356–57, 372–76, 416–20.

54. King (1970); Toy (1955): 133; Platt (1982): 39; Forde-Johnston (1977): 95–96; and A.H. Thompson (1912): 180–81.

55. Fino (1970): 307–10 and Toy (1955): 139.

56. Fino (1970): 343–47; Toy (1955): 137–39; and Platt (1982): 52.

57. Coad (1995); R. Brown (1954: 38, 49–51, 67–68, 83–84; 1974); Toy (1955): 84; Platt (1982): 43–46; Forde-Johnston (1977): 86–87; Brown, Colvin, and Taylor (1963): I: 65, 78; and Taylor (1958): 113.

58. Salet (1938); Toy (1955): 136–37; and Fino (1970): 408–11.

59. Van den Broucke (2003); Toy (1955): 128–31; Fino (1970): 327–30; Dieulafoy (1898); and Héliot (1962): 53–75. An itemized listing of the castle-building costs for Château-Gaillard can be found in Contamine (1984): 110.

60. On the additions to the White Tower see R. Brown (1989f): 168–76. On the additions to the castle at Ghent see Callebaut (1981); Laleman (2008); and Fino (1970): 368–71.

61. Because of the importance of these castles several works have discussed them. See in particular Taylor (1986) (which is a reprinting of Brown, Colvin, and Taylor [1963]: I: 293–408, II: 1027–39); Humphries (1983); Gravett (2007); Edwards (1946): 15–81; Taylor (1977: 265–92; 1961: 104–33; 1958: 111–19); Prestwich (1988): 207–16; Toy (1955): 164–72; R. Brown (1954): 61–81; Forde-Johnston (1977): 108–15; Platt (1983): 63–79; and the articles in Williams and Kenyon (2010).

62. On the Master James of St. George see Taylor (1950): 433–57.

63. On Conway Castle see Taylor (1986: 45–62; 1958: 115–16); Edwards (1946): 37–43; Toy (1955): 167–68; R. Brown (1954): 74; and Platt (1982): 71. On Caernarvon Castle see Taylor (1986: 77–103; 1958: 117–18); Edwards (1946): 43–52; Toy (1955): 167–68; R. Brown (1954): 74; and Platt (1982): 71–75.

64. See Wheatley (2010) for the latest discussion of this question.

65. Prestwich (1988): 214.

CHAPTER 10

URBAN
FORTIFICATIONS
AND
FORTIFIED
RESIDENCES

CASTLES CONTINUED TO BE BUILT WELL INTO THE EARLY MODERN PERIOD, especially in those areas threatened by foreign invasion or civil unrest. But the notion of castles as fortified structures did change. No longer did medieval castle builders deem it necessary or even desirable to construct heavily fortified complexes like those in the Holy Land and Europe.

There is no question that the high cost of large fortifications deterred some kings and nobles from continuing to build castles as their ancestors had. After all, Edward I had nearly bankrupted the English treasury to build his castles in Wales.[1] But that was not the only question: whether the castle complexes had truly fulfilled the defensive purposes for which they had been constructed also concerned those building fortifications in the late Middle Ages. Some very expensive castles had not held out for too long. After all, Château-Gaillard, a very expensive castle indeed, had fallen less than five years after it was constructed, and after less than one year of siege. It would be besieged and captured no fewer than three more times before the end of the Middle Ages.[2] Other castles met similar fates. Sometimes enemy forces merely avoided the castles, knowing that their garrisons were often not strong enough, or foolish enough, to leave their protective walls to pursue an evading army.[3]

Perhaps this is why so many earlier castles fell into disrepair by the fourteenth and fifteenth centuries. There were reports of weak and derelict castles everywhere in Europe during those two centuries. For example in 1341, Criccieth Castle in northern Wales was reported to be so weak that its doors could scarcely hold up to the wind, and this despite extensive late-thirteenth-century repairs to the structure.[4] In 1405, the ducal castle of Vannes in Brittany, known as La Motte, was in such disrepair that its walls were being used as a quarry for other construction projects in the town.[5] The same thing was happening to the walls of the castle at Worcester, which had fallen out of use in the thirteenth century and was being quarried to repair the town walls in the fifteenth century.[6] In fact, the ruination of many once strong and powerful castles in England had become so evident in the early sixteenth century that when John Leland made a tour of the island he became obsessed with the plight of the derelict castles. He found himself unable to understand how so many monuments of medieval military strength had fallen into such disuse and disrepair. Of the 258 castles whose condition Leland comments on, 30 were partially derelict and 137 were completely in ruin. Only 91 were still being used.[7]

FORTIFIED RESIDENCES

By the middle of the thirteenth century, castle builders began more and more to disregard the defensive aspects of the structure and to emphasize comfort and luxury in their place. A late medieval castle had first to be architecturally beautiful. No longer would a simple, plain, and dark keep or castle complex hidden behind huge walls suffice to meet the aesthetic demands of its owner.[8] Even those fortresses built ostensibly as defenses against invasion, such as Bodiam, Cooling, and Queensborough in England, Clisson, Rambures, Hunandaye, and Vincennes in France, and La Callahora in Spain, did not sacrifice comfort for that defense.[9]

The outside of these new castles needed to be decorative, original in design, and opulent enough to impress any observer of the extraordinary wealth and high social standing of their inhabitants. Walls were pierced more frequently with windows and were often capped with decorative cornices. Windows and moldings were embellished with lavish sculpture and trim. The buttresses, crenellations, barbicans, and ramparts, while still functional, became more beautiful. Moats, now often filled with water, included lilies and other water flora; some even had a flock of swans or other water birds. Many castles had attached hunting parks.[10]

The insides of these castles were also elegant. Halls were large enough to accommodate banquets and other celebratory functions, and they were better lit than earlier castles by the larger windows, built into the castle walls. Apartments were also larger and more comfortable, each usually having its own *garderobe* and fireplace, and some even with recessed storage areas for clothes. These apartments were also more numerous than in earlier castles, with as many as 40 and 50 included in the larger residences.[11]

Most fortified residences had chapels within them, and because the chaplain had become a regular member of the household, they also included his lodgings.[12] Since these castles also served as the administrative centers for their owner's business enterprises, they contained elaborate offices for the lord and his staff,[13] and, as some castle owners were responsible for administering justice in their lands, they often had courtrooms and small prisons, the latter located in the basements or lower levels.[14] Finally, while it seems that garrisons of troops were generally missing from late medieval castles, frequently they were replaced by an army of domestic servants, whose quarters were included in the overall structure.

Defensibility was not entirely forgotten. Some rural fortified residences continued to be built in inaccessible places, and some bailey walls were still large, crenellated, and lined with towers. Entrances remained protected by barbicans and large gatehouses, while large moats, far wider and deeper than earlier castle ditches, increased the overall defensibility of the building.[15] Gunports were also added to many late-fourteenth- and fifteenth-century castles. Still, as so many late medieval fortresses were smaller and weaker than earlier fortifications, even those meant to withstand foreign attack or to inhibit civil war did not rival the castles built in previous centuries.[16]

There were two styles of rural fortified residences built in the late Middle Ages. The first, and less numerous, resembled the earlier castle complex, although was neither as large or as defensible. Like those built earlier they consisted of large bailey walls lined with towers that sometimes enclosed a keep. A famous example of this type of fortification was built at Bodiam in southern England between 1386 and 1390. Erected by Sir Edward Dalyngrigge—a veteran who had greatly profited from the Hundred Years' War—for the purpose of defending the region against a French assault, the castle attempted to combine the defensive qualities of earlier castles, the latest technological advances, and the comfort required by an aristocratic owner. Its walls were built in a rectangular shape, with round towers projecting out from those walls on each

Fig. 10.1: Bodiam Castle, England (late fourteenth century).
Photo by the author.

corner. The eastern, western, and southern walls were protected by intermediate square towers, with the intermediate tower on the southern side serving also as a secondary entrance. In the middle of the northern wall stood a large gatehouse flanked by two square towers guarding the primary entrance into the residence. This gatehouse, machicolated on the parapet level and containing gunports, held three sets of barriers, each consisting of a portcullis and heavy door. Perhaps the most defensive feature of the castle was its large, water-filled moat, which completely surrounded the structure. It could be crossed only by a single L-shaped causeway containing three drawbridges and a barbican leading into the main gatehouse, or by a narrower straight causeway with a single drawbridge into the secondary entrance.

There was no keep at Bodiam Castle. The owner's residence was built along the walls, ringing a rectangular courtyard in a two-story series of apartments and offices that included a large hall, kitchen, buttery, pantry, and chapel. Some military quarters were also included at Bodiam, but these were small and may have served only to house Dalyngrigge's personal retinue rather than a garrison of regular troops. Although not as extravagant as in some late-medieval castles, the domestic quarters at Bodiam were quite comfortable. All chambers were quite large and well lit, and each contained its own *garderobe*. The most elaborate of these suites, located on the main floor near the gatehouse, was reserved for Dalyngrigge himself. There were several other apartments that provided lodging not only to Dalyngrigge's own family and servants, but also to a large number of guests when needed.[17]

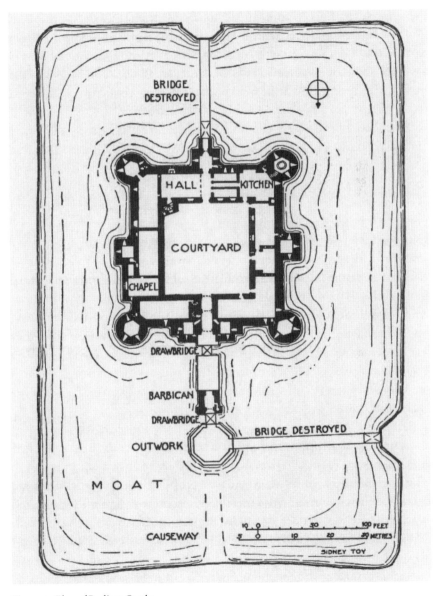

Fig. 10.2: Plan of Bodiam Castle.

Toy (1955): 218.

Another example of this type of late medieval fortification was built at Pierrefonds in France. Constructed at about the same time as Bodiam Castle, between 1390 and 1400, this castle served as the primary residence of Louis d'Orleans, duke of Valois and brother of King Charles VI. Although reconstructed with some historical imagination by the famous nineteenth-century French architect Eugène-Emmanuel Viollet-le-Duc, the elements of the medieval Pierrefonds castle can still be determined.[18] Pierrefonds imitated earlier castles, with high walls and projecting round corner towers. Round towers, 38 meters in height and named after classical heroes, were also built onto the middle of each wall. The castle was constructed on a promontory of land protected on three sides by steep escarpments and surrounded by a thin outer wall, with entrance gained only by climbing a ramp, entering a gate in the outer wall, and traversing a narrow terrace along the entire length of the inner wall before crossing under a barbican and across a drawbridge. It is evident that, built in this way, the Valois Castle at Pierrefonds was seen as a very defensive fortification, but its interior structures also emphasized the rich comfort expected by a powerful brother of the king. It contained a number of large, richly decorated suites and halls surrounding an almost rectangular courtyard and a many-storied square keep that jutted into the courtyard from the southern wall.[19]

A second, more numerous style of late medieval rural fortification was the tower house. Here the imitation was not of the castle complex, but of the earlier rectangular castle keep. In essence, these tower houses were, as the name implies, residences built as towers. Although there were many variations, they were generally rectangular in shape and stood two to five stories high, with an area of between 6 and 18 square meters. They were also permanent residences of their owners, staff, and servants, containing several apartments and other chambers arranged on the various stories.[20]

Defense in these fortifications, while not entirely neglected, was less evident and seemingly much less important than comfort and luxury. Except for their size, crenellated roofs, and the often inaccessible terrain on which they were built, these fortified residences would have provided little protection against a concerted enemy attack.[21] However, as they also were sometimes constructed in areas of potential warfare, e.g., along the border of Scotland and in the duchies of Brittany, Picardy, and Gascony in France, their defensive worth is probably underestimated.[22]

Again two examples, one in England and one in France, should suffice to illustrate this style of fortified residence. In England, there may have been no finer example of a tower house than that built in 1433–38 by Ralph Lord Cromwell at Tattershall in Lincolnshire. It was a rectangular structure built of brick, with a stone base and stone dressings and measuring 18.3 by 24.4 meters in area and 36.6 meters in height. Inside there were four stories and a basement. Each story consisted of a richly decorated and well-lit large hall, 12.2 by 6.1 meters in size, with several smaller chambers leading from it.

Defensibility at Tattershall seemed of little concern to its builders. The structure was tall and contained four crenellated octagonal corner turrets rising from the roof, but the construction in brick with three poorly guarded entrances leading onto the main floor certainly displayed weaknesses against attack. This is further shown by the lack of any kitchen facilities in the main edifice, indicating that cooking was done in another building apart from the fortified residence itself. The castle had little chance of surviving a prolonged siege by a large army, yet it would provide perfectly adequate defense against a smaller band without artillery.[23]

In France, an example of the tower house can be found at Rambures in Picardy. The Rambures Castle, begun in 1421 but not finished until 1470, was not a large fortress. Rather than being rectangular in shape, it was polygonal and consisted of six round towers attached to each other by a series of doorways. The four corner towers, larger than the two inner wall towers, were quite small, measuring 12 meters in diameter and 20 meters in height. Inside the castle, there were six complete, but short, stories, with two underground, both below the level of the outside moat. The chambers, encompassing the entire area of each tower level, were large, but not as elegant or as well decorated as those of other tower houses.

At the same time, Rambures may have been better prepared for defense than other tower houses, like Tattershall, for not only was it surrounded by a large moat, but it also had fairly thick walls (three meters thick) with several gunports added at the second-floor level. In addition, each of the six towers could easily be shut off from the others. Finally, it was built entirely of brick and thus was significantly stronger against gunpowder artillery bombardment than a fortification built of facing stones built around a rubble-and-mortar core.[24]

During the late Middle Ages, fortified residences were frequently built in towns, where wealthy individuals, both noble and non-noble, desired security for their families and possessions similar to that of the rural castle. Urban fortified residences were not primarily expected to withstand a foreign invasion; instead, the large amount of urban unrest and the local governments' limited ability to keep the peace necessitated protection of their wealthy owners. Urban castles also often served as centers of the political, economic, and social power of the prosperous towns.[25]

Most urban fortified residences were built in styles similar to the rural fortified residences, with some imitating tower houses and others built around a courtyard. In most cases urban castles were much smaller than their rural models, although, when built for a prince or another local governor, an urban fortified residence was often as large as or larger than a similar fortification built in the country. For example, the residence of the Sforza dukes in Milan was a very large walled fortress lined with towers and surrounded by a moat (traversed by no fewer than 62 drawbridges). It also included a barracks large enough to house between 800 and 1,200 mercenary soldiers.[26] The Este family fortress in Ferrara, known also as the Castle of Saint Michele or Castello Estense, built in 1385 (although heavily restored after a fire in 1544), had, like the Sforza Palace in Milan, four corner towers around a large central fortified core. Three entrances with drawbridges were protected by brick ravelins, while apartments, kitchens, chambers, galleries, halls, a chapel, and even a dungeon and garden were all included in the structure.[27]

Like those in the countryside, the builders of urban fortified residences often sought comfort at the expense of defensibility. The housing of the owner's family in a style that indicated a wealthy and prosperous social standing was of primary importance. Large and opulent apartments, kitchens, halls, and servants' quarters were all found within these castle walls. At the same time, many urban fortified residences included offices, shops, and warehouses in support of the owner's business.[28] Because of the smaller confines of the town, few of these urban fortresses could be guarded by outside walls, moats, barbicans, or ramparts. This did not mean that defense was totally neglected, however. Most urban fortified residences were protected by fortified gates and guarded entrances, towers, gunports, and even "murder-holes" in the walls and ceilings of entrances, through which pitch, as well as other substances, could be dropped on attacking enemies.[29]

TOWN WALLS

Fortified residences were neither the most numerous nor the most important fortifications built during the late Middle Ages; instead, that was the town wall.

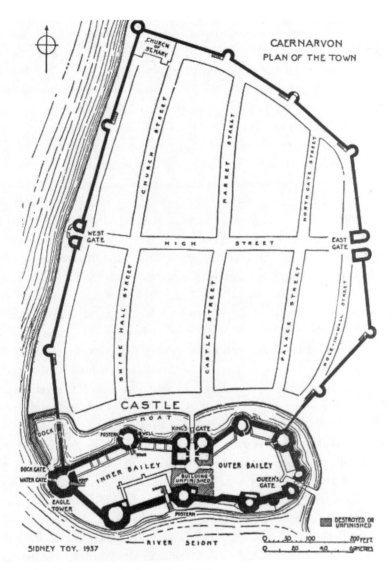

Fig. 10.3: Plan of Caernarvon Castle and Town Walls.

Toy (1955): 180.

Before the fifteenth century, only a few new town walls had been constructed. Some towns relied on the old, although usually well-maintained, Roman walls to meet their defensive needs, while other urban areas were often protected only by a ditch and earthen rampart.[30] In Germany in 1200, for example, there were only 12 walled towns, and 9 of these were Roman walls.[31]

Still, these fortifications seem to have met the needs of most towns until at least the thirteenth century, when towns began to grow in number, population, and wealth. By then, several towns had grown beyond their older defenses, forming unprotected suburbs.[32] Other towns that saw their size and development grow rapidly because of their increased industrial or trade prosperity had never been completely surrounded by walls. Even Paris, the largest and most populated town of Western Europe, was not completely enclosed until the mid-fourteenth century.[33] By this time, however, town governments had begun to recognize the need for new fortifications. Local violence, civil uprisings, and foreign invasions all threatened the security and prosperity of those living within their boundaries. The answer was either to repair and extend earlier medieval or Roman walls or, if this was not possible, to build new ones.[34]

At first this seems to have been done without much cost, using only the resources of the town treasury. Masonry was salvaged from old buildings, lands were confiscated "for the public good," and the goods and services of many within the town, especially masons, were levied for the construction of walls.[35] However, in some places this was insufficient to build the strong fortifications that most towns required. Extra funds were needed to complete the enclosure of the town with a fortified wall. In these cases, money could be obtained by an added taxation of the townspeople (a *murage*). The walls at Caernarvon and Conwy, for example, were paid for by a levy on goods sold within the town, and at Nantes, Rennes, and Fougères, the construction of the walls was paid for by a tax on alcoholic beverages.[36] Funds for building town walls could also be granted by the king or another governing person. The walls of Canterbury were built in part by a *murage* grant from the archbishop; and in 1367, the king of France allowed one-quarter of all royal taxes raised in a town that was building walls to be used for their construction.[37]

During the late Middle Ages, so many towns built walls that, by the end of the fifteenth century, few notable towns were without sizeable fortifications surrounding them. In England, perhaps the least populated medieval kingdom in Western Europe, it is estimated that between 108 and 200 towns acquired walls during the fourteenth and fifteenth centuries. The total number of walled towns in France, Germany, Italy, Spain, and the Low Countries was much higher.[38]

The principal defensive feature of these fortifications was the wall itself. Those surrounding London were 10.67 meters high, Caernarvon 8.53 meters high, Conwy 7.32 meters high, and Carcassone between 7 and 8 meters high.[39] They were also very wide, most measuring nearly 2 meters in thickness.[40] They were also usually extremely long. Those enclosing French towns were usually more than 2,000 meters in length, with the walls of Amiens, Chartres, and Provins measuring more than 3,000 meters and the walls of Rouen measuring more than 4,000 meters.[41] Town walls in England were often shorter, as the towns themselves were smaller, with the walls at Conwy and Caernarvon measuring only 1,280 and 731 meters, respectively, although larger towns, such as York and London, had walls that rivaled the length of the largest in France. The walls surrounding York were more than 4,800 meters in length.[42] Because of the length of the walls, the areas enclosed were also very impressive. The walls of Yarmouth enclosed an area of nearly 54 hectares, of Winchester an area of nearly 56 hectares, and of Rennes an area of 62 hectares.[43]

Almost all town walls were crenellated and had ramparts or wall-walks wide enough to support archers or gunners.[44] Some walls were surrounded by wide and deep ditches, filled with caltrops, thick metal spikes, and other hindrances,[45] and some were doubled, such as at Carcassone, with two sets of walls surrounding the city.[46] All of these features added to the walls' defensibility, but the most important defensive additions were the towers standing at regular intervals along the walls and the fortified gates that limited access to the town enclosure. Most town walls incorporated a number of towers placed at intervals of 40 to 60 meters. The walls at Canterbury had 24 towers, Conwy 21, Carcassone 25, and Southampton 29.[47] These towers had various shapes, although they were usually circular, horseshoe- or square-shaped.[48] They were also often taller than their walls, perhaps by as much as 20 to 30 meters, with Carcassone again the primary example, and were filled with arrow slits and gunports.[49] Entrance through these walls into the town was limited, usually by means of strongly fortified gates. These gates were rarely numerous, again with defensibility in mind: Caernarvon was entered through only two gates, Conwy through three gates, and York through four gates.[50] However, some towns with large markets or industries, such as Ghent and Southampton, needed and had more entrances.[51] Like castle gates, entrances into town walls provided a strong defense for their inhabitants. Some were flanked by large towers, while others were towers themselves. Many were pierced by numerous arrow slits and, after the late fourteenth century, gunports, and some also included a barbican. Doors were constructed from wood reinforced by iron bars and covered with leather to protect against fire. In front of the doors were one or more portcullises.[52] Finally, because these gates were the only part of the fortification seen by most travelers, many were decorated as a sign of the town's prosperity.[53]

Most town walls were constructed using the same materials as castle walls— facing stones enclosing a rubble core of large stones and mortar—although by the late fourteenth and fifteenth centuries some walls, like those surrounding the town of Hull, were built using bricks.[54] The construction of these fortifications often took a long time, up to five decades for some town walls, with others, such as those surrounding Coventry and Canterbury, taking more than a century to complete.[55]

Town walls always impressed late medieval observers with their strength and their defensive capabilities.[56] However, for modern historians there is some debate as to their military effectiveness. Some claim that walls which surrounded most late-medieval urban areas were weak defensively and failed to protect their towns' inhabitants. They point to the large number of walled towns that fell to the sieges and bombardments of late-medieval warfare.[57] Also, because these fortifications were so expensive, some towns were unable to complete their walls, or to extend them to cover their suburbs,[58] and some also were unable to keep them in good condition; the walls of Alnwick, Richmond, Warwick, Southampton, Chester, and even York had all fallen into ruin before 1500. Southampton's walls were in such poor condition in 1460 that a contemporary writer described them as "so feeble that they may not resist any gunshot, and so thin that no man may stand on them to make any resistance or defense."[59] Even Christine de Pisan, writing in the early fifteenth century, was forced to admit that most walls built to defend the towns of her time were not as good as those built by the Romans centuries before.[60]

Other historians are less critical of fourteenth- and fifteenth-century town walls. They note the many towns that adequately defended themselves against sieges and even gunpowder artillery bombardments of the later Middle Ages, forcing their besiegers to withdraw without conquering them, such as Orléans and Paris in 1429, La Charité and Compiègne in 1430, Calais in 1436, Belgrade in 1456, Neuss in 1475, and Rhodes in 1480.[61] Furthermore, the fact that many town walls continued in strength into the sixteenth and seventeenth centuries, and indeed remained the principal fortification of those centuries, also seems to denote a defensive achievement that cannot be criticized too harshly.[62]

THE INFLUENCE OF
GUNPOWDER WEAPONS

BY THE END OF THE FOURTEENTH CENTURY, IT WAS APPARENT THAT GUNpowder weapons were changing siege tactics and, consequently, fortification construction had to adapt to them. From shortly after their invention, guns began to be used in sieges. They were possibly used in 1338 at the siege of Cambrai, in 1340 at Tournai and Quesnoy, in 1342 at Rennes and Hennebout, and almost certainly at Calais in 1346–47. But on all of these occasions their use was rather limited, especially in comparison to other siege machines.

Gunpowder weapons continued to be used to attack fortifications throughout the fourteenth century, and by the end of the century they had begun to have some successes in breaching them. In 1374, the French used guns to bring down the town walls of Saint-Saveur-le-Vicomte, and in 1377, Philip the Bold, Duke of Burgundy, used them to penetrate the wooden walls of the fortress of Odruik. At the beginning of the fifteenth century, no castle or town wall was safe from bombardment, and castles, such as Berwick in 1405, and towns, such as Harfleur in 1415, seem to have been fairly easily taken by attackers who used gunpowder weapons. Up to this time, some sieges were brought to a conclusion more quickly by gunpowder bombardment. Where it once could have taken more than a year to capture a heavily fortified and well-stocked town or castle, it might now take less than one month to capture one. Perhaps the most famous defeat by bombardment in the early history of gunpowder weapons was the city of Constantinople, the great walls of which fell in 1453, some contemporary sources suggest, due to the continual and sustained attack.[63]

Naturally, this threat of attack by gunpowder weapons influenced those responsible for the construction or maintenance of fortifications. Military leaders, as well as fortification architects and engineers, quickly realized that traditional medieval castles and town walls, with their tall, flat surfaces, made easy targets for guns, especially for the large-caliber bombards so frequently used in sieges of the period. The tall walls of medieval fortifications had not been built to sustain the continual barrage on a single area that the new gunpowder weapons could deliver, and in fact the relative thinness of the base of these walls, as well as the height of the walls, invariably made it easier to breach these fortifications.[64]

It was both too expensive and too time-consuming to rebuild all fortifications to meet the attacks of gunpowder weapons. Therefore, the initial move was to outfit them with their own gunpowder artillery as a defense. Gunpowder weapons began to be delivered to castles and town walls by the middle of the fourteenth century, but guns mounted on the tops of castle and town walls made little sense as they could not effectively defend the wall below them, an area that was most likely to be attacked.[65] This meant that the wall itself needed to be pierced with gunports so that defending fire could be more directly aimed at attacking artillery. This may have occurred as early as 1347, when the gate at the castle of Bioule was recorded as having been defended on its first floor by two men firing cannons,[66] but even so, the idea did not become popular in England until at least 1365 and in France until after 1380. Germany, Italy, and Spain may not have constructed gunports in their fortifications until even later than this.[67]

Once gunports had become popular in England and France, however, a large number of fortifications, both castles and town walls, received them. In England, gunports were added to Quarr Abbey on the Isle of Wight in 1365–66 (perhaps their earliest English use), to Queensborough Castle in 1373, to Assheton's Tower at Porchester in 1379, to Carisbrooke Castle in 1379–80, to the Canterbury town wall in 1380, to Cooling Castle in 1381, to Southampton Castle in 1382–86, to Saltwood Castle in 1383, to the Norwich town wall in 1385, to Bodiam Castle in 1386, and to the Winchester town wall in 1390.[68] In France, gunports were added more slowly and in smaller numbers. Besides those that may have existed at Bioule Castle, it is only the gunports in the town wall of Mont-Saint-Michel and at the castles of Blanquefort and Saint-Malo that can be confirmed to have been built before 1400.[69] Others were not built until after 1412, with the towns of Paris and Rennes receiving their gunports in 1415 and 1418, respectively.[70] However, gunport construction in France increased through the end of the Middle Ages, while in England it declined drastically after 1420.[71]

In the late fourteenth century most gunports were shaped like inverted keyholes with circular openings for guns below vertical slits. This may indicate that they were initially nothing more than arrow slits adapted for gunpowder weapons by adding a circular opening to the bottom, as fifteenth century gunports were usually built without the vertical slit; however, some architectural historians contend that the slits were there merely to facilitate the sighting of the weapon.[72] Gunports were also quite small: the slits ranged in length between 381 and 813 millimeters and in width between 65 and 152 millimeters, while the circular openings ranged between 127 and 305 millimeters in diameter. Although some gunports were built higher in towers, especially after 1400, most were built near to the ground, generally no higher than 1 meter from the inside floor.[73]

The number and distribution of gunports around the fortifications varied greatly. Sometimes there were very few gunports in a fortress, perhaps only one or two, while other fortifications, especially those built in the fifteenth century, contained a much larger number. For example, Raglan Castle, built c.1450, contained no fewer than 32 gunports.[74] Most also were located in the fortification's gates and towers. This allowed them to provide some flanking fire along the wall and causeways, although this may have been of limited effect, as most gunports allowed less than a 45-degree angle of fire.[75]

The small size of these gunports meant that the large guns could not be used for defense of the fortification. This can also be seen in the small size of the gunport embrasures on which these guns were mounted, most of which were less than 70 centimeters long. This allowed only the smallest of mounted gunpowder weapons or handheld guns to be fired from these gunports.[76] Still, gunports alone could not supply sufficient defense against most gunpowder artillery bombardments, especially as those guns had become much more powerful and accurate by the beginning of the fifteenth century and even more by the beginning of the sixteenth century. Other methods of improving defense were needed.

Some towns and castles tried to meet this threat by thickening their walls with piles of earth behind them. While this did add protection to the walls so that they could not be easily breached in some instances, it was not always successful. The earthen rampart exerted a heavy pressure on the wall and weakened the masonry instead of strengthening it. As Philip, Duke of Cleves, noted at the end of the fifteenth century, "whenever the guns batter the wall, the earth tumbles down with the masonry, which makes it all the easier for the enemy to climb into the breach."[77] Other walls were thickened with more masonry instead of earth. Or a separate, shorter wall, known as a *faussebray*, was added slightly in front of the main walls, usually no more than two to three meters, to take the impact of gunshots that might hit the more vulnerable base of the walls.[78] Finally, some walls had a sloping *glacis* of masonry added to their front to deflect gunshots, avoiding direct impact on the flat wall. However, these additions were often very expensive and therefore not generally obtainable for many towns or castle owners whose resources were often limited.[79] Still others tried to increase the size of the ditches surrounding their fortifications, noting the relative security against bombardment of large moated fortresses, such as Bodiam, Kenilworth, or Caerphilly castles.[80] The most impressive increase of this sort was at Rhodes where, between the Ottoman Turkish sieges of 1480 and 1522, the moat was doubled in size, from roughly 23 meters to more than 50 meters. In fact, in three sizeable places along the moat at Rhodes the size was increased so much that islands of earth made from, on average, 10 meters of the former moat edges were left as additional fortifications, *tenailles*, between the walls and the new moat edges.[81] But these were even more expensive than most townspeople or castle owners could afford.

Some builders tried to increase the defense of castles and town walls by adding new fortifications to the existing defensive structures and then filling them with defensive gunpowder artillery and missile troops. In essence the theory behind these was the same as that of gunports, facing guns with guns, except that they were entirely separate from the castles and town walls themselves, and thus their defeat did not necessarily mean the collapse of a fortification. Generally, these were built in two styles. The first style was the low earthwork defense, known as a *boulevard*, which was typically placed before a vulnerable gate or wall. Its defense derived from its large number of guns (which increased the amount of defensive firepower), its low height (which made it easier to fire), and its earthen walls (which more readily absorbed the impact of stone and metal cannonballs). It seems to have been particularly popular in mid-fifteenth-century France among fortresses that were more open to gunpowder artillery bombardment.[82] Perhaps the most famous medieval *boulevards* were those that stood outside the fortified bridgehead called the Tourelles, at Orléans, which was attacked first by the English, led by Thomas Montagu, earl of Salisbury, in 1428, and then by the French, led by (among others) Joan of Arc, in 1429. Built in 1426, these *boulevards* were filled with gunpowder weapons and missile troops. Both fell, but only after numerous assaults. According to the contemporary *Journal du siège de Orléans*, in order for Joan of Arc's soldiers to capture the *boulevard*, they made "many marvelous assaults, during which many marvelous feats of arms were performed . . . [and] many Frenchmen were killed or wounded."[83]

The second style was the artillery tower. This was usually newly constructed tower, again filled with a large number of gunpowder weapons, which was added to the most exposed part of a fortress. Its purpose was nearly the same as the *boulevard*, both to increase the amount of defensive firepower and to add flanking fire to a vulnerable wall or gate, but it was generally much taller and constructed of stone. The artillery tower was also usually round in shape to provide no flat surfaces to enemy gunfire. It soon became the preferred artillery fortification added to castles and town walls, and was in fact built well into the early modern period. (*Boulevard* construction had ceased for the most part by the end of the fifteenth century).[84]

Certainly the most varied, if not also the most numerous, artillery towers can be found at Rhodes in the eastern Mediterranean. Following their successful defense of the city in 1480, the Knights Hospitaller, who controlled the city, were determined to add artillery towers at every angle and vulnerable spot along the landward sides of the walls. (The seaward side was guarded by three fortresses at the end of moles that jutted into the harbor, these having received their own updating and rebuilding, and by heavy chains running between them.) The result over the next 40 years was the construction of more than 10 new towers and one new gate, the reconstruction of 3 older gates, and the refitting of all the other towers to withstand the gunpowder artillery that the Hospitallers were certain would be the result of a second Ottoman siege. These included the massive St. George bastion, built originally in 1481 under the direction of Grand Master Pierre d'Aubusson, and rebuilt in 1496 by that same Grand Master, who had recently been appointed cardinal of Asia. This huge five-sided structure was topped by a large number of artillery platforms facing in all directions, from which the largest of gunpowder weapons could fire at opponents on the moat opposite them. Inside the bastion were two stories of chambers filled with gunports. From these, medium-sized and small guns could be fired down the moat. Perhaps because of its size and the number of guns that the St. George bastion contained, it was not attacked during the 1522 siege, when the Ottoman Turks finally did return. This time they captured Rhodes; large artillery towers and numerous guns simply could not compensate for the seemingly endless supply of Turkish troops and artillery or the determination of their Sultan, Suleyman I the Magnificent.[85]

Yet none of these additions to existing fortifications provided complete security against gunpowder artillery attack, as was made clear at Rhodes in 1522, and by the end of the fifteenth century it was recognized that traditional medieval fortifications, even with a number of additions, could not provide adequate defense against a gunpowder weapon attack on their inhabitants. A more elaborate system of fortifications was needed, a system where walls could withstand the constant impact of stone or metal cannonballs while at the same time offering its own gunpowder artillery bombardment against those besiegers.

Known as the *trace italienne*, because of its appearance in numerous early-sixteenth-century Italian city-states, this system of artillery fortifications may have originated in Leon Battista Alberti's *De re aedificatoria* (*On Construction*), written in the 1440s (although it was not popular until after its 1485 printing). Alberti contends:

1) that fortification walls facing gunpowder weapons should be both short enough to easily see the ground below them and wide enough to withstand the impact of cannonballs;

2) that artillery towers projecting at an angle beyond the walls should be added to the fortification—this would not only protect the fortification itself but also keep offensive guns at bay and cover blind spots along the fortress walls;

3) that angled bastions projecting out at regular intervals from the fortress walls be built giving increased flanking cross-fire along the surface of those walls;

4) that as time passed further refinements should be added to the fortification: wide and deep ditches along the walls to keep enemy artillery at a distance and to cut down on mining with detached casements or bastions (called *ravelins*) built beyond those ditches to further impede enemy artillery attacks; and

5) that extensions should be built to these fortifications, complete with crownworks or hornworks, to protect outside strategic areas.[86]

The *trace italienne* completely changed the future of fortification construction. Few tall castles and town walls would be newly built as defenses against foreign invasion or domestic rebellion. Already by the end of the fifteenth century, the Italian fortifications of Sarazana, Avezzano, and Ostia Antica had begun to adapt Alberti's ideas in their construction. However, it was not until after 1494, when Charles VIII's invasion of Italy would show the vulnerability of medieval fortifications to artillery bombardment, that most *trace italienne* artillery fortifications began to appear, and they would continue to be built into the nineteenth century.[87]

Notes

1. Platt (1982): 85.

2. Toy (1955): 161–62 and Mercier-Sivadjian and Sivadjian (1985): 38.

3. Allmand (1988): 77.

4. Stenton (1960): 119.

5. M. Jones (1981): 153.

6. M.W. Thompson (1987): 19–20.

7. M.W. Thompson (1987): 104, 171–78. See also Dobson (1977): 5.

8. M. Johnson (2002) and Morley (1981): 104–5.

9. M.W. Thompson (1987): 17, 29–30; Brown, Colvin, and Taylor (1963): II: 802; Fino (1970): 421–23, 438–41; M. Jones (1981): 178–80; and Monreal y Tejada (1999).

10. Morley (1981): 113.
11. Morley (1981): 107–11 and Toy (1955): 228–29.
12. Morley (1981): 107 and Toy (1955): 230.
13. Morley (1981): 113.
14. Toy (1955): 230–31.
15. Prestwich (1982): 176 and D. Turner (1986): 168–69. However, Vale (1986): 136–37 and M.W. Thompson (1987): 3 claim that defense was always the primary interest of the builders of these fortified residences.
16. R. Brown (1954): 89–91; D. Turner (1986): 268; and Vale (1986): 138.
17. D. Turner (1986); Toy (1955): 218–20; R. Brown (1954): 94–96; Platt (1982): 114–18; Forde-Johnston (1977): 120–23; and Taylor (1958): 121–22.
18. Viollet-le-Duc (1883). A recent re-examination of Viollet-le-Duc's work is Midant (2002): 107–19, which convincingly restores the reputation of the restoration work at Pierresfonds.
19. Fino (1970): 412–15 and Toy (1955): 222–23.
20. Platt (1982): 278–91.
21. Toy (1955): 212–28; M.W. Thompson (1987): 17–18, 22–26; Forde-Johnston (1977): 127; and M. Jones (1981): 177.
22. On the Scottish tower houses see Cruden (1960): 100–143; R. Brown (1954): 91–92; Brown, Colvin, and Taylor (1963): I: 235–36; and Prestwich (1982): 174–75. For France see M.W. Thompson (1987): 3 and M. Jones (1981): 172–80.
23. Toy (1955): 225–26; Platt (1982): 169–73; M.W. Thompson (1987: 87–91; 1981: 156–62); and Forde-Johnston (1977): 130–33.
24. Fino (1977): 421–23 and M.W. Thompson (1987): 29–30.
25. English (1984): 175, 190–91.
26. Martines (1979): 221–22. See Toy (1955): 212–13, 216–18 for other examples of princely urban fortified residences.
27. Bentini and Borella (2002) and Di Francesco and Borella (1998).
28. English (1984): 183–84 and Brucker (1969): 35–38.
29. English (1984): 185 and Eltis (1989): 100.
30. Stephenson (1933): 188–92; Kenyon (1990): 183; Jones and Bond (1987): 112; and Allmand (1988): 77.
31. Stephenson (1933): 12.
32. Stephenson (1933): 24.
33. Stephenson (1933): 26.
34. Stephenson (1933): 23; Forde-Johnston (1977): 134; Guillerme (1988): 49; Frere, Stow, and Bennett (1982): 91; and Rörig (1967): 169.
35. Contamine (1978); H. Turner (1971): 28–46; and Allmand (1988): 77–78.

36. Forde-Johnston (1977): 137 and M. Jones (1981): 171–72.
37. Frere, Stow, and Bennett (1982): 91 and Allmand (1988): 77–78. See also Kenyon (1990): 183–84; Dobson (1977): 6 and Forde-Johnston (1977): 134.
38. Kenyon (1990): 183; Platt (1976): 41; and M. Jones (1981): 153–55.
39. H. Turner (1971): 156, 211–13; Forde-Johnston (1977): 134–36; and Fino (1970): 334–35.
40. The walls of Conway were two meters thick (H. Turner [1971]: 212–13 and Forde-Johnston [1977]: 134–35), while the walls at Canterbury were 1.78 meters thick (Frere, Stow, and Bennett 1982: 91).
41. Guillerme (1988): 49 and M. Jones (1981): 153–55.
42. An extremely detailed study is Inventory (1972). For a more concise discussion see H. Turner (1971): 141, 211–13; and Forde-Johnston (1977): 134–36.
43. H. Turner (1971): 141, 179; and M. Jones (1981): 153.
44. H. Turner (1971): 61–66 and Frere, Stow, and Bennett (1982): 91.
45. Christine de Pisan (1932): 138; Kenyon (1990): 197–99; Fino (1970): 334; and Frere, Stow, and Bennett (1982): 91.
46. Fino (1970): 334–35. See also Christine de Pisan (1932): 136.
47. H. Turner (1971): 60–62, 211; Forde-Johnston (1977): 134–35, 141; and Fino (1970): 334–35.
48. H. Turner (1971): 59 and Kenyon (1990): 195–97.
49. Fino (1970): 334–35.
50. H. Turner (1971): 66–72, 211–13; Kenyon (1990): 191–95; and Forde-Johnston (1977): 134–36.
51. Nicholas (1987): 70 and Forde-Johnston (1977): 141.
52. H. Turner (1971): 66–72 and Christine de Pisan (1932): 137–38.
53. Guillerme (1988): 49.
54. Kenyon (1990): 186–89; Frere, Stow, and Bennett (1982): 23; and Platt (1976): 42.
55. Kenyon (1990): 184; Platt (1976): 44; and Frere, Stow, and Bennett (1982): 91.
56. See, for example, the description of Harfleur in 1415 given by the anonymous author of the *Gesta Henrici quinti* (Taylor and Roskell [1975]:29–31) and the description of early-fifteenth-century Arras given by Enguerran de Monstrelet ([1857–62]:III:22).
57. Allmand (1988): 79.
58. See, for example, Ipswich and King's Lynn in England (Platt [1976]:42–43) and Fagnano and Venice in Italy (Mallett and Hale [1984]:89).
59. Dobson (1977): 6–7 and Platt (1976): 44.
60. Christine de Pisan (1932): 136.
61. M. Jones (1988): 236 and DeVries (2005a).
62. Parker (1988): 7–16.
63. Although DeVries (1996b) has suggested that it was not the guns themselves that brought about the surrender.

64. This is certainly the theory of Rogers (1993): 262–67, 275 and Parker (1988): 6–44, but DeVries (2005b) disputes this.

65. O'Neil (1960): 4–5, 10–11, 22; and Renn (1968): 302–3.

66. Contamine (1984): 202.

67. DeVries (1995): 233.

68. Kenyon (1981): 206–12; DeVries (1995): 233; DeVries (2005a): 38–39; Renn (1968): 301–02; O'Neil (1960): 9–11, 17–18, 20; Brown, Colvin, and Taylor (1963): II: 594, 801–2, 844; Frere, Stow, and Bennett (1982): 23; and D. Turner (1986): 270–72.

69. DeVries (1995): 233–34; Contamine (1984): 202; Vale (1981): 133; and M. Jones (1981): 174.

70. Douet-d'Arcq (1863–64): II: 32–33; M. Jones (1981): 175; and DeVries (1995): 134.

71. Contamine (1984): 202–3; Kenyon (1981): 232; and DeVries (1995): 235–37.

72. O'Neil (1960): 12–13; Kenyon (1981): 207; DeVries (1995: 235–36; 2005a: 44–45). Kirby Muxloe Castle does have fifteenth-century gunports that have the muzzle hole apart from the slit. See Toy (1955): 237.

73. O'Neil (1960): 7–11, 17–20, 29–30, 37; Kenyon (1981): 207–8; Kenyon (1987): 143–60; DeVries (1995: 235–37; 2005: 45–47); Renn (1968): 301; Leguay (1988): 185; and Frere, Stow, and Bennett (1982): 117.

74. Kenyon (1987): 162.

75. DeVries (1995): 236; Kenyon (1981): 209; and Frere, Stow, and Bennett (1982): 117.

76. Kenyon (1981): 207; DeVries (1995): 236–37; and DeVries (2005a).

77. Duffy (1979): 2; Eltis (1989): 94; and DeVries (1995): 237.

78. The best example of this can still be seen surrounding most of the walls of Rhodes. See Smith and DeVries (2011).

79. Contamine (1984): 204 and DeVries (1995): 237.

80. Fino (1970): 297–300 and D. Turner (1986): 269.

81. Smith and DeVries (2011).

82. Fino (1970): 295–96; Contamine (1984): 204; Leguay (1981): 171–72, 185–86; M. Jones (1981): 176; Vale (1981): 133; DeVries (1995: 237–38; 2005a: 49–52).

83. Journal (1896): 84–85. See also DeVries (1999a: 60–62, 80–86; 2005a: 50–53).

84. DeVries (1995: 239; 2005a: 54–57); H. Turner (1971): 60, 165; Contamine (1984): 204; Brown, Colvin, and Taylor (1963): II: 606; Fino (1970): 294–95; Vale (1981): 133; Leguay (1981): 187; M. Jones (1981): 175–76; and Hale (1965): 479.

85. Smith and DeVries (2011).

86. Alberti (1988). See also Hale (1965): 471–81; Parker (1988): 8–11; and Contamine (1984): 204–5.

87. Hale (1965, 1977); Pepper and Adams (1986); and Duffy (1979).

PART IV

Warships

MAN'S EARLIEST SHIPS WERE SMALL VESSELS USED FOR TRANSPORTATION and trade. These were probably rafts, floats, or dugout canoes—as Lionel Casson writes, "whatever [men] could find that would keep them afloat."[1] The technology was simple. Boats such as these were constructed using the most accessible materials—reeds, light wood, bark, or animal skins—and were fashioned with the most rudimentary skills. They were made to sail only on rivers or along coasts of seas and lakes, as their hulls were not constructed to withstand high waves or bad weather.[2]

Nor could they hold much cargo. But as the population of the ancient world began to increase, the need for larger trading ventures also increased, and the least expensive means of transportation for these ventures was on water. Therefore, larger ships were built to accommodate larger cargoes, and these vessels also began to take more risks, traveling where earlier ships had been unable to go. By the third millennium BCE in Egypt, ships had become so large that they were able to ferry large blocks of stone along the Nile River from quarries to building sites, and a thousand years later similar vessels measuring more than 70 meters in length and 25 meters in width carried obelisks down the Nile from their quarries at Aswan.[3]

Initially, at least, these ships were constructed using similar materials to earlier vessels. The design of these vessels also changed little from their predecessors. Even when shipwrights had become more expert in their construction and began using more substantial materials, ship design did not differ much from earlier boats. The earliest planked ships were flat-bottomed and square-ended and were constructed in the clinker-style. First, a keel plank (or planks) was laid that formed the centerline of the hull. From there, on both sides, other short planks were added, fastened to each other and to the keel planks by dowels, mortises and tenons, wooden clamps, or a combination of these. These short planks continued to be added until the shell of the vessel had been completed. Gunwales, crossbeams, and deck planks were then attached to the hull to strengthen it. A pole mast, equipped with a single, loose-fitting, square, papyrus or cloth sail, was also often present, although most ships were powered principally by oarsmen, paddlers, or punters. Steering was accomplished by one or more steering oars placed near or at the stern of the ship.[4] This mode of construction would remain popular well into the Middle Ages.

It is difficult to determine when the first warships appeared in the ancient world. Some historians theorize that as cargo ships grew larger and trade became more prosperous, piracy also began to flourish. This theory may indeed be valid, but there is little evidence either to support it or in fact to counter it. For it is not until c.1400 BCE that an artistic source possibly showing a warship is found: a painting on a Mycenaean vase from the eastern coast of Greece depicting a curved stem-post characteristic of later Greek galleys.[5]

It is not until at least two centuries later that an Egyptian source depicts a military engagement at sea: a large carving on the side of a temple portrays a naval battle fought on the Nile between the Egyptian fleet and ships from barbarian invaders known only as "Sea Peoples." From this source it can be determined that the numbers and sizes of the ships of both—for they are identical in the carving—were impressive and that their hulls were no longer square-ended but rounded. They were also decorated, with a lion's head adorning most of the prow posts. Lookouts were placed on the top of the mast, and rowers were protected by a high bulwark attached to the hull. Perhaps most important was the fact that the loose-fitting sail common on all ancient ships was now outfitted with brails, i.e., lines for controlling the area of the sails exposed to the winds, which could be used to shorten the sails and add maneuverability. There are no long-range weapons depicted in this carving for use in battle at sea; the only means of fighting appears to have been the grappling of opposing ships, by means of a grappling iron or hook, and then the imitation of a land battle on both decks.[6]

The first successful style of warship to appear in large numbers in the ancient world was the oared warship or galley. While it was probably first invented sometime between 725 and 680 BCE by the Phoenicians — who developed both a single-banked oared warship known as a penteconter and a two-banked warship known as a bireme[7]—it was the Greeks who made this the most famous warship of the ancient world, and with whom it is most often associated. In the fifth century BCE the Greeks added a third bank of oars to the galley, thus creating a trireme, and with it controlled the Mediterranean Sea until long after Alexander the Great's empire had split into its various parts and fallen.[8]

The first ancient oared warships were low-hulled and flat, with crews of 25 oarsmen rowing on each side of the vessel (in combat the oarsmen became archers). However, this one level of oarsmen did not produce much speed, and therefore there was a move to equip ships with several banks of oarsmen— hence the creation of biremes, triremes, and even larger vessels. Of these, the best and most common were the triremes, which measured approximately 35 meters long and 3.5 meters wide and carried a crew of 170 oarsmen—31 oars- men on the top bank of oars on both sides and 27 on all of the lower banks.

The weapon of most ancient oared warships was not the grappling iron but the ram. The invention of the ram gave the oared warship the added ability to attack an opposing ship. It is believed that the first ram was attached to a warship between 1200 and 1000 BCE but that it was not used effectively until 600 BCE, when the Greeks began to fit all of their oared warships with them. Initially, the ram was simply an extension of the keel, but later this was changed both in shape and size, leading eventually to a down-turned three-pronged ram covered with metal sheeting. At least this is the design of the single extant ram found in 1980 in the sea off the coast of Israel near Athlit. Dating to the second century BCE, this ram was bronze and was meant to be placed over a wooden extension of the keel.[9] The ram remained in use until 121–22 CE, with the Romans discarding it as a naval weapon, choosing instead to return to the grappling iron and pseudo-land battle for naval warfare, although the ram would return once again in the early Byzantine Empire, although to a rela- tively limited extent.

Ancient oarsmen/sailors were not slaves or prisoners. This modern concept is drawn from late medieval and early modern history, but it is inaccurate for much of the ancient world. For the Greeks at least, much pride was taken in their rowing skill. Only the best athletes could be oarsmen for the triremes, and they frequently held competitions to determine which crew was the stron- gest and fastest. It would be later, in the Roman Empire, that free oarsmen were replaced by slaves and prisoners.[10]

During the two centuries when the Roman Republic controlled the Mediterranean, the second and first centuries BCE, there was little change from the warships common in the eastern part of the Mediterranean. These were the ships that opposed each other in the naval battle of Actium, fought in 31 BCE between the Roman fleet of Octavian and the Roman/Egyptian fleet of Marc Antony and Cleopatra. There Octavian, mixing his triremes with larger warships, known as "sixes," defeated Antony and Cleopatra's triremes and "tens," securing for himself the sole leadership of Rome: the emperorship.

Actium was the last large naval battle for three hundred years. For most of the history of the Roman Empire there was no need for a large naval force. By the end of the first century BCE, the entire Mediterranean Sea was under imperial control and crossings of the English Channel and Black Sea were unhindered by opposing fleets. The Roman navy was used for little more than transportation, communication, and control of piracy. For these duties, the trireme was too large, bulky, and slow. A lighter, more maneuverable warship was needed, and this was provided by the liburnian.

The liburnian, which took its name from a piratical tribe that lived among the islands of the Dalmatian coast and are credited with its invention, was a sleek and fast galley fitted with two banks of oars and a main mast with a square sail. Its use in pirate attacks on imperial fleets had been so impressive that by 36 BCE the Roman navy began to build them for its own use. Soon they had become the primary ship of the fleet, as shown by their frequent appearance on Trajan's Column and other artistic sources. Although triremes reappeared for a time during the civil wars of the early fourth century CE, the liburnian remained the warship of the Roman Empire until its fall.[11] It also became the archetype for the two-banked Byzantine dromon, the primary warship of that empire until its fall in the fifteenth century. The dromon, 40 to 50 meters in length, contained two banks of 25 oars on each side.[12]

The following section discusses medieval warships, although despite this focus it describes all medieval ships: while on occasion ships specific to warfare were constructed, it was more common throughout the Middle Ages to use cargo ships for naval conflicts. At times alterations were made to these ships to outfit them for fighting, but most often they were simply used as they were. When the wars were completed, these ships generally returned to carrying cargo. Two chapters divide this section chronologically. The first discusses early medieval ships, i.e., vessels built before the Crusades. The second discusses high and late medieval ships. Technological changes that would allow very late medieval sailors to explore the coast of Africa and the open Atlantic Ocean are

addressed in this chapter. These would lead not only to the voyages of exploration, but also to the development of the large, multi-masted, multi-sailed ship
filled with banks of cannon. By the mid-sixteenth century, navies and naval
warfare would resemble very little their ancient or medieval ancestors.

Notes

1. Casson (1971): 1.
2. See Casson (1971): 3–10.
3. See Casson (1971): 11–42 and Bass (1972): 11–36.
4. Casson (1971): 13–16.
5. Casson (1971): 31–32.
6. Casson (1971): 36–38.
7. See Casson (1971): 54–65 and Anderson (1962): 1–5.
8. Casson (1971): 77–140 and Hale (2009).
9. Linder (1987) and Casson, Steffy and Linder (1990). See also Basch and Frost (1975).
10. On the Greek oared warship see Foley and Soedel (1981); Casson (1971): 77–140; Anderson (1962): 6–30; DeVries and Katzev (1972): 37–64; and Steffy (1980). A Greek trireme has been reconstructed and is currently commissioned in the Greek navy. This has greatly increased our knowledge about its construction and sailing capabilities.
11. Casson (1971): 141–47; Anderson (1962): 31–36; and Unger (1981): 236.
12. Dolley (1948): 48–53; Unger (1980): 43–46; Casson (1971): 148–54; Lewis (1951): 30–32, 72–75; van Doorninck (1972); Pryor (1988): 57–61; and Anderson (1962): 36–41. On the dromon the best study, perhaps the only study that need ever be written, is the massive Pryor and Jeffreys (2006).

CHAPTER II

EARLY
MEDIEVAL
WARSHIPS

LATE ROMAN AND EARLY
MEDIEVAL SHIPS

THE INITIAL BARBARIAN INVASIONS DID NOT ALTER ROMAN NAVAL STRATEGY. With the possible exception of the Suevi, who began their invasions on the southern shores of the Baltic Sea and may have sailed to the northwestern shores of Iberia, all invasions of the Empire were land-based and required no warships. It was not until the Vandals crossed from Spain to North Africa and the Visigoths from Italy to Spain in the early fifth century that the Mediterranean was invaded, and it is unlikely that the ships used in these crossings were built for naval conflict.[1] Similarly, the invasions of Britain by the Angles, Saxons, and Jutes in the fifth century were probably accomplished by using ships only for transportation and trade, and not for warfare, although the near contemporary Gildas does identify them as *cyuls*, "that is . . . ships of war, with their sails wafted by the wind."[2] A vessel like that uncovered at Sutton Hoo, narrow and not too long, may have been used.[3]

Once established in North Africa, the Vandals built a pirate fleet that preyed on Mediterranean shipping and was used in the 455 invasion of Italy. But it is uncertain what type of warships the Vandals used in these operations, or even if they were similar to those used at the same time by the Romans. Their tactics appear to be different, however, as a passage written by the sixth-century Byzantine historian Procopius illustrates:

> But the Vandals... raised their sails and, taking in tow the boats which... they had made ready with no men in them, they sailed against the enemy [the Romans]. And when they came near, they set fire to the boats which they were towing, when their sails were bellied by the wind, and let them go against the Roman fleet. And since there were a great number of ships there, these boats easily spread fire wherever they struck.... And already the Vandals too were at hand ramming and sinking the ships, and making booty of such of the soldiers as attempted to escape, and of their arms as well.[4]

By 500, the Vandal naval threat had ended, defeated finally by the Byzantine forces under Belisarius.[5] In Western Europe, the barbarians, unaccustomed to fighting on the sea, had established their kingdoms without navies. Even the great Charlemagne felt no need to outfit a navy until near the end of his reign, and it was not until the reigns of his son and grandsons that this navy was put into use against the Arabs and the Vikings.[6]

It was in fact these two threats that again led to the construction of warships. In the Mediterranean the naval threat to Europe came from Muslim Arab fleets. While the barbarian tribes conquered the western part of the Roman Empire, the Byzantine Empire inherited the eastern part, including the Middle East. However, this dominance ended with the rise of Islam in the sixth and seventh centuries. By 710 Mohammed and his followers had conquered all of the Middle East, North Africa, Spain, and Persia, and much of India. Only the Byzantines and the Franks were able to stop their further progress. In conquering these lands, many ports in the Mediterranean were taken, and with them many ships. These were used later to attack other regions, as the Muslims continued their onslaughts on Europe.

The first Arab navy dates to about 651, when Muawiyah, the governor of Syria (and later caliph of the Umayyad Empire) gathered the ships captured from conquered Mediterranean ports and armed them for war. His initial target was the almost completely unprotected island of Cyprus; it fell quickly. Other Mediterranean targets were taken equally as fast. Between 672 and 678, a large Arab navy even attempted an attack on the Byzantine capital,

Constantinople, and, although this ultimately failed, with the Byzantines almost completely destroying the attacking fleet, it showed the strength and designs of Arab sea captains. (A second attack on Constantinople followed in 717–18, but it too proved to be unsuccessful.)[7]

The Arab (and later Arab-Egyptian) navy continued to play a major role in the Mediterranean until the end of the Middle Ages. The technology of early Arab ships is difficult to ascertain, since few illustrations of Arab ships before the thirteenth century exist. But, according to contemporary sources, their tactics were similar to those of the Byzantine navy, and perhaps their maritime technology was like that of the Byzantines as well. What is known is that the Arab vessels were oared warships, especially built for raiding, and less well crafted for battle.[8]

This did not change until the early ninth century. Largely because of Byzantine political unrest, which resulted in a decline in naval power, the Arabs again began to exert their naval might. Sicily, Crete, Cyprus (which had earlier been reconquered by the Byzantines), Corsica, Sardinia, and the Balearic Islands all fell in quick succession. In turn, naval bases were established on these Mediterranean islands from which frequent raids against the rest of Europe, especially Southern Italy, were undertaken. While it seems that many of these ships, especially the larger ones, continued to resemble the Byzantine dromons, others were smaller and often powered by the lateen (or triangular) sail rather than by oar. Larger warships also began to use Greek Fire and catapults as weapons in battle. This would be the nature of the Arab fleet until the middle of the eleventh century.[9]

VIKING SHIPS

In Northern Europe at the end of the eighth century, the Vikings began to attack the lands across the sea from their Scandinavian homelands. These attacks were completely unanticipated by a European populace that did not believe it possible for anyone at the time to make ships capable of raiding their coasts. As the English scholar Alcuin wrote to Aethelred, the king of Northumbria, concerning the Viking raid on the Lindisfarne monastery in 793: "Lo, it is nearly 350 years that we and our fathers have inhabited this most lovely land, and never before has such terror appeared in Britain as we have suffered from a pagan race, nor was it thought that such an inroad from the sea could be made."[10] These raids proved to be very profitable and would continue, with varying intensity, for the next three centuries. The ship, the primary means of transportation for the Viking raids, once again gained prominence in military matters.

Historians have many questions concerning Viking shipbuilding and naval tactics. Fortunately, not only is there a large number of written sources, especially Scandinavian sagas, describing the adventures of Viking sailors/raiders, but there has also been a significant number of Viking ships excavated by archaeologists, which have added to our knowledge of their construction and use at sea.

Scandinavian ships were not always capable of raiding the coasts of other European lands. In the Early Middle Ages, these vessels had little potential for open-sea sailing and were probably not unlike boats constructed elsewhere in Europe. They had a relatively shallow hull and were built in a clinker-style, i.e., in a manner similar to the shipbuilding techniques of the ancients. Loose planks were laid to serve as a deck. Early on they also contained no strong keel, and they were thus unable to carry a mast, using oars as their sole means of power. However, this changed in the early eighth century, when ships with strong keels began to be built. These keels allowed a deeper, flatter, and longer hull to be constructed. They also allowed the placement of a heavy mast, perhaps as long as 12 meters. The new hull strength, depth, and length made it possible for the raids that began later in the century.[11]

Many ships took part in the Viking raids over the following centuries. They varied in size and, seemingly, in purpose. Some were quite large in length and width—the Gokstad ship was 23 meters long and 5.2 meters wide, and the Skuldelev longship was 28 meters long (its width cannot be estimated because of the bad state of preservation)—but shallow in depth, which has indicated to some historians that they were built as warships. Others were considerably smaller in length and width, but larger in depth, perhaps suggesting that they were vessels that would be used chiefly for transporting cargo. All Vikings ships, however, may have participated in the very profitable raids, as they were needed only for transporting men to and from their raiding destination and not for combat on the sea.

The Viking ship could be rowed, with most large vessels being equipped with oarlocks cut into both sides of the hull, which would accommodate as many as 50–60 seamen. It was also equipped with a large square sail. The sail did not add anything to the maneuverability of the ship, but it did add considerable speed. The Viking ship was steered by a single rudder attached to one side near the stern.[12]

Most Viking ships cannot be considered "true" warships, if the definition is determined by whether they fought naval engagements. There were simply

Fig. 11.1: Oseburg Viking ship, c. 815–820.

Viking Ship Museum, Oslo, Norway / Ancient Art and Architecture Collection Ltd. / The Bridgeman Art Library International.

not many battles to be fought on sea. One of the exceptions was the battle of Svoldr, fought in 1000 between the powerful king of Norway, Olaf Tryggvason, and a consortium of opponents, which included King Swein Forkbeard of Denmark, King Olof of Sweden, and the Earl Eric, a rebellious noble vassal of Olaf Tryggvason. From the description given in later sagas, the tactics of the Viking forces appear to have been little different than those of the Romans.

The king of Norway had perhaps the greatest fleet of his day; included in it were such large prize longships—known collectively as *drekkars* or dragon ships—as the *Long Serpent*, *Short Serpent*, and *Crane*. However, this fleet had never fought in a naval battle before. At Svoldr, his consortium of opponents lured Olaf into a trap and forced him to do battle. The two fleets approached each other, grappled together, and then fought a long and violent battle with edged weapons and bows on the decks of all vessels. Arrows and spears flew, and axes were swung. Finally, the battle came down to a single combat between Olaf's Norwegians on board the *Long Serpent* and Eric's Norwegians on board his ship, *Iron Beard*. Ultimately, Eric's forces gained the upper hand. Most of Olaf's Vikings were slain, and he jumped overboard and was drowned.[13]

Because of the political turmoil of most European states during the centuries in which the Vikings raided, few competent attempts at naval opposition against them were made. Only the English were successfully able to counter the Viking navy by building ships of their own. This was begun as early as 851, when West Saxon ships opposed Viking raiders, but it did not become an earnest effort until the reign of Alfred the Great. Alfred, perhaps recognizing the largely unrecognized potential for naval defense against the Vikings, built a large fleet early in his reign. They were successful against a Viking flotilla in the summer of 875, and again in 882 and 885, and they may have been one of the causes of the peace between the English and the Vikings that followed for more than a decade. Finally, in 896 as the Vikings threatened England once again, Alfred's fleet was enlarged. The *Anglo-Saxon Chronicle* reports:

> Then King Alfred had "long ships" built to oppose the Danish warships. They were almost twice as long as the others. Some had sixty oars, some more. They were both swifter and steadier and also higher than the others. They were built neither on the Frisian nor the Danish pattern, but as it seemed to himself that they could be most useful.[14]

No sooner were these ships constructed than they were used in several successful naval conflicts against the Vikings. That these ships were unlike those opposing them is recorded, but how different, or in fact what exactly they were like, has not been confirmed by archaeological excavation.[15]

WILLIAM THE CONQUEROR'S FLEET

The Viking threat diminished in the tenth and eleventh centuries. But it did not end completely until 1066, when Harald Hardrada "the Hard Ruler," king of Norway, led a large fleet across the sea in an attempt to conquer England. He and most of his companions met their deaths at the battle of Stamford Bridge, defeated by the king of England, Harold Godwinson; the remnants of the Viking force returned to their homeland in a much smaller fleet. This was to be the last major naval undertaking of the Scandinavians.[16] But it was not to be the last attack on England in 1066, for later that same year, William, duke of Normandy, also attacked England, this time defeating Harold Godwinson and conquering the kingdom.

Fig. 11.2: William the Conqueror's ships crossing the English Channel, from the Bayeux Tapestry.

The Bridgeman Art Library International / With special authorization of the city of Bayeux Giraudon.

For this journey William needed many ships—contemporary numbers vary between 696 and 3,000—to transport an army of at least 5,000, and perhaps as many as 10,000 soldiers, accompanied by 2,000 to 3,000 horses. These needed only to be troop and horse carriers, however, as the once vaunted navy of the Anglo-Saxons had declined in power and thus would provide little opposition to a naval assault on the island.[17] It has been commonly thought that these vessels were built by William the Conqueror in Norman harbors, using Viking cargo or transport ship designs.[18] But recently this view has been challenged.

The first challenge, that of Bernard Bachrach, claims that William, in acquiring the ships needed to transport his army, was faced not only with the difficulty of procuring vessels to transport his troops, but also, because his army was cavalry-based, of procuring vessels to transport their horses. This could be accomplished only by constructing an entire new fleet of specially built horse transports or by using the same ships for both horses and men. The Bayeux Tapestry shows that men and horses traveled together in similar vessels, but this source, especially in depicting the Norman fleet, is fraught with problems. For example, no horse stalls are depicted, although, in Bachrach's interpretation, "these are absolutely necessary if horses are to be transported by sea without injuring themselves or each other."

Nor does it appear that the technology for transporting horses across the sea was known in northern Europe at this time. Certainly, Bachrach contends, there is no evidence to show that Viking ships were capable of this type of transportation, nor were any others at this time. But this was William's plan of assault, so he had to look elsewhere for his fleet; he found it only with Byzantine shipwrights, whose construction of horse transports was found to be precisely what William desired. These shipwrights were thus brought north to design his horse transports, while the remainder of his troops were transported to England by more conventional vessels acquired from Norman and Flemish owners.[19]

Carroll Gillmor, in answering Bachrach, returns to the thesis that William the Conqueror's ships were of northern European design, although not Viking. She suggests that there is an "unreliability of standardization" to be faced when studying the Norman fleet of 1066. Based on archaeological evidence and the depiction of the transport vessels portrayed on the Bayeux Tapestry, the Norman invasion fleet can have been composed only of sailing ships native to the Northern Sea coastal region (primarily Normandy and Flanders) rather than rowed vessels similar to those of the Vikings, and it was definitely "not a necessity to import the designs of Mediterranean vessels." It also seems certain that most of these ships were procured rather than constructed for the invasion. Furthermore, this "lack of standardization" also meant that while "the number of ships cannot be established with any certainty," the numbers themselves should be reduced, perhaps as low as the twelfth-century chronicler Wace's estimate of 700, an estimate much lower in number than other more contemporary Anglo-Norman chroniclers.[20]

Finally with J. Neumann's article, "Hydrographic and Ship-Hydrodynamic Aspects of the Norman Invasion, AD 1066," the argument comes full circle. Although Neumann is more concerned with the shape of the Norman ships and their capabilities against heavy Channel winds than he is in the origin of their design and construction, he does conclude that they could have been designed after the traditional Viking transport ships of the day. Indeed, their dimensions—which he estimates to have been 12.5 meters in length, with a length-to-beam ratio of 4.5 based on his hydrographic and hydrodynamic calculations—are not dissimilar to most of the Viking transport vessels that have been excavated. Nor is their estimated sail size, 4 or 5 square meters set on a 7–8-meter-high mast, different from those estimated to have been on the same Viking transport ships. Viking-style warships were too long and slender to have

been used for transporting horses and men, although some of these were probably used by William to protect his fleet.[21]

Notes

1. Lewis and Runyan (1985): 9–10.
2. Gildas (1978): 23.
3. Lewis and Runyan (1985): 12 and M. Jones (1987): 62–69. On the Sutton Hoo boat see
   P. Marsden (1972): 123–24.
4. Quoted in Lewis and Runyan (1985): 10–11. See also Lewis (1951): 18–19 and Rodgers
   (1940): 6–9.
5. Rodgers (1940): 9–14.
6. Lewis and Runyan (1985): 62–63.
7. Hourani (1995): 53–60.
8. Hourani (1995): 87–113. Hourani takes most of his evidence of Arab naval technology from
   pre-Islamic and Byzantine sources.
9. Lewis (1951): 54–78, 100–115, 132–63, 192–98; Lewis and Runyan (1985): 41–50; Nicolle
   (1989); Kreutz (1976); Unger (1980): 99–100; Pryor (1988): 28–29; and Rodgers (1940):
   30–40. On the Byzantine naval effort against the Arabs see Lewis and Runyan (1985):
   24–39; Unger (1980): 52–55, 96–98; and Stratos (1980).
10. Hooper (1989): 203 and Rodgers (1940): 72.
11. Atkinson (1979) and Durham (2002). On the excavated ships see Olsen and Crumlin-
    Pedersen (1990) and Sjøvold (1985).
12. See Atkinson (1979); Durham (2002); Crumlin-Pedersen (1981); Binns (1981); Christensen
    (1972); Unger (1980): 75–96; G. Jones (1968): 182–90; Lewis and Runyan (1985): 92–99;
    and Rodgers (1940): 69–87. On the Viking sail specifically see Gillmer (1979) and
    Christensen (1979).
13. Atkinson (1979): 41–44. See also Lewis and Runyan (1985): 95–99. For the *Long Serpent* see
    Rodgers (1940): 73–76. Other Viking naval battles include Aarhus (1044), Nisaa (1062),
    and Gotha River (1159). On these see Rodgers (1940): 80–86.
14. As quoted in Lewis and Runyan (1985): 94.
15. See Hooper (1989): 203–4; Hollister (1962): 103; and Lewis and Runyan (1985): 94.
16. DeVries (1999b).
17. See Hollister (1962): 103–26 and Hooper (1989).
18. See, for example, Lewis and Runyan (1985): 94–95 and Douglas (1964): 189–90.
19. B. Bachrach (1985b).
20. Gillmor (1985).
21. Neumann (1989).

CHAPTER 12

HIGH AND
LATE
MEDIEVAL
WARSHIPS

CRUSADER SHIPS

WHILE THE VIKING INVASIONS OF EUROPE AND THE NORMAN CONQUEST OF England were relatively small naval expeditions, the Crusades represented a far greater task. The First Crusade traveled to the Holy Land across land, needing naval assistance only to cross the Bosporus Strait next to Constantinople; such assistance was provided by the Byzantines. But even before the Crusaders captured Jerusalem and had established their kingdoms—in fact, as they were marching down the coastline from Antioch to Jerusalem—ships were required for delivering supplies, reinforcements, and pilgrims.[1] For the most part this requirement was filled by cargo and transport vessels; however, the capture of coastal towns and the protection of the cargo fleets necessitated warships as well.

Before the Crusades, most Europeans thought little about the Mediterranean, unless they lived around it. Many in the early Middle Ages made their living from that sea, but few had any links, economic or otherwise, with anyone who lived on the other side of it. What were once vibrant trading routes between North Africa, Egypt, the Middle East, and Anatolia and Europe had little if any traffic. Nor was the sea that had once hosted great Egyptian, Greek, Roman, and Carthaginian war fleets the site of much naval activity during those many centuries.

This state of affairs persisted for a long while after Rome fell. Late Carolingian fleets were weak and small, and voyages made by them were usually into the North Sea and English Channel—where they faced Frisians and Scandinavians—rather than into the Mediterranean. There, before the turn of the first millennium, only the Pisans in Italy and the Catalans in Spain were able to muster enough naval strength to make conquests of nearby islands: Corsica by the Pisans and the Balearic Islands by the Catalans. These were but short-lived conquests before the islands were recaptured by superior Byzantine and North African naval forces.[2]

However, this began to change somewhat in the late tenth and early eleventh centuries, when two Italian cities, Venice and Naples, began to construct fleets and develop trade links with Byzantine and Muslim lands in the Middle East and North Africa. Increased prosperity was almost immediate, and this encouraged other Italian coastal cities to also construct their own fleets. Soon Pisa and Genoa had joined Venice and Naples in a contest for control of the Mediterranean, a contest that quickly developed into several military conflicts, some small—what one might describe as piracy: disrupting trade, capturing ships, etc.—and others much larger—as when the Pisans and Genoese provided naval assistance to the Normans for their successful invasions of Sicily and Southern Italy, including Naples.[3] The Italian interest in and dominance of the Mediterranean had been born and would continue to provide huge economic benefits throughout the Crusades, with Venice and Genoa profiting extensively from the transportation of men and supplies to and from the Holy Land.

Most of the ships used for this purpose during the early Crusades were relatively small vessels of various designs, commonly referred to as coasters because of their tendency to keep close to the shore. But a journey to the Holy Land around the coast from Italy took weeks; it was much shorter to sail directly from one spot to the other, perhaps with a stop-over in Cyprus. But the Mediterranean Sea was not always calm, and small coasters were likely to flounder should they try the open-sea journey. This would require larger vessels, which were capable of carrying larger and heavier loads for longer voyages. These were either two-masted sailing ships outfitted with lateen sails, called nefs or naves, which were favored by the Genoese and Pisans (similar vessels in the north were known as hulks), or galleys, which, descended from Byzantine dromons, used two banks of oars for power, although they were also fitted with either one or two masts of lateen sails, which were favored by the Venetians and Neapolitans.[4] Sometimes larger ships were built, such as Saladin's three-masted galley, which is recorded as being capable of carrying "a hundred camel-loads of arms of every kind: great heaps of arbalests (crossbows), bows, spears, and arrows" as well as "seven Saracen emirs and eight hundred chosen Turks," and was also equipped with Greek Fire. But ships of this size were very rare and usually associated with only the highest and wealthiest leaders.[5]

These were not specially built warships, but cargo vessels modified for naval warfare. The modifications were usually minor, though. Rams were attached to galleys, and *ballistae* and small trebuchets could be mounted on the decks and castles (wooden turret-like superstructures attached to the aft and sometimes the fore of the ship).

But the best weapon on almost all ships was the personnel sailing aboard them. All sailors and even some oarsmen—although a large contingent would need to maneuver their galleys during battle—could be used both as missile troops when fighting at a distance and as marines when grappled and fighting at close quarters. By the end of the twelfth century, crossbowmen had become so adept at fighting from ships that they could even shoot their bows effectively from the rigging and crows' nests of their vessels (although reloading might have been difficult in such a position).[6] Still, despite the constant hostilities that followed the Christian victories in the First Crusade for the next two centuries, major naval battles remained rare, with piracy, minor skirmishes, and amphibious operations still the chief military duties of naval vessels.[7] The only large conflicts fought between Christian and Muslim navies during this period were in 1123, when a Venetian fleet defeated the Fatamid Egyptian navy near Ascalon, and in 1191, when Richard I of England's ships defeated Saladin's fleet near Acre, the latter conflict also seeing the destruction of the large galley mentioned above.[8]

THIRTEENTH-CENTURY SHIPS

The thirteenth century saw a substantial increase in the number of naval conflicts, especially on the Mediterranean. While Naples had ceased being a naval power by the beginning of the century, and Pisan fleets were also declining rapidly in numbers and influence, Genoa and Venice had greatly increased the sizes of their fleets and, more importantly, their desire to dominate maritime trade in the Mediterranean. Added to their naval hostility was the emerging competition of new, powerful, and bellicose Aragonese fleets, especially those from Barcelona and Catalonia.[9] Theirs were sizeable naval forces, so powerful in fact that by the middle of the century King James I of Aragon was able to launch successful conquests of the Balearic Islands and Valencia.[10]

The northern European seas remained comparatively peaceful. This was, in large part, due to the absence of large royal, ducal, or comital fleets. However, the amount of piracy and privateering increased markedly, especially in the English Channel and Baltic Sea, with warships from England, France, Germany, Scandinavia, and the Low Countries preying continually on opposing ships and even ports. Of course, much of this piracy was state-sponsored, directed at enemies or potential enemies. In fact, the piracy between France and England was so intense that in 1285 it developed into more serious naval warfare, which continued on and off until the end of the fourteenth century.[11]

Perhaps the bellicose temperament of the century was established at its very beginning when a combined land and naval attack of Constantinople succeeded in destroying almost all of the ships of the Byzantines, a blow to that empire's naval power from which it would never recover. Called, rather erroneously, the Fourth Crusade, as an attack on Eastern Christians is hardly what "taking the cross" was meant to achieve, the amphibious landing and conquest of the Byzantine capital by western European warriors not only put a European king on the imperial throne until 1261, but also gave the Venetians, who had transported and incited the Fourth Crusaders, a virtual monopoly over the eastern half of the Mediterranean. The western half was fought over by Venice, Genoa, Pisa, and Aragon, with Genoa being the most successful.[12]

This made Venice and Genoa the two dominant naval powers in the Mediterranean, and therefore it should come as little surprise that they fought several naval wars against each other over the next three centuries. Between 1253 and 1270 these included large sea battles off the coast of Acre, Tyre, Settepozzi, and Trepani. In these Venice achieved more victories than losses, largely because of Genoese tactical ineptitude. However, Genoa's assistance to the Byzantines in recovering Constantinople in 1261 may have far exceeded any defeats it suffered, especially as the grateful emperor Michael VIII Palaeologos granted them the formerly Venetian-held trade monopoly with the empire, which the Genoese held until the city's ultimate fall to the Ottoman Turks in 1453. They also provided the naval support for Charles of Anjou's successful conquest of Naples and southern Italy in 1281 (won despite the destruction of the also allied Angevin-French fleet by the Aragonese at the Bay of Naples in 1282). The Genoese followed this by destroying the Pisan fleet at Meloria in 1284, and by fighting a second naval war against the Venetians between

1294 and 1299, with battles fought at Lapazzo and Curzola, as well as several smaller engagements, all of which they won.[13]

Almost all of the engagements in these wars were fought on the open sea, the first such naval warfare. It differed from the coastal battles of the ancient world and thus has given rise to the belief among some historians that it was during the High Middle Ages that modern naval strategy and tactics originated, although this was before the invention and use of naval gunpowder weapons.[14] More important, however, may be the question of what such incessant naval warfare cost the Crusader kingdoms in the Holy Land. For without a strong, secure Mediterranean fleet, it was difficult for the Crusaders to gain necessary supplies and reinforcements. Jerusalem had fallen to Saladin in 1187, before most of the inter-European Mediterranean warfare began; however, especially after the capture of Acre in 1191, the coast remained under Crusader control until the middle of the thirteenth century. But from 1265 on, the coastal cities began to fall quickly to the Mamluks: Caesarea, Haifa, and Arsuf in 1265, Antioch in 1268, Tripoli in 1289, and Acre, the last vestige of the Crusader kingdoms in the Holy Land, in 1291.[15] In addition, both of French king Louis IX's Crusades, sometimes referred to as the Sixth and Seventh Crusades, launched against Egypt and Tunis in 1248 and 1270 respectively, failed to gain even small victories.[16] While it would be difficult, and perhaps even foolhardy, to try to make a causal link between the European naval wars in the Mediterranean and the defeats of these Crusades and the Crusader kingdoms—especially as the victory of the Mamluks over the Ilkhanid Mongols at the battle of Ayn-Jalut in 1260, which gave the Mamluks a huge amount of military confidence, has a much more direct tie—the disruption of supplies and reinforcements and the loss of naval protection for the Crusaders that resulted from these wars must also be recognized.

Galleys built in the thirteenth century were little changed in function, style, or technology from those constructed the century before, although some began to be made larger. These, known as great galleys, measured around 39 meters long and 5.2 meters wide, with a draft of 1.3–1.7 meters when fully laden. Their masts were as much as 22 meters tall. Most galleys, even great galleys, continued to have only two banks of oars on each side, although the Venetians did construct some with three banks during the century, and most had one or two masts. (While these vessels are often referred to as biremes and triremes in contemporary sources, their similarity to ancient galleys has not been established.) Galleys also usually carried a very large crew, larger than earlier medieval oared warships; for example, Venetian galleys of the period carried a crew of 158, 139 of whom manned the oars, with others serving as officers, guard, marines, and crossbowmen. The number of oarsmen sometimes differed greatly between vessels, with Flemish and Spanish galleys often employing more oarsmen than Italian galleys. The increased number also might explain the move to using slaves, convicts, and prisoners of war as rowers; this became more frequent during this period and later until, at the end of the Middle Ages, almost all galleys, especially great galleys, were oared this way.[17]

Added to the galley as a thirteenth-century warship was the galleon (also called a *galea* and *galiotte*). This was a smaller vessel than the galley and was sometimes known simply as a light galley. It also seems to have been built in the same way as the galley, with both oars and sails for propulsion, but carried a smaller crew—Venetian galleons carried 126 men (101 of whom were rowers). Also, three oarsmen per oar generally rowed the galleon, while two men per oar rowed the galley.[18]

Galleys also served as cargo ships and were capable of carrying sizeable cargoes, with the great galley, for example, able to carry 130–145 tons of cargo. Most often they operated in the Mediterranean, carrying spices, Eastern goods, and pilgrims, but galleys from Flanders traveling to England, Scotland, and along the Atlantic and Mediterranean coasts to Italy were not unknown.[19] However, galleys as cargo ships were limited by the space needed for the large numbers of oarsmen and their personal possessions, so most cargo continued to be transported by large round sailing ships, even on the Mediterranean. Two-masted nefs and hulks, sometimes as large as 500 or 600 tons, remained the dominant round-ship of the early thirteenth century, but by the end of the century their dominance had been replaced by the *taurides* (or *tarides*), larger multiple-masted cargo ships of Middle Eastern design, and by the cog, a ship designed in northern Europe principally to transport large amounts of cargo through the more turbulent Baltic Sea, English Channel, and Atlantic Ocean. The *taurides* were little more than larger versions of the earlier nefs, primarily using lateen rigs for propulsion, and their prominence was short lived as they quickly became surpassed by the superior capabilities of the cog as both a cargo ship and a warship.[20]

Indeed, no medieval ship may have been as influential as the cog. Little is known about its origin, although it may have developed out of smaller coastal vessels prominent in England, Friesland, and Scandinavia, but it is certain that by the middle of the thirteenth century it had become the dominant sailing vessel throughout the medieval world, in the northern seas, Atlantic, and Mediterranean. Initially, the cog was a small ship, with a length of 25–30 meters, a width of no more than 9.5 meters, and a draft of between 3 and 4 meters, yet it could carry as much or more cargo than other much larger ships, sometimes as much as 300 tons, while being operated by a smaller crew. But it also had the potential to increase in size, and as the trading needs of Europe in the thirteenth century and later rose, the size of the cog increased, seemingly without much increase in construction costs or crew size. Its single, large, square sail also provided sufficient propulsion to deliver its load quickly, yet its high freeboard allowed it to be able to withstand treacherous, heavy winds and waves, including those in the Atlantic Ocean. High castles could also be added to both its fore and aft decks, giving it sufficient defensibility to stand alone against pirates and other warships. This made it practically a warship in its own right—although it had few offensive naval capabilities before the invention of gunpowder weapons—cutting down substantially on the need for other, more militarily capable ships to sail in convoy to protect it. All of this added up to a striking savings in maritime freight costs.[21]

The weapons on board thirteenth-century ships were little different from those of the eleventh and twelfth centuries, with the personal arms of the crew still the dominant weapons used against opposing vessels. According to a 1225 Venetian law, these were to be a broad sword, dagger, and two lances or long lances—a helmet and shield were also required—but this may not have been indicative of all sailors' arms of the period.[22] Crossbows certainly continued to provide both the best offense and defense against opposing warships, and, according to Frederic C. Lane, the nautical use of the crossbow increased substantially with the use of the double-castled cog. This can be seen most clearly in the large number of regulations, like the one above, given in the thirteenth and fourteenth centuries requiring either that a special body of crossbowmen be present on board all ships or that any mate or sailor above a certain rank be outfitted with a crossbow in addition to his other personal arms. Some large crossbows and *ballistae* may also have been mounted on the deck of these ships.[23] A few ships also carried trebuchets on their castles, but the use of these seems to have been limited to firing on fortifications or to hurling burning projectiles at distant ships.[24]

Most naval warfare continued to be close-quarter combat between sailors of grappled vessels. This was the type of fighting that Bernat Desclot reports took place in a battle within the port of Malta between the Catalan navy and the Southern French navy of Charles of Anjou:

... the battle was great and hard with lances, and with stones and lime [used to blind opponents] and bolts from the crossbows; and it was mostly from the galleys of the Provençals that came so many lances and stones and so much lime onto the galleys of the Catalans, that all the galleys and sea were covered. Then the admiral of the King of Aragon said to the men of the galley he was in, and they said it from one galley to the other, that they should not throw any weapons, only bolts from the crossbows, and that they should think to cover themselves well and resist the missiles. This word went through all the Catalan galleys; and so it was that they did not throw any weapons, but they took cover and withstood the missiles which came from the galleys of the Provençals, of lances and stones and lime, so dense that it was frightful to see. But the crossbows of both sides shot; so that the snapping of the crossbows was so strong that it was terrible to hear. The battle went on until noon [it had begun at sunrise] with neither one party nor the other knowing which had the advantage, until the galleys of the Provençals had exhausted the lances, the stones and the lime and began to throw the rammers and the mortars [used to pulverize the lime]. When the Catalans saw that they were throwing the rammers and mortars, they learned that they had exhausted all their weapons and then they cried: "Arago— via sus." And they took strength and fought them with great vigor and threw their lances of ash with hardened points ... and hunting darts and hurled them so hard that neither defenses nor shields helped, all were pierced; even the deck of the galley was pierced one side to the other.[25]

TECHNOLOGICAL INNOVATIONS

The first major technological innovation that altered, and significantly improved, ships was the adoption of skeleton or carvel construction, which seems to have taken place in the eleventh or twelfth century. Prior to this time all ships, both those used as warships and those used as cargo vessels, were built in the clinker style. But with the rise of maritime trade and the need for ships to carry more cargo, shipwrights began to realize that larger cargo vessels were needed. However, the size of ship was severely limited by the fact that the clinker-built hull was capable of rising only to the height governed by the strength of the planks forming its shell. The carvel style of construction reversed the order of building the shell and skeleton after the keel of the ship was laid: instead of a plank shell being attached directly to the keel, a heavy timber skeleton framework of ribs was attached first and then planks affixed to it. This greatly increased the strength of the hull, which allowed it to be built higher, enabling the construction of larger and deeper vessels. Still, no matter how innovative this new construction technique was, it took nearly a century before most ships, including warships, began to be made this way. Even then, some northern shipwrights resisted change and continued to build clinker-style vessels into the fifteenth century, including the extremely large English warship of Henry V, the *Grace Dieu*, built in 1418. Perhaps this was why the *Grace Dieu* sailed on only one voyage and then remained moored in the Hamble River until 1439, when it was hit by lightning and burned to the water level. Its remains are still visible just below the surface. The carvel-style construction, perhaps more than any other shipbuilding innovation, allowed for the construction of the large ships needed for Atlantic and Pacific exploration.[26]

In what order the next two technological innovations—the introduction of the stern rudder and the invention of the compass—appeared is not known, although they both seem to have come from the thirteenth-century Mediterranean.

The sternpost rudder, an invention that may have accompanied the development of the cog in the thirteenth century, quickly proved to be far superior to the traditional dual steering oars that had piloted earlier ships. Using a sternpost rudder a ship could turn much more quickly and in a much smaller place, allowing it to be much more easily maneuvered through water, even through the most turbulent waves. Ships also no longer needed to rely on their lateen rigs for direction and could replace these with the more powerful square sails, which added considerably to their speed.[27]

Appearing about the same time, the primitive boxed compass, its origins and provenance debated, completely changed the navigational method of medieval ships. Earlier navigation was based on the stars, astrolabes, and inaccurate maps. While latitude could be correctly determined, longitude could not. It was difficult to sail ships on cloudy nights, and they could not sail in

Fig. 12.1: *St. Nicholas Rebuking the Tempest*, painted by Bicci di Lorenzo (1375–1452), early fifteenth century.

winter. The compass allowed for year-round sailing in almost any weather condition. It also allowed for the making of more accurate portolan charts, which appeared in the early fourteenth century and enabled a vessel to sail more easily on open sea.[28]

The final technological advancement of the Middle Ages related to warships was the mounting of guns on board ship. Until the early to mid-fifteenth century, shipboard guns were little different from those used on land, except that they were almost always small with removable chambers, perhaps comparable in size and, essentially, function to those initially placed in fortifications. But as the fifteenth century progressed, shipboard guns became more specific in both use and technology.

While we have little direct evidence, many of the guns used on board ships in the fifteenth century were breech loaders—the powder contained in a removable chamber wedged into the rear of the barrel after the ammunition had been loaded. This avoided the need to bring the gun back into the ship to reload the meant that the gunner did not put himself at risk. These guns, if they were small, were also sometimes mounted on a swivel so that they could be more easily aimed, especially when used as anti-personnel guns to repel boarders. [29] The late fifteenth century Tudor warship, the *Sovereign*, was equipped with over 140 swivel guns, all of them quite small in size, distributed all round her decks.[30]

As the fifteenth century progressed there also appears to have been a move to mount larger guns in ships but this could not be easily accomplished until the invention of the gunport—a rectangular opening in the side of the ship through which the cannon could be mounted. Although traditionally said to have been invented by a French shipwright named Descharges in 1501, it is more likely that gunports were developed in the later fifteenth century. They were certainly used on English ships of the beginning of the sixteenth century as shown by the development of large wrought-iron cannons mounted on wheeled carriages, call port pieces. [31]

By the first decades of the sixteenth century very large guns firing both stone and cast-iron ammunition were being used extensively on ships, especially those of Northern Europe. Further changes in ship construction, resulting in large carvel-built vessels with more gundecks and a flat transom stern, continued throughout the sixteenth century, leading to the ships which were capable of firing a broadside—the way that ships fought one another up until the coming of the modern battleship. [32]

LATER MEDIEVAL SHIPS

Surprisingly, considering how much warfare occurred during the last two centuries of the Middle Ages, there was comparatively little naval warfare. The number of major conflicts at sea decreased, as did even the number of minor conflicts, i.e., single ship combat, piracy (both state-sponsored and not), skirmishing, trade disputes, and so on.

However, the fourteenth century did not start out as one of naval peace, with wars in both northern European seas and the Mediterranean continuing from the previous century. In the north, especially in the English Channel off Normandy and Flanders, the fleets of Edward I of England and Philip IV of France continued to spar against each other without decisive conclusion. Both had large treasuries, with which they could build a large number of their own ships and also buy the services of others, the English primarily using ships, captains, and sailors from the various Low Countries principalities, and the French using primarily those from the Iberian kingdoms. Edward and Philip were also powerful kings who saw negotiation and compromise with each other as weakness. They actually did not like each other personally, an enmity not helped even by the marriage of Philip's daughter, Isabella, to Edward's son, Edward (later King Edward II), a union that would produce the military headache of the next century and half: the so-called Hundred Years' War. [33]

In the Mediterranean, during the first half of the fourteenth century, Venice and Genoa continued to fight sporadically against each other, whether it was a new war, a continuation of the war (or wars) begun in the thirteenth century or a side-theater of the war that Venice was also then fighting with Byzantium. This matters only for historical interpretation, and for the fact that it is in this war that Marco Polo was taken prisoner, which allowed him to dictate his memoirs to fellow prisoner, Rustichello. However it is classified, the warfare ended in a draw, an indecisiveness that ensured the continuation of the fighting.

This continuation occurred in 1350 and again in 1378 (the third and fourth Venetian-Genoese wars, if counted separately). Ostensibly, the 1350 war was fought for the reason that earlier Venetian-Genoese wars had: Genoese trading in the eastern Mediterranean. Venice was allied with Aragon, which had its own conflict with the Genoese over trading in the western Mediterranean, Byzantium, and Pisa (although the latter would never be a naval factor after its defeat by Genoa at Meloria in 1284), and Genoa was allied with the upstart Ottoman Turks. But most of the actual fighting was between Venetian and Genoese ships. Both sides fought to a draw at the battle of the Bosporus in 1352, although the amount of destruction that had been done to its fleet forced Venice to withdraw from the region and restored Genoa to its trading monopoly with Byzantium. They then traded victories at the battles of Alghero and Zonklon in 1354 and signed a peace a year later.

Therefore it came as little surprise when fighting broke out again in 1378. Frequently called the War of Chioggia, it was started over possession of the island of Tenedos in the eastern Mediterranean. In the initial battles, Cape d'Anzio, Traù, and Pola, fought in 1378–79, little was decided, although the Genoese did claim victory, which perhaps gave them too much confidence, as in the following year they boldly took their fleet into the Venetian lagoon only to be defeated in a much larger battle fought off Chioggia. Their fleet almost completely destroyed, the Genose limped to the Peace of Turin (1381), their proud naval history essentially ended in a single afternoon.[34]

Throughout the rest of the Mediterranean the seas remained peaceful during the fourteenth century. Part of this was certainly due to the natural disasters that paralyzed Europe—the Famine of 1315–17 and the Black Death of 1346–49—during which time maritime traffic declined markedly (especially as ships were thought to be primarily responsible for spreading the plague), and part also to man-made disasters—the Bardi and Peruzzi bank failures in the 1340s, the Hundred Years' War, Flemish and Italian trade decline, and so on.

But also to be considered were the changes in design and construction of ships that made attacking these vessels no longer a simple feat. Piracy was ubiquitous; it always would be, and in fact it would significantly increase during the later fifteenth century with the rise of powerful Ottoman and Mamluk navies whose state-sponsored piracy against European ships would more than match the state-sponsored piracy of those ships against them. But it was harder and more expensive for smaller, non-state-sponsored ships (for they were rarely fleets—although that, too, would change in the early sixteenth century with, among others the Barbarossa brothers[35]) to compete with the new, larger, and better-armed vessels. Perhaps economics could also be credited for the low number of national naval conflicts. As Pisa had proved in 1284 and Genoa in 1380, the loss of a fleet was difficult to recover from; building new ships was expensive and time-consuming, during which time other, non-military maritime activities, i.e., trade and fishing, ceased. Peace allowed for recovery, the building of larger fleets, and increased trade and prosperity. Even though there would be a slight resurgence in naval activity during the 1420s and 1430s, again between Genoa and Venice, the Mediterranean remained relatively calm until around 1480.[36]

This peace permitted Venice, Aragon, and, at least until 1460, Genoa to strengthen their maritime empires and even to recover some of their previously lost territories. Venice especially grew strong during this period, with large mainland holdings along the Italian peninsula, on the Dalmatian coast, in Greece and the eastern Mediterranean islands, including Crete and Cyprus, and a fleet that grew to an estimated 80 galleys and 300 sailing ships, the largest in the Mediterranean. (Only Ottoman Turkey would eventually compete with Venice in the east.)

Venice's strength in the eastern Mediterranean was nearly equaled by that of Aragon in the western Mediterranean. Naples, Southern Italy, Sicily, Sardinia, Valencia, and Catalonia had been added during the long reign of Alfonso V the Magnificent (1396–1458); Castile was united to the kingdom by the marriage between Alfonso's grandson, Ferdinand II, and Isabella in 1469; and Grenada was captured in 1492. This allowed Aragonese ships to travel virtually without danger around the Mediterranean between the Italian and Iberian peninsulas. Only Portugal competed with them in the Atlantic, which allowed Aragonese fleets free access to whatever lay to the west, and resulted, also in 1492, in Columbus's voyage to the "new world."[37]

The Mediterranean peace also gave rise to new maritime powers. One of these, Florence, interestingly, did not lie on the sea but grew into a minor naval power after its conquest of Pisa in 1406. At the same time, the French, Burgundians (also landlocked), and the Knights Hospitaller also began to build their own fleets and to develop their own naval power. But no new naval power arose more quickly or had more impact than Portugal. With Aragon dominating the western Mediterranean, the Portuguese, under, among others, the able leadership of Prince Henry the Navigator, took a new approach to naval activity. Instead of venturing east into the Mediterranean, the Portuguese went south to the islands of the Atlantic, conquering Madeira, the Cape Verdes, and the Azores by 1410, and into Atlantic North Africa, conquering Ceuta in 1415 and adding to that throughout the century until, by 1471, Portugal had complete control of Tangiers and all the Moroccan ports south to Agadir. Traveling farther to the south along the African continent, by 1480 the Portuguese had reached the coasts of Guinea, Ghana, Nigeria, and the Congo, and, by 1487, Bartholomeu Diaz had landed at the Cape of Good Hope. Eleven years later, Vasco da Gama sailed around Africa and landed in India.[38]

In the Indian Ocean the Portuguese encountered another European naval power, the Ottoman Empire, which had arrived there through a much more direct route, overland and down the Arabian Gulf and Red Sea, but had the same goal in mind: trying to find an alternative to the Silk Road, which had essentially, if not actually, been closed due to the bellicosity of the Mongol warlords who controlled it. A secondary, although also similar, reason for the Ottoman presence was to seek converts for their religion, in this case Islam, as it was for the Portuguese to seek converts for their religion, Christianity.

The rise of the Ottoman Turks had been meteoric. Little more than a small tribe led by a central Asian Minor Turkish dynast, Ghazi Osman, in 1300, by the time the Portuguese ran into them off Africa and India shortly after 1500 they had come to be one of the most dominant political, military, and naval powers in the world. They had conquered all of Asia Minor, although not completely defeating the Byzantine Empire until 1453 when Sultan Mehmed II conquered Constantinople. By that time they had also captured Bulgaria, Macedonia, Greece, Montenegro, Bosnia, Albania, Herzegovina, and Serbia; soundly defeated two pan-European "Crusader" forces sent to stop their progress—at Nicopolis in 1396 and Varna in 1444; outlasted the Timurid Mongols under Tamerlane, after an initial setback at the battle of Ankara in 1402, where they had been defeated and their Sultan, Bayezid I, captured (after being paraded around the Timurid lands in a cage for more than a year, he committed suicide by banging his head repeatedly into the metal bars of his cage); and survived several inheritance crises. Only the Hospitallers on Rhodes, the Serbs in Belgrade, and the Hungarians had halted Ottoman progress, although they would not be able to hold out past 1527.

Before 1453 almost all of the Ottoman conquests had been land-based operations, with few ships needed, other than for transporting men and supplies. Indeed, the Ottoman navy before the middle of the fifteenth century probably had more riverine than open-sea vessels. It even had difficulty keeping European ships from running the very meager blockade they had set up around Constantinople in 1453. However, Constantinople's conqueror, Mehmed II, was determined to change this and, within a decade at most, had built a navy that could compete with any others in the world. Quickly, Eastern Mediterranean islands began to fall. Rhodes held out through his and his two successors' reigns, but, after being resoundingly defeated in the 1499–1503 war against them, Venice kept only Crete and Cyprus by submitting to the harshest, and most expensive, peace treaties. Mehmed's grandson, Selim I, used an even larger and more powerful fleet to defeat the Mamluks and conquer Aleppo, Damascus, Cairo, Syria, Israel, and Egypt in 1516–17, and his great-grandson, Suleyman I the Magnificent, took an even larger and more powerful navy even farther, into the central and western Mediterranean, where he terrorized European and North African foes into the 1570s.[39]

In northern Europe, the conflict of the late thirteenth and early fourteenth centuries between France and England developed by the middle of the fourteenth century into the Hundred Years' War. From its outset naval warfare became a prominent, if not frequent, feature of this war. The first major engagement, fought at Sluys in 1340, was a naval battle, with the navy of Edward III sweeping down on the moored French and mercenary Iberian and Genoese fleet with, as contemporary chronicler Geoffrey le Baker writes, "the wind and sun at his back and the flow of the tide with him." The English prevailed and the French fleet was either captured or destroyed. They would prevail again over a much smaller French-employed Castilian fleet at the battle of Winchelsea in 1350. Together these victories allowed the English almost unhindered access to the Channel, and they used this freedom to transport large armies back and forth across the water, which helped achieve further victories at Crécy, Calais, Poitiers, and elsewhere. But the French eventually recovered and, again with the help of mercenary Castilian ships and sailors, at the battle of La Rochelle, fought in 1372, they responded with an impressive victory against the English, destroying most of the latter's fleet, but also leaving their own fleet in ruin. This Pyrrhic victory for the French, coupled with the financial problems of both them and English—for example, after the death of Edward III in 1377 the English were forced to sell off many of their ships to pay the royal debts—essentially meant the end of the naval phase of the Hundred Years' War. This decline continued into and throughout most of the fifteenth century, with neither France nor England desiring to engage each other on the sea, although piracy and privateering continued to be sponsored by the two kingdoms against each other until well past the end of the war.[40]

The cog continued to be the most prominent ship of the late Middle Ages, especially in the north, both as a cargo vessel and as a warship. So dominant were cogs in England, for example, that they made up more than 57 percent of the vessels in that navy between 1337 and 1360.[41] Their popularity also extended to the Mediterranean, but there the great galley continued to be a most favored cargo and warship, as it would into the eighteenth century. Its long, thin shape was perfect for the relative calm of the Mediterranean, its speed ensured by capable oarsmen—although these began increasingly to be replaced by enforced rowers—and lateen sails. Some galleys also had square sails. Galleys were also known in northern Europe, with several involved in the naval battles of the early Hundred Years' War.[42] One interesting reference to galleys comes from Burgundian Duke Philip the Good's construction of five galleys in Antwerp to deliver a large dowry of arms and armor, together with his niece, for her marriage to King James II of Scotland in 1449.

By the fifteenth century, other vessels also began to appear. One was the balinger, a small-oared cargo ship of indeterminate design, although probably similar to a barge, which served as a coastal cargo transport primarily along the English, French, Low Countries, and Scandinavian coasts.[43] A second was the extremely large northern European buss, the principal herring fishing ship of the growing Dutch fleet.[44] And a third new ship was the caravel, a two-masted ship of Middle Eastern and North African influence, which used lateen and square sails together to allow for both speed and maneuverability. It was 20–30 meters long, 4–5 meters wide, with a shallow draft and a cargo capacity of 50 tons or more (150–200 tons by the end of the fifteenth century), and it could also travel long distances with relative ease. The caravel was favored by the Portuguese and Spanish for their lengthy voyages of exploration, with Columbus's *Nina* and *Pinta* being the most famous examples.[45]

However, the most important new ship of the fifteenth century, as both a cargo ship and a warship, was without doubt the carrack. Essentially a modification of the cog, the carrack (sometimes erroneously called a nef in the fifteenth century) was a large ship with two and later three or four masts. Its enormous size, sometimes as large as 38 meters long and 12 meters wide, with a previously unprecedented cargo capability of 1,000 to 1,400 tons, made it an excellent

Fig. 12.2: *Expedition of Duc de Bourbon to Barbery*, from the *Chroniques de Froissart*, late fifteenth century.

The Bridgeman Art Library International. BL Harley MS 4379, f60v.

cargo ship, capable of carrying heavy bulk cargoes, while its carvel construction, sternpost rudder, and multiple sails allowed it to withstand both Atlantic and Mediterranean travel. Like the cog, primarily a cargo ship, the carrack was also capable of easily being both warship and cargo vessel, and was often outfitted with fore and aft castles on which could be set crossbowmen and cannon. By the end of the fifteenth century, the carrack, which counted Columbus's flagship the *Santa Maria* among its number, had already replaced the cog as the ship of choice among late medieval admirals and sailors, and it would become the model of the great sailing ship-of-the-line of the early modern era.[46]

What made the carrack the great vessel that it became was that it took the earlier naval technological innovations—compass, carvel construction, and sternpost rudder—and in the fifteenth century added the innovation of full-rigging. Full-rigging—"the great invention of European ship design," as Richard W.

Unger characterizes it—was the mixture of both lateen and square sails together on board the ship. Generally, this meant that while the fore- and mainmasts of the carrack held one or two large square sails apiece, giving the ship more speed, the mizzenmast was fitted with a lateen sail providing extra maneuverability. At the end of the century, a small square sail was also often attached to the bowsprit as a headsail for even further handling control. Full-rigging enabled the ship to be controlled more easily and with greater power, features required for a vessel to endure the frequently inhospitable Atlantic coastal waters of Europe and Africa as well the high waves and harsh winds of open sea travel.[47]

Notes

1. Lewis and Runyan (1985): 64–65, 115; Rodgers (1940): 53–58; and Unger (1980): 120.

2. Lewis and Runyan (1985): 62–63.

3. Lewis and Runyan (1985): 63–64.

4. The most extensive discussions of the Crusader nef can be found in Pryor (1982; 1984; 1988: 32–34; 1990); Steffy (1981); Unger (1980: 123–27; 1981: 237–38). The best description of a galley built from around 1000 to 1250 can be found in Unger (1980): 121–22.

5. As quoted in Lewis and Runyan (1985): 75–76. On other, more traditional Muslim ships facing the Crusaders see Nicolle (1989): 170–75.

6. Lewis and Runyan (1985): 68–69 and Pryor (1988): 75–76.

7. For a chronology of Crusader–Muslim naval conflict between 1099 and 1126, see Hamblin (1986).

8. Lewis and Runyan (1985): 75–76 and Pryor (1988): 115–30. On the 1123 defeat of the Fatamid navy, see Hamblin (1986): 83.

9. Lewis and Runyan (1985): 69–70.

10. Lewis and Runyan (1985): 69–70.

11. Lewis and Runyan (1985): 121–23. See also Freeman (1980) and Rodgers (1940): 81–95.

12. Lewis and Runyan (1985): 70–72 and Dotson (1981b): 87. For a description of the naval operation at Constantinople see Queller (1980) and Rodgers (1940): 117–28.

13. Lewis and Runyan (1985): 70–76 and Rodgers (1940): 128–42. On the first Genoese–Venetian war, see Dotson (1981b). On the Aragonese naval battles of the thirteenth century, see Pryor (1983).

14. See, for example, Lewis and Runyan (1985): 77.

15. Lewis and Runyan (1985): 76–77.

16. Lewis and Runyan (1985): 76–77 and Unger (1980): 123–25.

17. Robbert (1969): 142–43; Laures (1987): 19–20; Mott (1990): 110–11; Pryor (1988): 64–66; Unger (1980: 121, 176–82; 1981: 238–40); Lewis and Runyan (1985): 74; and Rodgers

(1940): 110–16. On the Venetian construction of triremes, see Lane (1963b). On English galleys of the thirteenth century, see Anderson (1962): 42–51.

18. Robbert (1969): 143; Mott (1990): 104–8; Pryor (1988): 66–67; and Unger (1980): 176–82. Numbers of crewmen also varied on these smaller oared vessels.

19. Unger (1980): 176–82.

20. Pryor (1982): 103–25; Lewis and Runyan (1985): 74; Unger (1980): 123–25; and Rodgers (1940): 112.

21. Unger (1980: 138–46, 150–51; 1981: 242–47); Ellmers (1979); and Lewis and Runyan (1985): 74–75. On the defensibility of the cog see Unger (1981): 235.

22. Robbert (1969): 141 and F.W. Brooks (1928): 126. A 1255 Venetian law altered this to require all seamen to be equipped with a sword, shield, dagger, three lances or javelins, a helmet or cap, and a battle jacket. See Lane (1969–70): 162.

23. Lane (1969–70); F.W. Brooks (1928): 121–25; and Laures (1987): 26–27.

24. F.W. Brooks (1928): 119–20 and Robbert (1969): 143.

25. As quoted in Laures (1987): 26.

26. Unger (1980): 120–21, 129, 225–26; and Anderson (1962): 43.

27. Unger (1980): 141–43 and Lewis and Runyan (1985): 74–75.

28. Marcus (1956); Lane (1963a); Unger (1980): 130–31, 174; and Lewis and Runyan (1985): 74–75.

29. DeVries (1990a).

30. Hutchinson (1994): 160. For another example, the placement of guns on the *Leyde* in 1477, see Jongkees (1986): 79–80.

31. Smith (1993; 1995).

32. DeVries (1998a) and Friel (1995): 154–56.

33. Freeman (1980) and Reid (1960).

34. Lewis and Runyan (1985): 77–78; Lane (1977): 188–201; and Dotson (2001).

35. Crowley (2008).

36. Lewis and Runyan (1985): 78–81.

37. Lewis and Runyan (1985): 79–82, 148–49.

38. Lewis and Runyan (1985): 81, 145–48; DeVries (2010); Russell-Wood (1998); and Diffie and Winius (1978). On the Portuguese conquest of Atlantic Morocco see Cook (1994), and the biography of choice on Prince Henry the Navigator is Russell (2000).

39. DeVries (2010); Inalcik (1973); and Imber (2009).

40. See Richmond (1971); Runyan (1986); Sherborne (1967); Rodgers (1940): 95–105; and Lewis and Runyan (1985): 123–28, 149. On the battle of Sluys see DeVries (1996b). On the French use of Castilian mercenaries during the first part of the Hundred Years' War see Lewis and Runyan (1985): 133–34.

41. Unger (1980): 162–71, 182–87; Lane (1934): 37–50; Runyan (1986): 93–96; Burwash (1947): 117–21; Sandurra (1972): 214; and Lewis and Runyan (1985): 82–83, 137–38.

42. Mallett (1967); Dotson (1981a); Tinniswood (1949); Anderson (1928; 1962: 52–55); Mott (1987); Lane (1963c; 1934: 1–34); Unger (1980): 176–82, 192–93, 209–11; Sandurra (1972): 209–10; Pryor (1988): 66–70; Law (1987): 114–17; and Runyan (1986): 96–97.

43. Sherborne (1977); Burwash (1947): 101–17; Unger (1980: 171–72; 1981: 247–48); and Lewis and Runyan (1985): 137–38, 158.

44. Unger (1980): 206–9; Lewis and Runyan (1985): 158–59; and Unger (1973): 394–97.

45. Unger (1980): 212–14, 231; Lewis and Runyan (1985): 82–83, 159; and Law (1987): 121–22. For English caravels see Burwash (1947): 128–31.

46. Unger (1980): 220–21, 228–31; Lewis and Runyan (1985): 82–83, 159–63; and Sandurra (1972): 214. On the carrack's defensibility see Unger (1981): 235.

47. Unger (1980: 216–20, 226–27; 1981: 247–48).

CONCLUSION

IN THE MIDDLE OF THE FIFTEENTH CENTURY THE WORLD CHANGED. THE year 1453 was an extraordinary one: it saw the end of the Hundred Years' War, marking the rise of French and the decline of English European power. All English holdings in France were lost, except for Calais, which would stay English for another century. The same year also saw the Ottoman Turks conquer Constantinople, ending more than eleven centuries of Byzantine presence in the eastern Mediterranean and at the same time capping a Turkish war of conquest in that region that had begun in the first years of the fourteenth century. This also no doubt gave the Ottoman Turks greater confidence in pursuing conquests in central and southern Europe, Persia, the Middle East, Egypt, and North Africa, although confidence was rarely the Turks' problem. The year 1453 also saw the technological innovation of gunpowder begin to change, if not quite to revolutionize, warfare, and witnessed the printing press bring education and the written word to more and more people, as well as numerous shipbuilding inventions and changes that would take European culture, religion, disease, and warfare to the rest of the globe. Less than 40 years later, in 1492, the Genoese admiral Christopher Columbus piloting a Spanish ship sailed west across the Atlantic Ocean to explore the Caribbean islands; later voyages would take him to other islands and along the coast of South America. His voyages opened a floodgate of later western explorations.

In 1498, Vasco Da Gama passed the southernmost point of Africa and sailed to India. And, by 1519, Ferdinand Magellan's ships, if actually not their admiral (who had been killed and eaten in the Philippines), would travel around the entire globe.

But, while 1453 did see an end to two wars, what it did not see was an end to all wars. Only a little more than 40 years later, in 1494, Charles VIII took his army through Italy on a journey of punishment against the kingdom of Naples, then rebelling against his cousin, the duke of Savoy. Although this was not his primary purpose, the theretofore relatively free Italian city-states suddenly realized that their independence was basically dependent on the larger and more militarily powerful kingdoms of Europe being involved in turmoil elsewhere to keep them away from the vulnerable Italian land mass. But they could not put away old rivalries and disputes to unite against either Charles VIII's campaign or any other campaign that would follow in the next 55 years. The so-called Italian Wars would destroy much of the urban and rural economic wealth of Italy and, by their end in 1559, would also essentially end the progress in human art and thought that historians later called the Renaissance.

Only when these larger military entities saw that the Christian religious monopoly was being threatened did they turn away from Italy and begin to fight their own people and, eventually, anyone who dared oppose Catholicism. The Wars of Religion would further change Europe and, by extension, because of the global European presence, the whole world. Wars became even crueler than before. What had once been somewhat regulated by chivalry and the "laws or war," even in conflicts between Christianity and Islam, now deteriorated into a ruthlessness that was once ascribed to Huns or Vikings or Mongols, soldiers who, as they had come from the fringes of civilization, simply did not understand how wars should be fought.

As this was happening, most medieval military technologies were becoming quickly outmoded. Edged weapons would always have their place; indeed, daggers are still carried by soldiers as back-ups to their guns, bullets, and explosives. But while swords and spears lingered into the nineteenth century, there is no place for them on today's battlefield. Well before they were gone, maces, hammers, staff weapons, bows, and crossbows had disappeared into storage spaces and eventually dumps or museums. Armor, too, disappeared, as it became too expensive to outfit the increasingly valueless common soldier. Strangely, though, it has returned, although lightweight Kevlar has replaced the much heavier iron. Even before the demise of medieval arms and armor, catapults had ceased to be built, except, in modern times, by scout troops, high-school classes, and re-enactors. Recently, the University of Virginia engineering honors program spent two years studying and building a copy of Leonardo da Vinci's *ballista*, both out of respect and as a search for historical knowledge, but not out of any practicality. With catapults went other siege machines, while Greek Fire gave way to better understood, safer, and more secure incendiaries, and gunpowder yielded to smokeless powder and eventually to chemical propellants. Fortifications, which had already been on the decline by the end of the Middle Ages, eventually became little more than piles of stones, although some persist as hotels and homes, with a large amount of remodeling and updating, of course.

Of all the medieval technologies that lingered into the early modern world, though, it was probably the wooden warship that lasted the longest. Galleys were still being rowed around the Mediterranean in the early nineteenth century, and sailing ships lasted until the end of the nineteenth century. Even then, they did not completely disappear. While having none of their earlier purposes and being also substantially smaller in size, both continue to provide vehicles for sports, in particular Olympic sports—in perhaps an ironic connection to where much medieval military technology began: the ancient world.

BIBLIOGRAPHY

Abels, Richard P. 1988. *Lordship and Military Obligation in Anglo-Saxon England*. Berkeley, Los Angeles: University of California Press.

Abels, Richard P. 1998. *Alfred the Great: War, Kingship and Culture in Anglo-Saxon England*. London: Longman.

Addyman, P. V. 1972. "Excavations at Baile Hill, York." *Château Gaillard* 5:7–12.

Addyman, P.V. Nicholas Pearson, and Dominic Tweddle. 1982. "The Coppergate Helmet." *Antiquity* 56:189–94.

Alberti, Leon Battista. 1988. *On the Art of Building in Ten Books*. Trans. J. Rykwert, N. Leach and R. Tavernor. Cambridge, MA: MIT Press.

Allmand, Christopher. 1988. *The Hundred Years War: England and France at War, c.1300–c.1450*. Cambridge: Cambridge University Press.

Alm, Josef. 1994. *European Crossbows: A Survey*. Trans. H. Bartlett Wells. Ed. G.M. Wilson. London: Trustees of the Royal Armouries.

Anderson, R. C. 1928. "English Galleys in 1295." *Mariner's Mirror* 14:220–41.

———. 1962. *Oared Fighting Ships from Classical Times to the Age of Steam*. London: Percival Marshall.

Anglim, Simon, Phyllis G. Jestice, Rob S. Rice, Scott M. Rusch, and John Serrati. 2002. *Fighting Techniques of the Ancient World, 3000 BC–AD 500*. London: Greenhill Books.

Anglo, Sydney. 2000. *The Martial Arts of Renaissance Europe*. New Haven: Yale University Press.

Aparcio, Guitart. Cristóbal. 2003. *El castillo de Loarre*. 3rd ed. Leon: Editorial Everest.

Apollinaris, Sidonius. 1963. *Poems and Letters. Trans. W.B. Anderson*. 2 vols. Cambridge, MA: Harvard University Press.

Araguas, Philippe. 1979. "Les châteaux des marches de Catalogne et Ribagorce (950–1100)." *Bulletin Monumental* 137:205–34.

Ascherl, Rosemary. 1988. "The Technology of Chivalry in Reality and Romance." In *The Study of Chivalry*, ed. H. Chickering and T. H. Seiler, 263–311. Kalamazoo: Medieval Institute Publications.

Ashdown, Charles H. 1925. *Armour and Weapons in the Middle Ages*. London: The Holland Press.

Atkinson, Ian. 1979. *The Viking Ships*. Cambridge: Cambridge University Press.

Awty, Brian G. 2003. "The Breakthrough of the 1540s in the Casting of Iron Ordnance." *Journal of the Ordnance Society* 15:19–27.

Baatz, Dietwulf. 1978. "Recent Finds in Ancient Artillery." *Britannia* 9:1–17. http://dx.doi. org/10.2307/525936.

Bachrach, Bernard S. 1969. "The Rise of Armorican Chivalry." *Technology and Culture* 10 (2): 166–71. http://dx.doi.org/10.2307/3101476.

———. 1970a. "Charles Martel, Mounted Shock Combat, The Stirrup, and Feudalism." *Studies in Medieval and Renaissance History* 7:47–75.

———. 1970b. "Procopius, Agathias and the Frankish Military." *Speculum* 45 (3): 435–41. http://dx.doi.org/10.2307/2853502.

———. 1972. *Merovingian Military Organization, 481–751*. Minneapolis: University of Minnesota Press.

———. 1974. "Military Organization in Aquitaine under the Early Carolingians." *Speculum* 49 (1): 1–33. http://dx.doi.org/10.2307/2856549.

———. 1975. "Early Medieval Fortifications in the 'West' of France: A Revised Technical Vocabulary." *Technology and Culture* 16 (4): 531–69. http://dx.doi.org/10.2307/3103434.

———. 1976. "A Study in Feudal Politics: Relations between Fulk Nerra and William the Great, 995–1030." *Viator* 7:113–21.

———. 1979. "Fortifications and Military Tactics: Fulk Nerra's Strongholds circa 1000." *Technology and Culture* 20 (3): 531–49. http://dx.doi.org/10.2307/3103815.

———. 1983. "The Angevin Strategy of Castle Building in the Reign of Fulk Nerra, 987–1040." *American Historical Review* 88 (3): 533–60. http://dx.doi.org/10.2307/1864586.

———. 1984. "The Cost of Castle Building: The Case of the Tower at Langeais, 992–994." In *The Medieval Castle: Romance and Reality*, ed. K. Reyerson and F. Powe, 47–65. Dubuque, Iowa: Kendall/Hunt Publishing Company.

———. 1985a. "Animals and Warfare in Early Medieval Europe." In *L'uomo di fronte al mondo animale nell'alto medioevo*. Settimane di studio del centro italiano di studi sull'alto medioevo, XXXI. Spoleto: Centro Italiano di Studi sull'alto Medioevo. 707–51.

———. 1985b. "On the Origins of William the Conqueror's Horse Transports." *Technology and Culture* 26 (3): 505–31. http://dx.doi.org/10.2307/3104851.

———. 1988. "*Caballus et Callarius* in Medieval Warfare." In *The Study of Chivalry*, ed. H. Chickering and T. H. Seiler, 173–211. Kalamazoo: Medieval Institute Publications.

———. 1993. *Fulk Nerra, the Neo-Roman Consul, 987–1040: A Political Biography of the Angevin Count*. Berkeley and Los Angeles: University of California Press.

———. 1994. "Medieval Siege Warfare: A Reconnaissance." *Journal of Military History* 58 (1): 119–33. http://dx.doi.org/10.2307/2944182.

Bachrach, Bernard, and Rutherford Aris. 1990. "Military Technology and Garrison Organization: Some Observations on Anglo-Saxon Military Thinking in Light of the Burghal Hidage." *Technology and Culture* 31 (1): 1–17. http://dx.doi.org/10.2307/3105758.

Bachrach, David S. 2004a. "Crossbows for the King: The Crossbow during the Reigns of John and Henry III of England." *Technology and Culture* 45 (1): 102–19. http://dx.doi. org/10.1353/tech.2004.0003.

————. 2004b. "The Military Administration of England: The Royal Artillery (1216–1272)." *Journal of Military History* 68 (4): 1083–104. http://dx.doi.org/10.1353/jmh.2004.0163.

————. 2006a. "Crossbows for the King, Part II: The Crossbow during the Reign of Edward I of England." *Technology and Culture* 47 (1): 81–90. http://dx.doi.org/10.1353/tech.2006.0055.

————. 2006b. "English Artillery, 1189–1307: The Implications of Terminology." *English Historical Review* 121:1408–30.

Bacon, Roger. 1912. "Part of the Opus tertium." Ed. A.G. Little. *British Society of Franciscan Studies* 4.

Barber, Richard. 1982. *The Knight and Chivalry*. New York: Harper and Row.

Barber, Richard, and Juliet Barker. 1989. *Tournaments: Jousts, Chivalry and Pageants in the Middle Ages*. New York: Weidenfeld and Nicolson.

Barbier, Pierre. 1968. *La France féodale*. Vol. I: Chateaux-forts et eglises fortifiées. Saint-Brieuc: Les presses bretonnes.

Barbour, John. 1997. *The Bruce*. Ed. and trans. A.A.M. Duncan. Edinburgh: Canongate.

Barker, John W. 1966. *Justinian and the Later Roman Empire*. Madison: University of Wisconsin Press.

Barker, Juliet R.V. 1986. *The Tournament in England, 1100–1400*. Wolfesboro: The Boydell Press.

Barker, Philip. 1979. "The Plumbatae from Wroxeter." In *Aspects of the "De rebus bellicis": Papers Presented to Professor E.A. Thompson*, ed. M.W.C. Hassall, 97–99. BAR International Series, 63. Oxford: British Archaeological Reports.

Barrow, G. W. S. 1956. *Feudal Britain*. London: Edward Arnold.

Bartlett, Robert J. 1986. "Technique militaire et pouvoir politique, 900–1300." *Annales: économies, sociétés, civilisations* 41:1135–59.

Basch, Lucien, and Honor Frost. 1975. "Another Punic Wreck in Sicily: Its Ram." *International Journal of Nautical Archaeology and Underwater Exploration* 4 (2): 201–28. http://dx.doi.org/10.1111/j.1095-9270.1975.tb00915.x.

Basista, Michael. 2007. "Hybrid or Counterpoise? A Study of Transitional Trebuchets." *Journal of Medieval Military History* 5:33–55.

Bass, George F. 1972. "The Earliest Seafarers in the Mediterranean and the Near East." In *A History of Seafaring Based on Underwater Archaeology*. New York: Walker & Company. 11–36.

Bautier, Anne-Marie. 1976. "Contribution a l'histoire du cheval au moyen age." *Bulletin philologique et historique*: 209–49.

Beeler, John H. 1956. "Castles and Strategy in Norman and Early Angevin England." *Speculum* 31 (4): 581–601. http://dx.doi.org/10.2307/2850972.

————. 1966. *Warfare in England, 1066–1189*. Ithaca: Cornell University Press.

————. 1971. *Warfare in Feudal Europe, 730–1200*. Ithaca: Cornell University Press.

Bentini, Jadranka and Marco Borella. 2002. *Il Castello Estense*. Viterbo: BetaGamma Editrice.

Berthelot, Marcellin. 1891. "Les compositions incendiaires dans l'antiquité et au moyen âge." *Revue des Deux Mondes (Paris, France)* 4:786–822.

Binding, Günther. 1972. "Spätkarolingisch-ottonische Pfalzen und Bergen am Niederrhein." *Château Gaillard* 5:23–34.

Binns, Alan. 1981. "The Ships of the Vikings, were they 'Viking Ships'?" In *Proceedings of the Eighth Viking Congress*. Odense: Odense University Press.

Biringuccio, Vannoccio. 1959. *The Pirotechnia of Vannoccio Biringuccio: The Classic Sixteenth-Century Treatise on Metals and Metallurgy*. Trans. Cyril Stanley Smith and Martha Teach Gnudi. New York: Basic Books.

Bishop, M.C. and J.C. Coulston. 1989. *Roman Military Equipment*. Aylesbury: Shire.

Blair, Claude. 1958. *European Armour*. London: B.T. Batsford.

———. 2004. "The Milemete Guns." *Journal of the Ordnance Society* 16:5–18.

Bloch, Marc. 1961. *Feudal Society*. Trans. L.A. Manyon. 2 vols. Chicago: University of Chicago Press.

Boase, T. S. R. 1967. *Castles and Churches of the Crusading Kingdom*. London: Oxford University Press.

———. 1977. "Military Architecture in the Crusader States in Palestine and Syria." In *A History of the Crusades*. Philadelphia: American Philosophical Association Publications, and Madison: University of Wisconsin Press. 4:140–64.

Bolea Aguaron, F.J. 1983. *El castillo de Loarre*. Huesca: Imprenta Aguarón.

Bonde, Sheila. 1984. "Castle and Church Building at the Time of the Norman Conquest." In *The Medieval Castle: Romance and Reality*, ed. K. Reyerson and F. Powe, 84–91. Dubuque, Iowa: Kendall/Hunt Publishing Company.

Boot, Max. 2006. *War Made New: Technology, Warfare, and the Course of History, 1500 to Today*. New York: Gotham Books.

Boucher, Andy. 2007. *Ewyas Harold Castle*. Hereford: Archaeological Investigations Ltd.

Bowlus, Charles. 1978. "Warfare and Society in the Carolingian Ostmark." *Austrian History Yearbook* 14:3–28. http://dx.doi.org/10.1017/S0067237800008997.

Bowlus, Charles R. 2006. *The Battle of Lechfeld and its Aftermath, August 955: The End of the Age of Migrations in the Latin West*. Aldershot: Ashgate.

Boyer, Majorie Nice. 1976. *Medieval French Bridges: A History*. Cambridge, MA: Medieval Academy of America Publications.

Bradbury, Jim. 1985. *The Medieval Archer*. New York: St. Martin's Press.

———. 1992. *The Medieval Siege*. Woodbridge: The Boydell Press.

Brodie, Bernard and Fawn M. Brodie. 1973. *From Crossbow to H-Bomb*. 2nd. ed. Bloomington: Indiana University Press.

Brønsted, Johannes. 1960. *The Vikings*. Trans. K. Skov. Harmondsworth: Penguin Books.

Brooks, F. W. 1928. "Naval Armament in the Thirteenth Century." *Mariner's Mirror* 14:114–31.

Brooks, Nicholas P. 1971. "The Development of Military Obligations in Eighth- and Ninth-Century England." In *England Before the Conquest: Studies in Primary Sources Presented to Dorothy Whitelock*, ed. P. Clemoes and K. Hughes, 69–84. Cambridge: Cambridge University Press.

———. 1978. "Arms, Status and Warfare in Late-Saxon England." In *Ethelred the Unready: Papers from the Millenary Conference*, ed. D. Hill, 81–103. BAR British Series, 59. Oxford: British Archaeological Reports.

———. 1979. "England in the Ninth Century: The Crucible of Defeat," *Transactions of the Royal Historical Society*. 5th series 29:1–20.

Brown, Elizabeth A.R. 1974. "The Tyranny of a Construct: Feudalism and Historians of Medieval Europe." *American Historical Review* 79 (4): 1063–88. http://dx.doi.org/10.2307/1869563.

Brown, R. Allen. 1954. *English Medieval Castles*. London: B.T. Batsford.

———. 1974. *Dover Castle, Kent*. 2nd ed. London: Her Majesty's Stationery Office.

———. 1976. *English Castles*. 3rd ed. London: B.T. Batsford.

———. 1989a. "The Architecture of the Bayeux Tapestry." In *Castles, Conquest and Charters: Collected Papers*. 214–226. Woodbridge: The Boydell Press.

———. 1989b. "The Castles of the Conquest." In *Castles, Conquest and Charters: Collected Studies*. 65–74. Woodbridge: The Boydell Press.

———. 1989c. "An Historian's Approach to the Origins of the Castle in England." In *Castles, Conquest and Charters: Collected Papers*. 1–18. Woodbridge: The Boydell Press.

———. 1989d. "The Norman Conquest and the Genesis of English Castles." In *Castles, Conquest and Charters: Collected Papers*. 75–89. Woodbridge: The Boydell Press.

———. 1989e. "Royal Castle-Building in England, 1154–1216." In *Castles, Conquest and Charters: Collected Papers*. 19–64. Woodbridge: The Boydell Press.

———. 1989f. "Some Observations on the Tower of London." In *Castles, Conquest and Charters: Collected Papers*. 163–176. Woodbridge: The Boydell Press.

———. 1989g. "The White Tower of London." In *Castles, Conquest and Charters: Collected Papers*. 177–186. Woodbridge: The Boydell Press.

Brown, R. Allen, H.M. Colvin and A.J. Taylor. 1963. *The History of the King's Works*. Vol. 1 and 2: *The Middle Ages*. London: Her Majesty's Stationary Office.

Bruce-Mitford, Rupert. 1974a. "The Sutton Hoo Helmet – a New Reconstruction." In *Aspects of Anglo-Saxon Archaeology: Sutton Hoo and Other Discoveries*. 198–209. New York: Harper's Magazine Press.

———. 1974b. "The Benty Grange Helmet and Some Other Supposed Anglo-Saxon Helmets." In *Aspects of Anglo-Saxon Archaeology: Sutton Hoo and Other Discoveries*. 223–252. New York: Harper's Magazine Press.

Brucker, Gene. 1969. *Renaissance Florence*. Berkeley, Los Angeles: University of California Press.

Bruhn de Hoffmeyer, Ada. 1961. "Introduction to the History of the European Sword." *Gladius* 1: 30–75. http://dx.doi.org/10.3989/gladius.1961.212.

———. 1963. "From Mediaeval Sword to Renaissance Rapier." *Gladius* 2:5–68.

———. 1966. "Military Equipment in the Byzantine Manuscript of Scylitzes in the Biblioteca Nacional in Madrid." *Gladius* 5:1–160.

———. 1972. *The Bronze Age to the High Middle Ages*. Vol. I: Arms and Armour in Spain: A Short Survey. Madrid: Instituto de Estudios Sobre Armas Antiguas.

Brun, Robert. 1951. "Notes sur le commerce des armes a Avignon au xive siècle." *Bibliothèque de l'École des Chartes* 109 (2): 209–31. http://dx.doi.org/10.3406/bec.1951.449441.

Brunner, Heinrich. 1887. "Der Reiterdienst und die Anfänge des Lehnwesens." *Zeitschrift der Savigny-Stiftung fur Rechtsgeschichte. Germanistische Abteilung* 8:1–38.

Brusten, Charles. 1953. *L'armée Bourguignonne de 1465 à 1468*. Brussels: Fr. van Muysewinkel.

Bullough, D. A. 1965. *The Age of Charlemagne*. New York: Putnam.

———. 1970. "*Europae Pater*: Charlemagne and His Achievement in the Light of Recent Scholarship." *English Historical Review* 85:59–105.

Burne, Alfred H. 1955. *The Crecy War*. London: Eyre and Spottiswood.

———. 1956. *The Agincourt War*. London: Eyre and Spottiswood.

Burns, Robert I. 2004. "100,000 Crossbow Bolts for the Crusader King of Aragon." *Journal of Medieval Military History* 2:159–64.

Burns, Thomas. 1984. *A History of the Ostrogoths*. Bloomington: Indiana University Press.

Burwash, Dorothy. 1947. *English Merchant Shipping, 1460–1540*. Toronto: University of Toronto Press.

Bury, J. B. 1967. *The Invasion of Europe by the Barbarians*. New York: W.W. Norton and Company.

———. 1982. "The Early History of the Explosive Mine." *Fort* 10:23–30.

Butler, R. M. 1959. "Late Roman Town Walls in Gaul." *Archaeological Journal* 116:25–50.

Buttin, François. 1965. "La lance et l'arrêt de cuirasse." *Archaeologia* 99:77–178. http://dx.doi.org/10.1017/S0261340900011140.

Callebaut, Dirk. 1981. "La château des Comtes à Gand." *Château Gaillard* 11:45–54.

Capwell, Tobias. 2009. *The Illustrated Encyclopedia of Knives, Daggers and Bayonets*. London: Lorenz Books.

Carman, W. Y. 1955. *A History of Firearms from the Earliest Times to 1914*. London: Routledge & Kegan Paul.

Cary, M. and H. H. Scullard. 1975. *A History of Rome down to the Reign of Constantine*. 3rd ed. New York: St. Martin's Press.

Casson, Lionel. 1971. *Ships and Seamanship in the Ancient World*. Princeton: Princeton University Press.

Casson, Lionel, John Richard Steffy, and Elisha Linder. 1990. *The Athlit Ram*. College Station: Texas A&M Press.

Chaucer, Geoffrey. 1951. *The Canterbury Tales*. Trans. N. Coghill. Harmondsworth: Penguin Books.

Cheveddan, Paul E. 1995. "Artillery in Late Antiquity: Prelude to the Middle Ages." In *The Medieval City Under Siege*, ed. I. A. Corfis and M. Wolfe, 131–173. Woodbridge: The Boydell Press.

———. 1998. "The Hybrid Trebuchet: The Halfway Step to the Counterweight Trebuchet." In *On the Social Origins of Medieval Institutions: Essays in Honor of Joseph F. O'Callaghan*, ed. Donald J. Kagay and Theresa M. Vann, 179–222. Leiden: E.J. Brill.

———. 1990. "The Artillery Revolution of the Middle Ages: The Impact of the Trebuchet on the Development of Fortifications." Unpublished Paper.

———. 2000. "The Invention of the Counterweight Trebuchet: A Study in Cultural Diffusion." *Dumbarton Oaks Papers* 54:71–116. http://dx.doi.org/10.2307/1291833.

Cheveddan, Paul E., Les Eigenbrod, Vernard Foley, and Werner Soedel. 1995. "The Trebuchet." *Scientific American* 273 (July): 66–71. http://dx.doi.org/10.1038/scientificamerican0795-66.

Cheveddan, Paul E., Zvi Shiller, Samuel R. Gilbert, and Donald J. Kagay. 2000. "The Traction Trebuchet: A Triumph of Four Civilizations." *Viator* 31:433–86.

Christensen, Arne Emil. 1972. "Scandinavian Ships from Earliest Times to the Vikings." In *A History of Seafaring Based on Underwater Archaeology*, ed. George F. Bass, 159–179. New York: Walker & Company Bass.

———. 1979. "Viking Age Rigging, A Survey of Sources and Theories." In *The Archaeology of Medieval Ships and Harbours in Northern Europe: Papers Based on those Presented to an International Symposium on Boat and Ship Archaeology at Bremerhaven in 1979*. Ed. S. McGrail. BAR International Series, 66. Greenwich: British Archaeological Reports.

Chronique des Pays-Bas, de France, d'Angleterre et de Tournai. 1856. In *Corpus chronicorum Flandriae*, 3. Ed. J.J. de Smet. Brussels.

Cipolla, Carlo. 1965. *Guns and Sails in the Early Phase of European Expansion, 1400–1700*. London: Collins.

Cirlot, Juan-Eduardo. 1967. "La evolucion de la lanza en occidente (piezas de hierro de hallstatt al siglo xv)." *Gladius* 6:5–18.

Cirlot, Victoria. 1985. "Techniques guerrières en Catalogne féodale: le maniement de la lance." *Cahiers de civilisation médiévale (Xe–xiie siècle)* 28:35–43.

Clephan, R. Coltman. 1911. "The Ordnance of the Fourteenth and Fifteenth Centuries." *Archaeological Journal* 68:49–138.

Coad, Jonathan. 1995. *Book of Dover Castle and the Defences of Dover*. London: B.T. Batsford/ English Heritage.

Collins, Roger. 1983. *Early Medieval Spain: Unity in Diversity, 400–1000*. New York: St. Martin's Press.

Comnena, Anna. 1969. *The Alexiad*. Trans. E.R.A. Sewter. Harmondsworth: Penguin Books.

Contamine, Philippe. 1972. *Guerre, état et société à la fin du moyen âge: Etudes sur les armées des rois de France, 1337–1494*. Paris: Mouton.

———. 1978. "Les fortifications urbaines en France à la fin du Moyen Age: aspects financiers et économiques." *Revue historique* 260:23–47.

———. 1984. *War in the Middle Ages*. Trans. M. Jones. Oxford: Basil Blackwell.

Cook, Weston F. Jr. 1994. *The Hundred Years War for Morocco: Gunpowder and the Military Revolution in the Early Modern Muslim World*. Boulder: Westview Press.

Coulson, Charles L.H. 1976. "Fortresses and Social Responsibility in Late Carolingian France." *Zietschrift für Archäologie des Mittelalters* 4:29–36.

Coulston, J. C. 1988. "Three Legionaries at Croy Hill (Strathclyde)." In *Military Equipment and the Identity of Roman Soldiers*, ed. J. C. Coulston, 1–15. Oxford: British Archaeological Reports.

Coupland, Simon. 1990. "Carolingian Arms and Armor in the Ninth Century." *Viator* 20:29–50.

Crossley-Holland, Kevin, trans. and ed. 1979. *The Exeter Book Riddles*. Harmondsworth: Penguin Books.

Crouch, David. 2003. "The Historian, Lineage and Heraldry, 1050–1250." In *Heraldry, Pageantry and Social Display in Medieval England*. 17–38. Woodbridge: Boydell Press.

———. 2005. *Tournaments*. London: Hambledon and London.

Crowley, Roger. 2005. *Constantinople: The Last Great Siege, 1453*. London: Faber and Faber.

Crowley, Roger. 2008. *Empires of the Sea: The Siege of Malta, the Battle of Lepanto, and the Contest for the Center of the World*. New York: Random House.

Cruden, Stewart. 1960. *The Scottish Castle*. Edinburgh: Nelson.

Crumlin-Pedersen, Ole. 1981. "Viking Shipbuilding and Seamanship." *Proceedings of the Eighth Viking Congress*. Odense: Odense University Press.

Davis, R. H. C. 1970. *A History of Medieval Europe from Constantine to Saint Louis*. London: Longman.

———. 1983. "The Medieval Warhorse." In *Horses in European Economic History: A Preliminary Canter*, ed. F.M.L. Thompson, 4–20, 177–84. Reading: British Agricultural History Society.

———. 1989. *The Medieval Warhorse*. London: Thames and Hudson.

Davison, Brian K. 1967. "The Origins of the Castle in England: The Institute's Research Project." *Archaeological Journal* 124:202–11.

de Bouard, Michel. 1964. "Quelques données Françaises et Normandes concernant le problème de l'origine des mottes." *Château Gaillard* 2:19–26.

de Commynes, Philippe. 1969. *The Memoires of Philip de Commynes*. Ed. S. Kinser. Trans. I. Cazeaux. Vol. 1. Columbia: University of South Carolina Press.

de Lombares, Michel. 1984. *Histoire de l'artillerie Française*. Paris: Charles-Lavauzelle.

de Monstrelet, Enguerran. 1857–62. *Chronique*. Ed. L. Douet-d'Arcq. Société de l'histoire de France. Paris: Libraire Renouard.

de Pisan, Christine. 1932. *The Book of Fayettes of Armes and of Chyvalrye*. Ed. Trans. W. Caxton. A.T.P. Byles. Early English Text Society. London: Oxford University Press.

Dearden, Brian. 1988. "Charles the Bald's Fortified Bridge at Pîtres (Seine): Recent Archaeological Excavations." *Anglo-Norman Studies* 11:107–12.

Deschamps, Eustace. 1878–1903. *Oeuvres complètes*. 11 vols. Ed. Q. de Saint Hilaire and G. Raynaud. Société des anciens textes Française. Paris: Libraire Renouard.

DeVries, Keith, and Michael L. Katzev. 1972. "Greek, Etruscan and Phoenician Ships and Shipping." In *A History of Seafaring Based on Underwater Archaeology*, ed G.F. Bass, 37–64. London: Walker.

Deuchler, Florens. 1963. *Die Burgundebeute: Inventar der Beutestucke aus den Schlachten von Grandson, Murten und Nancy 1476/77*. Bern: Verlag Stämpfli & Cie.

DeVries, Kelly. 1987. *Perceptions of Victory and Defeat in the Southern Low Countries during the Fourteenth Century*. Unpublished Dissertation. University of Toronto.

———. 1990a. "A 1445 Reference to Shipboard Artillery." *Technology and Culture* 31 (4): 818–29. http://dx.doi.org/10.2307/3105909.

———. 1990b. "Military Surgical Practice and the Advent of Gunpowder Weaponry." *Canadian Bulletin of Medical History* 7:131–46.

———. 1991. "Hunger, Flemish Participation and the Flight of Philip VI: Contemporary Accounts of the Siege of Calais, 1346–47," *Studies in Medieval and Renaissance History* n.s 12:129–81.

———. 1995a. "Contemporary Views of Edward III's Failure at the Siege of Tournai, 1340." *Nottingham Medieval Studies* 39:70–105.

———. 1995b. "God, Admirals, Archery, and Flemings: Perceptions of Victory and Defeat at the Battle of Sluys, 1340." *American Neptune* 55:223–42.

———. 1995c. "The Impact of Gunpowder Weaponry on Siege Warfare in the Hundred Years War." In *The Medieval City Under Siege*, ed. Ivy A. Corfis and Michael Wolfe, 227–244. Woodbridge: The Boydell Press.

———. 1996a. "Gunpowder and Early Gunpowder Weapons." In *Gunpowder: The History of an International Technology*, ed. Brenda Buchanan, 121–35. Bath: University of Bath Press.

———. 1996b. "Gunpowder Weaponry at the Siege of Constantinople, 1453." In *War, Army and Society in the Eastern Mediterranean, 7th-16th Centuries*, ed. Yaacov Lev, 343–362. Leiden.

———. 1996c. *Infantry Warfare in the Early Fourteenth Century: Discipline, Tactics, and Technology.* Woodbridge: The Boydell Press.

———. 1997. "Catapults Are Not Atomic Bombs: Towards a Redefinition of 'Effectiveness' in Premodern Military Technology." *War in History* 4:475–91.

———. 1998a. "The Effectiveness of Fifteenth-Century Shipboard Artillery." *Mariner's Mirror* 84:389–99.

———. 1998b. "The Forgotten Battle of Bevershoutsveld, May 3, 1382: Technological Innovation and Military Significance." In *Armies, Chivalry and Warfare: Harlaxton Medieval Studies, VII*, ed. Matthew Strickland, 289–303. Stamford: Paul Watkins Publishing.

———. 1998c. "Gunpowder Weaponry and the Rise of the Early Modern State." *War in History* 5:127–45.

———. 1999a. *Joan of Arc: A Military Leader.* Stroud: Sutton Publishing.

———. 1999b. *The Norwegian Invasion of England in 1066.* Woodbridge: The Boydell Press.

———. 2001a. "15th-Century Weapons Dowry: The Weapons Dowry of Duke Philip the Good of Burgundy for the Marriage of Mary of Guelders and James II of Scotland in 1449." *Royal Armouries Yearbook* 6:22–31.

———. 2001b. "The Use of Gunpowder Weapons in the Wars of the Roses." In *Traditions and Transformations in Late Medieval England*, ed. Douglas Biggs, Sharon D. Michalove, and A. Compton Reeves, 21–38. Leiden: Brill.

———. 2003. "Reassessment of the Gun Illustrated in the Walter de Milemete and Pseudo-Aristotle Manuscripts." *Journal of the Ordnance Society* 15:5–17.

———. 2004. "The Failure of Philip the Good to Fulfill His Crusade Promise of 1454." In *The Medieval Crusade*, ed. Susan Ridyard, 157–170. Woodbridge: The Boydell Press.

———. 2005a. "Facing the New Military Technology: Non-*Trace Italienne* Anti-Gunpowder Weaponry Defenses, 1350–1550." In *Heirs of Archimedes: Science and the Art of War through the Age of Enlightenment*, ed. Brett Steele and Tamara Dorland, 37–71. Cambridge: The MIT Press.

———. 2005b. "'The Walls Come Tumbling Down': The Myth of Fortification Vulnerability to Early Gunpowder Weapons." In *The Hundred Years War*, ed. L.J. Andrew Villalon and Donald Kagay, 429–46. Leiden: Brill.

———. 2007. "The Introduction and Use of the Pavise in the Hundred Years War." *Arms and Armour* 4 (2): 93–100. http://dx.doi.org/10.1179/174962607X229834.

———. 2009. "Conquering the Conqueror at Belgrade (1456) and Rhodes (1480): Irregular Soldiers for an Uncommon Defense." In *A Guerra, Revista de História das Ideias* 30: 219–32.

———. 2010. "Warfare and the International State System." In *European Warfare, 1350–1750*, ed. Frank Tallett and D. J. B. Trim, 27–49. Cambridge: Cambridge University Press.

DeVries, Kelly, Martin Dougherty, Iain Dickie, Phyllis G. Jestice, and Christer Jorgensen. 2006. *Battles of the Medieval World, 1000–1500: From Hastings to Constantinople.* New York: Barnes and Noble Books.

DeVries, Kelly, and Robert Douglas Smith. 2006. "Removable Powder Chambers in Early Gunpowder Weapons." In *Gunpowder, Explosives and the State: A Technological History*, ed. Brenda Buchanan, 251–265. Aldershot: Ashgate.

Deyres, Marcel. 1974. "Les châteaux de Foulque Nerra." *Bulletin monumental* 132:7–28.

Dickinson, Tania. F.S.A. Härke, and Heinrich Härke. 1992. *Early Anglo-Saxon Shields.* In *Archaeologia* 110, 1–94; rpt. London: The Society of Antiquaries of London.

Dieulafoy, M. 1898. *Le Château Gaillard et l'architecture militaire au XIIIe siècle.* Paris: Libraire C. Klincksieck.

Diffie, Bailey W. and George D. Winius. 1978. *Foundations of Portuguese Empire, 1415–1850.* Minneapolis: University of Minnesota Press.

Di Francesco, Carla, and Marco Borella. 1988. *Ferrara: The Estense City.* Modena: Italcards.

Dobson, R.B. 1977. "Urban Decline in Late Medieval England," *Transactions of the Royal Historical Society.* 5th series 27:1–22.

Dolley, R. H. 1948. "The Warships of the Later Roman Empire." *Journal of Roman Studies* 38:47–53. http://dx.doi.org/10.2307/298170.

Dotson, John E. 1981a. "Merchant and Naval Influences on Galley Design at Venice and Genoa in the Fourteenth Century." In *New Aspects of Naval History*, ed. C. L. Symonds, 20–32. Annapolis: Naval Institute Press.

———. 1981b. "Naval Strategy in the First Genoese-Venetian War, 1257–1270." *American Neptune* 46:84–90.

———. 2001. "Foundations of Venetian Naval Strategy from Pietro II Orseolo to the Battle of Zonchio." *Viator* 32:113–25.

Douet-d'Arcq, L, ed. 1863–64. *Choix de pièces inédites relatives au règne de Charles VI.* Société de l'histoire de France. Paris: Libraire Renouard.

Douglas, David C. 1964. *William the Conqueror.* Berkeley, Los Angeles: University of California Press.

Drew, Katherine Fischer. 1964. "The Carolingian Military Frontier in Italy." *Traditio* 20:437–47.

Dubled, H. 1976. "L'artillerie royale Française à l'époque de Charles VII et au début du règne de Louis XI (1437–1469): Les frères Bureau," *Memorial de l'artillerie Française* 50:555–637.

Duby, Georges. 1958. "La Féodalité? Une mentalité médiévale," *Annales: économies, sociétés, civilisations* 13:765–71.

———. 1980. "The Origins of Knighthood." In *The Chivalrous Society.* Trans. C. Postan. 158–170. Berkeley, Los Angeles: University of California Press.

Duckett, Eleanor Shipley. 1956. *Alfred the Great: The King and His England.* Chicago: University of Chicago Press.

Duffy, Christopher. 1979. *Siege Warfare: The Fortress in the Early Modern World, 1494–1660.* London: Routledge & Kegan Paul.

Durham, Keith. 2002. *Viking Longship.* London: Osprey.

Eaves, Ian. 1989. "On the Remains of a Jack of Plate Excavated from Beeston Castle in Cheshire." *Journal of the Arms and Armour Society* 13:81–154.

Edwards, J. Goronwy. 1946. "Edward I's Castle-Building in Wales," *Proceedings of the British Academy* 32:15–81.

Ellenblum, Ronnie. 2007. *Crusader Castles and Modern Histories*. Cambridge: Cambridge University Press. http://dx.doi.org/10.1017/cbo9780511497247

Ellis, Henry. 1833. *A General Introduction to the Domesday Book*. 2 vols. London: Eyre & Spottiswood.

Ellis Davidson, H. R. 1962. *The Sword in Anglo-Saxon England: Its Archaeology and Literature*. Oxford: Clarendon Press.

———. 1973. "The Secret Weapon of Byzantium." *Byzantinische Zeitschrift* 66:61–74.

Ellmers, Detlev. 1979. "The Cog of Bremen and Related Boats." In *The Archaeology of Medieval Ships and Harbours in Northern Europe*, ed. S. McGrail, 1–15. BAR International Series, 66. Oxford: British Archaeological Reports.

Eltis, David. 1989. "Towns and Defence in Later Medieval Germany." *Nottingham Medieval Studies* 33:91–103.

English, Edward D. 1984. "Urban Castles in Medieval Siena: The Sources and Images of Power." In *The Medieval Castle: Romance and Reality*, ed. K. Reyerson and F. Powe, 175–198. Dubuque, Iowa: Kendall/Hunt Publishing Company.

Engstrom, Robert, Scott Michael Lankton, and Audrey Lesher-Engstrom. 1990. *A Modern Replication Based on the Pattern-Welded Sword of Sutton Hoo*. Kalamazoo: Medieval Institute Publications.

Enlart, Camille. 1916. *Le costume*. Vol. III: Manuel d'archéologie Française. Paris: Auguste Picard.

Esper, Thomas. 1965. "The Replacement of the Longbow by Firearms in the English Army." *Technology and Culture* 6 (3): 382–93. http://dx.doi.org/10.2307/3101785.

Ferrill, Arther. 1985. *The Origins of War from the Stone Age to Alexander the Great*. London: Thames and Hudson.

———. 1986. *The Fall of the Roman Empire: The Military Explanation*. London: Thames and Hudson.

ffoulkes, Charles. 1912. *The Armourer and His Craft*. London: Methuen.

Fields, Nic. 2004. *Troy c. 1700–1250 BC*. London: Osprey.

Fino, J.-F. 1964. "Notes sur la production du fer et la fabrication des armes en France au moyen-age." *Gladius* 3: 47–66. http://dx.doi.org/10.3989/gladius.1964.201.

———. 1970. *Forteresses de la France médiévale*. Paris: Éditions A. & J. Picard.

———. 1972. "Machines et jet médiévales." *Gladius* 10:25–43.

———. 1974. "L'artillerie en France à la fin du moyen age." *Gladius* 12:13–31.

Fletcher, Richard. 1989. *The Quest for El Cid*. Oxford: Oxford University Press.

Flori, Jean. 1988. "Encore l'usage de la lance ... La technique du combat chevaleresque vers l'an 1100." *Cahiers de civilisation médiévale (Xe-XIIe siècle)* 31:213–40.

Foley, Vernard, George Palmer, and Werner Soedel. 1985. "The Crossbow." *Scientific American* 252 (January): 104–10. http://dx.doi.org/10.1038/scientificamerican0185-104.

Foley, Vernard, and Werner Soedel. 1981. "Ancient Oared Warships." *Scientific American* 244 (April): 148–63. http://dx.doi.org/10.1038/scientificamerican0481-148.

Foote, Peter G. and David M. Wilson. 1970. *The Viking Achievement*. New York: Praeger.

Forbes, R. J. 1955. *Studies in Ancient Technology*. Leiden: E.J. Brill.

Forde-Johnston, J. 1977. *Castles and Fortifications of Britain and Ireland*. London: J.M. Dent & Sons.

Forgeng, Jeffrey L. 2003. *The Medieval Art of Swordsmanship: A Facsimile and Translation of Europe's Oldest Personal Combat Treatise, Royal Armouries MS. I.33*. Leeds/Union City: Royal Armouries/Chivalry Bookshelf.

Fournier, Gabriel. 1974. "Les campagnes de Pépin le bref en Auvergne et la question des fortifications rurales au VIIIe siècle." *Francia* 2:123–35.

———. 1978. *Le château dans la France médiévale*. Paris: Aubier Montaigne.

Fox, Cyril. 1955. *Offa's Dyke: a Field Survey of the Western Frontier Works of Mercia in the Seventh and Eighth Centuries AD*. London: British Academy.

France, John. 1999. *Western Warfare in the Age of the Crusades, 1000–1300*. Ithaca: Cornell University Press.

Freely, John. 1998. *Istanbul: The Imperial City*. London: Penguin Books.

Freeman, A. Z. 1980. "Wooden Walls: The English Navy in the Reign of Edward I." In *Changing Interpretations and New Sources in Naval History*, ed. R.W. Love Jr., 58–67. New York: Garland Publishing.

Frere, S. S. S. Stow, and P. Bennett. 1982. *The Archaeology of Canterbury. Vol. II: Excavations on the Roman and Medieval Defences of Canterbury*. Maidstone. Kent Archaeological Society.

Friel, Ian. 1995. *The Good Ship: Ships, Shipbuilding and Technology in England, 1200–1520*. Baltimore: The Johns Hopkins University Press.

Froissart, Jean. 1888. *Chroniques*. Ed. S. Luce. Vol. 8. Société de l'histoire de France. Paris: Libraire Renouard.

Gaier, Claude. *Art et organisation militaires dans la principauté de Liège et dans le comté de Looz au moyen âge*. Académie Royale de Belgique, Classe des Lettres: Mémoires, 59, V. 3. Brussels: Palais des académies.

———. 1973. *L'industrie et le commerce des armes dans les anciennes principautés Belges du XIIIme à la fin du XVme siècle*. Paris: Société d'Edition «les belles lettres.»

———. 1978. "L'invincibilité anglaise et le grande arc après la guerre de Cent ans: un mythe tenace," *Tijdschrift voor gescheidenis* 91:378–85.

———. 1983. "Armes et armures dans l'oeuvre épique et historique de Jean d'Outremeuse (XIVe siècle)." *Gladius* 16:11–43.

Ganshof, François Louis. 1964. *Feudalism*. Trans. P. Grierson. 3rd ed. New York: Harper and Row.

———. 1968. *Frankish Institutions under Charlemagne*. Trans. B. and M. Lyon, New York: W.W. Norton & Company.

Garnier, Joseph. 1895. *L'artillerie des duc de Bourgogne d'après les documents conserves aux archives de la Côte d'Or*. Paris: Honoré Champion.

Geary, Patrick J. 1988. *Before France and Germany: The Creation and Transformation of the Merovingian World*. Oxford: Oxford University Press.

Gildas. 1978. *Gildas: The Ruin of Britain and Other Works*. Trans. Michael Winterbottom. Totowa: Rowman and Littlefield.

Giles of Rome. 1968. *De regimine principium libri III*. Frankfurt: Minerva G.M.B.H.

Gille, Bertrand. 1966. *Engineers of the Renaissance*. Cambridge, MA: MIT Press.

Gillmer, Thomas. 1979. "The Capability of the Single Square Sail Rig: A Technical Assessment." In *The Archaeology of Medieval Ships and Harbours in Northern Europe: Papers Based on those Presented to an International Symposium on Boat and Ship Archaeology at Bremerhaven in 1979*. Ed. S. McGrail. BAR International Series, 66. Greenwich: British Archaeological Reports.

Gillmor, Carroll. 1981. "The Introduction of the Traction Trebuchet into the Latin West." *Viator* 12:1–8.

———. 1982. "European Cavalry." In *Dictionary of the Middle Ages*, ed. J. R. Strayer, 200–208. New York: Scribners. II.

———. 1985. "Naval Logistics of the Cross-Channel Operation, 1066." *Anglo-Norman Studies* 7:221–43.

———. 1988. "The Logistics of Fortified Bridge Building on the Seine under Charles the Bald." *Anglo-Norman Studies* 11:87–106.

Giraud, J. B. 1895, 1899. *Documents pour servir à l'histoire de l'armement au moyen âge et à la Renaissance*. 2 vols. Lyon: J.B. Giraud.

Goldsworthy, Adrian. 2009. *How Rome Fell*. New Haven: Yale University Press.

Goodman, Anthony. 1981. *The Wars of the Roses: Military Activity and English Society, 1452–97.* London: Routledge & Kegan Paul.

Gravett, Christopher. 2007. *The Castles of Edward I in Wales, 1277–1307.* London: Osprey.

Gregory of Tours. 1974. *The History of the Franks.* Trans. L. Thorpe. Harmondsworth: Penguin Books.

Guillerme, André E. 1988. *The Age of Water: The Urban Environment in the North of France, AD 300–1800.* College Station, Texas: Texas A&M University Press.

Guilmartin, John Francis, Jr. 1974. *Gunpowder and Galleys: Changing Technology and Mediterranean Warfare at Sea in the Sixteenth Century.* Cambridge: Cambridge University Press.

Gwei-Djen, Lu, Joseph Needham, and Phan Chi-Hsing. 1988. "The Oldest Representation of a Bombard." *Technology and Culture* 29 (3): 594–605. http://dx.doi.org/10.2307/3105275.

Hacker, Barton C. 1968. "Greek Catapults and Catapult Technology: Science, Technology, and War in the Ancient World." *Technology and Culture* 9 (1): 34–50. http://dx.doi.org/10.2307/3102042.

Haldon, J. and M. Byrne. 1977. "A Possible Solution to the Problem of Greek Fire." *Byzantinische Zeitschrift* 70 (1): 91–9. http://dx.doi.org/10.1515/byzs.1977.70.1.91.

Hale, J. R. 1965. "The Early Development of the Bastion: an Italian Chronology, c.1450–c.1534." In *Europe in the Late Middle Ages*, ed. J. R. Hale, J. R. L. Highfield, and B. Smalley, 466–494. Evanston: Northwestern University Press.

———. 1966. "Gunpowder and the Renaissance: An Essay in the History of Ideas." In *From Renaissance to Counter-Reformation: Essays in Honour of Garrett Mattingly*, ed. C. H. Carter, 113–144. London: Jonathan Cape.

———. 1977. *Renaissance Fortification: Art or Engineering?* London: Thames and Hudson.

Hale, John R. 2009. *Lords of the Sea: The Epic Story of the Athenian Navy and the Birth of Democracy.* New York: Viking.

Hall, A. R. 1957. "Military Technology." In *A History of Technology*, ed. C. Singer et al., II:695–730, III:347–82. Oxford: Clarendon Press.

Hall, Bert. 1979. *The So-called "Manuscript of the Hussite Wars' Engineer" and Its Technological Milieu: A Study and Edition of "Codex Latinus Monacensis" 197, part 1.* Wiesbaden: Dr. Ludwig Reichert Verlag.

———. 1983. "Cast Iron in Late Medieval England: A Re-examination." In *Historical Metallurgy Notes: Early Ironmaking.* 76, #855:66–71.

———. 1997. *Weapons and Warfare in Renaissance Europe: Gunpowder, Technology, and Tactics.* Baltimore: The Johns Hopkins University Press.

Hall, Nicholas. 1998. "Building and Firing a Replica *Mary Rose* Port Piece." *Royal Armouries Yearbook* 3:57–66.

Halsall, Guy. 2007. *Barbarian Migrations and the Roman West, 376–568.* Cambridge: Cambridge University Press.

Hamblin, William. 1986. "The Fatimid Navy during the Crusades: 1099–1124." *American Neptune* 46:77–83.

Hamer, Richard, trans. 1970. *A Choice of Anglo-Saxon Verse.* London: Faber and Faber.

Hanson, Victor Davis. 1989. *The Western Way of War: Infantry Battle in Classical Greece.* Oxford: Oxford University Press.

Härke, Heinrich. 1989. "Knives in Early Saxon Burials: Blade Length and Age at Death." *Medieval Archaeology* 33:144–8.

———. 1990. "'Warrior Graves'? The Background of the Anglo-Saxon Weapon Burial Rite." *Past & Present* 126 (1): 22–43. http://dx.doi.org/10.1093/past/126.1.22.

Harmuth, Egon. 1979. "Belt Spanners for Crossbows: Some Notes on What Were Once the Most Widely Used Spanning Devices, Though They Came to Be Virtually Forgotten." In

Art, Arms and Armour: An International Anthology. Vol I: *1979–80,* ed. Robert Held, 1979, pp. 100–07. Chiasso: Acquafresca Editrice.

Heather, Peter. 2006. *The Fall of the Roman Empire: A New History of Rome and the Barbarians.* Oxford: Oxford University Press.

Héliot, Pierre. 1962. "Le Château-Gaillard et les fortresses des XIIe et XIIIe siècles." *Château Gaillard* 1:53–75.

———. 1966. "Les châteaux-forts en France du Xe au XIIe siècle à la lumière de travaux récents." *Journal des savants.* 483–515.

———. 1974. "Origins du donjon résidential et les donjons-palais romans de France et d'Angleterre." *Cahiers de civilisation médiévale* 17:217–34.

Herben, Stephen J. 1937. "Arms and Armor in Chaucer." *Speculum* 12 (4): 475–87. http://dx.doi.org/10.2307/2849302.

Higham, Robert and Philip Barker. 1995. *Timber Castles.* Mechanicsburg: Stackpole Books.

———. 2000. *Hen Domen Montgomery: A Timber Castle on the English-Welsh Border.* Exeter: University of Exeter Press.

Hill, David. 1969. "The Burghal Hidage: The Establishment of a Text." *Medieval Archaeology* 13:84–92.

———. 1979. "Siege-craft from the Sixth to the Tenth Century." In *Aspects of the "De rebus bellicis": Papers Presented to Professor E.A. Thompson,* ed. M.W.C. Hassall, 111–17. BAR International Series, 63. Oxford: British Archaeological Reports.

Hill, David, and Alexander R. Rumble, eds. 1996. *The Defence of Wessex: The Burghal Hidage and Anglo-Saxon Fortifications.* Manchester: Manchester University Press.

Hill, David, and Margaret Worthington. 2009. *Offa's Dyke.* Stroud. History Press.

Hill, Donald R. 1973. "Trebuchets." *Viator* 4:99–114.

Hilton, R. H. and P. H. Sawyer. 1963. "Technical Determinism: The Stirrup and the Plough." *Past & Present* 24 (1): 90–100. http://dx.doi.org/10.1093/past/24.1.95.

Hollister, C. Warren. 1962. *Anglo-Saxon Military Institutions on the Eve of the Norman Invasion.* Oxford: Clarendon Press.

Homer. 1950. *The Iliad.* Trans. E.V. Rieu. Harmondsworth: Penguin Books.

Hooper, Nicholas. 1989. "Some Observations on the Navy in Late Anglo-Saxon England." In *Studies in Medieval History Presented to R. Allen Brown,* ed. C. Harper-Bill, C. J. Holdsworth, and J. L. Nelson, 203–213. Woodbridge: The Boydell Press.

Hope-Taylor, Brian. 1956. "The Norman Motte at Abinger, Surrey, and its Wooden Castle." In *Recent Archaeological Excavations in Britain,* ed. R. L. S. Bruce-Mitford. New York: Macmillan.

Hotz, Walter. 1981. *Pfalzen und Burgen der Stauferzeit. Geschichte und Gestalt.* Darmstadt: Wissenschaftliche Buchgesellschaft.

Hourani, G. F. 1995. *Arab Seafaring in the Indian Ocean in Ancient and Early Medieval Times.* Princeton: Princeton University.

Humphries, Peter H. 1983. *Castles of Edward the First in Wales.* London: Her Majesty's Stationery Office.

Hunt, Peter. 2007. "Military Forces." In *The Cambridge History of Greek and Roman Warfare.* 2 vols, ed. Philip Sabin, Hans van Wees, and Michael Whitby, 108–146. Cambridge: Cambridge University Press.

Hunt, Tony. 1981. "The Emergence of the Knight in France and England, 1000–1200." In *Knighthood in Medieval Literature,* ed. W.H. Jackson, 1–22. Woodbridge: The Boydell Press.

Hutchinson, Gillian. 1994. *Medieval Ships and Shipping*. Rutherford: Fairleigh Dickinson University Press.

Huuri, Kalervo. 1941. *Zur Geschichte des mittelalterichen Geschützwesens*. Helsinki: Societas Orientalis Fennia.

Imber, Colin. 2009. *The Ottoman Empire, 1300–1650*. 2nd ed. Houndmills: Palgrave Macmillan.

Inalcik, Halil. 1973. *The Ottoman Empire: The Classical Age, 1300–1600*. Trans. Norman Itzkowitz and Colin Imber. New York: Praeger Publishers.

[Inventaire]. 1855. "Inventaire de la bastille de l'an 1428," *Revue archéologique* 12:321–49.

[Inventory]. 1972. *Inventory of the Historical Monuments in the City of York, An. II: The Defences*. London: Royal Commission on Historical Monuments.

Jacob, E. F. 1947. *Henry V and the Invasion of France*. London: Hodder and Stoughton Limited.

James, Montague Rhodes, ed. 1913. *The Treatise of Walter de Milemete*. London: The Roxburghe Club.

Jessop, Oliver. 1996. "A New Artefact Typology for the Study of Medieval Arrowheads." *Medieval Archaeology* 40:192–205.

Johnson, Matthew. 2002. *Behind the Castle Gate: From Medieval to Renaissance*. London: Routledge.

Johnson, Stephen. 1983. *Late Roman Fortifications*. Totowa, N.J.: Barnes & Noble.

Jones, Gwyn. 1968. *A History of the Vikings*. Oxford: Oxford University Press.

Jones, Michael. 1981. "The Defence of Medieval Brittany: A Survey of the Establishment of Fortified Towns, Castles and Frontiers from the Gallo-Roman Period to the End of the Middle Ages." *Archaeological Journal* 138:149–204.

———. 1988. *The Creation of Brittany: A Late Medieval State*. New York: Hambledon Press.

Jones, Michael E. 1987. "The Logistics of the Anglo-Saxon Invasions." In *Naval History: The Sixth Symposium of the United States Naval Academy*, ed. D.M. Masterson, 62–69. Wilmington: Scholarly Resources.

Jones, M. J. and C. J. Bond. 1987. "Urban Defences." In *Urban Archaeology in Britain*, ed. J. Schofield and R. Leech. London: Council for British Archaeology.

Jongkees, A.G. 1986. "Armement et action d'une flotte de guerre: la contribution des comtés maritimes à l'armée générale des pays de Par-Deçà en 1477." *Publications du centre Européen d'études Bourguignonnes (xive–xvie s.)* 26:71–86.

Journal du siège d'Orléans, 1428–1429. 1896. Ed. Paul Charpentier and Charles Cussard. Orleans: Libraire R. Houzé.

Justinian. 1987. *Justinian's Institutes*. Ed. P. Kruger, Trans. P. Birks and G. Mcleod. Ithaca: Cornell University Press.

Keegan, John. 1978. *The Face of Battle: A Study of Agincourt, Waterloo and the Somme*. Harmondsworth: Penguin Books.

Keen, Maurice. 1984. *Chivalry*. New Haven: Yale University Press.

Kennedy, Hugh. 1994. *Crusader Castles*. Cambridge: Cambridge University Press.

———. 2006. "The Military Revolution and the Early Islamic State." In *Noble Ideals and Bloody Realities: Warfare in the Middle Ages*, ed. Niall Christie and Maya Yazigi, 197–208. Leiden: Brill.

Kenyon, John R. 1981. "Early Artillery Fortifications in England and Wales: A Preliminary Survey and Reappraisal." *Archaeological Journal* 138:205–40.

———. 1987. "The Gunloops at Raglan Castle, Gwent." In *Castles in Wales and the Marches: Essays in Honour of D.J. Cathcart King*, ed. J. R. Kenyon and R. Avent, 143–160. Cardiff: University of Wales Press.

———. 1990. *Medieval Fortifications*. New York: St. Martin's Press.

Kern, Paul Bentley. 1999. *Ancient Siege Warfare*. London: Souvenir Press.

King, D.J. Cathcart. 1970. "Pembroke Castle." *Archaeologia Cambrensis* 127:75–121.

———. 1972. "The Field Archaeology of Mottes in England and Wales: Eine kurze überzicht." *Château Gaillard* 5:101–12.

———. 1988. *The Castle in England and Wales: An Interpretative History*. Portland: Aeropagitica Press.

Kramer, Gerhard W. 2001. *The Firework Book [Das Feuerwerkbuch]: Gunpowder in Medieval Germany*. Trans. Klaus Leibnitz. In *The Journal of Arms and Armour Society* 17.1 (March).

Krenn, Peter, ed. 1989. *Von Alten Handfeuerwaffen: Entwicklung, Technik, Leistung*. Graz: Landeszeughaus.

Krenn, Peter, Paul Kalaus, and Bert Hall. 1995. "Material Culture and Military History: Test-Firing Early Modern Small Arms." *Material History Review* 42 (Fall): 101–9.

Kreutz, Barbara M. 1976. "Ships, Shipping, and the Implications of Change in the Early Medieval Mediterranean." *Viator* 7:79–109.

Kritovoulos. 1954. *History of Mehmed the Conqueror*. Trans. Charles T. Riggs. Princeton: Princeton University Press.

Kuphal, E., ed. 1957. "Der Neusser Kugelbrief von 1475." In *Aus Mittelalter und Neuzeit: Festschrift Gerhard Kallen*. Bonn. 155–57.

Kyeser, Conrad. 1967. *Bellifortis*. Ed. G. Quarg. Dusseldorf: VDI Verlag.

Laleman, Marie Christine. 2008. "Middeleeuwse kastelen in Gent." *Handelingen der Maatschappij voor Geschiedenis en Oudheidkunde te Gent* 62:5–42.

Landels, J. G. 1978. *Engineering in the Ancient World*. London: Chatto & Windus.

Lander, James. 1984. *Roman Stone Fortifications: Variation and Change from the First Century AD to the Fourth*. BAR International Series, 206. Oxford: British Archaeological Reports.

Lane, Frederic C. 1934. *Venetian Ships and Shipbuilders of the Renaissance*. Baltimore: Johns Hopkins University Press.

———. 1963a. "The Economic Meaning of the Invention of the Compass." *American Historical Review* 68 (3): 605–17. http://dx.doi.org/10.2307/1847032.

———. 1963b. "From Biremes to Triremes." *Mariner's Mirror* 29:48–50.

———. 1963c. "Venetian Merchant Galleys, 1300–34: Private and Communal Operation." *Speculum* 38 (2): 179–205. http://dx.doi.org/10.2307/2852449.

———. 1969–70. "The Crossbow in the Nautical Revolution of the Middle Ages." *Explorations in Economic History* 7 (1–2): 161–71. http://dx.doi.org/10.1016/0014-4983(69)90052-7.

———. 1973. "Naval Actions and Fleet Organization, 1499–1502." In *Renaissance Venice*, ed. John R. Hale, 146–173. Totowa: Rowan and Littlefield.

———. 1977. *Venice: A Maritime Republic*. Baltimore: Johns Hopkins University Press.

Lapper, Ivan, and Geoffrey Parnell. 2000. *Landmarks in History: The Tower of London, A 2000-Year History*. Oxford: Osprey Publishing.

Larsen, Henrietta M. 1940. "The Armor Business in the Middle Ages." *Business History Review* 14:49–64.

Laures, Federico Foerster. 1987. "The Warships of the Kings of Aragon and their Fighting Tactics during the 13th and 14th Centuries AD." *International Journal of Nautical Archaeology and Underwater Exploration* 16 (1): 19–29. http://dx.doi.org/10.1111/j.1095-9270.1987.tb01239.x.

Law, John. 1987. "Technology and Heterogeneous Engineering: The Case of Portuguese Expansion." In *The Social Construction of Technological Systems: New Directions in the Sociology and History of Technology*, ed. W. E. Bijker, T. P. Hughes, and T. J. Pinch, 111–134. Cambridge, MA: MIT Press.

Lawrence, T. E. 1988. *Crusader Castles*. Oxford: Clarendon Press.

Le Patourel, John. 1976. *The Norman Empire*. Oxford: Clarendon Press.

Leguay, Jean-Pierre. 1988. *Un réseau urbain au moyen age: les villes du duché de Bretagne aux XIVème et XVème siècles*. Paris: Maloine S.A.

Leo VI. 2010. *The Taktika of Leo VI*. Ed. and trans. George T. Dennis. Dumbarton Oaks Texts, 12. Washington: Dumbarton Oaks.

["Lettre"]. 1846–47. "Lettre sur la bataille de Castillon en Perigord, 19 juillet 1453." *Bibliothèque de l'École des Chartes* 8:245–7.

Lewis, Archibald R. 1951. *Naval Power and Trade in the Mediterranean, A.D. 500–1100*. Princeton: Princeton University Press.

Lewis, Archibald R. and Timothy J. Runyan. 1985. *European Naval and Maritime History, 300–1500*. Bloomington: Indiana University Press.

Leyser, Karl. 1965. "The Battle at the Lech, 955: A Study in Tenth-Century Warfare." *History (Historical Association (Great Britain))* 50 (168): 1–25. http://dx.doi.org/10.1111/j.1468-229X.1965.tb01113.x.

Linder, Elisha. 1987. "New Evidence for the Study of Warships and Naval Warfare in Antiquity Based on the Discovery of the Athlit Bronze Ram." In *Naval History: The Sixth Symposium of the United States Naval Academy*, 20–25. Wilmington: Scholarly Resources.

Lindsay, Jack. 1974. *The Normans and Their World*. London: Hart-Davis, MacGibbon.

Littauer, Mary Aitken. 1981. "Early Stirrups." *Antiquity* 55:99–105.

"Le livre des trahisons de France envers la maison de Bourgogne." 1873. In *Chroniques relatives à l'histoire de la Belgique sous la domination des ducs de Bourgogne (textes Français)*, ed. Kervyn de Lettenhove. Brussels: F. Hayez.

Lomax, Derek W. 1978. *The Reconquest of Spain*. London: Longman.

Long, Pamela O. and Alex Roland. 1994. "Military Secrecy in Antiquity and Early Medieval Europe: A Critical Reassessment." *History and Technology* 11 (2): 259–90. http://dx.doi.org/10.1080/07341519408581866.

Loomis, Roger Sherman, and Laura Hibbard Loomis, trans. 1957. *Medieval Romances*. New York: The Modern Library.

Lot, Ferdinand. 1961. *The End of the Ancient World and the Beginnings of the Middle Ages*. New York: Harper and Row.

Luttwak, Edward N. 1976. *The Grand Strategy of the Roman Empire*. Baltimore: Johns Hopkins University Press.

Lyon, Bryce. 1987. "The Role of Cavalry in Medieval Warfare: Horses, Horses All Around and Not a One to Use." *Mededelingen van de Koninklijke Academie voor Wetenschappen, Letteren en Schone Kunsten van Belgie* 49:77–90.

Macartney, C. A. 1930. *The Magyars in the Ninth Century*. Cambridge: Cambridge University Press.

Mallett, M. E. 1967. *Florentine Galleys in the Fifteenth Century*. Oxford: Clarendon Press.

Mallett, M. E. and J. R. Hale. 1984. *The Military Organization of a Renaissance State: Venice c. 1400 to 1617*. Cambridge: Cambridge University Press. http://dx.doi.org/10.1017/CBO9780511562686

Mann, James. 1933. "Notes on the Armour worn in Spain from the Tenth to the Fifteenth Century." *Archaeologia* 83:285–305. http://dx.doi.org/10.1017/S0261340900005440.

———. 1957. "Arms and Armour". In *The Bayeux Tapestry: A Comprehensive Survey*. 2nd ed. Ed. Frank M. Stenton, 56–69. London: Phaidon Press.

———. 1958. "Arms and Armour." In *Medieval England*, ed. A. L. Poole, 314–337. Oxford: Clarendon Press.

———. 1962. *European Arms and Armour*. Vol. II: *Arms*. Wallace Collection Catalogues. London: Trustees of the Wallace Collection.

Marcus, G. J. 1956. "The Mariner's Compass: Its Influence upon Navigation in the Later Middle Ages." *History (Historical Association (Great Britain))* 41 (141–143): 16–24. http://dx.doi. org/10.1111/j.1468-229X.1956.tb02163.x.

Marsden, E. W. 1969. *Greek and Roman Artillery: Historical Development*. Oxford: Clarendon Press.

———. 1971. *Greek and Roman Artillery: Technical Treatises*. Oxford: Clarendon Press.

Marsden, Peter. 1972. "Ships of the Roman Period and After in Britain." In *A History of Seafaring Based on Underwater Archaeology*, ed. George F. Bass, 113–131. New York: Walker & Company.

Marshall, Rosalind K. 1993. *Mary I*. London: HMSO.

Martines, Lauro. 1979. *Power and Imagination: City-States in Renaissance Italy*. New York: Alfred A. Knopf.

McGuffie, T. H. 1955. "The Long-bow as a Decisive Weapon." *History Today* 5:737–41.

McKisack, May. 1959. *The Fourteenth Century, 1307–1399*. The Oxford History of England. Oxford: Clarendon Press.

McKitterick, Rosamund. 1983. *The Frankish Kingdoms under the Carolingians, 751–987*. London: Longman.

McNeill, William H. 1982. *The Pursuit of Power: Technology, Armed Force and Society since AD 1000*. Chicago: University of Chicago Press.

Mercier-Sivadjian, Eve and J.-L. Sivadjian. 1985. *Châteaux du moyen âge en France*. Paris: Libraire Larousse.

Midant, Jean-Paul. 2002. *Viollet-le-Duc: The French Gothic Revival*. Paris: L'Aventurine.

Monreal y Tejada, Luis. 1999. *Medieval Castles of Spain*. Trans. Lucilla Watson. Cologne: Könemann.

Morley, Beric M. 1981. "Aspects of Fourteenth-Century Castle Design." In *Collectanea historica: Essays in Memory of Stuart Rigold*, ed. A. Detsicas, 104–13. Maidstone: Kent Archaeological Society.

Mortimer, Richard. 1986. "Knights and Knighthood in Germany in the Central Middle Ages." In *The Ideals and Practice of Medieval Knighthood I*, ed. C. Harper-Bill and R. Harvey, 86–103. Woodbridge: The Boydell Press.

Mott, Lawrence V. 1987. "Square-Rigged Galleys of the Late Fifteenth Century." *Mariner's Mirror* 73:49–54.

———. 1990. "Ships of the 13th-century Catalan Navy." *International Journal of Nautical Archaeology and Underwater Exploration* 19 (2): 101–12. http://dx.doi.org/10.1111/ j.1095-9270.1990.tb00241.x.

Müller-Wiener, Wolfgang. 1966. *Castles of the Crusaders*. Trans. J.M. Brownjohn. New York: McGraw-Hill.

Mumford, Lewis. 1934. *Technics and Civilization*. New York: Harcourt, Brace and Company.

Musset, Lucien. 1965. *Les invasions. Le second assaut contre l'Europe Chrétienne (VIIe–XIe siècles)*. Paris: Presses universitaires de France.

Myers, A.R., ed. 1966. *English Historical Documents*. Vol. 4: *1327–1485*. Rpt. London: Routledge.

Needham, Joseph. 1976. "China's Trebuchets, Manned and Counterweighted." In *On Pre-Modern Technology and Science: Studies in Honor of Lynn White, Jr.*, ed. B.S. Hall and D.C. West, 107–45. Malibu: Undena Publications.

———. 1985. *Gunpowder as the Fourth Power, East and West*. Hong Kong: Hong Kong University Press.

———. 1986. *Chemistry and Chemical Technology. Part 7: Military Technology: The Gunpowder Epic*. Vol. 5. Science and Civilisation in China. Cambridge: Cambridge University Press.

Nelson, Janet. 1989. "Ninth-Century Knighthood: The Evidence of Nithard." In *Studies in Medieval History Presented to R. Allen Brown*, ed. C. Harper-Bill, C. J. Holdsworth, and J. Nelson, 255–266. Woodbridge: The Boydell Press.

Neumann, J. 1989. "Hydrographic and Ship-Hydrodynamic Aspects of the Norman Invasion, AD 1066." *Anglo-Norman Studies* 11:221–43.

[Neuss]. *Neuss, Burgund und das Reich*. 1975. Neuss: Gesellschaft für Buchdruckerei AG.

Newhall, Richard Ager. 1924. *The English Conquest of Normandy, 1416–1424: A Study in Fifteenth Century Warfare*. New Haven: Yale University Press.

Nicholas, David. 1987. *The Metamorphosis of a Medieval City: Ghent in the Age of the Arteveldes, 1302–1390*. Lincoln: University of Nebraska Press.

Nickel, Helmut. 1982. "Bow and Arrow/Crossbow." In *Dictionary of the Middle Ages*, ed. J. R. Strayer, 350–354. New York: Scribner. II.

Nicolle, David C. 1980. "The Impact of the European Couched Lance on Muslim Military Tradition." *Journal of the Arms and Armour Society* 10:6–40.

——. 1988. *Arms and Armour of the Crusading Era, 1050–1350*. White Plains: Kraus International Publications.

——. 1989. "Shipping in Islamic Art: Seventh through Sixteenth Century AD." *American Neptune* 49:168–97.

——. 2002. "Jawshan, Cuirie and Coats-of-Plates: An Alternative Line of Development for Hardened Leather Armour." In *Companion to Medieval Arms and Armour*, ed. David Nicolle, 179–221. Woodbridge: The Boydell Press.

——. 2006. *The Third Crusade: Richard the Lionheart, Saladin and the Struggle for Jerusalem*. London: Osprey.

Norman, A. V. B. 1975. "Notes on Some Early Representations of Guns and on Ribaudekins." *Journal of the Arms and Armour Society* 8 (3): 234–7.

Nossov, Konstantin. 2005. *Ancient and Medieval Siege Weapons: A Fully Illustrated Guide to Siege Weapons and Tactics*. Staplehurst: Spellmount.

Oakeshott, R. Ewart. 1964. *The Sword in the Age of Chivalry*. New York: Frederick A. Praeger.

——. 1980. *European Weapons and Armour: From the Renaissance to the Industrial Revolution*. London: Luttersworth Press.

——. 1991. *Records of the Medieval Sword*. Woodbridge: The Boydell Press.

O'Callaghan, Joseph F. 2003. *Reconquest and Crusade in Medieval Spain*. Philadelphia: University of Pennsylvania Press.

O'Connell, Robert L. 1989. *Of Arms and Men: A History of War, Weapons, and Aggression*. Oxford: Oxford University Press.

Ogilvy, J. D. A. 1966. "The Stirrup and Feudalism." *University of Colorado Studies: Series in Language and Literature* 10:1–13.

Olsen, Olaf, and Ole Crumlin-Pedersen. 1990. *Fünf Wikingerschiffe aus Roskilde Fjord*. 2nd ed. Roskilde: Vikingeskibshallen.

Oman, Charles W.C. 1924. *A History of the Art of War in the Middle Ages*. 2 vols. London: Methuen.

O'Neil, B. H. St. J. 1960. *Castles and Cannon: A Study of Early Artillery Fortifications in England*. Oxford: Clarendon Press.

Painter, Sidney. 1935. "English Castles in the Early Middle Ages: Their Number, Location, and Legal Position." *Speculum* 10 (3): 321–32. http://dx.doi.org/10.2307/2848384.

Parker, Geoffrey. 1988. *The Military Revolution: Military Innovation and the Rise of the West, 1500–1800*. Cambridge: Cambridge University Press.

Partington, J. R. 1960. *A History of Greek Fire and Gunpowder*. Cambridge, W. Heffer & Sons.

————. 1999. *A History of Greek Fire and Gunpowder*. Baltimore: Johns Hopkins University Press.

Payne-Gallwey, Ralph. 1903. *The Crossbow*. London: Longmans, Green.

Pedersen, Anne. 2002. "Scandinavian Weaponry in the Tenth Century: The Example of Denmark." In *Companion to Medieval Arms and Armour*, ed. David Nicolle, 25–35. Woodbridge: The Boydell Press.

Peirce, Ian. 1986. "The Knight, His Arms and Armour in the Eleventh and Twelfth Centuries." In *The Ideals and Practice of Medieval Knighthood*, ed. C. Harper-Bill and R. Harvey, 152–164. Woodbridge: The Boydell Press.

————. 2002. *Swords of the Viking Age*. Woodbridge: The Boydell Press.

Pentz, P. 1988. "A Medieval Workshop for Producing 'Greek Fire' Grenades." *Antiquity* 62: 88–93.

Pepper, Simon. 1995. "Castles and Cannon in the Naples Campaign of 1494–95." In *The French Descent into Renaissance Italy, 1494–95: Antecedents and Effects*, ed. David Abulafia, 263–293. Aldershot: Ashgate.

Pepper, Simon, and Nicholas Adams. 1986. *Firearms and Fortifications: Military Architecture and Siege Warfare in Sixteenth-Century Siena*. Chicago: University of Chicago Press.

Phillips, Jonathan. 2008. *The Second Crusade: Extending Frontiers of Christendom*. New Haven: Yale University Press.

Pike, Andrew. 2009. *Church of St. Bartholomew, Richard's Castle, Herefordshire*. London: The Churches Conservation Trust.

Platt, Colin. 1976. *The English Medieval Town*. London: David McKay Company.

————. 1982. *The Castle in Medieval England and Wales*. New York: Charles Scribner's Sons.

Poertner, Rudolf. 1975. *The Vikings: Rise and Fall of the Norse Sea Kings*. London: St. James Press.

Powers, James F. 1988. *A Society Organized for War: The Iberian Municipal Militias in the Central Middle Ages, 1000–1284*. Berkeley and Los Angeles: University of California Press.

Powicke, Michael. 1962. *Military Obligation in Medieval England*. Oxford: Clarendon Press.

Prager, Frank D. and Gustina Scaglia. 1972. *Mariano Taccola and His Book "De ingeneis."* Cambridge, MA: MIT Press.

Prawer, Joshua. 1980. *Crusader Institutions*. Oxford: Clarendon Press.

Prestwich, Michael. 1980. *The Three Edwards: War and State in England, 1272–1377*. London: Weidenfeld & Nicolson.

————. 1982. "English Castles in the Reign of Edward II." *Journal of Medieval History* 8 (2): 159–78. http://dx.doi.org/10.1016/0304-4181(82)90047-1.

————. 1988. *Edward I*. Berkeley, Los Angeles: University of California Press.

Pryor, John H. 1982. "Transportation of Horses by Sea during the Era of the Crusades: Eighth Century to 1285 A.D." *Mariner's Mirror* 68:9–27, 103–25.

————. 1983. "The Naval Battles of Roger of Lauria." *Journal of Medieval History* 9 (3): 179–216. http://dx.doi.org/10.1016/0304-4181(83)90031-3.

————. 1984. "The Naval Architecture of Crusader Transport Ships: A Reconstruction of Some Archetypes for Round-hulled Sailing Ships." *Mariner's Mirror* 70:171–219, 275–92, 363–86.

————. 1988. *Geography, Technology, and War: Studies in the Maritime History of the Mediterranean, 649–1571*. Cambridge: Cambridge University Press.

————. 1990. "The Naval Architecture of Crusader Transport Ships and Horse Transports Revisited." *Mariner's Mirror* 76:255–73.

Pryor, John H. and Elizabeth M. Jeffreys. 2006. *Age of the* DROMON: *The Byzantine Navy, ca. 500–1204*. Leiden: Brill.

Purton, Peter. 2010a. *A History of the Early Medieval Siege, c.450–1200*. Woodbridge: Boydell Press.

————. 2010b. *A History of the Late Medieval Siege, 1200–1500*. Woodbridge: Boydell Press.

Queller, Donald. 1980. "Combined Arms Operations and the Latin Conquest of Constantinople." In *Changing Interpretations and New Sources in Naval History: Papers from the Third U.S. Naval Academy History Symposium*, ed. R.W. Love, Jr., 45–57. New York: Garland Publishing.

Radford, C.A. Ralegh. 1970. "The Later Pre-Conquest Boroughs and their Defences." *Medieval Archaeology* 14:83–103.

Reid, W. Stanford. 1960. "Sea-power in the Anglo-Scottish War, 1296–1328." *Mariner's Mirror* 46:7–23.

Religieux de Saint-Denis. 1839–52. *Chronique*. Ed. L. Bellaguet. 6 vols. Paris: Crapelet.

Renn, Derek F. 1960. "The Anglo-Norman Keep, 1066–1138." *Journal of the British Archaeology Association*. 3rd series, 23:1–23.

———. 1968. "The Earliest Gunports in Britain?" *Archaeological Journal* 125:301–3.

———. 1973. *Norman Castles in Britain*. 2nd ed. London: J. Baker.

Richardson, Thom. 1997. "The Introduction of Plate Armour in Medieval Europe." *Royal Armouries Yearbook* 2:40–5.

———. 2007. "Pavises in the Royal Armouries Collection." *Arms and Armour* 4 (2): 101–8. http://dx.doi.org/10.1179/174962607X229843.

Riché, Pierre. 1983. *Daily Life in the World of Charlemagne*. Trans. J. McNamara. Philadelphia: University of Pennsylvania Press.

Richmond, C. F. 1971. "The War at Sea." In *The Hundred Years War*, ed. K. Fowler, 96–121. London: Macmillan.

Robbert, Louise Buenger. 1969. "A Venetian Naval Expedition of 1224." In *Economy, Society, and Government in Medieval Italy: Essays in Memory of Robert L. Reynolds*, ed. D. Herlihy, R. S. Lopez, and V. Slessarev, 141–151. Kent: Kent State University Press.

Robinson, H. Russell. 1975. *The Armour of Imperial Rome*. New York: Scribner.

Rodgers, William Ledyard. 1940. *Naval Warfare Under Oars, 4th to 16th Centuries*. Annapolis: Naval Institute Press.

Rogers, Clifford J. 1993. "The Military Revolutions of the Hundred Years War." *Journal of Military History* 57 (2): 241–78. http://dx.doi.org/10.2307/2944058.

———. 1998. "The Efficacy of the English Longbow: A Reply to Kelly DeVries." *War in History* 5:233–42.

Roland, Alex. 1992. "Secrecy, Technology, and War: Greek Fire and the Defense of Byzantium, 678–1204," *Technology and Culture* 33:655–79.

Rörig, Fritz. 1967. *The Medieval Town*. Berkeley, Los Angeles: University of California Press.

Ross, D. J. A. 1951. "Plein sa hanste." *Medium Aevum* 20:1–10.

———. 1963. "L'originalité de 'Turoldus': le maniement de la lance," *Cahiers de civilisation médiévale* 6:127–38.

Runciman, Steven. 1964. *A History of the Crusades*. 3 vols. New York: Harper and Row.

———. 1965. *The Fall of Constantinople, 1453*. Cambridge: Cambridge University Press.

Runyan, Timothy J. 1986. "Ships and Fleets in Anglo-French Warfare, 1337–1360." *American Neptune* 46:91–9.

Russell, Peter. 2000. *Henry the Navigator: A Life*. New Haven: Yale University Press.

Russell-Wood, A.-J. 1998. *A World on the Move: The Portuguese in Africa, Asia, and America, 1415–1808*. Baltimore: The Johns Hopkins University Press.

Salet, Francis. 1938. "Najac." *Congrès archéologique de France* 100:170–202.

Sandurra, Enrico. 1972. "The Maritime Republics: Medieval and Renaissance Ships in Italy." In *A History of Seafaring Based on Underwater Archaeology*, ed. George F. Bass, 205–224. New York: Walker & Company Bass.

Sawyer, P. H. 1962. *The Age of the Vikings*. London: Edward Arnold.

———. 1982. *Kings and Vikings*. London: Methuen & Co.

Setton, Kenneth M. et al., eds. 1955–1990. *A History of the Crusades*. 7 vols. Philadelphia: American Philosophical Association Publications, and Madison: University of Wisconsin Press.

Sherborne, J. W. 1967. "The English Navy: Shipping and Manpower 1369–1389." *Past & Present* 37:163–75. http://dx.doi.org/10.1093/past/37.1.163.

———. 1977. "English Barges and Balingers of the Late Fourteenth Century." *Mariner's Mirror* 63:109–14.

Sherlock, David. 1979. "*Plumbatae*--A Note on the Method of Manufacture." In *Aspects of the "De rebus bellicis": Papers Presented to Professor E.A. Thompson*, ed., 101–02. M.W.C. Hassall. BAR International Series, 63. Oxford: British Archaeological Reports.

Sicking, Louis. 2010. "Naval Warfare in Europe, *c.* 1330–*c.* 1680." In *European Warfare, 1350–1750*, ed. Frank Tallett and D. J. B. Trim, 236–263. Cambridge: Cambridge University Press.

Sjøvold, Thorleif. 1985. *The Viking Ships in Oslo*. Oslo: Universitetets Oldsaksamling.

Smail, R. C. 1951. "Crusaders' Castles of the Twelfth Century." *Cambridge Historical Journal* 10:133–49.

———. 1956. *Crusading Warfare, 1097–1193*. Cambridge: Cambridge University Press.

Smith, Robert Douglas. 1993. "Port Pieces: The Use of Wrought-Iron Guns in the Sixteenth Century." *Journal of the Ordnance Society* 5:1–10.

———. 1995. "Wrought-iron Swivel Guns." In *The Archaeology of Ships of War*, ed. M. Bound, 104–113. Oxford: British Archaeological Reports.

———. 1999. "The Reconstruction and Firing Trials of a Replica of a 14th Century Cannon." *Royal Armouries Yearbook* 4:86–94.

———. 2000. "The Technology of Wrought-Iron Artillery." *Royal Armouries Yearbook* 5:68–79.

———. 2010. *Rewriting the History of Gunpowder*. Nykobing: Middelaldercentret.

Smith, Robert Douglas, and Ruth Rhynas Brown. 1989. *Mons Meg and Her Sisters*. London: Trustees of the Royal Armouries.

Smith, Robert Douglas, and Kelly DeVries. 2005. *The Artillery of the Dukes of Burgundy, 1363–1477*. Woodbridge: The Boydell Press.

———. 2011. *The Sieges of Rhodes: A New History*. Stroud: History Press.

Soedel, Werner, and Vernard Foley. 1979. "Ancient Catapults." *Scientific American* 240 (March): 150–61. http://dx.doi.org/10.1038/scientificamerican0379-150.

Sommé, Monique. 1991. "L'armée Bourguignonne au siège de Calais de 1436." In *Guerre et société en France, en Angleterre et en Bourgogne XIVe–XVe siècle*. Eds. Philippe Contamine et al., 197–219. Lille: Centre d'histoire de la région du Nord et de l'Europe du Nord-Ouest.

Steffy, J. Richard. 1980. "The Greek Ship: New Evidence through Nautical Archaeology." In *Changing Interpretations and New Sources in Naval History: Papers from the Third United States Naval Academy History Symposium*, ed. R.M. Love, Jr. New York: Garland Publishing.

———. 1981. "The Medieval Cargo Ship: Evidence from Nautical Archaeology." In *New Aspects of Naval History*, ed. C. L. Symonds, 13–19. Annapolis: Naval Institute Press.

Stenton, Frank. 1957. *The Bayeux Tapestry: A Comprehensive Survey*. 2nd ed. London: Phaidon Press.

———. 1960. "The Development of the Castle in England and Wales." In *Social Life in Medieval England*, ed. G. Barraclough, 96–123. London: Routledge & Kegan Paul.

———. 1961. *The First Century of English Feudalism, 1066–1166*. 2nd ed. Oxford: Clarendon Press.

———. 1971. *Anglo-Saxon England*. 3rd ed. Oxford: Clarendon Press.

Stephenson, Carl. 1933. *Borough and Town: A Study of Urban Origins in England*. Cambridge, MA: Medieval Academy of America.

———. 1942. *Mediaeval Feudalism*. Ithaca: Cornell University Press.

Stone, John. 2004. "Technology, Society, and the Infantry Revolution in the Fourteenth Century." *Journal of Military History* 68 (2): 361–80. http://dx.doi.org/10.1353/jmh.2004.0076.

Stork, Nancy Porter. 1990. *Through a Gloss Darkly: Aldhelm's Riddles in the British Library MS Royal 12.C.XXIII*. Toronto: Pontifical Institute of Mediaeval Studies Press.

Stratos, Andreas N. 1980. "The Naval Engagement at Phoenix." In *Charanis Studies: Essays in Honor of Peter Charanis*, ed. A. E. Laiou-Thomadakis, 221–247. New Brunswick: Rutgers University Press.

Strauss, Barry. 2006. *The Trojan War: A New History*. New York: Simon and Schuster.

Strayer, Joseph R. 1965. *Feudalism*. Princeton: Princeton University Press.

———. 1985. "Feudalism." In *Dictionary of the Middle Ages*, ed. J. R. Strayer, 52–57. New York: Scribners. V.

Strickland, Matthew, and Robert Hardy. 2005. *The Great Warbow: From Hastings to the Mary Rose*. Stroud: Sutton Publishing.

Sumption, Jonathan. 1978. *The Albigensian Crusade*. London: Faber and Faber.

Szwejkowski, W. Ted. 1990. "A Full Size Working Model of a Medieval Traction Trebuchet." Unpublished Paper.

Tacitus. 1970. *The Agricola and the Germania*. Trans. H. Mattingly. Harmondsworth: Penguin Books.

Talhoffer, Hans. 2000. *Medieval Combat: A Fifteenth-Century Illustrated Manual of Swordfighting and Close-Quarter Combat*. Trans. and ed. Mark Rector. London: Greenhill Books.

Taylor, Arnold J. 1950. "Master James of St. George." *English Historical Review* 65: 433–57. http://dx.doi.org/10.1093/ehr/LXV.CCLVII.433.

———. 1958. "Military Architecture." In *Medieval England*. vol. 1., ed. A. L. Poole, 98–127. Oxford: Clarendon Press.

———. 1961. "Castle-Building in Wales in the Later Thirteenth Century: The Prelude to Construction." In *Studies in Building History: Essays in Recognition of the Work of B.H.St.J. O'Neil*. 104–133. London: Odhams Press.

———. 1977. "Castle-Building in Thirteenth-Century Wales and Savoy." *Proceedings of the British Academy* 63:265–92.

———. 1986. *The Welsh Castles of Edward I*. London: The Hambledon Press.

———. 1989. "Master Bertram, Ingeniatoris Regis." In *Studies in Medieval History Presented to R. Allen Brown*, 289–315. Woodbridge: Boydell.

Taylor, Frank, and John S. Roskell, trans. and eds. 1975. *Gesta Henrici quinti*. Oxford: Clarendon Press.

Thielmans, Marie-Rose. 1966. *Bourgogne et Angleterre: Relations politiques et économiques entre les Pays-Bas Bourguignonnes et l'Angleterre, 1435–1467*. Brussels: Presses universitaires de Bruxelles.

Thompson, A. Hamilton. 1912. *Military Architecture in Medieval England*. London: H. Frowde.

Thompson, E. A. ed. 1952. *A Roman Reformer and Inventor*. Oxford: Oxford University Press.

Thompson, E. A. 1958. "Early Germanic Warfare." *Past & Present* 14 (1): 22–31. http://dx.doi.org/10.1093/past/14.1.2.

———. 1982. *Romans and Barbarians: The Decline of the Western Empire*. Madison: University of Wisconsin Press.

Thompson, M. W. 1960. "Recent Excavations in the Keep of Farnham Castle, Surrey." *Medieval Archaeology* 4:81–94.

———. 1961. "Motte Substructures." *Medieval Archaeology* 5:305–6.

———. 1981. "The Architectural Significance of the Building Works of Ralph, Lord Cromwell (1394–1456)." In *Collectanea historica: Essays in Memory of Stuart Rigold*, ed. A. Detsicas, 156–62. Maidstone: Kent Archaeological Society.

———. 1987. *The Decline of the Castle*. Cambridge: Cambridge University Press.

Thordeman, Bengt. 1939. *Armour from the Battle of Wisby, 1361*. 2 vols. Stockholm: Kungl. Vitterhets Historie och Antikvitets Akedemien.

———. 1944. *Invasion på Gotland, 1361: Dikt och verklighet*. Stockholm: Hugo Gebers Förlag.

Thorne, P. F. 1982. "Clubs and Maces in the Bayeux Tapestry." *History Today* 32:48–50.

Tinniswood, T. 1949. "English Galleys, 1272-1377." *Mariner's Mirror* 35:276–92.

Tittmann, Wilfried. 1983. "Der Mythos vom 'Schwarzen' Berthold." *Waffen- und Kostümkunde* 25: 17–30.

———. 2005. "The Guns of Archbishop Baldwin of Trier 1331/32 and the Guns in the Milemete Manuscripts of 1326/27: Some Critical Comments." *Journal of the Ordnance Society* 17:5–23.

Toy, Sidney. 1955. *A History of Fortification from 3000 BC to AD 1700*. London: Heineman.

Troso, Mario. 1988. *Le armi in asta: delle fanterie europee (1000–1500)*. Novara: Istituto Geographico de Agostini.

Tudela, William of and an Anonymous Successor. 1996. *The Song of the Cathar Wars: A History of the Albigensian Crusade*. Trans. Janet Shirley. Aldershot: Ashgate.

Turner, D. J. 1986. "Bodiam, Sussex: True Castle or Old Soldier's Dream House?" In *England in the Fourteenth Century: Proceedings of the 1985 Harlaxton Symposium*, ed. W.J. Ormond, 267–79. Woodbridge: The Boydell Press.

Turner, Hilary L. 1971. *Town Defences in England and Wales: An Architectural and Documentary Study, AD 900–1500*. London: John Barker.

Tweddle, Dominic. 1984. *The Coppergate Helmet*. York: York Archaeological Trust.

———. 1992. *The Anglian Helmet from 16–22 Coppergate*. 2 vols. York: York Archaeological Trust.

Unger, Richard W. 1973. "Dutch Ship Design in the Fifteenth and Sixteenth Centuries." *Viator* 4:387–411.

———. 1980. *The Ship in Medieval Economy, 600–1600*. Montreal: McGill-Queens University Press.

———. 1981. "Warships and Cargo Ships in Medieval Europe." *Technology and Culture* 22 (2): 233–52. http://dx.doi.org/10.2307/3104899.

Vale, M. G. A. 1974. *Charles VII*. Berkeley, Los Angeles: University of California Press.

———. 1975. "New Techniques and Old Ideas: The Impact of Artillery on War and Chivalry at the End of the Hundred Years War." In *War, Literature and Politics in the Late Middle Ages: Essays in Honour of G.W. Coopland*, ed. C. T. Allmand, 57–72. Liverpool: University of Liverpool Press.

———. 1981. *War and Chivalry: Warfare and Aristocratic Culture in England, France and Burgundy at the End of the Middle Ages*. London: Duckworth.

———. 1986. "Seigneurial Fortification and Private War in Later Medieval Gascony." In *Gentry and Lesser Nobility in Later Medieval Europe*, ed. M. Jones, 133–158. Gloucester: A. Sutton.

van Creveld, Martin. 1989. *Technology and War: From 2000 BC to the Present*. New York: The Free Press.

van den Broucke, Serge. 2003. "Château-Gaillard: The Mighty Lock of Normandy's Gate." *Medieval History Magazine* 1 (3): 18–25.

van Doorninck, Frederick. 1972. "Byzantium, Mistress of the Sea, 330–641." In *A History of Seafaring Based on Underwater Archaeology*, ed. George F. Bass, 133–57. New York: Walker & Company.

van Emden, Wolfgang. 1984. "The Castle in Some Works of Medieval Literature." In *The Medieval Castle: Romance and Reality*, ed. K. Reyerson and F. Powe, 1–26. Dubuque, Iowa: Kendall/Hunt Publishing Company.

Vaughan, Richard. 1962. *Philip the Bold: The Formation of the Burgundian State*. London: Longman.

———. 1966. *John the Fearless: The Growth of Burgundian Power*. London: Longman.

———. 1970. *Philip the Good: The Apogee of Burgundy*. London: Longman.

———. 1973. *Charles the Bold: The Last Valois Duke of Burgundy*. London: Longman.

Verbruggen, J. F. 1947. "La tactique militaire des armées de chevaliers." *Revue du Nord* 29:161–80.

———. 1950. "Note sur le sens des mots *castrum, castellum*, et quelques autres expressions qui désignent des fortifications." *Revue Belge de Philologie et d'Histoire. Belgisch Tijdschrift voor Philologie en Geschiedenis* 28 (1): 147–55. http://dx.doi.org/10.3406/rbph.1950.1864.

———. 1977. "De goedendag," *Militaria Belgica*: 65–70.

Vercauteren, F. 1936. "Comment s'est-on défendu, au IXe siècle dans l'empire franc contre les invasions normandes?" *Annales du XXXe Congrès de la Féderation archéologique et historique de Belgique*. 117–32.

Viollet-le-Duc, Eugène-Emmanuel. 1883. *Description et histoire du Château du Pierrefonds*. Paris: A. Morel et Cie.

Virgil. *The Essential Aeneid*. 2006. Trans. Stanley Lombardo. Indianapolis: Hackett Publishing.

von Petrikovits, Harald. 1971. "Fortifications in the North-Western Roman Empire from the Third to the Fifth Centuries AD." *Journal of Roman Studies* 61:178–218. http://dx.doi.org/10.2307/300017.

Vyronis, Speros, Jr. 1981. "The Evolution of Slavic Society and the Slavic Invasions in Greece: The First Major Slavic Attack on Thessaloniki, AD 597." *Hesperia* 50 (4): 378–90. http://dx.doi.org/10.2307/147879.

Waldman, John. 2005. *Hafted Weapons in Medieval and Renaissance Europe: The Evolution of European Staff Weapons between 1200 and 1650*. Leiden: Brill.

Wallace-Hadrill, J. M. 1962. "Gothia and Romania." In *The Long-Haired Kings*, 25–48. New York: Methuen & Co.

Webster, Graham. 1985. *The Roman Imperial Army of the First and Second Centuries*. London: A. & C. Black.

Wheatley, Abigail. 2010. "Caernarfon Castle and its Mythology." In *The Impact of the Edwardian Castles in Wales: The Proceedings of a Conference Held at Bangor University, 7–9 September 2007*. Ed. Diane M. Williams and John R. Kenyon. Oxford: Oxbow Books.

White, K. D. 1984. *Greek and Roman Technology*. Ithaca: Cornell University Press.

White, Lynn, Jr. 1962. *Medieval Technology and Social Change*. Oxford: Oxford University Press.

Williams, Alan R. 1977. "Methods of Manufacture of Swords in Medieval Europe: Illustrated by the Metallography of Some Examples." *Gladius* 13: 75–101. http://dx.doi.org/10.3989/gladius.1977.146.

———. 1980. "The Manufacture of Mail in Medieval Europe: A Technical Note." *Gladius* 15:105–34.

———. 2003. *The Knight and the Blast Furnace: A History of the Metallurgy of Armour in the Middle Ages and the Early Modern Period*. Leiden: Brill.

Williams, Diane M. and John R. Kenyon, eds. 2010. *The Impact of the Edwardian Castles in Wales: The Proceedings of a Conference held at Bangor University, 7–9 September 2007*. Oxford: Oxbow Books.

Wilson, David M. 1965. "Some Neglected Late Anglo-Saxon Swords." *Medieval Archaeology* 9:32–54.

Wilson, Guy M. 2007. "What's in a Name? One Foot and Two Foot Crossbows." In *ICOMAM 50: Papers on Arms and Military History, 1957–2007*, 300–25. Leeds: Basiliscoe Press.

Wolfram, Herwig. 1988. *History of the Goths*. Trans. T.J. Dunlap. Berkeley, Los Angeles: University of California Press.

Wood, Michael. 1985. *In Search of the Trojan War*. New York: Facts on File Publications.

Wright, Quincy. 1964. *A Study of War*. 2nd ed. Chicago: University of Chicago Press.

Yadin, Yigael. 1969. *The Story of Masada*. New York: Random House.

INDEX

Brown, Elizabeth A.R., 99
Brunner, Heinrich, 101–103, 110, 111, 112
buckler, 90
Bullough, D.A., criticism of White's
    thesis, 109
burhs, 202–204
buss, 314
byrnie, Carolingian, 62–63, 64
Byzantines
    armor, 58
    fortresses, 236–238, 245
    navy, 291, 302

Caernarvon castle, 254–256, 269, 270–271
Calais, 166–167
cannon
    chambers in, 152
    development, 151–152, 154
    manufacture, 147–149
    projectiles, 153–154
    on ships, 147
    in sieges, 140–144
    transport, 154–155
cannonballs, 154
caparison, 72
capitulare missorum, 11, 61
caravel, 314
Carcassone, 270–271
cargo ships
    Crusades' support, 299, 300–301
    as modified warships, 300–301
    style and construction, 307
    types, 304–305, 314–315
Carolingians. *See also* Charlemagne
    armor and helmet, 62–63
    bow, 37
    in Catalonia, 226
    cavalry, 110–111
    fortifications, 197–200, 204–207
    shield, 62, 63
    spear, 11
    sword, 19–20
carrack, 314–315, 316
carvel construction, 306–307
cast iron, in gunpowder weapons, 148
castellogie, 184
casting, cannons, 154
castles. *See also* motte-and-bailey castles;
    stone castles

Byzantine-style, 236–238
    comfort in, 262–263, 268
    complexes, 247–251, 252
    earth-and-timber, 211, 223
    keep-and-bailey, 228–229
    lordship, 251
    as residences, 228, 229, 230, 232
    rural, 196–197
    urban, 267–268
Catalonia, 225–226
catapult
    Alexandrian, 119–120
    barbarians, 121–123
    effectiveness, 120–121
    invention and improvements, 117,
        118–119, 120
    non-torsion, 117–119
    Romans, 120, 121–122
    torsion, 117–123
Catholic Church, and gunpowder
    weapons, 157–158
cavalry
    in Carolingian army, 110–111
    costs and formation, 105
    feudalism and, 102–104
    helmet, 56
    shield, 66, 89–90
    spear and lance, 11–15
    stirrup, 105
cervellière, 71, 87
Chanson de la croisade albigenoise, 128
Charlemagne. *See also* Carolingians
    armor, 61–63
    army policy and decrees, 10–11, 37, 61–62
    bow, 37
    Catalonia, 226
    fortifications, 197–198
    spread of feudalism, 105
Charles Martel, 102–103, 105, 110–111,
    112, 226
Charles the Bold, 158–159
Charles VII, 159
Charles VIII, 320
Chastel Blanc, 236
Château-Gaillard, 249–250, 261
Chaucer, Geoffrey, 31, 33, 84
chausses, 70
cheiroballistra, 120
cinquedea dagger, 27

handheld firearms, 145–146
Harold Godwinson, 65, 294
haubergeon, 64, 83
hauberk, 64–65, 68–70, 72, 75
heater shield, 70
helm. *See* great helm
helmet
    Anglo-Saxons, 59–60
    Bayeux Tapestry, 65, 67, 71
    Carolingians, 62, 63
    crests on, 87
    late medieval, 86–89
    Roman, 56
    tenth and eleventh centuries, 63
    thirteenth century, 71–72
    twelfth century, 67
    visor, 88–89
Henry V, 142
heraldry on armor, 73–74
hoop and stave construction, 148–149
hoplon, 54
horseman's axe, 18
horsemen. *See* cavalry
horses
    armor, 72–73, 90–93
    in feudalism's origin, 101–105
    naval transport, 295–296
Houdan castle, 245
Hundred Years' War, 313–314, 319
Hungarians, 200, 201

incendiary weapons. *See also* Greek Fire;
    gunpowder weapons
    cannonballs, 154
infantry
    armor, late medieval, 85–93
    Franks, 101–102
    helmet, 56
    shield, 66, 90
    spear, 11, 14–15
    staff-weapon, 28–29
iron, for gunpowder weapons, 148–149
Italy, 300–302, 320

jack, 86
Jebail Castle, 236
Jericho fortifications, 183–184

John, Archbishop of Thessaloniki, 122–123
John the Fearless, 158
Josephus, 121

Kallinikos, 129
Keegan, John, 39
keep. *See also* rectangular tower keep castles
    castle complexes, 247, 248–250
    keep-and-bailey castles, 229
    round or multi-angular, 245–247
    stone castles, 224, 225, 226–228
keep-and-bailey castles, 228–229
kettenmorgenstern, 30
kettle hat, 71–72, 87
kite shield, 66, 67, 70
Klappvisier, 88
knights, 85
Krak des Chevaliers, 238–240
Kritovoulos, 156

ladder, 167–169
lance, 8–15
    couched, 12–14
    in tournaments, 14
lance-rest, 77
landlords, 99–100
Langeais castle, 224–225
leg armor, 83
legharness, 83
Leo VI, 130–131
liburnian, 286
light galley, 304
Loarre Castle, 242–243
longbow, 38–41, 42, 146
lordship castles, 251
lorica hamata, 56–57
lorica segmentata, 55
lorica squamata, 56

mace, 30–32
mail armor, 64–65, 68–70, 72, 75
mail coif, 70, 71, 76, 78
mail leggings, 70
manganum, 125
mangonel, 125
maritime conflicts. *See* naval conflicts
    and engagements

maritime trade, 299–300, 301, 310
Martel, Charles, 102–103, 105, 110–111, 112, 226
McKitterick, Rosamond, 198–199
Mesolithic Age, 2
metal
for gunpowder weapons, 147–149, 154
in projectiles, 153–154
middle class, rise of, 256
military flail, 30
mining of fortifications, 115–116, 177–179
misericordia dagger, 27
moat, 173–174, 275
Montbazon castle, 225
morgenstern, 30
morion, 87
motte, 217–218, 229
motte-and-bailey castles
Bayeux Tapestry, 214, 217, 218, 219, 220
construction techniques, 217–221
description and origins, 211–213
as model for stone castles, 228
substructure, 218–219
William the Conqueror and, 211, 214–217, 228
mounted shock combat, 11–14, 105, 108, 113
mufflers, 68
Muslims
in Crusades, 234, 240–241
in Europe, 225–226, 242–244, 290
naval fleet, 290–291

Najac Castle, 248–249
names for artillery, 149, 151
naval conflicts and engagements. *See also* warships
Actium, 286
close-quarter combat, 305–306
depiction, 284
England, 294–295, 309, 313–314
France, 309, 313–314
Greek Fire use, 129, 130–132
gunpowder weapons, 146–147
late medieval era, 309–314
rise, 300, 301–302
Venice and Genoa, 302–303, 309–311
Vikings, 292–294

naval power expansion, 311–313
neck and chin protection, 77, 78
Neumann, J., 296
Niger, Ralph, 67
non-torsion catapult, 117–119
Norman invasion and rule of England, 214–217, 228, 294–297
nose-guard, 65
Nur ad-Din, 240

oared warships, 284–285. *See also* galleys
oarsmen, 285
Ogilvy, J.D.A., criticism of White's thesis, 107–109
onager, 120
Orléans, 276
Ottoman Empire, 312–313, 319

Paleolithic Age, 2
palisade, in motte-and-bailey castles, 218–219
partizan, 30
pauldron, 81
pavise, 90
peasants, 99–100
Pembroke, 246
Pepin III, 105, 197
peytral, 90
Philip the Good, 158
Philippe de Commynes, 144
Pierre d'Aubusson, Grand Master, 277
Pierrefonds castle, 266
pike, 15
piracy, 300, 302, 310–311
Pîtres bridge, 205–206
plackart, 81
plate armor, 74–75, 78–84
illustrated, with terms, 80
pieces included, 79
styles and production, 79–81
plumbata, 5
polearm, 28–30
poleyn, 75, 77, 83
pollaxe, 30
pommel, of sword, 18, 19, 22, 23
Portugal, naval power, 311–312
pourpoint, 72
Procopius, 7–8, 121–122, 290